NO HOLDS BARRED

NO HOLDS BARRED

My *Life in Politics*

John C. Crosbie

with Geoffrey Stevens

Canadian Cataloguing in Publication Data

Crosbie, John, 1931-
No holds barred : my life in politics

ISBN 0-7710-2427-4

1. Crosbie, John, 1931– . 2. Canada – Politics and government –
1984-1993.* 3. Canada – Politics and government – 1963-1984.*
4. Cabinet ministers – Canada – Biography.* 5. Politicians –
Newfoundland – Biography.   I. Stevens, Geoffrey, 1942– .   II. Title.

FC631.C76A3 1997   971.064'7'092   C97-931202-7
FI034.3.C76A3 1997

The publishers acknowledge the support of the Canada Council for the
Arts and the Ontario Arts Council for their publishing program.

Set in Goudy by M&S, Toronto

Printed and bound in Canada

McClelland & Stewart Inc.
The Canadian Publishers
481 University Avenue
Toronto, Ontario
M5G 2E9

1 2 3 4 5 6   02 01 00 99 98 97

CONTENTS

To the memory of my grandfathers, Andrew G. Carnell, O.B.E.,
Deputy Mayor and Mayor of St. John's, 1929–49, and Sir John C.
Crosbie, M.H.A., Minister without Portfolio, 1909–17,
Minister of Shipping, 1918–19, and Minister of Finance of
Newfoundland, 1924–28

And to my granddaughters, Jane, Charlotte, Megan, Catherine,
Victoria, Amanda, Mary Margaret, and Rachel, and grandson,
John Alexander

A CROSBIE IN
NEWFOUNDLAND

I WAS BORN on January 30, 1931, in St. John's, then the capital of the Dominion of New-foundland – a proud and independent member of the British Commonwealth. I had the good fortune to be born into a proud and inde-pendent family – the second of three chil-dren of Jessie Carnell and Chesley Arthur Crosbie. My sister, Joan, was three years older, and my brother, Andrew, who would grow up to run (and ultimately to lose) the family businesses, was born two years after me.

The history of the Crosbie family is so intimately intertwined with the development of Newfoundland itself that, to me, family and homeland are virtually inseparable. The Crosbies trace their origins to Dumfries, in Scotland, where my great-great-grandfather Thomas Crosbie was born in 1796, the same year that Robbie Burns died in that town. In 1840, in the wake of a great cholera epidemic, and with the Highland "Clearances" creating population pressures as far away as Dumfries in the

Lowlands, Thomas sent his wife, Margaret, and their three sons to the New World, where they settled at Napan, in Miramichi, New Brunswick. A stonecutter by trade, Thomas stayed behind in Scotland, eventually joining his family in New Brunswick in 1843.*

Their youngest son, George Graham Crosbie, who was only five years old when his mother brought him to New Brunswick, was my great-grandfather. George became a plasterer, but he obviously had an entrepreneurial bent, because, in 1858, at the age of twenty-three, he left New Brunswick on his own to seek his fortune in Newfoundland. After a few years in Harbour Grace, he moved to the prosperous outport of Brigus, in Conception Bay, where he met and married Martha Ellen Chalker, the daughter of a cooper, and my great-grandmother. George quickly expanded his business beyond plastering, becoming a dealer in dry goods, groceries, and other supplies; running a sawmill; and later owning and operating ships. Meanwhile, he and Martha produced eight children, of whom my grandfather, John Chalker Crosbie – later Sir John Crosbie – was the second-youngest.

As steamships replaced wooden vessels, the economy of outports such as Brigus slowly collapsed, causing George Crosbie in 1884 to move his large family to St. John's, where he bought and operated the Central Hotel. The business flourished, and George purchased Clovelly Farm, outside St. John's, to supply his hotel's kitchen with fresh meat and produce. A great fire in the summer of 1892, however, destroyed two-thirds of St. John's, including two thousand houses, the major churches, the entire business district of the city, and five hotels, among them the Crosbies' Central Hotel. George quickly built a new and larger hotel, only to die suddenly, at age fifty-nine, just three months after it opened. As Michael Harris put it in his fine book *Rare Ambition: The Crosbies of Newfoundland*: "George Crosbie's real legacy was

---

* I am indebted to author–journalist Michael Harris for his early history of the Crosbie family: *Rare Ambition: The Crosbies of Newfoundland* (Toronto: Viking, 1992).

the remarkable children he left behind. In the generation to come they would build on their father's ambition, establishing not so much a dynasty, in the normal sense of the word, as a rough-and-tumble tradition of involvement that would put Crosbies at the heart of Newfoundland's affairs from that day forward. Up or down, they were a force to be reckoned with."*

The family enterprises passed into the hands of George's widow, Martha, and their daughter, Ellie. My grandfather John Chalker Crosbie worked in the hotel business for a time before deciding to try his hand in the most important business in the province, fish marketing. In his early twenties, he created a new firm, Crosbie and Company, to export fish to Spain and Portugal. He served his apprenticeship in the fish business working with his employees on the dock, salting fish, and becoming an expert on the seven grades of marketable salt fish. He learned about the markets and bought ships to carry fish to them, flying the red Crosbie "C" on a white pennant. The business prospered and, after just three years, my grandfather was able to buy out his partners and become the sole owner.

By 1909, John Crosbie was described by *Newfoundland Quarterly* as "one of the younger of our merchants, an aggressive and enterprising businessman" with "five splendid foreign-going vessels that freighted his fish to a variety of international destinations." The *Quarterly* said young Crosbie had won his place in the commercial world of St. John's "by sheer ability and perseverance."† By this time, he had branched out into marine and fire insurance, forming an association with brokers at Lloyd's of London.

As my grandfather's businesses grew, so did his family. In 1899, he married Mitchie Anne Manuel, a daughter of the leading merchant and shipbuilding family in the rugged outport community of Exploits Island, in Notre Dame Bay. They produced twelve children, of whom eleven survived infancy. My grandfather also

---

* Ibid., p. 45.
† Quoted in ibid., p. 63.

became the first Crosbie to venture into politics. In 1904, he ran for the House of Assembly as a Conservative in the rural district of Bay de Verde, losing by twelve votes. In the 1908 election, he ran again in the same district, but under the banner of the new People's Party, led by Edward Morris, and this time he was successful. John Chalker Crosbie was named minister without portfolio in the new Morris government and, with the exception of one loss, he was returned to office in each Newfoundland election until he retired from politics in 1928. As Minister of Shipping in 1917 and 1918, he was responsible for keeping the Newfoundland economy going through the later stages of the First World War, his service being recognized by King George V, who made him a Knight Commander of the Order of the British Empire in 1919. In 1924, Sir John Crosbie became Minister of Finance for Newfoundland, a post I, too, would hold a half-century later. In 1925, he founded one of his most successful enterprises, the Newfoundland Butter Company (later the Newfoundland Margarine Company), to manufacture margarine in Newfoundland.

My father, Chesley Arthur Crosbie – known to everyone in Newfoundland as "Ches" – was the fifth of the twelve offspring born to Sir John and Lady Mitchie Anne Crosbie. Like his father, Ches married young, being just twenty-one when he wed my future mother, Jessie Carnell, the beautiful, blue-eyed daughter of Andrew Carnell, a prominent St. John's carriage-maker and undertaker. Marriage into the Carnell clan meant I would have politics in my veins from both sides of the family, as Grandfather Carnell served for many years as the popular, colourful, and acerbic mayor of St. John's. I've been told that, if I got my ambition, drive, and tenacity from the Crosbie line, I inherited my political style and wit from Andy Carnell.

He was quite a character. On one occasion in the 1930s when Andy was driving his horse and carriage, carrying a coffin, an elderly gentleman, much the worse for wear, accosted him. Andy pulled up his horse to ask what this citizen wanted. The old man said that he had voted for Andy and now he wanted a job. Mayor Carnell drew himself up to his full height, looked down at his erstwhile supporter, and said: "Look here, I had to kiss your arse to get a vote and now you'll have to kiss my arse to get a job."

In this age of subservient, bootlicking politicians – an abject and woebegone lot, most of them – it is refreshing to note this measure of outspoken independence by an elected official!

I was twenty-one months old when Sir John Crosbie, who had a history of alcoholism, like a number of other Crosbie men through the generations, died in 1932, at the age of fifty-six. Sir John had built the Crosbie commercial empire, only to see his companies reduced to near-bankruptcy as the Great Depression deepened. My grandfather personally lost $250,000, a fortune in those days, in the 1929 stock-market crash.

Those were dark days for Newfoundland, as they were for the Crosbies. Between 1929 and 1931, the economy of Newfoundland was devastated as the fishery collapsed; a ten-million-dollar industry in 1929, the fishery was reduced to revenues of a mere three million dollars in 1931. By the spring of 1939, fully 30 per cent of my fellow Newfoundlanders were on relief, subsisting on a princely forty-two cents a week.[*] The Depression was the most grievous blow ever suffered by the economy and the people of Newfoundland – until the closure of the cod fishery sixty years later, which unfortunately occurred on my watch as Fisheries minister in Brian Mulroney's federal government.

Unable to meet its obligations, the Dominion of Newfoundland sank in red ink. It had to surrender its prized autonomy. In 1934, the government of the United Kingdom suspended responsible government and placed Newfoundland – "the lost Dominion," as they called it in London – under trusteeship, administered by an appointed Commission of Government.

---

[*] For an excellent explanation of the economy and financial situation of this period, see Peter Neary, *Newfoundland in the North Atlantic World, 1929–1949* (Montreal and Kingston: McGill-Queen's University Press, 1988).

It would take fifteen years, one world war, two referendums, the emergence of Joey Smallwood, and Confederation with Canada for Newfoundland to escape the dead hand of the British Home Office bureaucrats who comprised the Commission of Government.

By the time the Depression struck, our family had established itself as one of Newfoundland's most powerful clans. Newfoundland was not then, and is not now, a place where great family fortunes or immense pools of wealth can be amassed. While a family or a business may do well, the commercial environment is always perilous and there is no assurance that any individual or firm that does well one year will survive the next. Perhaps that's why the work ethic has always been vitally important to the Crosbies. My grandparents instilled it in their children, and they, in turn, instilled it in the members of my generation. Lady Crosbie put it plainly and bluntly in a letter she wrote to my uncle Bill Crosbie while he was away at school:

> Your duty to me and to yourself, your name and the family, to your father, whose work and money make it possible for you to go to university, is to work seriously at the course you have chosen – don't let yourself be side-tracked and take on too many other interests that will not leave you time for the important work, however good they may be in themselves. Keep an open mind, study from the viewpoint of the onlooker, judge people by their conduct, what they do more than what they say. Times are changing, men's thoughts are changing. By the time you get through university, you will be able to bring a trained mind to think about things as they are. One of the hardest things in life is to think. So many just leave the thinking-out of things to others.

It was taken for granted in my family that every Crosbie had a duty to work seriously at whatever endeavour he or she chose. If our family had more money or influence than other families, it meant we had more opportunities than other children; it also meant we were expected to work harder to justify our good fortune.

The death of Sir John left my father, Ches, then twenty-seven and the oldest of five sons, his four older siblings all being girls, to take over the family businesses. Like the others, Dad was hard-working and unassuming, treated his employees fairly, and went about his business without airs or pretensions. Despite his youth, he made a positive impression in 1934 on Sir John Hope Simpson, Commissioner of Natural Resources in the Commission of Government, and his wife, Lady "Quita" Hope Simpson. "Ches is not beloved of the rest of 'Water St.,'" Lady Hope Simpson wrote after meeting my father. "He is a keen, good businessman, but he is not greedy or selfish. He sees the men's side & is sympathetic & generous in his treatment of them." Her husband found Ches Crosbie "rather a rough diamond, but very straight and strong."*

My father needed all his strength and perseverance as the Depression worsened. Still centred on the fishery, the Crosbie enterprises were shaken to their very foundations. They would have gone bankrupt had my grandfather not, providentially, taken out a $300,000 life-insurance policy a few months before his death. Lady Crosbie allowed my father and his brothers to use the insurance money to refinance the Crosbie companies, which gradually prospered again in salt fish, shipping, insurance, margarine, and whaling and sealing. Ches Crosbie also pioneered deep-sea trawling in Newfoundland, and the development of the herring fishery through the use of purse-seine vessels, processing herring into fish meal and oil at Quigley's Cove, near Corner Brook, on the west coast of Newfoundland. Other Crosbie companies bottled soft drinks and brewed beer.

---

* Peter Neary, ed., *White Tie and Decorations: Sir John and Lady Hope Simpson in Newfoundland, 1934–1936* (Toronto: University of Toronto Press, 1996), pp. 83 and 85. For a marvellous firsthand account of the Newfoundland people in the 1930s, I recommend this collection of letters.

Later, he went into general construction, lease-back financing, and airlines, with the initiation of the bush air service that grew into Eastern Provincial Airways. In all of these enterprises, he demonstrated the virtues of entrepreneurship and risk-taking. His losses, particularly in the development of the herring fishery, were offset by gains in other business ventures, but he never ceased taking calculated risks.

St. John's was a small, tight, isolated community when I was growing up, with a population of 39,886 in 1935, growing to 44,603 by the end of the Second World War. The city huddled on towering Signal Hill and the Southside Hills around the harbour, whose narrow entrance was known, naturally enough, as the "Narrows." There were few roads outside the city, as the sea served as the highway to all Newfoundland outports.

The houses in St. John's were wood, painted bright colours, and heated by coal or wood. Like Newfoundland itself, the capital was poor, with a number of slum areas. It was a fairly primitive place. A lot of people used to spit, to hawk – you would see them doing so on the sidewalk at any time of day or night. Many chewed tobacco. I think their deportment must have had something to do with income levels or poverty, because public spitting is not something you see at all these days.

Everybody seemed to be employed at something, but they did not make much money. We had a cook and a maid. The maid lived in and was paid about fifteen dollars a month plus room and board. This changed fairly rapidly after Confederation with Canada, because, as the people got more income and more cash, they didn't want to do domestic work. Within ten years of Confederation in 1949, it was practically impossible to get a maid, whereas before Confederation it was fairly easy because women's options were limited, especially if they came from the fishing outports.

I lived on Water Street West until 1941, when my father bought our home at 18 Rennies Mill Road, in the east end of the city, from the estate of my great-aunt Ellie Bell. During those years, we took the streetcar to Bishop Feild College, a school for boys, each school day, and spent many happy hours playing cowboys and Indians, softball, baseball, tiddley, marbles, and other children's games with our friends from Sudbury, Water, and Leslie streets. Behind our house was Lester's Field, then ideal for sliding and skiing and all other kinds of outdoor games.

On fine weekends, we might go out the Topsail Highway for a "boil-up" on Conception Bay. (A "boil-up" was what mainlanders would call a picnic; it got its name from the old kettle that was always taken along to boil water for tea.) On St. George's Day, which was the opening of the lobster season every year, Dad would drive us down to St. Joseph's, or somewhere along St. Mary's Bay, to buy lobster from the fishermen. We would fill the car trunk with lobster to bring back for a feast that evening. In July and August, we moved to our summer home on Hogan's Pond, sixteen kilometres from the city, where swimming, boating, and exploring occupied our summer days.

Growing up, I never experienced any resentment or jealousy directed at the family because of our affluence or prominence. Other people might expect you to be a Little Lord Fauntleroy, but wealth was never a factor around our house. We weren't like some Canadian or American millionaires or multi-millionaires living in Toronto or Boston. This was Newfoundland in the 1930s and 1940s. There was no ostentatious display of wealth, no extravagant living, no yachts or Rolls-Royces.

We had motor cars, and we had a pretty good house, but not a mansion by any means. We knew we were better off than other people. We were privileged in that sense and didn't feel vulnerable. But there was no feeling of being rich or aristocratic. Whatever wealth there was in Newfoundland was middle class. No one in Newfoundland in those days amassed great wealth. It was only too easy to lose a lot of money overnight in the fishery. The business empires that flourished in St. John's when I was a youngster are long gone. There are hardly any left from even thirty years ago.

Later on, Joey Smallwood would try to stir up feelings against the merchants of Water Street, but that never brushed off much on us because my father wasn't a Water Street merchant per se. He wasn't a retailer. An independent entrepreneur and risk-taker, he was never one of the crowd. All the Crosbies – his father, his brothers, and himself – were looked on as being regular people. They took an interest in their employees and treated them properly.

One Sunday, Dad and I drove over to the Newfoundland Homogenized Fish Plant on the south side of St. John's. As we were walking back to the car, we were intercepted by a derelict who asked my father, "Mr. Crosbie, what about a dollar for a cup of coffee?" Dad reached into his pocket and pulled out a twenty-dollar bill, which he handed to the old fellow, saying, "Here, boy, take this and go out and have a damn good drunk for yourself." I've seldom seen such a look of pure joy on anyone's face as that derelict showed before shuffling off.

On another occasion, the Old Man showed his sterner side. There was a labour dispute, and my father was on Crosbie's wharf debating the issues with leaders of the stevedores, dozens of union members crowding around to listen. As the discussion grew more heated, the men pressed forward, closing Dad in the centre of their circle and walking or pushing him towards the end of the wharf, with the intention of forcing him right into the harbour. As they neared the end, or head, of the wharf, my father grabbed two of the labour leaders by their ties and collars and said, "Now, boys, if you want me to go for a swim, you're coming with me. I can swim, and I only hope to God that you can, too." The crowd stopped in their tracks.

I had a very warm and protected life in the large Crosbie and Carnell families. These were years filled with tradition, family events, companionship, and fun. My father had four brothers and six sisters who had survived childhood, and my mother had two brothers and three sisters, giving us a total of fifteen aunts and uncles, plus their assorted spouses and children, whom we saw frequently.

The large clan boasted a number of strong characters. I've already mentioned my maternal grandfather, Andy Carnell. Of my father's brothers and sisters, George, known as "Gentleman George," or "The Count," managed the Newfoundland Margarine Company. He was a tall, good-looking man; had a heart of gold; and was well liked. He was assisted at the Newfoundland Margarine operation by Uncle Jack, who had a degree from the Ontario Agricultural College, now the University of Guelph. Jack, who was short, stout, gruff, generous, and popular, died in his early forties because of a heart condition. Uncle Percy was a tall, florid man who worked with my father at Crosbie and Company, supervising the salt-codfish, insurance, and shipping activities of the group. Percy had a very serious drinking problem, but stopped using alcohol just in time to save his life. At the Crosbie businesses, he was known as "Mr. Percy"; Dad was "Mr. Ches"; and Uncle Bill was "Mr. Bill."

Percy was hard for non-Newfoundlanders to understand because he spoke very quickly with a guttural accent. He did a lot of business in the salt-fish trade with importers in Puerto Rico, and often went there on vacation and to represent the Crosbie interests. He spent many hours there with his main sales agent. They could converse all day and all evening, apparently understanding each other perfectly, although Percy spoke no Spanish and the agent spoke no English.

Bill, the youngest in my father's family, served overseas in the Canadian Army during the Second World War, rising to the rank of major and being awarded the DSO. Bill was a great favourite of all the family because he, like Uncle Geoff Carnell, was a genuine war hero. When he left the army, Bill began to study law at Osgoode Hall in Toronto. This lasted only until Christmas of his first year because he found school too boring after his experiences in the war. He chose to return to Newfoundland to work with my father.

But, while he was in Toronto, Bill lived at the Zeta Psi fraternity house on St. George Street. I remember visiting him there when I was about thirteen and staying for the weekend in his room on the top floor of the old building. The Zetes were notorious hell-raisers. When I awoke on Monday morning, the room was full of smoke, and Bill wasn't in his bed. I found him in the communal bathroom, chatting with his friends and having a drink while they shaved. I pointed out that the building was filled with smoke. Unconcerned, Bill told me there was nothing to worry about, that there was a fire in the kitchen, which the fire department would look after. Sure enough, when I looked out the window, there were two or three fire engines, and many firemen dashing around. Bill told me to get washed and dressed and we would go out for a good breakfast. We did, but it was a long time before my clothes lost the smell of smoke.

My father's sisters were all women of character and determination who could hold their own with any man and were never shy about expressing their opinions. My aunt Vera, who married Albert Perlin, the most prominent journalist in Newfoundland in his day, was a woman of strong will and great talent who did a magnificent job for retarded children in Newfoundland and Labrador, spearheading the formation of an association to look after their interests. Aunt Margaret was the family *femme fatale*. She remained unmarried throughout the war, although she had, according to family gossip, many romantic entanglements and misfortunes.

In St. John's, on Sundays and at Christmas, we had dinner at Granny Carnell's or the Carnell family came for Christmas dinner at our home, while, in the afternoon, fifty or sixty Crosbie relatives would gather at the residence of Lady Crosbie to meet Santy Claus, who distributed family gifts to the delighted recipients. A deep sense of family tradition, family loyalty, and family support grew from these activities, and even today all of the Crosbie aunts, uncles, cousins, nieces, and nephews, some seventy or eighty of them, gather for lunch on New Year's Day.

My father, Ches, was five foot ten inches tall, with broad shoulders and a deep chest, a moustache, and thinning hair; he was as strong as a bull, and a man of action. He played and worked hard, but he was absolutely fair and level with his employees and business associates. With him, you always knew where you stood. When he was sober, he had a very engaging personality, and was a good conversationalist, full of anecdotes and stories, and a pleasure to be with. He changed when he went on one of his periodic drinking binges. It might start with one sherry or one drink, but, within two or three days, he would be off on what we then called a "bat" – a bender that might last for a week or ten days. Drunk, he was a different person and could be quite nasty if crossed.

I adored my father but used to suffer intensely when he was on one of his "bats" since I hated seeing him make a fool of himself in front of others. When he wasn't drinking, he was a kind man, and was very attentive to his mother and loyal to his family.

My mother, Jessie, was a lovely woman with an independent streak of her own. She was not going to be dominated by the Crosbies, and she resented the pre-eminence of Lady Crosbie in the family and the fact that the matriarch expected all her sons to show up at her home for lunch every Thursday. There was also an underlying tension between my father and my mother, which my brother and sister and I, as children will, were quick to note. She did not want him away from home as much as he was, and she certainly did not want him ever to drink. Her attitude was perfectly understandable. But she was a hard woman. Even when Dad was behaving himself, Mother would insist on reminding him of his falls from grace – reminders that he certainly resented. She could never bring herself to let bygones be bygones, or to concede that Dad, as much as he might have wished otherwise, was unable to control his drinking.

Occasionally, Dad would take Andrew and me with him for a boys' weekend alone. I remember one particular weekend in our early teens when Dad and his brother Jack took us and Jack's sons to a summer cottage on the Salmonier Line, about fifty or sixty kilometres from St. John's. We had strict instructions from our fathers that anything that occurred during the weekend was not to be revealed at home. Dad and Jack started to drink and, before long, a party began that continued long after we boys had turned in. I remember hearing a lot of noise during the night, and voices calling out for Ches. Apparently Dad had disappeared, and search parties were organized to look for him. The searchers were unsuccessful and eventually returned to the cottage, where they found Dad calmly having another drink. He'd climbed up on the roof of the building and hidden there while the search parties went off to look for him. He thought this was a great joke.

The next morning, I went into the kitchen and sat down on what I thought was a pile of coats on the day bed, only to find that I was sitting on Uncle Jack, snoring away as he slept off the night's revelry.

Despite this father–son camaraderie, I wasn't close to my father in the sense that we ever revealed our innermost thoughts to each other. We were opposites in temperament and personality – I was much more like a Carnell than a Crosbie – and each of us found it very hard to unburden himself to the other.

As I grew up, I was determined to merit the approval of my mother and father, and to meet the exacting standards set by the Crosbie and Carnell families: Work hard. Show initiative. Look after yourself. Rally around to defend your brothers and sisters and your family when they are under attack. Treat people fairly. Look after the underdog, and oppose bullying wherever you find it. The Carnells and the Crosbies provided a marvellous atmosphere for youngsters to find and to develop themselves. We had to sink or swim, depending on our own brains, ability, determination, and effort – and we knew there wasn't anything we couldn't do or accomplish if we put our mind to it. Being part of such a large, interesting, and demanding family was one of the great influences of my life.

I grew up as a studious youth, interested in books and reading. (I had my first eyeglasses by the time I was eight.) History and politics were my great interests, and I still remember reading the *St. John's Daily News* on September 1, 1939, with its huge headline and story describing the invasion of Poland by Hitler's Germany and, on September 3, the declaration of war by Great Britain. From 1939 to 1945, St. John's harbour was filled with ships assembling for convoys – navy corvettes, destroyers, frigates, and cruisers. Ships damaged by torpedoes were a frequent sight at anchor. Entertainment of, and hospitality for, the visiting Canadian, British, American, Free French, and other Allied servicemen was a constant feature of life in St. John's.

This hospitality came in various forms and intensities. One of my more vivid memories of the war years is climbing with my friend Noel Goodridge to the roof of the Goodridge home at Rennies Mill Road and Riverview Avenue. There, Noel, later a distinguished Chief Justice of the Newfoundland Supreme Court, and I, a future minister of the Crown, would watch with intense adolescent interest as Allied servicemen and their Newfoundland girlfriends made love in the grass of Bannerman Park across the street.

The war wrought great changes in Newfoundland, apart altogether from the fact that many thousands of Newfoundlanders were serving in the armed forces of Britain and Canada, in the overseas forestry unit, in the Newfoundland militia home-defence force, and in the merchant marine. Its location made Newfoundland strategically essential to the defence of continental North America and the United Kingdom and led to its becoming the bastion of the North American forward defence. In 1940, Canadian Forces were stationed in Newfoundland, and Canada built and controlled air bases at Torbay and Goose Bay, with an immense naval base at St. John's and at Bay Bulls. The Gander air base, built by the United Kingdom just before the war, played a major role in the ferrying of aircraft across the Atlantic and in convoy defence.

In 1941–42, Newfoundland's role changed because of the U-boat war in the Atlantic. St. John's became the home of the Newfoundland Escort Force as the principal western base and turn-around port for convoy-escort ships. St. John's was the resupply, refuel, and crew-rest base for as many as twenty-three destroyers, thirty-six frigates, and fifty-two corvettes at various times throughout the war. We all thought, however, that the war had come too close to home when two submarine attacks sank ships anchored at Bell Island, in Conception Bay, barely three kilometres from our summer home at Hogan's Pond.*

On September 2, 1940, the United States and the United Kingdom signed the Leased Bases for Destroyers Agreement, under which the United States acquired the right to lease bases in Newfoundland, Bermuda, and the West Indies for ninety-nine years in return for fifty old U.S. destroyers. The result was the construction of Fort Pepperell, an army base, at St. John's; a navy and air force base at Argentia; and an air base at Stephenville, on the west coast of Newfoundland.

All this wartime activity had enormous consequences in Newfoundland. Almost overnight, millions of dollars poured into the local economy from defence projects and from free-spending servicemen. By 1942, twenty thousand Newfoundlanders (one-fifth of the male workforce) were working on base construction. Government revenues soared from $12.5 million in 1939–40 to $33.4 million in 1944–45. A cumulative budget deficit of $18.0 million in the six years up to 1940 was transformed into a cumulative surplus of $32.5 million in the war years. Suddenly freed from debt, Newfoundland even advanced a $12.3-million interest-free loan to Britain. And, as Newfoundland became self-supporting again, it was natural that the Commission of Government should lose its legitimacy.

During the war, my father was gone much of the time, tending to the affairs of Crosbie and Company Limited, including the development of the herring fishery on Newfoundland's west coast and the building and operating of a herring-oil and fish-meal dehydrating plant in Bay of Islands. His other interests included whaling and sealing, trawling for cod and other ground-fish, and managing Gaden's Limited, which bottled Coca-Cola and other soft drinks. The soft-drink business prospered mightily through the boom years of the war, thanks to the

---

* The story of the sinkings, on September 5 and November 2, 1942, is told by Stephen Neary in *The Enemy on Our Doorstep* (St. John's: Jesperson Press, 1994).

presence of so many Americans. In addition, my father served as commander of an anti-submarine craft with the Royal Canadian Navy Volunteer Reserve – the "Wavy Navy" – in Bay of Islands.

As the war ended, it was decided that I should go away to St. Andrew's College, in Aurora, Ontario, just north of Toronto, the school my father and uncles had attended in the 1920s.

My mother and I flew from St. John's to Toronto on Trans-Canada Airlines, now Air Canada, a flight that took almost twelve hours on a fourteen-passenger Lockheed 10-A aircraft that landed at Gander, Stephenville, Sydney, Halifax, Moncton, and Montreal before finally reaching Toronto – grim-looking, dour, forbidding, dowdy, and definitely not a fun-loving kind of place for a spirited young Newfoundlander.

As I recall, I was the only student from Newfoundland in my first year at St. Andrew's. Then my brother, Andrew, came up, and with him Frank Moores, who later became premier of Newfoundland. Frank's father, Sy Moores, had a fresh-fish plant, one of the early fish-processing factories. Until then, all the fish business in Newfoundland was salt fish – the Crosbies had a big salt-fish operation at Harbour Grace – but Sy Moores was among the first to establish a plant to process fresh fish into fillets and blocks for, mainly, the U.S. market.

I didn't know Frank well before St. Andrew's. The first time I met him was when there was a big fire in Harbour Grace. The town was literally burning down. Dad and I drove over to see what was happening and found the Moores fish plant gutted. When Frank came to St. Andrew's, he was a year or two behind me, and therefore I didn't really notice him.

In the summers, I went back to Newfoundland. The Old Man used to provide something for Andrew and me to do for twenty-five dollars a week, or whatever the going rate was. I worked at the herring-reduction plant in Bay of Islands, usually timekeeping or some other job that wasn't too onerous. We made meal and oil from herring at the plant, so it was a pretty smelly place. My father spent a fair amount of time at the herring plant and, when he was there, he stayed at the Glynmill Inn, in Corner

Brook. Mrs. Vatcher, who ran the inn, insisted that Dad remove his stinking work clothes and boots and leave them outside the back door. She provided a dressing-gown for him to change into. The Old Man put up with her regimen, although he didn't like it at all. One day, he filled two small sacks with rotting herring meal and stuffed them down the back of a sofa in the bridal suite. The sofa was against a radiator, and it was two weeks before Mrs. Vatcher figured out where the incredible stench was coming from.

Whenever Dad visited the herring plant, he couldn't resist needling a worker named Russ. One day, Russ had slid down a cable in the plant, but the wires at the bottom of the cable were bent up in the shape of a hook. When Russ hit the wires, they sliced open his scrotum, and he might have lost his testicles if Ted Perlin, who ran the plant, hadn't sewed him up on the spot. Every time the Old Man saw Russ after that, he'd torment him by asking, "How's your bag today, Russ?" One night, Russ grabbed a herring knife and chased my father around the plant until some of the workers managed to disarm him.

I also spent a couple of summers at our whaling factory up in Williamsport. I would go out in the whale-catchers or help carve up the whales. Whales had to be flensed, then dragged over to where the meat would go in the boilers or cookers. It was fairly skilled work. Later on, I did construction work for one or other of the Crosbie enterprises. After I went on to Queen's University, I got summer jobs with the Newfoundland Department of Municipal Affairs, because my thesis at Queen's was on local government in Newfoundland.

I was never under any pressure to go into the family businesses. From the time I started to think – at the age of ten or twelve – I knew I wanted to be a lawyer and go into politics. The two seemed to fit together. And that was fine with Dad. Andrew was going to go into the family business. He was always interested in it and wasn't that great academically. Not that I was much of a scholar in high school: I was terrible in mathematics and hated it. Chemistry and physics I also despised. I didn't much like languages, leaving history and English as the two subjects I enjoyed.

While I was away at boarding-school from 1945 to 1949, political life was returning to Newfoundland. There had been no time limit set in 1934 on how long the Commission of Government would last. By 1945, with Newfoundland's financial position stabilized thanks to the war effort, British prime minister Clement Attlee announced that a National Convention would be elected in Newfoundland to advise – advise, not decide – on the Dominion's constitutional future.

The election was held on June 21, 1946, with the candidates running as independents without political-party identification. In St. John's City West, twelve candidates put their names forward, but the general low level of public interest was revealed when candidates in eight rural districts were elected by acclamation. In Bonavista Centre, Joseph R. Smallwood was elected with the widest margin of any candidate, with 2,129 votes, to 277 votes for his only opponent. In St. John's City West, my father, Ches, led the poll with 5,770 votes, the largest number for any candidate in the election.

Dad's slogan for the election was "Give Ches a Chance." St. John's voters responded positively to that suggestion, but the National Convention itself was dominated by Smallwood and his personal crusade for Confederation with Canada. His efforts paid off when the U.K. government, ignoring the majority vote of the convention, announced in 1948 that Confederation with Canada would be included as a choice in a referendum to be held on June 3. The ballot gave three choices: continuation of the Commission of Government for a further three years; Confederation with Canada; or a return to responsible government as it existed in 1933.

Like many of his peers in the St. John's business and legal establishment, Ches Crosbie supported a return to responsible government. He had no objection to Newfoundland's joining Canada, but he believed firmly that, before Newfoundland decided to take such a final step, it should have the Commission of Government replaced by responsible government – to leave Newfoundland free to negotiate the best possible deal for itself, whether with Canada, with the United States, or with neither. The United Kingdom favoured the annexation of Newfoundland to Canada. It was my father's view that a return to responsible government was a necessary first step as Newfoundland embarked on the road back to political autonomy.

Far away, in Aurora, Ontario, I followed events in Newfoundland as closely as I could through the newspapers and letters from home. As a seventeen-year-old Newfoundland patriot, I endorsed my father's point of view completely and defended it on many occasions. At Christmas, in 1946, the *Saint Andrew's College Review* published my patriotic verse "To Newfoundland Unfettered," which made my views clear:

> For years they fought to make their country free.
> They were the men who fought for what was theirs.
> They always knew and loved their foe, the sea.
> For there they fished, and learned through all its cares.
> But now they did not have the right to hold
> An office, and their vote was held in fee
> Because an unpaid debt had left them sold
> Into a low domain with no man free.
> But now are rising men who loved their land,
> Who soon will try to govern once again
> Their native country, belov'd Newfoundland.
> Led by these men 'tis hoped to break that chain
> Of bondage. Up true Newfoundlander! Rise
> And fight once more to win proud freedom's prize!

The political situation changed completely just three months before the referendum, when Ches Crosbie announced the launching of the Party for Economic Union with the United States, with himself as president. He had been persuaded to do this by a group of younger, aggressive businessmen, including broadcasters Geoff Stirling and Don Jamieson (later a federal

Liberal cabinet minister). As economic union with the United States was not one of the three referendum choices, the new party had to campaign for responsible government as the first step in achieving its goal of a free-trade arrangement with the United States. My father might have been a great politician, perhaps as influential as his father, Sir John Crosbie, had been, but Dad had a fatal flaw: he had no knack for public speaking. Without the ability to communicate effectively, he could never be successful in politics.

Even so, the Party for Economic Union nearly carried the responsible-government cause to victory using the slogan "For a brighter tomorrow – vote for Economic Union with the United States today." Economic union with the United States was a concept that I always thought was sensible – not only for Newfoundland, but for Canada as well. That is why I included free trade with the United States as one of my main policy proposals when I ran for the leadership of the federal Progressive Conservative party in 1983 – thirty-five years after my father founded the Economic Union party in Newfoundland. That is also why, as a member of Brian Mulroney's government in Ottawa, I vigorously promoted Canada–U.S. free trade, and then North American free trade. Free trade created a big controversy for cultural reasons more than for economic ones. The Canadian concern about the United States and how it is going to affect our cultural values comes largely from Toronto. It comes from the cultural literati, the encyclopedia pedlars, all those people who have a direct interest in protecting their writing, or performing, or whatever they do, from U.S. competition.

Newfoundland was always a free-trade area. We were a little country that traded with everyone, worldwide. Every merchant in the fish business had to be an expert on currency and foreign markets and vessels and sailing and business customs all over the world. To us, free trade was just a matter of common sense.

In Newfoundland, the June 3, 1948, referendum was inconclusive. Responsible government took 69,400 votes, to 64,066 for Confederation with Canada, and 22,311 for the Commission of Government. As the politically astute recognized, the result heavily favoured a confederate victory in the run-off referendum seven weeks later.

I was now in a position to participate in this intense political conflict. Back from boarding-school for the summer, I was assigned to work in the apartment of Geoff Stirling on Topsail Road, in St. John's, where equipment had been rigged up to enable the responsible government/economic union forces to listen in on long-distance radio-telephone calls between confederates in Newfoundland and their contacts in mainland Canada. The object was to prove our suspicions that Smallwood and the confederates were being secretly financed by the Government of Canada or the Liberal Party of Canada. I didn't uncover the desired proof, but I did get to listen in on some amusing and intimate conversations – philanderers talking to their married girl-friends, that sort of thing.

In the second referendum, held on July 22, 1948, Newfoundlanders voted by 78,323 votes to 71,344 to join Canada in preference to returning to responsible government (and, quite possibly, economic union with the United States). Confederation had prevailed, barely, and the Smallwood era had begun! Appointed by the governor as a member of the delegation to negotiate the Terms of Union with Canada, my father was a lonely hold-out, refusing, in the end, to sign the agreement. The next spring, however, Newfoundland officially became the tenth province of Canada, with the charismatic, despotic, corruptible Joey Smallwood as its first premier.

Newfoundlanders' wicked sense of humour shone through in a post-referendum incident that occurred as the British governor, Sir Gordon MacDonald, was leaving to return to the United Kingdom. A dour Methodist and one-time Labour MP, Sir Gordon was a highly unpopular figure among those who: (a) supported responsible government; (b) favoured strong spirits; or (c) played cards – categories into one or more of which virtually every Newfoundlander fell. Governor MacDonald supported total abstinence, was opposed to card-playing, and was seen as a confederate supporter who encouraged Protestants to vote for Confederation with Canada on the ground that Newfoundland's Roman Catholic hierarchy supported responsible government.

The *St. John's Evening Telegram* unwittingly published this poetic farewell to Sir Gordon from an anonymous Newfoundland patriot who used the initials "E.A.":

A Farewell!
The prayers of countless thousands sent
Heavenwards to speed thy safe return
Ennobled as thou art with duty well performed
Bringing peace, security and joy
Among the peoples of this New Found Land.
So saddened and depressed until your presence
Taught us to discern and helped decide what's best for
All on whom fortune had not smiled.
Remember if you will the kindness and the love
Devotion and the rest that we the people have for Thee –
Farewell!

Thousands of copies of the paper were sold before the embarrassed editors discovered that they'd been duped. The first letter of each line, read vertically, spelled: THE BASTARD. But anticonfederates throughout Newfoundland were greatly cheered by this affront to the martinet from the mother country and were in a much better mood to accept becoming Canadians a few weeks later.

Meanwhile, at St. Andrew's College, kidding Newfoundlanders about events back home was a popular sport. Much to my chagrin, I found myself christened "Canada Crosbie." I naturally resisted this appellation, by giving a poke in the chops to anyone who called me that – as long as he was smaller than I was. If he was bigger, I was inclined to ignore the slight.

On the night of March 31, 1949, with the whole student body assembled in the dining-hall, they announced they would sing "O Canada" in my honour on the occasion of Newfoundland's joining Confederation that day. So the school got up and sang the anthem, and then I got my brother, Andrew, and Frank Moores over, and we sang a rousing rendition of "The Ode to Newfoundland," earning thunderous applause from all assembled. Perhaps Confederation would not be so bad after all, I thought.

So it was that, on March 31, 1949, while I was completing Grade 13 at St. Andrew's College, in Aurora, Ontario, Newfoundland became part of Canada. At eighteen, I became, reluctantly, a Canadian.

2

LOVE AND POLITICS

Courtesy Roy Peterson, Vancouver Sun

THE TRAUMATIC EVENTS of 1948 and 1949 in Newfoundland – two referendums and entry into Confederation with Canada – coincided with a period of great change and development in my own life. In the space of four years, I progressed from being a schoolboy who couldn't cope with math and science, to being something of a scholar. I set my sights on a life in politics and the law. And I fell in love and married. By the time I finished my studies, I was a father, and a career in public life beckoned.

No one pushed me to go to university. There was no tradition of scholarship in the Crosbie family. Most of the men were hard workers, not slackers, but no one would ever have accused them of being academically inclined. Neither my father nor his father before him went to university. One of my uncles, John Chalker (Jack) Crosbie, had a degree in agriculture, and another uncle, Bill Crosbie, had dropped out of law school, but they were the exceptions. There were some very bright women in the family, but in those days in Newfoundland, qualified women – my future wife being an example – didn't go to university. They went to high school, took jobs in offices, and waited to get married.

My brother, Andrew, finished St. Andrew's College in Ontario, but, after a few months in the United States, at Boston University, he, too, decided to return to Newfoundland to enter the family businesses. When our father, Ches Crosbie, died in 1962, Andrew and Uncle Percy Crosbie took over the various enterprises, which they ran successfully for the next two decades, at their peak employing 2,200 people.

There was no compelling reason why I chose to attend Queen's University in Kingston, Ontario. I was against going to Toronto, because I didn't want to be in a big city. Kingston was a smaller, more rural place, and Queen's was supposed to have a very good department of political science. I was interested in that and in economics.

∾

Between the two referendums, held on June 3 and July 22, 1948, I fell in love. I met Jane Furneaux, a fine-looking, lively girl at a friend's birthday party at a place called "Pop In" at Topsail, west of St. John's, on Conception Bay. We were both seventeen in that summer of 1948, the summer before my last year at St. Andrew's. (Jane, I confess, has a different recollection of the beginning of our relationship. She says she first met me when we were both in kindergarten, and she has memories of me being beastly to the little girls at the school, teasing them and making them cry and howl by locking them in the coat-room. Obviously, I failed to embrace politically correct principles at a very early age!)

They used to have parties in those days for young teenagers, dancing parties. You would have a program dance, something to eat, and so on. So that's where I saw Jane. I got her card and filled it out in a romantic manner, including the last dance, which was the signal that I wanted to take her home at the end of the evening.

She thought I was wonderful, naturally. So I fell for her, naturally. I took her home that first evening, but we didn't get there until about 2:30 in the morning because we had to drive all over the countryside to drop others off. A couple of days later, she came to our summer place on Hogan's Pond, where we went swimming. Jane went off the wrong side of the dock and cut her foot on a sharp rock, so the Old Man had to take her into the hospital to get stitches in her foot.

I courted her all that summer. Her father, Dr. John Furneaux, had been the sole veterinary surgeon in private practice in the St. John's area all during the war, and he and his family were very well known and popular in the community. When I returned to St. Andrew's, I was very much in love, and have stayed in that condition ever since. We had a routine: we wrote to each other every Sunday and Wednesday for the next four years. Then, on September 8, 1952, at the start of my fourth year at Queen's, we were married.

Jane has been a marvellous companion for me, and a tower of strength in all my activities, when I have been up and when I have been down. The Roman writer Publius said, "A pleasant companion reduces the length of the journey." Jane has vastly reduced the length of the journey and made it not only a pleasant, but also a far more worthwhile one.

We were only twenty-one, and there was a general air of disapproval about marrying so young. Probably no one thought the marriage would last. My father didn't say much; he had been the same age when he married my mother.

After the wedding and a short honeymoon, I went back for my last year at Queen's. By Christmas, we learned Jane was pregnant. We found a place to rent in Kingston that was owned by an elderly spinster. She had a bedroom, and we shared a kitchen and bathroom with her. She was a weird old soul, but it was quiet there. In June, we went back to Newfoundland, where our son Ches was born.

I found university to be a great liberation since I no longer had to try to master subjects that I didn't find absorbing, including math and science. Instead, I could pursue my real interests, English and history, as well as political studies and economics. At Queen's, they had outstanding teachers in these areas, including Professors J.A. Corry and John Meisel in political science, and Professor Frank Knox in economics.

I spent four very happy and useful years at Queen's, graduating in 1953 with a Bachelor of Arts degree, with first-class honours in political science. Along the way I received a number of scholarships in history and political science, and I graduated with the University Medal in Politics and a fellowship for post-graduate studies, which I declined because I wanted to study law.

I was delighted twenty-three years later when our eldest son, Ches, graduated from Queen's, not only winning the University Medal in Politics, but also becoming a Rhodes Scholar for Newfoundland. Both our second son, Michael, and daughter, Beth, are graduates of Queen's, with Michael graduating in both arts and law.

At Queen's, I was active in a number of extracurricular areas and was president of the Queen's Liberal party for several years. Following Confederation with Canada, the Crosbie family had to choose a political affiliation. My father and three of his brothers decided to become Liberals, while a fifth brother, George, like many responsible-government supporters, gave his allegiance to the Progressive Conservatives. I felt I was a liberal democrat. My later experiences, however, taught me that what counts with political parties is not their name, but what they do or whom they are led by.

In the fall of 1953, we went off to Halifax, where I entered Dalhousie Law School. We got a comfortable house close to the university for about a hundred dollars a month. Because we had a house, we got to hold a lot of parties.

In the summers, we returned to St. John's, where I worked with lawyer Doug Hunt to prepare submissions from the government of Newfoundland to a federal royal commission on

Canadian coastal shipping. I also assisted Hunt, later Mr. Justice Hunt of the Newfoundland Supreme Court, in researching Newfoundland's case for a revision of the financial Terms of Union with Canada. Under Term 29, the federal government was required to appoint a royal commission to review whether, after eight years of Confederation, Newfoundland still needed special transitional assistance to enable it to maintain a level of public services comparable to that of the three Maritime provinces. The federal McNair royal commission recommended these transitional payments be eight million dollars a year. The Diefenbaker government's announcement that it would cut off the payments as of 1962 created a rage in Newfoundland that influenced politics in the province for several years, until Ottawa relented and agreed to continue paying eight million dollars a year indefinitely.

We had three very pleasant and productive years at Dalhousie and in Halifax. The law school then, as it is now, was a first-rate place to learn, with relatively small classes and an accessible faculty. I did well scholastically and, of the seven scholarships available to graduating students, I won five and tied for a sixth. I was the University Medallist in law and was awarded the Viscount Bennett Fellowship for post-graduate study by the Canadian Bar Association. The fellowship could be taken anywhere, so Jane and I decided to take our two sons – our second, Michael, being only a month old – to England, where I would pursue my legal studies at the London School of Economics (LSE).

We got a place right in the centre of London, at Rutland Gate, which was opposite Hyde Park, just behind Brompton Road, where Harrod's was. It was a fascinating period to be in Europe. It was the time of Suez, the political destruction of Anthony Eden, and the Hungarian Revolution.

Jane loved London, but LSE was a mistake for me. They weren't really teaching me anything new or different, so I gave up classes at Christmas. But I wanted to be in London to soak up the atmosphere. I would drop three-year-old Ches off at nursery school in the morning, then take the Number 9 bus to the LSE library, which was very good. I spent some time with a firm of insurance brokers that Crosbie and Company represented in Newfoundland, and I'd go to Steamship Mutual, which used to cover our third-party risks in their claims department. I just wanted to learn how they handled their business. Or I'd visit the courts and sit in on interesting cases, then go home and tell Jane what I'd heard. She still has vivid memories of my accounts of a celebrated prosecution involving the then-notorious crime of sodomy, and another case in which a midget sued a circus over injuries suffered in an elephant stampede.

∾

While I was rounding out my education, my father, Ches, having wisely decided that active politics was not for him, was devoting himself full-time to the various Crosbie businesses. When Newfoundland joined Canada in March 1949, Dad – who had campaigned unsuccessfully for economic union between Newfoundland and the United States – was in Brazil checking on the operations of a margarine-manufacturing enterprise that Crosbie and Company owned in São Paulo. In the early 1930s, the Crosbies had sold a shipload of salt fish to Brazil, but, before payment could be received, Brazil had imposed complete foreign-exchange controls. Unable to get his money out of Brazil, my father invested the money in a margarine plant there. He was eventually able to sell the plant and repatriate most of the money to Canada.

Dad had winners and losers in business. He continued to invest very considerable sums of money in the development of the herring- and capelin-catching and -processing industry. The herring-processing operations were carried on by Newfoundland Dehydrating Process Company, and the catching of herring by Herring Unlimited. Unfortunately, it wasn't only the herring that were unlimited, but the financial losses as well. The eventual bill for pioneering this industry in Newfoundland was a million dollars written off. The whaling enterprise at

Williamsport, in White Bay, had to cease operations in the 1950s, when whaling was prohibited in Canada, but it was no longer profitable in any event. A money-maker for the family continued to be Gaden's Limited, which manufactured and distributed Coca-Cola and other soft drinks, and was run in association with Bavarian Brewing Limited, one of the three breweries in Newfoundland, in which the Old Man was an equal partner with Charles Bell and Edgar Hickman.

In 1949, my father founded Eastern Provincial Airways with Eric Blackwood, who later sold his shares to Dad. Starting with a single Norseman aircraft, the company grew, with charters and mail contracts, until it became the major regional airline in Atlantic Canada. In 1963, Eastern Provincial amalgamated with Maritime Central Airways, and my brother, Andrew, sold out to Harry Steele's Newfoundland Capital Corporation in 1980.

Also in 1949, Dad became involved in the engineering and construction business through Newfoundland Engineering and Construction Company (NECCO) Limited, which became a major contractor to the government of Newfoundland. NECCO entered into lease-back financing projects, including the building and leasing back to the provincial government of a major extension to Grace General Hospital in St. John's; the nurses' residence and training centre attached to the General Hospital in St. John's; and Confederation Building, the seat of the provincial government. The Crosbie group was involved as well in a widespread insurance business, in national and international shipping through Chimo Shipping Limited, the distribution of machinery and building supplies, real estate developments in western Labrador, a sugar refinery, building supplies, and wholesale and retail drug companies.

In the early 1980s, with my brother, Andrew, struggling with high interest rates, tight financial conditions caused by the recession of those years, and his personal battle with alcoholism, the Crosbie business empire came tumbling down. By that time, I had no investment in, or any connection with, any of the enterprises of this business conglomerate, having sold whatever interests I held in the late 1960s because of my involvement in politics. However, I am proud to see that Andrew's sons are continuing the family tradition of entrepreneurial activity and risk-taking in various enterprises, including the offshore oil and gas industry.

∾

Had it not been for John Diefenbaker, my life and career might have taken a different turn. Jack Pickersgill, then Newfoundland's representative in the Liberal cabinet in Ottawa, offered me a job on his personal staff once I returned from my post-graduate studies in the United Kingdom. But Diefenbaker and the Tories formed a minority government in the election of June 1957, and "Pic" was out. This rudely settled the question of what I would do when I finished my year in London. On July 2, 1957, Jane and I, together with Ches and Michael, arrived back by ship, and I promptly enrolled as an articling clerk with the law firm of Barron and Lewis in St. John's. I wrote the bar exam and was called to the bar of Newfoundland in October the same year. At age twenty-six, it was long past time for me to start earning a living. My wage was twenty-five dollars a week.

Jane and I settled in a house in Kings Bridge Court. In the fall, we moved from there to Forest Road, where my uncle Jack Crosbie had a great house. They turned the second floor into a separate apartment, and we took that for a year. The situation was not without peril, however. They had two big concrete posts at the end of the driveway. I used to regularly ram the car into one of the posts when arriving home after a late night. Whether the cause was alcohol or astigmatism, I clipped those posts frequently.

Once I was admitted to the Newfoundland bar, I began to do the legal work for the Crosbie interests, becoming a director of the various companies, and corporate secretary to most of them. From time to time, I would have to see Joey Smallwood on behalf of the family. In fact, I did some legal work, incorporating two or three companies for him. I could see the way he operated and, like businessmen who had dealings with the provincial government, I knew he was corruptible. But, although the general public was aware that he was autocratic and a demagogue, they probably didn't realize in those days that he was corrupt.

In the spring of 1958, I left Barron and Lewis to form a partnership with Fintan J. Aylward, who had been a year ahead of me at Dalhousie – and who I later, as federal Minister of Justice, took pleasure in appointing to the Supreme Court of Newfoundland. In our first month together, we managed to net $250 each, and we never looked back. We carried on as Aylward and Crosbie for a number of years. Then we went with Derek Lewis, later a Liberal senator, to form Lewis, Aylward and Crosbie.

I remained interested in politics, even working as a poll captain for Smallwood in the 1959 provincial election. Meanwhile, the federal Liberal party was struggling to rehabilitate itself following Diefenbaker's landslide win in 1958. I attended the now-legendary "thinkers'" conference on national problems held by Liberals in Kingston, Ontario, in September 1960. As a politically ambitious young lawyer from remote Newfoundland, I enjoyed rubbing shoulders and minds with the leading Liberal lights from across Canada, none of whom felt comfortable being out of power.

Working up my credentials as a "loyal Liberal" in anticipation of embarking on a political career of my own, I nevertheless felt pulled in two directions. I was increasingly uneasy over Smallwood's domineering and dictatorial tendencies; his madcap economic-development policy; his crushing of the International Woodworkers of America union, which he feared would become a political power in the province, and his breaking of the 1959 Newfoundland loggers' strike. His behaviour during that strike was despicable. I couldn't approve of Smallwood's ruthless way of operating, nor did I approve of the atmosphere he created whereby businessmen were expected to kiss his arse and give him gifts in order to get fat, untendered, cost-plus government contracts. The Crosbies were not above reproach in this regard. Our construction company, NECCO Limited, built an indoor swimming-pool for him at Russwood Ranch, where he lived; no invoice was ever submitted, of course. Competitors built his house or furnished goods for him. But, if that was the system, I couldn't very well undermine my family's business by making a public fuss about corruption. I couldn't ignore the unusual and friendly relationship that existed between my father and Joey, one that continued until my father's death, or the increasingly close business relationship between the Crosbie enterprises, directed by Andrew and Percy Crosbie, and the Smallwood administration.

The last occasion when I spoke to my father was near the end of his life. A serious binge drinker, he also had a heart condition. The long-standing difficulties between him and my mother had worsened. He left her, then divorced her in Nevada. Dad married Alice Squires, a widow, and they were planning to fly to Hawaii for their honeymoon. As it turned out, he had a heart attack on the aircraft and died in Honolulu on Boxing Day 1962.

Before he left Newfoundland for the last time, Dad came to see me at our country place at Hogan's Pond. It was unusual for him to give me advice, but he gave me some that day – and he repeated it at the airport when we said goodbye. He knew I was thinking of running for election with Smallwood. He told me, "Never, ever. Don't you ever run with Smallwood. You'll regret it if you do, so I'm trying to warn you." He sensed that I was too independent and too stubborn by nature to remain subservient to Smallwood if I joined his government. He knew Smallwood well and he knew me, and he knew the two of us would not be able to live together.

It was the best advice Dad ever gave me. And I ignored it.

I was so anxious to get involved in public life that I thought I might start my career by running for St. John's city council in the fall of 1965. In Newfoundland, a Liberal didn't do anything without clearing it first with Joey. When I asked him what he thought, his first reaction was that municipal government wasn't worth the time spent on it. "What do you want to be involved in water and sewerage for?" he asked. However, on further reflection, he said he thought it would give me an opportunity to discover whether I had any public appeal. Jane and I made a trip to a Commonwealth law conference in Australia, and, while we were away, I got antsy wanting to get back. I was so anxious that I didn't even want to stop in Fiji and Hawaii on the way home. I couldn't wait for the municipal election.

As there was a feeling among the public that the city was far too secretive in its deliberations, I and my supporters devised the slogan "You have a right to know," which struck a very responsive chord. This is always a good campaign slogan: *You have a right to know*. Of course, I made a point after I got elected of trying to make sure the public didn't know everything, but the slogan was a good one. *You have a right to know*. I recommend it. It fits almost anyone and any campaign, any time, anywhere!

Most of my time in the municipal election was spent meeting voters on the waterfront, at the dockyard, and at other work-places. This was a valuable experience because, by nature, I was more reserved than effusive. But my first political adventure turned out very well. In city-wide voting, I received 7,419 votes, or 71 per cent of the votes cast, and was declared deputy mayor by virtue of being the councillor receiving the greatest vote. I was launched on my political career.

In my seven months as deputy mayor, the only burning issue to come before the council was fluoridation of the municipal water supply. I was on the side of the fluoridationists, but the measure died on a four–three vote.

∾

Not far from the backwater of civic politics, a storm was brewing. Smallwood was laying the ground for a provincial election in the fall of 1966. His Liberals had won thirty-four of forty-two seats in the previous election. He would, he decided, go to the people with a whole slate of new, younger faces in a bid to wipe out the opposition completely. He proclaimed accomplishments galore and made extravagant promises. He claimed credit for the completion of the Trans-Canada Highway, even though Ottawa had paid for 90 per cent of it. He declared 1966 to be "Come Home Year" for all former Newfoundlanders to revisit the province to witness the miracles that had been wrought by Saint Joey. He promised a third pulp and paper mill, to be located at Come By Chance; a linerboard mill for Stephenville; a new phosphorus-manufacturing plant for Long Harbour, in Placentia Bay; a new education scheme under which the province would pay the tuition fees for all full-time students at Memorial University, and, what's more, provide fourth- and fifth-year students with salaries of fifty or a hundred dollars a month. Negotiations with Quebec would enable Newfoundland to tap the gigantic hydro resources of Churchill Falls, in Labrador. And on and on. It was breathtaking!

When he interviewed prospective Liberal candidates, Smallwood used as bait the suggestion that he was going into his last election. The leadership of the party – and the premiership – would then be open to any ambitious Liberal, young or old, such aspirants having a much better chance, of course, if they had experience as a member of the House of Assembly or as a member of his cabinet.

Inevitably, as it now seems, Smallwood invited me to his Russwood Ranch home to outline his plans and to discuss my political future. He fed me the line about it being his last election; he said he was going forward with as many new, young candidates as he could; and he declared his successor would be chosen by a great democratic convention. If I had ambitions in that direction, I should run in the coming election and accept membership in his cabinet. It was all very flattering. In truth, however, I was receptive to his flattery, and Smallwood didn't need to spread the persuasion on very thickly.

I may have been a pigeon waiting to be plucked, but I wasn't a complete dummy. I guessed that, if he was using this line on me, I wasn't the only one. (As it turned out, I was right. Clyde Wells, later the premier of Newfoundland; Ed Roberts, a future provincial Liberal leader; and Alex Hickman, who became chief justice of the province, were all seduced by Joey's pitch that year.)

At the time, the Newfoundland Liberal party existed in name only. There was no Liberal party; there was only the Smallwood party. There was no possible way a person could do anything as a Liberal without Joey's say-so, because *he* was the party. No one campaigned for a Liberal nomination. It would have been absurd. If Joey said you were the candidate, you were – and if he said you weren't, you weren't.

So I made my first major political mistake – by allowing my ambition and my impatience to overcome my common sense and the warnings I had received from my father and other family members. I accepted Joey's invitation. I agreed to be his candidate. And I was honoured to be appointed his Minister of Municipal Affairs and Housing before the election had even been called.

I should have known better. And I should have known it as soon as I learned that Smallwood had not bothered to advise the incumbent Minister of Municipal Affairs, Beaton J. Abbott, that he was losing his job to me. Nor did he feel it necessary to take the trouble to notify another minister, Neddy Spencer, that he was being dropped from the cabinet altogether.

After all, they could hear all about it on the radio, couldn't they? And that's how they found out.

3

JOEY

Yardley Jones, Montreal Star

MY FAMILY'S RELATIONSHIP with Joey Smallwood was long, tangled, ambiguous, frequently acrimonious, and ultimately destructive. My father, Ches Crosbie, financed some of Joey's early publishing and business ventures. Yet the two men clashed bitterly over Confederation with Canada. Smallwood had a burning vision of Newfoundland as the tenth province of Canada. My father led the campaign for Newfoundland to be an independent nation in an economic union with the United States.

My father, and later my brother, Andrew, used their relationship with Joey to help build the Crosbie business empire. Yet Andrew had the guts to break with Smallwood to support my attempt to wrest the Liberal leadership from him – only to run back to Joey's side when I joined the Progressive Conservatives.

As for me, thanks to Smallwood I entered provincial politics in 1966 at the top, being appointed Minister of Municipal Affairs and Housing in his cabinet even before I sought election to the

House of Assembly. Later I also served as his Minister of Health. I spent most of the next few years, however, fighting to rid the province of Smallwood and to undo the damage he and his legions of Liberal brothel-creepers had done to Newfoundland.

Most Newfoundlanders and mainlanders saw Joey Smallwood as he wanted them to see him – as a peppery little populist, a dreamer and visionary, a Newfoundland patriot, and a selfless servant of his people who dedicated his life to pursuing the elusive grail of economic development and prosperity for all. Thousands of Newfoundlanders revered him as they would a saint; many were buried with his picture in their coffin. But they didn't see, or didn't want to see, the real Smallwood. Joey was no saint, far from it. He was a demagogue and a despot. Never in Canadian history has so much raw political power been concentrated in the hands of one person as it was in his from the moment Newfoundland joined Canada in 1949 until we finally drove him from office twenty-three years later. And seldom has political power been used for such venal and corrupt ends as it was by Smallwood.

He was more than a despot. He was corrupt. "The only living Father of Confederation" (as he loved to style himself) not only betrayed the trust and stole the dreams of the people of our poor province, but also stole their money, living like a colonial King Tut on bribes and kickbacks from people who did business with his government. We could have put Smallwood on trial after my old schoolboy friend Frank Moores and the Tories took over in 1972. Maybe we should have. But Frank didn't have the stomach for putting a living legend behind bars. As a senior member of Frank's cabinet, I'm not sure I had the stomach for it either.

"Joey" – the man who, like Liberace, Cher, and Madonna, came to be known by one name – was born Joseph Roberts Smallwood at Gambo, on Bonavista Bay, on December 24, 1900, to Charles and Minnie Smallwood during a period when his father was surveying lumber for a mill once owned by Joey's grandfather. When Joey was five months old, the family returned to St. John's, where he grew up. So Joey was never really a "bayman," as he presented himself once he got into politics. He was as much a "townie" (a resident of St. John's, the capital) as I was.

He was one of thirteen children, and the children grew up in an atmosphere of constant poverty and frequent changes of housing. Assisted financially by an uncle, he attended Bishop Feild College, the boys' school in St. John's in which I would later be enrolled, but he left when he was fifteen. He got a job as a newspaper reporter, eventually working his way up to Newfoundland's leading paper, the *St. John's Evening Telegram.*

In the Roaring Twenties, Joey was in New York City pursuing socialism, writing, and experiencing life. After five years there, he returned to Newfoundland, where he organized unions, edited a Liberal party paper, and tasted defeat as a Liberal candidate in Bonavista South in the Newfoundland election of 1932 as the United Newfoundland Party routed Sir Richard Squires's Liberals. It would be Smallwood's only personal defeat at the polls in a political career spanning forty years.

After spending three years trying to organize a fishermen's co-operative union in Bonavista, he moved back to St. John's, where he conceived the idea for an extremely ambitious publishing project about Newfoundland's history, geography, and folklore. This project, which culminated in the publication of *The Book of Newfoundland,* was a risky venture in the Depression. Smallwood went to see my father, who was aptly described by Harold Horwood in his 1989 book, *Joey,* as "an adventurous businessman who in the course of his short lifetime made and lost fortunes in everything from whale blubber to Coca-Cola," who "put money not only into sound, imaginative ventures, but also into unlikely ones, big and small. . . . who was the kind of free-enterprise gambler who would back anything that looked as if it might have a chance of success," and who "had passionate feelings about Newfoundland. If someone proposed a scheme that looked good for his little sea-girt isle, he'd back the scheme to the best of his ability."

Ches Crosbie was, as Horwood saw him, a limited man, with little education and no gift for public appearances, "but with daring and courage and a heart that was in the right place."* So Dad agreed to underwrite Joey's great *Book of Newfoundland* venture, not only covering the cost of printing the first two volumes, but providing offices on the top floor of the Crosbie Building, and a secretary and typists to help in the work. My father provided most of the $25,000 it cost to produce the handsome set with a print run of ten thousand. Even at a price of five dollars, few Newfoundlanders could afford the two-volume set when it came out in 1937, and copies remained in a warehouse until the 1940s, when Canadian and American servicemen snapped them up as souvenirs to send home to their families.

In trying to explain the rapport that existed between my father, a gruff, free-wheeling entrepreneur, industrialist, and risk-taker, and Joey Smallwood, a voluble, hard-working union organizer and political activist, I conclude that they were kindred spirits in their love for their island homeland and in their desire to see Newfoundland develop, grow, and prosper. Or, as Joey wrote in the first volume of *The Book of Newfoundland*, "Governments come and go, depressions come and go. The Newfoundlander possesses more than his needed share of fighting spirit; his country possesses a more than generous share of God-given wealth. The combination is irresistible."† Other than a deep, abiding love of Newfoundland, my father and Joey Smallwood didn't seem to have anything in common.

The Book of Newfoundland was a remarkable feat, but it was in radio where Joey really made his name. Calling himself "The Barrelman," he hosted a program dedicated to "making Newfoundland better known to Newfoundlanders." It was one of the most popular pre-Confederation radio programs, as Smallwood spun

---

* Harold Horwood, *Joey* (Toronto: Stoddart, 1989), p. 61.
† Joseph R. Smallwood, *The Book of Newfoundland* (St. John's: Newfoundland Book Publishers, 1937), Vol. 1, p. 3.

stories of and about Newfoundland – and Newfoundlanders listened spellbound.

After six years on radio, Smallwood went to Dad again for money. He proposed to move to Gander, where he would establish a piggery – a farm on which he would raise pigs for the wartime messes of British, Canadian, and American forces stationed at Gander, which was then the western base of the Atlantic Ferry Command and site of one of the largest and busiest airports in the world. Dad agreed to provide the financing for the piggery, which was soon producing two thousand carcasses a year to feed Allied servicemen.

At the age of forty-five, Smallwood was in the right place at the right time when, the war over, British prime minister Clement Attlee announced plans for the election of a National Convention to advise on Newfoundland's constitutional future. Joey didn't hesitate for a second. His name was well known; his voice was recognized in every home in Newfoundland. Confederation with Canada would be a popular cause. It would be *his* cause. Many others joined him in the fight to make Newfoundland part of Canada. From London, the British government provided behind-the-scenes encouragement. From Ottawa, the Canadian government and the federal Liberal party sent under-the-table financial support. But the cause was Joey's, and the victory, when it came, after two referendums in Newfoundland in 1948, was his. When Newfoundland officially became the tenth province on the last day of March 1949, it was Joseph Roberts Smallwood, undeniably the greatest politician Newfoundland had ever known, who became its first premier.

From the day he took office, Smallwood proclaimed economic development to be his highest priority. "Newfoundland must develop or perish; we cannot stand still," he declared. He created a Department of Economic Development, with himself as minister. Throughout his twenty-three years as premier, he remained steadfast in his pursuit of development and jobs for Newfoundlanders.

My sister, Joan, and me.

The figures in the foreground are, from left to right, me aged about four, with Joan, Andrew, and our mother, Jessie.

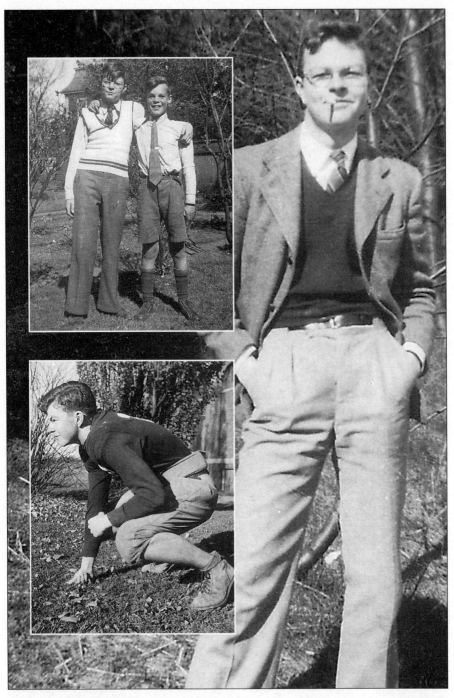

Inset above: During the war years, with Noel Goodridge, right, later chief justice of Newfoundland. *Inset below*: In a football crouch at St. Andrew's. *Background*: Aged 16.

FOR A BRIGHTER TO-MORROW

Economic Union With The United States Can Be Brought About

The Geneva Agreement Does Not Prevent the Formation of Such Unions

The Geneva Agreement Encourages the Making of Such Unions

U.S. Bases in Newfoundland Have Led to A Great Friendship Between Our Two Countries

The United States Wants Newfoundland Fish

The United States Wants Newfoundland Paper

The United States MUST HAVE Newfoundland Iron Ore

We Have What The United States Wants—The United States Has What We Want

We Can Get Together If You
VOTE
RESPONSIBLE GOVERNMENT
ON THE BALLOT PAPER

COMMISSION OF GOVERNMENT	
for a period of five years	
CONFEDERATION WITH CANADA	
RESPONSIBLE GOVERNMENT	**X**
as it existed in 1933	

CHES CROSBIE, President
Party For Economic Union With the United States

WHY WE MUST
VOTE
RESPONSIBLE GOVERNMENT
TO GET
ECONOMIC UNITED STATES UNION

The National Convention voted to send a delegation to Washington.

THE BRITISH GOVERNMENT
ANSWERED
YOU MUST GET YOUR OWN GOVT. FIRST !

The London Delegation asked if we could go to Washington.

THE BRITISH GOVERNMENT
ANSWERED
YOU MUST GET YOUR OWN GOVT. FIRST !

When asked to put Economic Union on the Ballot Paper

THE BRITISH GOVERNMENT
ANSWERED
YOU MUST GET YOUR OWN GOVT. FIRST !

That is why we must

VOTE
RESPONSIBLE GOVERNMENT
TO GET

ECONOMIC UNION MEANS:

Free trade between Newfoundland and the United States.

Newfoundland exports of fish, paper, minerals, etc., will enter the United States duty free.

American goods will enter Newfoundland duty free.

THIS WOULD MEAN:

Greater security for our primary producers—the fishermen, miners and loggers of Newfoundland.

Unheard of development of our fresh fish industry, which is entirely dependent upon the United States market.

Development of our natural resources by millions of dollars of American capital.

Newfoundland's greatest chance for the full development of Labrador.

DEVELOPMENT OF OUR FISHERIES AND OTHER NATURAL RESOURCES WILL MEAN:

A higher standard of living than ever before for all our people.

A higher standard of living than is possible under any other system.

More American dollars in our people's pockets.

More good food in our people's cupboards.

Security

Freedom from want.

A job for every Newfoundlander.

A bright future for all Newfoundland children.

A richer Newfoundland, with full employment.

A full share of the good things in life.

A happier Newfoundland, with a higher standard of living.

A brighter to-morrow.

That Is Why You MUST
VOTE
RESPONSIBLE GOVERNMENT
ON THE BALLOT PAPER

COMMISSION OF GOVERNMENT	
for a period of five years	
CONFEDERATION WITH CANADA	
RESPONSIBLE GOVERNMENT	**X**
as it existed in 1933	

ECONOMIC UNION WITH UNITED STATES

I inherited my father's belief in the virtue of free trade and accepted union with Canada reluctantly.

Our wedding picture with our parents on either side.

Graduation from Dalhousie Law School, Law Ball, Lord Nelson Hotel, October 23, 1953.

Jessie and Ches on their way to Europe aboard the *Queen Mary*, spring 1954.

Launching at Port Weller, Ontario, of the M.V. *Sir John Crosbie* in the early 1960s. From left: Ches Crosbie, unidentified, Joey Smallwood, Percy Crosbie, and three officials of Port Weller Drydocks Ltd.

Tootons Studios

St. John's City council meeting, January 1966, with the newly elected deputy mayor at the mayor's right hand.

Above: Opening the Avalon Mall in St. John's. Al Vardy is at the podium. Les Curtis is seated in the first row behind him. I was then Minister of Municipal Affairs. *Right:* As a delegate to the Liberal leadership convention held in Ottawa in spring 1968. Lester Pearson, about to be replaced as leader and prime minister by Pierre Trudeau, is in the foreground.

At Memorial Stadium in St. John's, October 1969, when I ran against Joey Smallwood for the leadership of the Newfoundland Liberal party. Being interviewed with Clyde Wells and entering the stadium (*below*) between ranks of Crosbie girls.

With Michael and Beth at about the time of the 1969 Newfoundland Liberal leadership convention.

With Jane and brother Andrew in 1972.

Unfortunately, he was an easy mark for every fast-talker, charlatan, or con man who blew into town with grandiose plans and empty pockets. Every promoter learned that Newfoundland was the place to head for if you had some crackpot scheme to flog. If you wanted a loan or a guarantee, you came here, to Newfoundland.

Smallwood listened as all these fellows spun images of the pots of gold that they assured him were waiting for the people of Newfoundland. And if the pots of gold contained a few pieces of silver for the premier or the Liberal party, well, so much the better as far as Joey was concerned.

He had no use for feasibility studies and cost-benefit analyses. If such studies or analyses were made and didn't support a project he liked, he simply ignored them and went ahead anyway. He committed the province to high-risk investments in foolhardy projects without demanding safeguards to protect the province's interests. He made deals without consulting his cabinet, which would find out only after the fact that the Premier had bought into another dream.

His develop-or-perish approach to government continued throughout his twenty-three years in power. In our first five years as a Canadian province, the Smallwood administration adopted a policy of subsidizing rapid economic development. Twenty new secondary industries were established, sixteen by firms from Germany. These were initiated by a shadowy Latvian economist, Alfred A. Valdmanis, whom Smallwood had met somewhere and hired to be Newfoundland's Director of Economic Development. Because of his personal relationship with the Premier, Valdmanis wielded enormous influence in the province between 1950 and 1953.

Valdmanis claimed to have all kinds of connections in Europe through whom to recruit industry for Newfoundland. He used to take Joey and some of his ministers over to Germany to meet industrialists there. After introducing Joey and the delegation, Valdmanis would speak to these investors in German. Right in front of Joey, Valdmanis would say, "Now, gentlemen, you understand there will have to be 10 per cent [of the provincial subsidy] paid over to me on behalf of the premier and his political party." And Smallwood would nod and smile, not understanding a word of what was being said.

A year or so later, one of the German outfits either told Smallwood or asked about this 10 per cent they were paying. Of course, if the 10 per cent had gone to Smallwood or the Liberal party, it would have been all right, but Valdmanis was keeping the money for himself. So Joey had to call in the Mounties. In the meantime, he'd been praising Valdmanis to the skies. He'd said he was going to raise statues to him on every street corner in the province. It was terribly embarrassing to Smallwood when he had to have his golden boy arrested. Valdmanis was convicted of defrauding the government; he spent some time in jail, dying not long after his release.

The cost of some of Joey's other gambles was staggering. Our small, impoverished province lost hundreds of millions of dollars in just two of his more reckless schemes: John C. Doyle's Canadian Javelin Limited linerboard mill at Stephenville, and John Shaheen's oil refinery at Come By Chance.

∾

Some people saw through Joey from the beginning. One of them was Sir Alexander Clutterbuck, who, as British high commissioner to Canada, toured the Atlantic provinces in 1950, the year after Newfoundland's entry into Confederation. In his report to London, he described his meeting with Smallwood, commenting that the Premier "obviously enjoys his position as the head of a 'one-man government' and commented to me on the benefits of 'democratic dictatorship,' which he said was only possible in a small place like Newfoundland." Clutterbuck also noted that Smallwood had described his economic policy as "make or break" – a course that the high commissioner thought had the potential to be a "lively embarrassment to the federal government."[*]

Clutterbuck was prescient. A "one-man government" with "make or break" economic policies! That described the Smallwood administration to a T. Over the years, not only did Joey embarrass the federal government, he betrayed the people of Newfoundland. But he was only half-right when he talked about his "democratic dictatorship." He was a dictator, but he was no democrat – especially as the years passed and he became hardened in his belief in his own infallibility.

∽

All of Smallwood's energy was devoted to politics and staying in power. He loved exercising power. He loved travelling around the world. He loved all the perks. He loved living well and he loved meeting other important people. Richard Nixon was one of his favourites.

He ruled like an absolute monarch. He attended the House of Assembly every second it was sitting, but he ignored everything that was said, except by himself. He treated his cabinet ministers with contempt. He controlled every facet of the Liberal provincial and federal parties in Newfoundland. He personally decided who would be the Liberal candidate in every riding in every provincial and federal election. There were no nominating conventions. Joey appointed the candidates himself. There were no local or district associations; no meetings were held; no members were elected to local executive bodies, provincially or federally. A provincial Liberal Association existed on paper; Smallwood appointed its president. If the federal Liberals were having a meeting in Ottawa, Joey picked the Newfoundland delegation.

---

[*] Quoted in Peter Neary's *Newfoundland in the North Atlantic World, 1929–1949* (Montreal and Kingston: McGill-Queen's University Press, 1988), p. 359.

He even decided which Newfoundlanders would be named to the Senate of Canada or to the Liberal cabinet in Ottawa. In 1967, he prevented Prime Minister Lester Pearson from promoting Newfoundland MP Don Jamieson to the cabinet. Smallwood astutely saw Jamieson as a threat to his hegemony. On the same occasion, he also vetoed Richard Cashin, an up-and-coming young Liberal back-bencher who Smallwood feared would become too popular in Newfoundland if he became a federal minister. Instead, Joey forced Pearson to appoint the lacklustre Charlie Granger, a member of Smallwood's own cabinet, to the job in Ottawa.

Smallwood's hold over the national party was based on the widespread belief, right or wrong, that federal candidates could get elected in Newfoundland only if they had the full and active support of Premier Smallwood, his organization, his road-paving crews, and so on. His hold was broken when he managed to deliver only one of the province's seven federal seats to the Liberals and their new leader, Pierre Trudeau, in 1968. It was only after Trudeau took over in Ottawa that Jamieson made it to the cabinet, where he served, prominently, for many years. Cashin never made it.

Joey Smallwood was a small man. A lot of leaders are short, and he was short and dynamic. He gave everything up for politics. Everything else was secondary – family relationships, sex; I think he gave it all up to devote himself to getting, keeping, and exercising power. He never stopped talking. He could talk all day and all night. A one-hour meeting with Smallwood might consist of Smallwood speaking non-stop for an hour.

Joey always claimed he was a teetotaller. He didn't drink hard liquor. Joey's father had been a heavy drinker, and this was probably the reason Joe didn't drink. But after he got to be premier, he found he enjoyed sherry. He had his own dining-room in the Confederation Building, and he always had sherry available before lunch, and after a while he got into liqueurs as well, but he didn't consider wine or liqueurs to be liquor. He became quite a connoisseur of wine. The liquor commission had a stock of wine that was brought in especially for Joey, very good wine. I remember one lunch when Bobby Brown, a big, independent Alberta oil producer, was down to see us. Joey got him into the liqueurs. Pretty soon they were smashing glasses in the fireplace in the dining-room and obviously getting tipsy.

I never saw him falling-down drunk, but I remember one night he came in the House of Assembly from a formal dinner all dressed up in white tie and tails. It was pretty obvious he'd been drinking. I was in Opposition then, so I got up on a point of order and asked the Speaker to note that the sergeant-at-arms had just come back. Joey was very offended. He didn't like having fun poked at him.

Stories about his dictatorial methods proliferated as the years passed. A man named Myles Murray was appointed to the Smallwood cabinet. Excited and eager to participate, he went to his first cabinet meeting and spoke enthusiastically about just about every matter that came up. As they walked out after the meeting, Joey put his arm around Myles.

"Well now, Myles, how did you like your first cabinet meeting?" he asked.

"Oh," said Myles, "it was wonderful, Premier, wonderful."

"Oh," said Joey, "and here I thought you hadn't enjoyed it, you were talking so much."

Myles got the message. He stayed in the cabinet for twelve years and seldom opened his mouth afterwards on any subject.

Under Smallwood, the Newfoundland House of Assembly didn't have an oral Question Period, although occasionally the Speaker might permit a question to be put to a minister. On one occasion, an Opposition member asked Max Lane, Smallwood's Minister of Fisheries, a question about some important matter. As Lane was getting to his feet, Smallwood turned, waved his hand, and said, "Sit down, Max!" Lane sank back in his seat without answering the question. Newfoundlanders have a quick sense of humour. The next morning, someone informed me that Max Lane had just had his tonsils removed. When I asked how he was, I was told he was not very well because it had been a most unusual operation. The doctors, or so they told me, had to remove Max's tonsils through his backside. When I asked why they had to go that way, I was told it was because "Joey wouldn't let him open his mouth!"

There was another character called Rossy Barbour. Rossy never made it to the cabinet, but he was a member of the House of Assembly, and he knew his place. One day, Joey was walking out of the Confederation Building, going down the front steps with a group around him, including Rossy, and Joey said, "Ross, did you fart?" He replied, "No sir, but I will if you want me to."

Some of the stories about Joey were funny. The not-so-funny thing about them was that they reflected reality. The reality was that Smallwood ruled by fear.

I saw that fear when I was running against Smallwood for the Liberal leadership in 1969. I went to see a storekeeper on the Burin Peninsula to see if I could get his support. His face turned white when I walked into his store, and he couldn't get me out of there fast enough. He held a licence from the provincial authority to sell beer in his store, and that could be quite lucrative. If I went in to see somebody who had a brewer's agent's licence, somebody in the liquor commission or one of Joey's people would call that evening to say that, if that person was ever seen talking to me again, it would be the end of his licence. Joey had informants in every community. There was always somebody who'd report where I went and whom I talked to.

It was characteristic of Smallwood that he could never conceive of any matter in which he would not act in the best interests of Newfoundland. He didn't recognize any possibility of conflict between any of his or his benefactors' private interests and the public interest of the province. He wasn't particularly secretive about it. He quite openly accepted gifts of great value from friends and associates, and from those who were doing business with the government of Newfoundland.

We had a system with liquor. Joey's friend Tony Mullowney ran the Newfoundland Liquor Commission, and favoured people got certain liquor agencies. That's where Senator Bill Petten and his father, Senator Ray, first made their money. Liquor and wine companies knew that, if they wanted to sell in Newfoundland, they should have somebody like the Pettens to act for them. They could get a licence only if Smallwood approved of them. It was the same with a licence to sell beer. They were all controlled by Smallwood through Mullowney, and they all had to pay the Liberal party.

His elaborate residence, Russwood Ranch, was located about eighty kilometres outside St. John's, on Roche's Line, on 1,400 hectares of Crown land that Joey had taken over for his own use. The house was paid for and furnished by friends and associates who did business with the provincial government, including the swimming-pool, which was constructed without charge by one of the Crosbie companies. Expensive gifts from such people as mining promoter Matthew Boylen and John C. Doyle, who held many concessions from the government, filled his residence. While claiming that he lived solely on his modest salary as premier, he enjoyed all the trappings of a wealthy man. He lacked for nothing.

Years later, Revenue Canada became interested in how Smallwood, who probably never made more than fifty thousand dollars a year, could afford to own a million-dollar home. Joey made a deal with the taxman under which he would turn Russwood over to the province for use as a museum after his death and he could continue to live there until he died. Around 1980, Smallwood wanted Brian Peckford, then the Conservative premier, to get the ownership of the house back for him, but Peckford wouldn't do it. After Clyde Wells, a Liberal, came to office, however, some arrangement must have been made to return the place to the Smallwood family, because Joey's granddaughter still lives at Russwood Ranch, raising sheep.

The most outrageous evidence of the crook in Smallwood involved the secret ownership of seven liquor stores leased to the Newfoundland Liquor Commission by the Royal Trust Company and/or Bankers' Trust Company. The annual rentals were very high; the leases were for twenty years, an exceptionally long period; and all obligations under the leases were assumed by the tenant, the liquor commission.

The total estimated cost of constructing these buildings – in Baie Verte, Clarenville, Deer Lake, Grand Bank, Marystown, Placentia, and St. Lawrence – was $175,000. The total annual rental was $74,192. Over the twenty years of the leases, the province would have to pay out $1,483,840 in rent, but, in addition, the government had to pay for heat, light, cleaning, interior repairs, exterior repairs, and municipal taxes. There was obviously a tremendous profit for the owners.

Who were the lucky owners of these buildings? The Premier claimed he did not know. He promised the House of Assembly he would find out, but he never did. It wasn't until the Moores Conservative administration took over in 1972 that we began to get answers. We appointed a royal commission to investigate. And, as many suspected, Joey Smallwood himself turned out to be a one-third owner of the seven liquor stores.

The two-member royal commission was chaired by Fabian O'Dea, a prominent lawyer and former lieutenant-governor of the province. In just six months – surely a speed record for any royal commission! – O'Dea investigated and reported. The report pulled aside the curtain of evasions and falsehoods that had hidden the sleazy business of the liquor-store leases. The seven leases were in the name of Bankers' Trust Company, a subsidiary of Toronto-based Royal Trust Company. But O'Dea quickly established that Bankers' Trust was just a front for the real owner of the buildings, a company called Investment Developers Limited (IDL).*

The commission found that IDL had the usual three subscriber shares. Two of those shares were transferred to Arthur Lundrigan, a big Newfoundland developer and pal of Joey's, and to Oliver (Al) Vardy, Smallwood's Deputy Minister for Economic

---

* See the *Report of the Royal Commission to Enquire into the Leasing of Premises for the Use of the Newfoundland Liquor Commission* (St. John's: Government of Newfoundland, 1972).

Development, Director of Tourism, and the Premier's closest, and arguably most corrupt, confidant in the government. The third share was held in trust by the company solicitor, who claimed not to know the identity of the third shareholder.

It was Vardy who blew the whistle on Smallwood. He testified that he and Lundrigan had formed IDL to make money for themselves and to provide for the financial security of their close friend Joey Smallwood. Vardy said he informed Smallwood of what they were doing, but that the affairs of IDL were never discussed with him thereafter. The commission did not believe Smallwood when he claimed that he was never a shareholder, had not consented to be a shareholder, and did not know he was a shareholder.

Evidence revealed that Smallwood had reported $11,720 in dividends from IDL on his 1970 income-tax return. Joey insisted he always signed his income-tax returns without reading them, a bit of nonsense that was demolished by his auditor, who testified he went over various portions of the 1970 return with Smallwood.

In its conclusions, the royal commission found that the rents paid by the Newfoundland Liquor Commission for the seven leases were high and that, generally, the rents the liquor authority was paying for its stores were higher than in any other province. And it found that Vardy and Lundrigan had used Smallwood's political position for their own advantage.

There was another, dirtier scandal hidden inside the liquor-lease scandal. The O'Dea Commission discovered that, beginning in April 1963, the Bank of Montreal had taken the shares of IDL as security for loans made jointly to Smallwood, Lundrigan, and Vardy. The three borrowed between $1.5 million and $1.6 million to purchase shares in the British Newfoundland Corporation (Brinco), a syndicate put together by the Rothschilds. They bought the shares at a time when Smallwood and his government were negotiating with Brinco to build the massive Churchill Falls hydro-electric development in Labrador.

In my view, the Bank of Montreal deserves a major share of the opprobrium. It was the province's banker at the time. It was also the banker for Brinco and for Arthur Lundrigan's companies. The bank knowingly made loans to the Premier; to Vardy, who held a position of high trust in the public service; and to Lundrigan, who was also a director of the Bank of Montreal. It made the loans knowing they would be used to buy shares in Brinco. It made them knowing that, with Brinco negotiating for the Churchill Falls project with Newfoundland and Quebec, these dealings posed an outrageous conflict of interest.

There's more to this sorry saga. When the Brinco shares did not perform well for the three cronies in corruption, the Bank of Montreal forgave them from having to repay hundreds of thousands of dollars of interest due on the loans. These deals involved the sort of corrupt behaviour that, by today's standards, would cause an elected leader, a public servant, and a bank director to be drummed from office and quite possibly clapped in prison.

The Bank of Montreal and Royal Trust were parties to conflict of interest, impropriety, corrupt behaviour, and malfeasance. They didn't seem to care. The Bank of Montreal's *laissez-faire* attitude was expressed in a letter its president wrote to Frank Moores confirming that it had forgiven repayment of interest on the loans: "It is difficult for this or any other bank to sit in judgment on the degree of propriety of financial transactions of persons in political life."

At one point in the hydro-electric negotiations, there had been a suggestion from Quebec that the governments of Quebec and Newfoundland should undertake the Churchill Falls project as partners, eliminating Brinco or any other private-sector participant. If this had been done, the impasse between Quebec and Newfoundland, which continues to this day, would not have occurred, and Newfoundland would have gained hundreds of millions of dollars in revenue now lost to Quebec. But Quebec's suggestion that they dump Brinco was turned down flat by Smallwood. Yet he couldn't possibly be impartial in making these decisions of immense importance to the province when he had a huge personal stake in ensuring that Brinco shares held their value.

Although the O'Dea Commission report revealed the most blatant and crass venality and conflict of interest in the history of twentieth-century Canadian politics, nothing much happened. No one in the Moores government, except me, wanted to pursue the matter. At the time, the province didn't have any conflict-of-interest legislation or regulations. Many in the new Tory government, including Frank Moores, didn't feel it would be wise politically to pursue questions of venality involving Smallwood. Given the reverence in which he was held for so many years, it would have been hard to find a Newfoundland jury that would convict him of anything, no matter the evidence. Both the Bank of Montreal and Royal Trust were large and powerful national institutions with a great deal of influence, and the government felt there was little, if anything, we could do about them. Federal banking regulators could have done something, but they chose to take no action about these shameful activities.

As Newfoundland's Finance minister, I arranged to terminate the seven liquor-store leases, and the government took over the buildings. We referred the question of criminal or civil action against Smallwood to the celebrated Toronto lawyer J.J. Robinette for an opinion, but no action was taken. Later, Moores said publicly that he thought the O'Dea Commission had been unfair in implicating Royal Trust in their report. He was convinced that "the company was totally honourable in every way," and he had no qualms about saying that. It was not an interpretation with which I could agree.

Had I been premier, I probably would have had Smallwood charged. But even I would have had to think twice about the perilous position we would have been in if we'd charged him and he wasn't convicted. Even if he was convicted, it would have been perilous, because probably half the island would have rioted. People whose dear-departed relatives were buried with his picture would not be happy to see Joey hauled off to jail. These were things we had to consider if we wanted to get re-elected. As for the Bank of Montreal, the question boiled down to this: Can they do us more damage than we can do to them? If the decision had been left to me, I think I would have done something about the bank.

The liquor leases, the conflict of interest, the malfeasance, and the serious dereliction of duty, all involving the Premier, faded quietly into history. The perpetrators survived the experience relatively unscathed. I haven't heard a word about these scandals since 1972, the year of the O'Dea Commission report. In recent years, of course, conflict of interest has become a media favourite. If these events occurred today, the reaction would probably be different.

Investigating the scandalous events of the later Smallwood years was like diving into a cesspool, and most people in politics decided this wasn't a healthy form of exercise. The public seemed to think that, if we pursued scandals, we were conducting a witch-hunt. It's the way the public thinks. The public assumes all politicians are crooks anyway.

4

IN THE TYRANT'S LAIR

I WAS THIRTY-FIVE years old when I let my ambition overwhelm my common sense and allowed Joey Smallwood, oh so easily, to talk me into entering his cabinet in 1966. I wanted to be premier that badly! After the first couple of cabinet meetings, however, I knew I was in for trouble. We would go in and sit around the table, and Smallwood would start to talk. He'd talk for the next hour, or maybe two hours, and everybody would look around wisely and nod their heads. There was nothing that could be called dialogue or discussion. A lot of the things he was doing, particularly in the economic-development field, I couldn't possibly agree with. Nobody but Joey knew what he was actually doing. In addition to being premier, he was Minister of Economic Development, but he would never have a report or analysis made. And some of it was cockamamie stuff. For example, we guaranteed the money for the Sea Mining Corporation project, a hare-brained scheme at Aguathuna, on the Port au Port Peninsula, which received $4.1 million for a manufacturing

Dennis Murphy, St. John's Daily News

plant that would supposedly turn sea water into magnesium. No feasibility study was made, and, of course, it wasn't feasible.

Chesley Pippy, a businessman pal of Smallwood's, came sniffing around for financial guarantees for the Newfoundland Steel Mill he built at Donovans, about eight kilometres outside St. John's. The cabinet couldn't get any satisfactory explanation of what the money was needed for or how it was going to enable the plant to perform better. Joey just told us Pippy was a supremely capable businessman and there was no point in questioning whether this funding would be used effectively or not. Joey knew that it would. The first feasibility study was made two years *after* the mill started operations. It eventually went bankrupt, taking about twelve million dollars out of the pocket of the Newfoundland taxpayer.

Such dubious proposals as hockey-stick factories, sawmills, wood factories, and the Custard Swept-Wing Aeroplane Manufacturing factory for Stephenville luckily never saw the light of day. But many enterprises – fish plants, breweries, and dozens of others – were given government guarantees or advances, and nearly all failed. Details were never given to the cabinet. In most cases, projects were announced by Smallwood without any cabinet discussion at all. It was a complete one-man show. Nobody else was allowed to say anything.

His administration was incredible. He personally wrote every word of every Speech from the Throne and Budget Speech. He wouldn't trust a mere Finance minister to write a Budget Speech. I remember being out at his palatial home, Russwood Ranch, one day while Joey, sitting in his reclining easy chair, dictated the entire Budget to his secretary, Betty Duff. He concocted all kinds of stuff out of thin air. Then he gave the speech to his Minister of Finance and told him to read it to the House of Assembly.*

---

* The best explanation of how Joey Smallwood acquired and wielded so much power is given by Herbert L. Pottle in *Newfoundland: Dawn without Light* (St. John's: Breakwater Books, 1979).

It was a remarkable characteristic of the Smallwood cabinet that there was no sense of collective responsibility for actions of the government. The principles of cabinet government established over the centuries in the United Kingdom made it clear that each member of a cabinet is equally and collectively responsible for all actions of the government. In the Smallwood cabinet, the members seemed to feel that Smallwood was responsible for everything and that they were responsible only for matters that came under their immediate jurisdiction as minister of a particular department.

There were some fine people in his cabinet, people I could respect, but they were not about to buck Joey. They didn't want to know what he was up to. I recall one minister, P.J. Lewis, on hearing of some government action announced by Smallwood, asking: "What's that fellow up to now?" – as though he and I could not be held responsible for whatever Smallwood did on behalf of the government.

I also remember a day when Joey set out deliberately to humiliate Arthur Monroe, who then owned Fishery Products Limited. Pioneers in the business of freezing fresh fish in Newfoundland, the company was having financial difficulties. They often got things financed through guarantees from the government and, in return, the government would take a mortgage on the fish plant or on the fishing vessels. But Arthur didn't always toe the line or sound supportive enough for Smallwood's liking. He acted a bit independent, as though he had a brain of his own. On this occasion, Joey had Monroe come into the cabinet meeting, and then behaved in a disgraceful manner towards him. "Now, you know, gentlemen," Smallwood said, "Mr. Monroe here and his company need a couple of million dollars. Should we give him a further guarantee or not? That's what he's here for. He's here like a trained seal, looking to us to toss him another bit of meat." He continued to insult and abuse poor old Monroe, who had to sit there and take it. There wasn't anything he could say without losing his chance of getting the funds his business needed to survive. I thought this was contemptible – in very poor taste and a crude piece of bullying!

Anyway, I knew well before election day in 1966 that my relationship with Smallwood was unlikely to be successful, but there was nothing I could do about it. I couldn't come in one month and leave the next. It was too late. It would have upset Joey's election plans, and he would have had to try to destroy me.

There was an incident involving Clyde Wells that illustrated the Smallwood style. At the cabinet meeting one afternoon, the Premier, as usual, opened proceedings by speaking for an hour or so before pausing for breath. Wells, who'd been appointed Minister of Labour at the same time I was made Minister of Municipal Affairs and Housing, still lived in Corner Brook, on the other side of the island, and to get home for the night he needed to catch the last flight at five o'clock. When Smallwood paused, Clyde interjected to say, "Excuse me, Premier, but it looks as though you may be starting on another long exposition and, before you do, I would like to ask to be excused as I have to catch a flight."

There were several unprecedented aspects to this intervention: First, the implication that the Premier might be long-winded; second, the suggestion that anyone would leave a cabinet meeting before the Premier had completely ventilated whatever he wished to expound upon; and, third, the idea that there could be anything more important than sitting around the cabinet table listening to the Premier had never been advanced before. The result was a Smallwood performance that would have won him an Oscar. His jaw dropped, then he looked around the table in a shocked and unbelieving manner and said:

> Gentlemen, can I believe my ears? I have never before had it suggested that I was wasting your time or that time could be better spent than in your sitting around this table discussing the affairs of the province. I have never before had a minister suggest I was taking too much time in explaining important details of public policy or asking for approval of a

course of action. Is there anyone else here that agrees with our colleague that I am wasting their time and that their time could be better spent elsewhere than in sitting around this table, which most people in the province would give their eye teeth to sit around conducting the affairs of their province?

Smallwood continued in this vein for at least another half-hour while the rest of us sat around the table, looking incredulous that anyone could possibly think that there might be something better to do than to sit, as we were, listening to the Premier. Clyde couldn't very well leave in the middle of the harangue, and so he missed his plane and had to stay overnight in St. John's.

∾

I was never on a warm or familiar basis with Smallwood. When he was alive, my father would call him "Joe" and he was "Ches." Smallwood always called me "John," but I called him "Premier" most of the time or "Mr. Smallwood." We never got any closer than that in my twenty-one months in the cabinet. I was his Minister of Municipal Affairs and Housing from 1966 to the fall of 1967, when he shuffled ministers and asked me to become Minister of Health with a mandate to prepare Newfoundland for the introduction of medicare.

He had a loud-speaker system connecting him to all his ministers. He could call down to my office without my being able to prevent it. The loud-speaker would come booming on. "John, are you there? John, are you there?" Then he'd ask me to do something. He'd press a button so that I could answer or have a conversation with him. Ministers couldn't call back up to his office to demand, "Premier, are you there?" It was a one-way system.

On the day of a provincial by-election in Gander, I was with Joey while he had a meeting in his office with Anglican canon Mark Genge, who later became a bishop, about problems in the community of Burgeo. The telephone rang for Smallwood. It was from a Liberal organizer in Glenwood, in Gander District. He informed Smallwood that the paving machines that had been resurfacing the main road through Glenwood had stopped paving at noon because it had started to rain, and they had not started up again. The citizens of Glenwood were extremely angry, saying that the government had stopped the paving even before the polls had closed, and they were going to show the government what a mistake they were making by treating the people with such contempt. So Joey went on that squawk-box of his, looking for Eric Jones, who was his Minister of Highways. He got Eric on the blower and he went berserk about the paving machines, about these "goddamn fools" out in Glenwood, and he ordered Eric to get on to them immediately and make the paving recommence. If they had a typhoon or a deluge or a cyclone, it didn't matter. The by-election was what mattered, and they were to pave those roads all day and not stop again. He really read the riot act to Eric. Now Canon Genge took all this in. He didn't get whatever he wanted for Burgeo from Smallwood, so he met the press and told them how astounded he'd been to hear Premier Smallwood humiliating one of his cabinet ministers. Of course, Joey went berserk again. He claimed it never happened, but he had to be careful. He couldn't attack an Anglican minister. As it happens, the paving machines didn't help. Joey's candidate lost the Gander by-election to a Tory.

∾

Smallwood wanted to win all forty-two seats in the House of Assembly in the 1966 provincial general election, which is why he went out of his way to recruit nineteen new and younger candidates. Of the nineteen, at least nine, including Clyde Wells and me, could be categorized as people with leadership aspirations.

I didn't have to worry about securing a nomination since all Liberal candidates in all electoral districts were appointed by Smallwood. My Progressive Conservative opponent in St. John's

West was Harvey Cole, a decent and hard-working Tory. I beat him by 4,054 votes to 2,980.

In this election, Smallwood was at the height of his political popularity. It's embarrassing, however, to revisit some of his campaign rhetoric. Here is what he told Newfoundlanders as the campaign began:

What a week! In nearly 500 years there has never been anything like it. There has never been anything even remotely like it. There may never be anything like it again. The Golden Week. Newfoundland's dream come true. Answers to our prayers. Newfoundland has hungered and thirsted for the Third Mill. Hungered and thirsted, ached and yearned and prayed. Like the child in the advertisement, "He'll never be happy 'til he gets it."

Grand Falls was such a gift from Heaven. Corner Brook was such a blessing to Newfoundland. All Newfoundlanders wanted that Third Mill. NOW WE HAVE GOT IT. AND THE FOURTH.

In one week, double the number of pulp and paper mills. On Tuesday, third mill – on Friday, fourth mill. A total capital investment of $180-million.

In the same week, a $33-million anhydrous ammonia plant. And still in the same week, a $40-million phosphorus plant at Long Harbour. Still in the same week, Newfoundland's first steel mill opened and put into operation.

And before you know it and crowning it all, Churchill [Falls]. . . . From here we go to industrial greatness. Cheap power will pour into this island from Churchill. It will come in staggering quantity. It will attract industry from both sides of the Atlantic. And create thousands more new jobs, and circulate millions more in wages, and strengthen still more the economy of our province. . . .

These are the great names, the magic words. All Liberal words. Pulp and paper; railway; electric power; cement; oil; phosphorus; mines; ammonia.

Liberal words. The noble framework of the Liberal vocabulary.

The voters caught some of Smallwood's enthusiasm. Although he didn't quite succeed in wiping out the opposition, he came close. The Liberals won thirty-nine seats, to three for the Progressive Conservatives.

Joey, however, proceeded to rule as though the tiny Opposition didn't exist. Not long after the election, the Opposition decided that it wanted to have a recorded vote on some issue, not just a show of hands. Gerry Ottenheimer, the Conservative leader, asked for a recorded vote, and Smallwood said, "No, it won't be a recorded vote." The Opposition asked, "Why won't there be a recorded vote?" "Because I have said there will not be a recorded vote," Smallwood replied. The only way to force a recorded vote in those days was for four members to stand. The Tories moved that a recorded vote be held, and the three of them stood up. I couldn't take this any more, so I stood up, too. No other Liberals stood, of course. If you'd put an electric prod under their seats, they wouldn't have stood up. My Liberal colleagues were dumbfounded. Smallwood couldn't see me because I was behind him. But the Speaker said there would be a recorded vote, so Joey turned around, and saw me. If looks could kill, I was dead. When we had the recorded vote, I voted with the government, of course.

But the episode turned my guts. I couldn't stand it. It was just an exhibition of raw power: *You can't have a recorded vote simply because I've decided you're not going have it.* Smallwood stayed in the House of Assembly every minute. If the Assembly was open, he was there. He wouldn't trust anyone else. He was there to watch and to observe and to make sure it was run the way he wanted it run.

In November 1967, Premier John Robarts of Ontario called together a "Confederation of Tomorrow" conference in Toronto to discuss constitutional disagreements between Quebec and the Government of Canada. This was a meeting of the ten provincial premiers and delegations, without the federal government. I was part of the Newfoundland delegation, and during the conference Smallwood was hospitalized for treatment of a detached retina. Before returning to St. John's, I visited him in the hospital. When I asked how he was doing and how he was feeling, he replied, "Very well. Disappointed?"

∾

At the federal Liberal leadership convention in Ottawa in April 1968, Smallwood put on one of his greatest performances. Lester Pearson had retired and it was assumed that Newfoundland's delegates would support Robert Winters, the Minister of Trade and Commerce, who had been the chief executive officer of Brinco, and had been friendly with and helpful to Smallwood during negotiations over the Churchill Falls hydro-electric project in Labrador. But friendship and gratitude count for less in politics than in any other field of endeavour. Smallwood was smitten with Pierre Trudeau, the Justice minister. Joey thought the party should choose a French Canadian to succeed the English-Canadian Pearson, and he felt that Trudeau had the personality, intelligence, and other attributes to win elections. He decided all Newfoundland delegates would support Trudeau.

This came as a surprise to many of our delegates. During convention week, the press broke a dramatic story of dissension in the Newfoundland delegation, and how many of the delegates would be supporting Winters, despite their premier's choice. Some even went on television to endorse Winters. Joey was not amused. Next morning, he summoned all Newfoundland voting delegates, alternates, and hangers-on to an emergency meeting. Smallwood was at the top of his form: "After all I have done for Newfoundland and for the Liberal Party in Newfoundland and for the members of that party in Newfoundland, and for everyone associated with the party in Newfoundland, including all those present, is this the way I am to be treated? Am I to be ignored, scorned, cast aside, treated as dirt, trampled on, by my own people gathered here in Ottawa? Is this my reward for all my many and loyal services to Newfoundland and to the Liberal Party?"

After listening to Joey's harangue for an hour or so, some of the delegates broke down and admitted that they were not worthy of Smallwood's trust and faith, but that they would now rally around and support Trudeau, as Joey had informed them it was in the interest of Newfoundland to do. They would follow the chief wherever he led them. It was Ready, aye ready! When their duty was pointed out to them as clearly as Joey had pointed it out, they knew what to do. They were followers and he was the leader. Unanimity was restored. As it was a secret ballot, I have no way of knowing how the delegates actually voted. My guess is the vast majority marked their X for Pierre Elliott Trudeau. I know I did.

∾

By this time, Smallwood had been our absolute leader for nearly twenty years, and he was completely paranoid. He thought that anybody who had any talent was burning with ambition for his job. He accused me of being consumed by ambition. To appreciate the full force of his paranoia, here is how he described me on radio after I left the Liberals:

The man is a political tragedy. He is a striking example of what can happen to a young man when he allows ambition – vaulting, overweening, immoderate, impatient, personal-career ambition – when he allows that to take uncontrolled possession of him. I would say quite definitely that his political reason is tottering. It's a sad case. . . .

Everybody in the House knows that we are faced by a hate-filled man. A man whose political reason is tottering. A man who is just a bagful of hate. A skinful of hate. He can't conceal it. He can't sit down, he can't stand still. He is doing one of two things in that House always: he is up on his feet talking or is walking out of the House. He can't sit there. He can't stay there. He gets up and gives a speech and he walks out. He comes back and stands up again and makes a speech. Twenty speeches in a day. He can't shut up. He can't hold his tongue. He can't close his mouth. He's so full of hate, so completely dominated by hate of me, that it's – look, it makes you ashamed to look at it. . . .

Now I am saying now, very publicly, that this man is a great, big – he must weigh two hundred pounds – he is two hundred pounds of vicious hate and, while I am alive on this earth – sometimes I am afraid, maybe I should have a bodyguard – while I'm alive on this earth, that man will hate me to my grave. Now, that is a diseased mind. That's political reason that is tottering – it's undermined. The man is a sad case, but in the meantime he is bedevilling the House of Assembly. He's just bedevilling it. He's turned it into a beer garden.

Even by Newfoundland's generous political standards, that was an uncommonly rough personal attack. If I'd really been burning with ambition, as Joey said I was, I would have acted completely differently. I would have been kissing his arse. I wouldn't have been getting him riled up. I would have wanted to get in line to succeed him, and the only way anyone could do that would be by arse-kissing, boot-licking, and doing whatever he wanted.

∽

What caused me to break with Smallwood had nothing to do with ambition. It had everything to do with the way he was running the province into an economic black hole. I'd become increasingly uneasy about his economic-development policies and the huge financial obligations he was exposing the province to. He guaranteed financing for literally dozens of projects without any independent studies as to their feasibility or viability. It seems astonishing, but he did not have a single economist on staff in the Department of Economic Development, of which he was the minister. Smallwood would announce a project as soon as it was suggested to him, without knowing whether it had any chance of succeeding. He would then be forced to make concession after concession to the promoters, since it would be an embarrassment to the government for a project not to go forward after it had been announced.

Our only real hope of getting Smallwood to change his madcap approach to economic development lay with the four-teen-member provincial Royal Commission into Economic Prospects for Newfoundland, which was appointed in 1964 and reported in 1968. The report was a devastating indictment of the Premier's approach to economic development. It empha-sized the need for feasibility studies and cost-benefit analyses before assistance was given to any project. Of course, sane think-ing like this was anathema to Smallwood. None of the royal commission's recommendations was accepted; as Smallwood declared: "Nine of the fourteen never read a word of the report. . . . they signed a blank paper. . . . it is 90 per cent trash and 10 per cent solid gold. It is full of partisanship and written with a purpose." The report vanished from sight and memory!

My greatest concern centred on the arrangements Smallwood was making with his two favourite promoters – John C. Doyle, the head of Canadian Javelin Limited, who proposed to build a linerboard mill at Stephenville, and John Shaheen, who dangled the dreams of a paper mill (known as the "third mill") plus a world-scale oil refinery, both at Come By Chance. I suggested to Smallwood that he appoint a cabinet committee to negotiate the detailed legal agreements with Doyle and Shaheen for these projects. Smallwood didn't think much of the idea, but he agreed, probably because he figured it would be a way to keep the "Kiddies Corner" of his cabinet out of his hair. He appointed three of us "kiddies" – Clyde Wells, Alex Hickman, and me – along with old-timer Leslie Curtis, to the committee. Curtis – who in his years as Minister of Justice had conducted a lucrative private law practice representing promoters who wanted Joey's ear and whose firm acted for both Shaheen and Doyle – never attended any of the committee meetings. Hickman, Wells, and I, however, held many meetings during 1967 and 1968 with Shaheen or Doyle, or their hirelings. Our objective was simply to try to ensure that some minimal protection was afforded to the government of Newfoundland in return for its huge financial contribution to their projects.

Both promoters regarded our cabinet committee as an irritant. Our meetings with them were formally correct, with an undercurrent of animosity. The two were on the phone to Smallwood a dozen times a day, and we knew that, if they had a major objection to something the committee wanted done, they'd go over our heads to the Premier. And they did.

The third mill project of Shaheen's Newfoundland Pulp and Chemical Limited never got off the ground because there wasn't enough wood available on the whole island of Newfoundland to supply it. Nevertheless, Smallwood guaranteed loans for Newfoundland Pulp and Chemical with which it constructed a building at Come By Chance in the period leading up to the 1966 election. The building was never completed, and Newfoundland lost the millions of dollars it guaranteed.

Because the third mill was never likely to become a reality, despite having been announced with great fanfare by Joey, our committee concentrated on the linerboard mill and the oil refinery. If Wells and I had had our way, we would have dumped both schemes and told the promoters to clear out and not come back. We were forced to deal with them because of Smallwood's desire that the projects proceed.

Wells and I decided we had to make a stand on the Come By Chance refinery. The agreement was completely one-sided, offering, as far as we could see, little economic benefit to Newfoundland, but posing great financial risks. Shaheen already had a sweetheart deal, and he tried to sweeten it with Smallwood's assistance. After months of tense negotiations, we finally obtained some small improvements in the agreement. Smallwood then suggested that Shaheen needed interim financing to launch the enterprise, despite all of the concessions the government had made.

The deal obligated Shaheen to invest ten million dollars in equity in the project once construction was completed, but he was not prepared to put any equity in or to arrange interim financing to initiate the project. And why should he, when his friend Premier Smallwood would arrange government-guaranteed loans for interim financing?

He told Joey he couldn't arrange interim financing and the government would have to guarantee the ten million dollars he needed. This was to be money advanced before Shaheen carried out any of his commitments under the agreement. It negated the value of the safeguards we had negotiated. First, Joey wanted to give him ten million dollars for interim financing. Then the amount was reduced to five million dollars because Wells, Hickman, and I were adamant that Shaheen not receive any interim financing at all. We thought the cabinet agreed with us. A couple of weeks later, however, when the question came back to cabinet, the amount was back up to ten million dollars. Shaheen had gone to Joey, and Joey, totally ignoring the cabinet, had made the commitment.

Shaheen's contempt for the brains, ability, or backbone of any of Smallwood's ministers was transparent. I was not prepared to accept such an arrangement or to work any longer under such humiliating circumstances. Nor was Clyde Wells. Alex Hickman was opposed to further concessions to Shaheen, but he wasn't willing to resign over it. I was ready to make a stand alone, but it was a great comfort to have Wells's support.

By now it was May 1968. Wells and I told the cabinet we were opposed to any interim financing at all for Shaheen. "We will not support this. If cabinet approves this, we're not supporting it. We'll oppose it." We had a huge row at the cabinet meeting, then Joey took us aside and said: "Now, think it over for three or four days, and come in and see me Monday morning and tell me whether you are still opposed to this."

Not trusting Smallwood, Clyde and I spent a couple of days preparing our resignation letters. I discussed my situation with my wife, Jane, my brother, Andrew, and my uncles Percy and Bill Crosbie, as well as with several close friends. Their conclusion was that I had to do what I thought was right, but everybody knew that this was a very serious step, with consequences that no one could foresee. My mind was made up, because I could no longer put up with the insane atmosphere of Smallwood's cabinet. I realized that any political future I might have would be seriously compromised, because Liberals prized what they called "loyalty" to the Liberal party. To complicate matters, the new national Liberal leader, Pierre Trudeau, had just called a Canadian general election for June 25, 1968.

On Monday morning, Clyde and I went to his office, and Smallwood asked if we'd changed our minds. We said we hadn't. So he produced two letters and said, "I'm dismissing you." I said, "Like fuck you are. Here's my letter of resignation." I flicked it right at him as he passed me my letter of dismissal. The treacherous devil had sent us off so he could have three or four days to figure out how he was going to handle our insubordination.

A quick glance at Smallwood's letter revealed the despicable tactic that he was attempting. As we left his office, Smallwood darted from his chair and vanished through the door that led from his office to the cabinet room. He had already called the news media there for a press conference to put out his own version of events. Clyde and I hurriedly decided to have a press conference at the Press Club. That the story was going to be a sensational one was obvious. It would have been a major story if two ministers had left Smallwood's cabinet at any time, even if their departure was relatively civilized, but, with the tactics Smallwood had chosen, there was going to be a monumental political battle.

My letter to Smallwood was five pages long, as I had tried to cover every point thoroughly. I wrote that I was resigning because I could no longer endure certain of Smallwood's policies and because I found it impossible to serve in an administration where the views of one man must always prevail. I said that the Come By Chance refinery dispute was just the latest of several instances where I disagreed with his policies, and that I could not continue to compromise on points where I had strong views as to what should be done in the interest of Newfoundland. So I was resigning from the government to sit in the Assembly as an independent Liberal.

Smallwood's letter to me contained three pages of clever but completely untrue suggestions and innuendoes about my allegedly having used my influence to try to obtain business for my "family's companies." The letter pointed out that government had paid my "family's construction company" more than fifty million dollars, presumably over many years, and that our airline company, Eastern Provincial Airways, had been helped by the government. He had detected a strange attitude in me during my months in his cabinet. An unnamed member of my family was said to have gone to New York City and called on John Shaheen and demanded the "contracts for your family's construction company and for your family's insurance company and also for certain shipping interests of your family." Another unidentified Crosbie allegedly telephoned Shaheen with similar demands and called on John C. Doyle to demand contracts with the linerboard mill. My relative, Smallwood claimed, was promised the insurance business for the mill. All of these "facts" were reported in detail to Smallwood, but he had given me the benefit of the doubt and chose to assume that all of this was going on without my knowledge. However, as I had persistently endeavoured to block the Come By Chance complex, Smallwood was forced to the unpleasant conclusion that I was taking positions in cabinet based on whether the promoters were willing to give business to Crosbie companies. He said he was compelled by these and other circumstances to ask for my immediate resignation.

When I entered provincial politics two years earlier, I realized I was vulnerable to allegations of conflict of interest because of the dominance of the government in the commercial life of a small province. So I sold to my brother all the shares I held in Eastern Provincial Airways, Crosbie and Company, Lease-Back Projects Limited, and Newfoundland Engineering and Construction Company Limited. I also resigned as an officer or director of all of these, which were the family companies most involved in business with the government of Newfoundland.

This precaution did not stop Smallwood. His letter showed the depths to which he could descend. There was no truth in any of his allegations. Crosbie companies, like others, were naturally interested in doing business with anyone who was proposing new development in the province. They probably contacted Doyle and Shaheen; it would have been odd if they hadn't done so. But at no time did anyone from my family or Crosbie-owned companies make demands or threats, or in any way suggest that the positions I took in cabinet could be influenced by business awarded to, or withheld from, these companies. This was a complete fabrication.

At his press conference, Smallwood made the mistake of naming the Crosbies whom he claimed had demanded and threatened and acted improperly in concert with me to obtain business from Shaheen and Doyle. They were my brother, Andrew, and our uncles Percy and Bill Crosbie. Because he made these charges in public, not in the House of Assembly, Smallwood's allegations were not privileged and he was not protected from libel or slander actions. I decided to sue Smallwood for defamation of character. Andrew, Percy, and Bill made it clear they, too, would take legal action against Smallwood. Andrew, in particular, quickly made Smallwood realize that he had to retract all his allegations or face a fight to the finish with all of the Crosbies, not just me.

After three days of negotiation, Smallwood retracted all allegations completely and without qualification. This meant that this issue, manufactured by Smallwood, was now out of the way so that the focus would be on the true reason for our resignations.

I had made my mind up that Smallwood was going. I wouldn't put up with being attacked like this and publicly lied about. I wouldn't succumb to a dictator. It was me or Smallwood. If it was the last thing I did, I intended to terminate Smallwood's political career. Anything that improved my chance of achieving that objective was what I was going to do.

5

IN PURSUIT OF
LEADERSHIP (1)

IT IS IMPOSSIBLE for anyone who has not been through what I went through with Joey Smallwood between 1966 and 1968 to understand the effect it had on my wife and family. I had ignored the wise advice of my father not to go into politics while Smallwood was still on the scene. I had allowed my political ambitions to outweigh my doubts about many of Smallwood's policies and his actions in running the government. I had spent twenty-one months working strenuously in an atmosphere that was stressful and distasteful. Now, having resigned from Smallwood's administration, I was engaged in a battle to salvage my reputation and to survive in politics.

I had jeopardized the businesses of my brother and uncles, none of whom had anything to gain by my involvement in politics, and all of whom had a great deal to lose as a result of my resignation and Smallwood's reaction to it. My family were there when I needed them, and never faltered in defending my character and reputation as well as their own. However nervous it must have made them, they understood why I was determined to bring about the end of the Smallwood administration.

Joey wasted no time in striking back at Wells and me. When the House of Assembly convened on the afternoon of our resignations, we discovered that our seats had been removed from the Government side, carried to the Opposition side near the four Progressive Conservative MHAs, and bolted to the floor – to make sure we didn't try to move them back. Smallwood had a Liberal member move a motion of confidence in the government, to be debated immediately. Joey forced every Liberal to declare support for him. No matter how awkward this was for many of them, they all fell in line. Those seeking cabinet positions were particularly critical of Clyde's and my reprehensible action.

Smallwood was scathing in the debate. He was beside himself, seeming almost possessed. He cut me to pieces. I didn't do well at all. To the people in the public gallery, I seemed shy and uncomfortable. I didn't project my voice. My delivery detracted badly from the clarity and effectiveness of what I had to say. In the end, remarkably, all forty-two members of the Assembly spoke. The debate went on until 2:00 A.M., ending in a May snowstorm, the bleakness of which matched my mood.

Odd though it may seem, I wasn't ready to leave the Liberal party. Indeed, I was quickly caught up in the June 25 federal election campaign, in which I made a point of campaigning for the Liberal candidate in my riding. I felt Smallwood would be most vulnerable if Wells and I maintained the principle that we could disagree with him and still be good Liberals, and that he had no authority to decree that we were no longer Liberals.

However, our resignations did incalculable damage to Liberal prospects in Newfoundland in the federal campaign. The election was no longer about Swinging Pierre and participatory democracy, but about Smallwood and authoritarianism. A tide that had started to turn with the Gander provincial by-election the year before was now ripping across Newfoundland. While the rest of Canada was revelling in Trudeaumania, we were swept up by Smallwoodphobia. Progressive Conservatives were elected in six of the seven Newfoundland seats, with Don Jamieson in Burin–Burgeo barely managing to defeat his unknown Tory opponent, a druggist who never bothered to campaign outside Port Aux Basques, where he lived. In the previous election, in 1965, the Liberals had taken all seven seats in Newfoundland, with 65 per cent of the popular vote. Now 84,419 Newfoundlanders had voted Tory, to just 68,549 for the Liberals. It was the greatest rebuke Joey had ever suffered. It was a political earthquake he could not ignore.

Not surprisingly, people began to speculate openly about Joey's future. He'd been premier for nineteen years. How much longer could he hang on? Would he jump, or would he have to be pushed? He kept saying he was ready to leave. "This is definitely my last," he told a rally in Corner Brook in 1966 –

Like I said before, in four years I'll be as old as Diefenbaker and that will surely be time to quit. Yes, this is my last election. A trail-blazer, that's what I have been. But, just about now, my trail-blazing has come to an end. I'll be 70 by the time the next election rolls around. Would Newfoundland want a 70-year-old premier? Especially when I have a group of young, smart Newfoundlanders in the cabinet. A leadership convention will be called and that's where the next leader will be chosen.

A few days after the 1968 federal election, however, Smallwood held a press conference to offer all kinds of reasons why "the tide has gone out." None assigned any blame to him. One reason was that Pentecostals had voted against Pierre Trudeau, because they believed he was a communist or a homosexual. No matter what fanciful reasons he advanced for the election catastrophe, Smallwood knew he had to act to recover momentum, so he announced there would be a great reorganization of the Liberal Party of Newfoundland to make it democratic. A Liberal Association would be organized in every electoral district. And there would be, in 1969, a great leadership convention to select a leader to succeed Joey, who would resign at that time – or so he said.

A reporter asked Smallwood whether he would accept a draft as leader. "No. Definitely not," he declared. "I will not accept the nomination. If I am nominated, I won't run, and if I am elected without being nominated, I won't serve."

Nothing could be clearer than that, but, as events would soon reveal, Smallwood never felt bound by declarations of his intentions. The next year, when he reversed himself, he told Robert Miller of the *Toronto Daily Star* that he intended to lead the party in the next couple of elections, adding: "Everybody forgets, or never notices, the little weasel words from little weasel politicians. I said I wanted to carry on for at least two years. At least. Don't those words mean anything? At least!"

As creation of the new, democratic Liberal party ostensibly began, skirmishing broke out over whether Wells and I were still Liberals and entitled to participate in the reform process. "I, the leader of the party, say he [Crosbie] is not," Smallwood said. "He may be a Liberal, in many ways he is indeed a Liberal, but he is not a member of the Liberal party." He said he would welcome me to resume a place in the party if I would affirm that "I am loyal to the Liberal party, the government, and the leader of the party." I responded by saying that, while I supported the Liberal party, I could not affirm loyalty to the current provincial leader. I said I would support the government in the Assembly, except when I disagreed with government policy in the economic-development areas outlined in my letter of resignation.

I had already decided to run for the leadership of the new, democratic Liberal party if the reforms announced by Smallwood were actually put in place. Obviously, I could not run unless I was a member of the party. Although I refused to affirm loyalty to Smallwood, I was accepted as a member.

∽

It was around this time that my friends and supporters brought my deficiencies as a public speaker to my attention. My speeches usually had good content, but my droning, monotone style meant people could not listen for long without their attention wandering. If I was going to unseat Joey Smallwood, I would have to do something about this. Jane had taken a Dale Carnegie course and she thought her instructor, Howie Young, could do something with me. I didn't take a Carnegie course, but every week or so some of us – Jane and I and our good friends Jim and Joan Roberts and Bob and Betty Young – would meet with Howie at one of our homes. Instead of dancing or playing cards, as other couples might, we took turns making speeches. Public speaking is very much like acting. You have to project yourself and adopt a role. You have to give a performance. With Howie's help, I soon acquired a lustier, more vivid way of speaking. This was the genesis of the John Crosbie speaking style that Canadians came to know in my years in Ottawa.

Jane tells me I've finally lived up to the quote under my photo in the Dalhousie University yearbook: "Even though vanquished, he will argue still." I like speaking. I like it too much. As Hubert Humphrey once said: "I've never made a speech that was too long. I've enjoyed them all." That's my problem. I entertain myself, and, the next thing I know, I'm going on too long. But I seem to have a flair for the short sound bites that television demands. I usually have no trouble thinking up a catchy line or phrase. You have to do that these days if you want to get on the air.

∾

I went to all the founding meetings of the new Liberal associations. It was an opportunity to meet party activists. From their ranks would come the delegates to the leadership convention in 1969. Smallwood attended and spoke at these meetings, too. His speeches were never under an hour in length, and I became an expert at observing his techniques and absorbing the punishment of listening to his endless repetition. Joey was a very good speaker in his day, but by now he was getting tiresome. He assumed everyone had the mentality of a two-year-old, and he repeated everything five or six times. Although many of the people still loved him, they recognized that the old ways had to change, and they liked the fact that Wells and I had the courage of our convictions and were unafraid to express our views. I was invited to speak at these meetings, until Joey had the new provincial executive rule that only the leader could address founding meetings. At the founding meeting for the district of Green Bay, a young teacher, Brian Peckford, was elected secretary. I spoke with him following the meeting and could see that he was the kind of person who could be very helpful to our cause. He later became one of my three full-time organizers for the leadership convention. Like thousands of other Liberals, he followed me into the Conservative party. He won a seat in the Assembly in 1972, becoming leader and premier in 1979 on the retirement of Frank Moores.

∾

There had to be something wrong with me for undertaking something as quixotic as running for the leadership of the party that Smallwood believed to be his and his alone. The convention was set for October 31 and November 1, 1969, in St. John's. Each district association was to send 24 elected delegates, plus 8 members of the district executive. Altogether, there would be 1,700 voting delegates.

By June that year, it was becoming obvious that I was going to win the convention easily if the only other serious candidate was Dr. Fred Rowe, a veteran Smallwood minister and confidant. Joey was going to be in the humiliating position of seeing me succeed him as leader and premier. But, while visiting Marystown that month, I received a telephone call from a party organizer and Smallwood supporter. She tipped me off that Joey was about to announce the postponement of the leadership convention for a year. I returned to St. John's immediately and passed this story to the news media, along with my demands that Smallwood carry out his repeated commitments to hold a convention in 1969, and that he resign and turn the leadership over to whomever was selected at the convention. Smallwood made a statement that he would like to put the leadership convention off, but that his decision on a postponement would be guided by the wishes of the new district Liberal associations. We quickly contacted all the district associations; twenty-six of them voted in favour of a convention in 1969, while only three voted to postpone it. A majority of active Liberals felt they had been promised a democratic party and a leadership convention, and they were going to have a leadership convention – or there would be hell to pay!

Even Smallwood realized he could not risk the political damage of a postponement. But the duplicitous little dodger had another card up his sleeve. He announced the convention would be held as promised and that he would resign as leader on the opening day – *but* that he would immediately put his name in nomination for re-election. Fred Rowe and Ross Barbour, a fringe candidate, immediately dropped out. I had to decide what to do.

It was obvious that my chances of winning a leadership contest against Smallwood were zilch. I'd have had to be a nut case to think I had any chance of beating Joey. He'd be able to call upon hundreds, even thousands, of people who were under some kind of obligation to him to work on his behalf. He had all the powers of the government of Newfoundland to exercise.

Reports of intimidation poured in. Beer distributors were given one half-hour to report to the Confederation Building; sawmill operators were told they would get no further timber limits if they didn't support Smallwood; fish-plant operators had their trucks weighed and their plants closed if they said they were going to support me; a fisherman was told by Smallwood that his application for a bounty to construct a longliner (a middle-distance fishing vessel) would be removed from the list if

he did not support Joey; men lost their jobs with the Newfoundland Power Commission.

Smallwood was determined to save the party, as he put it so
quaintly, from "falling into the wrong hands."

The people working with me wanted me to stay in the race. I
decided to continue, even though I realized I had no chance
of winning. I did have the option of joining the Progressive
Conservatives. Many Tories were urging me to do just that –
and to get ready to run for the leadership of their party. The
Conservative leader at the time was Gerry Ottenheimer, who'd
been involved in an unfortunate incident that had hurt him
badly politically. On a trip to Montreal, he was found in a whore-
house when the police raided it. It was widely suspected that
Gerry had been caught in a trap set up by a German fellow
who was in the entertainment and nightclub business in
Newfoundland. He allegedly did it as a favour to Joey's people,
but no one really knew. After the incident became public,
Ottenheimer resigned as the Tory leader.

But the Conservatives were nothing in those days. They
had only four members. The whole battle was within the Liberal
party, so I chose the option of carrying on. I figured it would cause
Smallwood more trouble if I fought the thing to the end. If I'd
joined the Tories then, I might well have won their leadership
and become premier in 1972 instead of Frank Moores. If so, I
might never have ended up in government in Ottawa. But this
was 1969, and I figured the Conservative option would always be
there and could be exercised later if it became obvious there was
no other way to terminate Smallwood's reign. I was consumed by
the need to end the kind of government that Newfoundland was
enduring, and that could be done effectively, I thought, only if I
continued on the course I had set.

My brother, Andrew, who was looking after the finances of
my campaign, recommended that I withdraw from the race. But
when I decided to stay in, Andrew, to his great credit, continued his support. He raised money or arranged financing for my

whole campaign, somehow managing not to burn all his bridges with Joey.

Political campaigns are expensive. Organizers had to be paid; travelling expenses of the candidate and his assistants and organizers had to be met; halls had to be rented; policy booklets printed; newspaper, radio and TV time bought. We had to hire buses to deliver supporters to the delegate-selection meetings. At the convention, entertainment suites and rivers of booze had to be provided, Crosbie girls had to be clothed in Crosbie costumes, Crosbie buttons had to be purchased. The expenses were unending. The Newfoundland leadership battle was no ordinary contest. It was like a general election fought in every electoral district of the province. I was locked in battle with a Smallwood machine that had been organizing and winning elections since 1949, a machine that used every shred of influence, power, and authority available to the government.

In our planning for the campaign, we had a budget of $150,000. When the campaign was over, I discovered it had cost more than $400,000, and there was a loan of $300,000 owed to the Bank of Montreal. According to Andrew, the final cost was in the area of $530,000. This was an astounding amount of money to spend in 1969; allowing for inflation, it would be the equivalent of $2.3 million today. The Smallwood campaign cost him $1 million – the equivalent of $4.4 million today. But, as premier, all his bills were paid by businesses that dealt with the provincial government; for example, his allocation of choice service-station sites along the Trans-Canada Highway resulted in a handsome contribution to his campaign. As the loser, with no favours to bestow, I had to find the money to repay the Bank of Montreal myself. I did it by selling the shares I owned in a number of family businesses, such as Chimo Shipping and Wabush Enterprises, to Andrew. Eventually, the $300,000 bank debt was paid off.

∽

In September 1969, I published my campaign booklet, *Building for the New Newfoundland – Priorities for Progress*. A 56-page document, it was distributed to 15,000 Liberal party members. Joey responded by personally writing a 175-page book, *To You with Affection from Joey*, which was sent to 100,000 Newfoundland households, at government expense.

Both my people and Joey's crowd bused people to delegate-selection meetings. The Pentecostals were a very fertile group for Smallwood. The pastor would arrive with a busload of these people, and they'd come into the meeting and all hold their cards and vote as a block. They were Smallwood's shock troops.

We got a nasty surprise in St. John's East, where Joey's people outvoted us. They carried them in on stretchers from the hospitals. There was one woman who came in on a stretcher – we called her "Blue Lips" because she looked like a corpse – to vote for Joey's slate. Then they carried her out again.

A few weeks before the convention, after all the slates had been chosen, Alex Hickman, Joey's Justice minister, announced he was going to be a candidate. Smallwood immediately fired him from the cabinet. Hickman's only hope was to persuade delegates that he was their one chance to unite the party. It was an appealing pitch. It could work, however, only if delegates who were pledged to Joey or me were prepared to switch to Hickman.

Hickman's entry, plus rumours my workers were circulating that many delegates elected on Joey's slates were secretly pledged to vote for me, caused Smallwood to take steps to enforce his delegates' commitments. The delegations elected on Smallwood slates in each district were summoned to appear at Russwood Ranch, where they were given a pledge to sign.

The delegates from Bell Island, for example, swore an affidavit: "We were elected to vote for Premier Smallwood in the leadership convention and this is exactly what we intend to do." They all signed their names to this solemn commitment. In the district of Port de Grave, delegates signed this statement: "We the undersigned delegates offered ourselves voluntarily to the registered

Liberals of Port-de-Grave district as Joey delegates and we were elected as such. We wish to assure all registered Liberals in Port-de-Grave district that we will not let them down but will carry out their wishes for us to vote for Premier Smallwood for leader. Recent developments have not changed our minds in the least." Then the names followed.

Joey had all these affidavits from Smallwood delegates published in the St. *John's Evening Telegram* a week before the convention. He didn't want anyone to think there was any chance that he was not going to be re-elected, and he wanted everyone to remember who would be in control after the convention.

When the convention opened at the St. John's Memorial Stadium, it was clear that the enmity between the Smallwood delegates and the rest of the delegates far exceeded the normal hard feelings among competing groups at a leadership convention. The race had become a civil war. There was no mixing: a Smallwood delegate would not go to a Crosbie hospitality suite, or vice versa. Smallwood delegates were followed and watched by Smallwood agents and kept from all contact with Crosbie delegates. Hundreds of Smallwood delegates were billeted on a ship, the M.V. *William Carson*, or on fourteen railway sleeper-cars during the convention to keep them away from my people.

The balloting came as no surprise. Smallwood received 1,070 votes, Crosbie 440, and Hickman 187, with 17 distributed among three other candidates. The crowd's reaction showed that the Liberal party was irrevocably split. Many of my younger supporters shocked older Liberals by shouting, "Seig Heil," and holding their right arms aloft in the Nazi salute. Some burned Liberal party membership cards on the spot. Smallwood's victory was, as John Frecker, a student-council president at Memorial University, put it, "the most vivid demonstration of a Pyrrhic victory since Greek times."

The one thing I had forgotten to do before the voting took place was to warn our youngest child, Beth, who was nine, that

I wasn't going to be leader. Naturally she thought her daddy was going to win and was terribly upset when the result was announced. We still have a photograph of her crying over Daddy's defeat.

6

The Defeat of Joey Smallwood

ANY POSSIBILITY, HOWEVER remote, of a rapprochement between Joey Smallwood and me vanished at the end of the tumultuous Newfoundland Liberal leadership convention in 1969. True to his vindictive form, Smallwood tried to embarrass his defeated opponents, Alex Hickman and me, by demanding that we come up on the platform and give him our public congratulations. Gritting our teeth, we did it – and, as he insisted, we moved that the vote be made unanimous.

I didn't really mind too much. My biggest fear at this point was that Joey would do the *right* thing – be magnanimous, be conciliatory, say all was forgiven, and invite everyone back into the party to bind up the wounds. I needn't have worried. The next day, Smallwood crowed to the media that he'd buried me ten feet deep. And he refused to take Hickman and Val Earle, who had supported Hickman, back into his cabinet. Instead of consolidating his victory, he deepened the divisions in the party and hardened the determination of his foes.

For those of us who had opposed Smallwood, the issue now was strategy. We held several heated meetings. In the end, Hickman and Earle decided that the only practical way to get rid of the little tyrant was by joining the four Tory members of the Assembly. One of our group, and only one, chose to go back to Smallwood. Nath Noel rejoined the Liberal caucus, became Deputy Speaker of the Assembly, and was later named to the Newfoundland Supreme Court.

My post-convention strategy was to continue, for the time being, to oppose Smallwood, as an independent Liberal. I still regarded myself as a Liberal; the Liberal party had an honoured place in Newfoundland history, and I wasn't about to let a despot drive me out of *my* party. I would do whatever would weaken Joey the most. In the unlikely event that he decided to step down voluntarily, our best chance of taking over and forming a government after the next election would be as Liberals. But, if and when it became clear that Joey intended to fight another election, we could either form our own party or join the Conservatives and drive Smallwood from office that way.

And that's how it unfolded. I spent the next two years as an independent Liberal, then joined Frank Moores and the Tories. After two general elections – in 1971 and 1972 – we finally finished Smallwood off.

Clyde Wells had already decided not to stand for election again, but he wasn't about to give up the struggle against Smallwood. He, Beaton Abbott, and Gerry Myrden went into Opposition with me as the Liberal Reform Group, with me as their chairman. We four Liberal Reformers, the six Conservatives, and Tom Burgess, the volatile politician from Labrador West who sat as an Independent Labrador member, comprised the Opposition to Smallwood. With eleven of us, five of whom had been ministers in Smallwood cabinets, we had the numbers and experience to be an effective fighting force. We knew where the government was vulnerable, where many bodies were buried, and we enjoyed a sympathetic news media. Day after day, we undermined the Government. For the first time in twenty years, Joey Smallwood faced an informed and effective Opposition!

He didn't make it easy for us. He ignored our Liberal Reform Group's requests for office space and secretarial help. He wouldn't even give us hooks on which to hang our coats and hats. When the session opened, he announced the Assembly would meet five afternoons and four nights a week. This was contrary to past practice, but Smallwood obviously intended to try to wear us down.

As always, he attended the Assembly every minute it was open, determined that his members make no mistakes that would give the reborn Opposition the slightest opening. Wednesday was private members' day, when we could introduce any subject we wanted to debate. We made sure that the right subjects were called, including the Shaheen oil-refinery project at Come By Chance and John C. Doyle's linerboard scheme at Stephenville. In both cases, the government had much to hide, and we had a great deal of information to unveil.

We introduced non-confidence motions, citing the failure of the government to provide the public with the facts on the financial status of the province. I got information that the government would not give to the Assembly by obtaining copies of their prospectus whenever they floated a bond issue in New York or London. In these prospectuses, the government had to disclose facts about its finances, guarantees, and other liabilities that might affect the credit of the province. By these means, I exposed the fact that they had guaranteed $66.1 million in loans to the linerboard mill, which was $13 million more than they were authorized by law to guarantee. The legislation did permit the government to exceed the $53-million limit, but only if the guarantee agreements were tabled in the Assembly within fifteen days. Smallwood had never tabled the agreements.

There still being no oral Question Period, I had to use written questions on the order paper to ferret out embarrassing or incriminating information. I asked whether any company incorporated in Liechtenstein had acquired rights to timber or mineral resources in Labrador and, if so, who the principals of that corporation were. The minister responsible, William Callahan, said he had no knowledge of any such an arrangement. This grew into one of the greatest scandals of the Smallwood years when it came out that Joey, without authority from the cabinet or the Assembly, had written a letter purporting to grant 26,000 square kilometres of timber rights in Labrador to Société Transshipping of Liechtenstein.

Another scandal that revealed malfeasance on the part of the government involved the Doyle-backed Atlantic Brewing Company, of Stephenville. This one stunned the Assembly and the public. Finding itself in desperate financial trouble, the brewery went to the government for help. It turned out that Atlantic Brewing not only received an exemption from provincial taxation, but failed to pay the duty of $2.70 per case that all brewing companies were supposed to remit to the Newfoundland Liquor Commission. Atlantic Brewing produced a letter, signed by Joey, granting them an exemption from taxes and duty, although the Premier had no legislative authority to grant such exemptions. The brewery owed the government $407,000. Smallwood's explanation was incredible and pitiful. He said the company's managing director had come to him asking for tax relief, and that he had told him to dictate a letter to Joey's secretary in a nearby office and that he would sign it. Smallwood maintained he just glanced at the letter and signed it, thinking it must be in order. He denied knowing the exact contents of the letter, even though it was on his letterhead. The explanation was simply not believable. Apart from Smallwood's letter, there was gross negligence, or worse, on the part of the liquor commission in its failure to collect the duty. The only credible explanation for the commission's failure was that Joey had instructed them to lay off his pal Doyle's company.

As our attacks on Smallwood continued, Ray Guy of the *St. John's Evening Telegram* amused his readers, delighted me, and infuriated Joey when he reproduced this bizarre exchange from Hansard:

Mr. Smallwood: "Mr. Speaker, I will not be shoved out, I was going out happily, joyfully going out to start a new career – travelling reporter. I love reporting and I love travelling and the combination is pretty irresistible. Travelling reporter. Under a magnificent offer to go anywhere I like in the world, well-paid, exciting, entrancing work that I am well able to do – that I well know how to do. I was looking forward to it when, suddenly, someone decided to boot me out.

"I was unreasonable enough to think that I had earned the right in the work I had done in the province, that I had earned the right not to be booted out. Unreasonable, you know. A sort of eccentric, a sort of peculiar makeup, I just decided that I had earned the right in Newfoundland not to be booted out, and when someone decided . . ."

Mr. Crosbie: "Will the premier permit a question?"

Mr. Smallwood: "Yes, sure."

Mr. Crosbie: "Was he forced to announce his pending retirement at Grand Falls in September, 1968? Was someone twisting his arm then?"

Mr. Smallwood: "No, nobody twisted my arm. I do not allow people to twist my arm or boot me out either. I do not allow anyone to boot. . . . I don't think anyone can boot me out.

"I refuse to allow anyone – I do not think there is anyone clever enough to boot me out. I do not think there is anyone brainy enough to boot me out. I do not think there is anyone smart enough politically or otherwise to boot me out. I do not think there is anyone capable of booting me out except the Newfoundland people.

"Ha, ha. They are all surprised. Surprised. Surprised. I was determined not to be booted out and I was right. I was not. And I am not going to be. If there is going to be any booting done I will not be on the end of the boot. I will be on the right end of the boot, not the wrong end.

"Oh! One day I will have a story to tell. What a story I will have to tell one day. What a story. The Hon. Gentleman will have no story to tell. Just a story of endless frustration. Frustration, defeat and embitterment. That is all. That is all. That is all. That is all. Because there is one cement they have on that side over there. . . ."

Mr. Crosbie: "They are all against us."

Mr. Smallwood: "That is all. That is it. That is the only cement that keeps them together. That gives them the only thing they have in common. They may mistrust each other. They may be jealous of each other. They may be afraid to turn their back, or even sideways to each other. But they have one thing in common: They do not like Joe."

Opposition morale soared when I caught the Government without a quorum in the Assembly. Noticing there were only three or four Liberals in the chamber, including Smallwood, I passed the word quietly to the other Opposition members to wander unobtrusively out of the chamber. The rules required the presence of fourteen members for a quorum. When there were only two of us left on the Opposition side, I informed the Deputy Speaker that there was no quorum. Under the rules, the Deputy Speaker had no choice but to adjourn the Assembly until the next afternoon.

I saw Smallwood, furious, leave his seat, and, thinking he would rush to see the Speaker, I did the same, clutching my rule book. I burst into the Speaker's office, just as Smallwood ran in through a door on the Government side. "We will meet tonight, George!" he shouted to Speaker George Clarke. When he spotted me, he jumped back, caught in the act of giving orders to the Speaker.

In my customary restrained and dignified manner, I endeavoured to make it clear to Speaker Clarke that, if he attempted to hold this night sitting, in contravention of the rules, he might expose himself to unpleasant consequences. "Look here, Clarke. You open this fucking House tonight and you're going out that fucking window," I reasoned with him. "You can be sure of that." We were up on the eighth floor and I said: "You're going out through that goddamn window. There's no way this House is meeting tonight. Now here's the rule book. Here's what it says." Now, I don't know whether he was swayed by my gentle logic, but he agreed: the Assembly was adjourned until the next afternoon.

What a celebration we had that evening! That was fun! We'd demonstrated that a determined minority could checkmate a bullying majority. Smallwood had lost control of the Assembly for the first time since Confederation in 1949. The Opposition had them on the run. Joey no longer dominated the House. Clyde Wells and I were easily able to catch him off balance and to match him in rhetoric or vituperation. The momentum was with us.

∾

Meanwhile, the Conservatives were choosing a new leader. Frank Moores had been elected to Parliament in June 1968, and the following year the Tories chose him to be their national president. In 1970, responding to a draft, he returned to Newfoundland to take over the Conservative leadership, succeeding Gerry Ottenheimer, who had resigned.

The Liberals had completed the fourth year of their five-year term, and Smallwood had to call an election in 1971 at the latest. Luckily for us, he didn't call it in 1970. Instead he chose to hang on, making the same mistake that the Trudeau Liberals made in 1978–79, and the Mulroney Conservatives in 1992–93. It's always a bad sign when a government goes beyond the fourth year, because it loses its options. Joey might have won in 1970, because, despite taking another year of pounding in the Assembly, he managed to come within a seat or two of winning in 1971.

Live television coverage came to the House of Assembly in 1971, and what a boon it was for the Opposition! I got the Government to bring John Shaheen and his cronies before the Assembly to answer questions about the refinery at Come By Chance. For three days, Clyde Wells and I and other Opposition members peppered Shaheen and the others with questions. Often Shaheen would refuse to answer a question, citing confidentiality. For three days, everybody in the province watched the blood-letting on television. The damage to the Government was incalculable.

∾

During that winter, Clyde Wells resigned his seat to return to his law practice in Corner Brook. Articulate, intelligent, fearless, independent, and a good speaker, he had been a tower of strength during my leadership campaign and in Opposition in the Assembly. Clyde was not an easy person, however. He was, and is, the kind of individual whose mind can never be changed once he has made it up. Having made up his mind that he was a Liberal, nothing could dissuade him. Joining the Conservatives was not an option. As Canadians learned during the Meech Lake constitutional débâcle, Wells can be stubborn and inflexible, a man of intractable principle. Sometimes this is a strength, as it was when we were fighting to end Smallwood's tyranny. At other times, it can be a crippling flaw, as it was when he destroyed the Meech Lake accord because of his inability to compromise his "principles" – or prejudices – in the greater interest of the Canadian nation.

∾

If there was any doubt that the Liberals were becoming unhinged, it was dispelled on the evening of May 27, 1971, when an event occurred that was unprecedented in the hundred-year history of the Newfoundland legislature. Bill Smallwood, son of the Premier and Liberal member for Green Bay, leaped across the floor of the Assembly and physically attacked Conservative William ("Witch-Hunt Willie") Marshall, the member for St. John's East. It was during a debate on the spending estimates of the Department of Social Services. The minister, Steve Neary, had annoyed Opposition members who were lawyers by insinuating that they were slum landlords. In response, Willie quoted a new magazine, *The Alternate Press*, whose first issue had appeared that day. The magazine suggested that many prominent people were slumlords and reported that Clara Smallwood, wife of Joey and mother of Bill, owned property on Bulley Street in St. John's, which she rented out, with the rent being paid monthly at the Premier's office. That was all anyone said about Clara Smallwood. "That's something I'm not going to put up with," Bill said, as he crossed the floor and struck Willie. The Speaker found Bill guilty of a serious breach of privilege and agreed that he be suspended for a week.

The next day, in his weekly "Conversations with the Premier" program on the radio, Joey made light of the incident, saying, "How does a young man sit there and listen to his mother being slandered?" He continued with other outrageous statements, and in the Assembly that afternoon I moved that Joey be cited for breaching the privileges of the Assembly by publicly condoning violence by one member against another. Speaker Clarke rejected my motion and, when he refused to permit me or Marshall to speak, I denounced him as a "tool of the government." That got me suspended for three days for unparliamentary language.

Several others were also suspended. When the rest of the Opposition boycotted the Assembly in protest, Smallwood rammed through sixty pieces of legislation, plus the government's annual spending estimates – with no Opposition members present. It was a breathtaking abuse of parliamentary process.

∽

A week later, I joined the Progressive Conservatives. Moores and I had been talking for some time, both at the Assembly and at his home. We agreed on a number of steps that would be taken by a Tory government. These included elimination of the worst abuses of the patronage system, creation of an independent board to hear appeals from all licensing decisions of the Newfoundland Liquor Commission and other agencies, introduction of conflict-of-interest legislation, and reform of the rules of the Assembly. Frank welcomed me warmly. I replied that Moores was now my leader, "and when Frank's roll is called up yonder, I'll be there."

I have never regretted joining the Conservative party. In Newfoundland, it was far more "liberal" than the Liberal party. The Tories had stood up to Joey's authoritarian rule and, having served their apprenticeship, they deserved an opportunity to govern. Many Liberals who had participated in the struggle to democratize their party joined me, and at least six ran for the Conservatives in the next two provincial elections.

Despite his earlier promises to step aside for a younger leader, Joey was sounding like an aged warhorse already harnessed for combat. I had not had a private conversation with him in three years, but one day, while I was having a cigarette – a filthy habit I have long since broken! – in a corridor outside the Assembly, Joey bumped into me. At first he recoiled, as though he had stepped on a snake.

"Hello," I said.

"I hate it, I hate it," he replied after a pause.

"You hate what, sir?"

"The god-damned House of Assembly. I hate it. When will it ever end?" he said.

"When you call an election?" I suggested.

"No," Joey said. "There won't be one yet. Unemployment is still too bad. But it'll improve in a couple of months. . . . I'm going to win thirty-eight or thirty-nine seats, you know . . . and Moores won't get elected in any riding."

Then Smallwood launched into my own political future: "You're a brainy, brainy lawyer. The brainiest in St. John's, but you've made a lot of mistakes. You shouldn't run in the next election. Stay out of it for a couple of years. If you do that people will forget your mistakes and only remember how brainy you are. . . . I haven't got anyone to succeed me here."

I took this to mean that if I stayed out of politics for a few years, Smallwood might allow me to succeed him. I said, "Why don't you give one of your cabinet boys a chance? They might do quite well."

But he replied, "No there's no one here, no one. I'll have to go outside, but there's no one outside. . . . No, I'm only leaving when I'm cock of the walk again. . . . I've just been reading a book on Diefenbaker. God how I hated that man. He was unfit to be prime minister, but they should have let him go decently."

∾

Having joined the Conservatives, I needed a new campaign song. The one I used during the Liberal leadership campaign, "John Is Every Inch a Liberal," would clearly not do. My friend Jim Roberts, a doctor who had fun writing verse, wrote a new song to suit my altered circumstances. Sung to the tune of "John Brown's Body," it was called "The St. John's West Tory Marching Song." The most popular verse was the seventh, which made reference to Joey's statement that he would never let the Liberal party fall into the wrong (meaning, my) hands. It went like this:

Now Johnnie's hands are wrong indeed and all his organs too,
But Frank has got an organ that is up and standing true,

So lump them both together and they'll give old Joe the
   screw,
Now Team go in and WIN!

CHORUS:
Tory, Tory; hallelujah,
Tory, Tory; hallelujah,
Tory, Tory; hallelujah,
His sole goes marching on.

∽

As election fever grew, problems continued to mount for the
government. There was a major labour-relations confrontation
at the Lake Fish Plant, in Burgeo, where the Fishermen, Food
and Allied Workers union, led by former Liberal MP Richard
Cashin, was involved in a major strike. We attacked a blatant
conflict of interest involving Joey's new Justice minister, John
Mahoney, who had been a partner in the law firm of Curtis,
Dawe, Mahoney and Fagan, where he had represented John C.
Doyle and John Shaheen in their negotiations with the
Smallwood government. His senior partner, Leslie Curtis, who,
as Justice minister before Mahoney, had negotiated on behalf of
the province with Doyle and Shaheen, was now representing
the two promoters in their negotiations with government –
meaning he was negotiating with his law partner Mahoney, with
Smallwood, and with the rest of the Liberal cabinet.

We also brought out the embarrassing fact that pressure had
been put on the Iron Ore Company of Canada, a very big
player in mining in Labrador, to dump the law firm that had
acted for them since the 1940s in favour of Curtis, Dawe,
Mahoney and Fagan. The company had been advised by an
unnamed senior member of the Newfoundland government
that their old law firm, Cook, Bartlett, was *persona non grata*
with the Smallwood government because one of the partners

in the firm, Senator Eric Cook, had supported me at the leadership convention.

∾

Without my being aware of it, Joey began to quietly court my brother, Andrew, to succeed him as Liberal leader and premier.

Andrew was two years younger than I. He was always loyal to me and supported me at crucial times. He stood by me when I quit Joey's cabinet. He managed my finances when I ran against Joey for the Liberal leadership. But Andrew considered himself to be a loyal Liberal, and I thought it unlikely that he would follow me to the Conservatives.

Joey knew there were tensions between Andrew and me, and he tried to exploit them by floating the idea in a few interviews that he might step down before the election if Andrew Crosbie was available to succeed him. When Andrew indicated the idea had some appeal, I asked him what the hell was going on. He told me that, although he wanted to remain a Liberal, he didn't intend to go into active politics. But the matter didn't end there, as I later learned. Andrew was invited to go to Montreal for a clandestine meeting with Oliver L. (Al) Vardy, Joey's right-hand man, who asked him to consider taking over from Smallwood. The day after his return to St. John's, Andrew was summoned to a meeting with Joey himself at Vardy's penthouse apartment. There, Joey made a stunning proposal. He invited my brother to go with him at once to meet the Lieutenant-Governor, who, Joey said, was standing by. The Lieutenant-Governor would accept Smallwood's resignation and swear Andrew in as premier, or so Joey claimed. He titillated Andrew with the idea of being premier, but Andrew declined the opportunity.

Even so, he was becoming increasingly active in politics. Barron Macdonald, his chief lieutenant, was actively campaigning for Smallwood and trying to recruit people who had supported my leadership bid to stand as Liberal candidates in the election. Andrew, it was reported, had agreed to be Smallwood's provincial campaign manager.

There had always been a love–hate relationship between Joey and the Crosbies. Joey liked Andrew, but I couldn't believe it when he made him his campaign manager. There I was, in the Opposition, whacking it to Joey every day, and he puts my brother in charge of the whole Liberal campaign. Smallwood, I'm sure, thought it was a good ploy that would undermine my influence. It wasn't hard to understand why Andrew had to try to keep his mug on one side of the fence and his wump on the other, but why Joey permitted him to get away with it, I don't know. It must have been because of his relationship with our father, who helped Joey out financially in the early years. It would have been more typical of Joey to crush Andrew by saying to him, "Look, you're not going to get one red cent, no business, nothing, if you don't get John to shut up." But he never tried that. I don't know why he didn't.

Of course, by using Andrew the way he did, he embarrassed me. He infuriated me. I made sure Andrew knew how I felt, and we were estranged for some time. But, after a few months, I realized he'd been in a hard spot and there wasn't a lot else he could have done. I'd put him in a very difficult situation, the poor devil, and we got back to our normal relationship. In later years, Andrew got cheesed off with Pierre Trudeau and started to support the Conservatives federally. He always gave money to both sides.

The Liberal strategy, agreed to by Smallwood, was that he let it be known that he planned to step down within a year or so. In so far as was possible, he was to take a back seat during the election to give the impression that there was a Liberal team in charge. I blew this strategy out of the water by letting the public know the Liberals wanted to "low-bridge" Joey. Smallwood, I said, was going to have to do what my brother told him to do. I wrote a rhyme and had great fun reciting it:

Oh where, oh where has the Premier gone?
Oh where, oh where can he be?

He has been the boss for twenty-two years
But now its Andrew C-r-o-s-b-i-e.

Smallwood went wild at this, making it clear to everyone that he was in charge and that he had every intention of serving another full five-year term.

Finally, out of time, Smallwood called the election for October 28, 1971. The Liberal party showed contempt for the intelligence of the electorate by using the slogan "Of course, I'm voting Liberal," together with campaign comic books, coloured 3-D pictures of Smallwood, a Smallwood mirror, and similar devices. They didn't present any program for the future. They refused to discuss the issues with candidates from other political parties and would not take part in open-line shows or go on television or radio with representatives of other parties.

Sensing the end was near, Joey grew desperate. He had awarded Basil Dobbin's Viking Construction a contract to pave a road on New World Island. At three o'clock one morning in mid-campaign, Basil was awakened by a phone call from a furious Smallwood. "I want you to pave ten more miles," the Premier screamed. It was fall, the ground was covered with snow, and Dobbin didn't have any paving equipment available. Smallwood didn't care. "Get the goddamn road paved. Buy the equipment. Get some asphalt and put it down on this bloody road." Dobbin didn't do it – and it was a good thing for him that he didn't. Joey was awarding contracts without authority, and, when the government changed, contractors who had done his bidding didn't get paid.

The Conservatives campaigned on the theme that it was time for a change. Our slogan was succinct and easily understood: "The Time Has Come!" Moores put together a fine slate of candidates. The party had new policies on resources, economic development, quality-of-life issues, and rural development. For once, the party was well financed. After all the years of opposition to Smallwood's Liberals, we had no shortage of issues.

Two weeks into the campaign, Joey made a neophyte's mistake when he asked a crowd of students at the College of Trades and Technology if they thought he was lying. Twelve hundred voices shouted: "YES!" Joey bolted from the auditorium.

A week later, four thousand cheering supporters – probably the biggest political rally in Newfoundland's history – tried to cram into Humber Gardens in Corner Brook to hear Moores and our candidate in the next riding, Tom Farrell. Motorcades – five hundred cars from the east and six hundred or seven hundred from the west – brought eager Tories to the event.

The election-day turnout of 90 per cent was phenomenal; the previous high was 76 per cent in the 1949 Confederation-year election. Our Conservative candidates took 52 per cent of the popular vote, to 44 per cent for the Liberals and 4 per cent for other parties and candidates. If the popular vote had been fairly reflected in seats, we would have had a clear Tory majority. But for years electoral districts had been gerrymandered to favour the Liberals. The capital, for example, was a Conservative strong-hold. St. John's North had 17,000 voters, St. John's East (Extern) 14,042, and St. John's West 10,838. Outside the city, however, Bell Island had 2,735 voters, Bay de Verde 3,321, White Bay South 4,585, and Fortune Bay 3,417. An outport vote was equal to at least two, and sometimes three or four, urban votes.

In Labrador West, the turnout was an unbelievable 110 per cent, with 6,491 people voting, although there were only 6,191 names on the voters' list. This discrepancy was supposedly explained by a procedure that allowed people not on the voters' list to be sworn in at the polling station.

With forty-two seats at stake, the Tories took twenty-one, the Liberals twenty, and Tom Burgess was elected in Labrador West for the New Labrador Party. In six districts, the margin of victory was fewer than one hundred votes.

Smallwood had no intention of going quietly. Or of going at all. He announced recounts in all districts where the Liberal candi-date was within a hundred votes of the Tory. In analysing the results, Joey concluded that too many people had voted; that it was not really a defeat since the total Liberal vote was a bit higher than it had been five years earlier; that 350 votes in the right districts would have delivered those seats to the Liberals and given him a majority; that many people would not vote the same way again; that the popular vote was quite meaningless because of the number of people who lived in St. John's (and whose votes, apparently, should not count); that he was going to retire voluntarily; and that he was going to continue to govern as though the election had not taken place, and not confine himself to routine matters, until recounts and court challenges were decided.

The six judicial recounts confirmed the election-night results. In St. Barbe South, the election-night count gave the Tories the seat by four votes. But when the ballot-box from the outport of Sally's Cove was opened in court for the recount, there were no ballot papers inside. The deputy returning officer testified that, after the ballots had been counted – it being a cold night in Sally's Cove – they decided to add them to the fire in the wood stove. So the ballots were burned.

The Liberals applied to the Newfoundland Supreme Court to order a new election in St. Barbe South. This meant Smallwood was able to hang on through November and December, until the Court gave its decision in mid-January. It awarded St. Barbe South to the Tories.

With the party standings now confirmed at twenty-one Conservatives, twenty Liberals, and one independent, the question was, what would the independent, Tom Burgess, do when the House of Assembly met? If he voted with the Liberals, there would be a tie, and if the Tories elected a Speaker from their ranks, the Liberals would be able to defeat a Conservative government twenty-one to twenty. If Burgess voted with the Tories, we would have a twenty-two–to–twenty majority, enough to control the Assembly, barely, after electing a Speaker.

But what would happen if the Liberals could persuade, by whatever means, an elected Conservative member to join them? Or what would happen if the Tories were able to entice a Liberal to support them?

Conspiracy and intrigue reigned from November 1971 until the second election in March 1972. No possibility, however remote, was left uncanvassed; no pressure was left unapplied; no inducement, however dubious, was left unoffered.

Burgess bathed happily in the limelight. The Liberals got to him first. He was flown from Labrador City to Stephenville by promoter John C. Doyle in an aircraft leased by Doyle from the Bank of Montreal. Smallwood's pal Arthur Lundrigan sent a jet to Stephenville to bring him the rest of the way to St. John's. Doyle also proceeded to St. John's, and checked in on the same floor of the Holiday Inn as Burgess. Burgess met with both Smallwood and Moores to see which party would offer him the most for his support. He issued a list of demands, including an exemption for Labrador from provincial gasoline tax; construction of water and sewerage facilities for the Labrador coast; more Labrador seats in the Assembly; a commitment not to run candidates against his New Labrador Party; and, of course, a cabinet post (or posts) for himself.

The problem with Burgess was that his support could never be bought. At best, he could be rented, and perhaps only by the hour. I opposed making any concessions whatsoever to him, believing him to be unstable and untrustworthy. His demands kept increasing. He wanted to be Minister of Mines, Agriculture and Resources. He wanted to control everything the government did in Labrador. He wanted a Trans-Labrador Highway. It was all ego stuff. In the next few weeks, he overplayed his hand until his cards became valueless.

I wrote a memorandum to Moores on the constitutional issues created by the election deadlock and enclosed a draft letter for him to give to Lieutenant-Governor John Harnum, citing the modern precedents and suggesting Smallwood should be invited to resign. If he refused, the Lieutenant-Governor should instruct the Liberal administration to convene the House of Assembly to see which party commanded the confidence of a majority of members. Moores also persuaded Burgess to forward a letter to the Lieutenant-Governor indicating he would vote with us in the Assembly and support us to form a government.

Meanwhile, Joey announced he would retire as Liberal leader. But he got to Burgess with the same old stuff – persuading him he would have a very good chance of succeeding him in the leadership. I don't know what Burgess may have received in the way of money. Anything was possible, because Doyle would certainly supply any funds needed. It was the craziest situation I've ever come across. Newfoundland was a laughing-stock to anyone in Canada who took notice. On January 31, 1972, Burgess announced he was going to go with the Liberals, after all, and would run for the leadership. He did, and was thrashed by Ed Roberts at the leadership convention in the next month.

On January 18, 1972, with Burgess not yet a Liberal, but not really a Tory supporter either, the first Progressive Conservative government of Newfoundland was sworn in. I was appointed to all the important economic portfolios – Minister of Finance, President of the Treasury Board, and Minister of Economic Development. We were in office at last! But could we govern?

Unfortunately, it's not possible for a leader to appoint every follower to a cabinet post. We had to contend with some bitterly disappointed caucus members. Within days, Hughie Shea, elected in St. John's South, announced that he would sit as an independent because Moores had left him out of the cabinet.

Shea was an eccentric. He ran a small store in the Goulds, a district of St. John's, and he had a highly exaggerated sense of his own value. He was very angry when Frank didn't put him in the cabinet, because he believed his constituents had elected him to be a minister, not a back-bencher. Then the Liberals got to him and promised him the sun, moon, and stars, and the next thing we knew Hughie announced he would cross the floor and sit with the Liberals. That happened on the same day that Burgess announced he would join the Liberals.

People have to understand our position. After nearly twenty-three years of Liberal administration, the Tory party couldn't

stand idly by and lose the government because of the eccentric-
ities of some members or because others were seduced by the
Liberals and their courtesans. So we struck back. Smallwood had
persuaded a local magistrate, Augustus Oldford, to leave the
bench to run as a Liberal in Fortune Bay in the October election. He defeated Val Earle of the Conservatives. Oldford
thought he would be joining a Liberal government; instead, he
found himself in Opposition with a doubtful future. But we
Conservatives were a forgiving lot. In exchange for Oldford's
resignation from the Assembly, we kindly reappointed him to
his old job on the bench.

We marked our scorecards – twenty Conservatives, nineteen
Liberals, one vacancy (Oldford), and two independents (Shea
and Burgess, both of whom were on their way to the Liberals).
When Shea and Burgess landed there, the tally would be twenty-
one Liberals, twenty Conservatives, and one vacancy. We weren't
out of the woods yet, not by a long shot.

Alex Dunphy had been elected for us in St. George's, on the
west coast of the island, and the Liberals made a strenuous effort
to get him to defect. This soon turned into a bizarre kidnap plot.
Poor Alex had a big drinking problem. He went to a national
Conservative convention in Ottawa in December, got drunk
there, and stayed drunk until late January. Alex actually admitted all this in an interview in the *St. John's Evening Telegram*. So
we knew Dunphy might be vulnerable to any stunts the Liberals
would try to pull. Dunphy had received offers to switch to the
Liberal party, and he speculated openly that he might receive as
much as fifty thousand dollars to make the switch. Ed Poole,
one of our boys on the west coast, was keeping an eye on Alex
for us. So was Alex's wife; she didn't want him to make a fool
of himself.

But Father Ron Kelly, the Roman Catholic priest in his district, was working on Dunphy for the Liberals. He talked him
into coming to St. John's to meet Joey to see what Joey could do
for him. God knows what Alex might have agreed to do if
Smallwood had got hold of him. Dunphy's wife called Poole to

say Alex had been picked up by a car owned by the Lundrigans and was being driven to Stephenville, where Arthur Lundrigan's plane would fly him to St. John's. This grotesque Grit conniving had to be thwarted! Alex was in no condition to make a decision about anything, let alone where he would sit in the House of Assembly.

Fortunately, Alex had dear friends who cared about him and wanted to do what was best for him. Us. Tom Farrell, who was in Frank's cabinet, was a medical doctor and tried to dissuade Alex from going to St. John's. As it was for his own good, we had some large and persuasive Tories meet the Lundrigans' plane, intercept Dunphy as he got off, and take him away for a few days to sober up. Unlike the Liberals, we weren't out to take advantage of him. We were his friends and we saved him from doing something he would regret. We kept him in seclusion until he dried out enough to return to his normal life, as a Progressive Conservative.

❧

The House of Assembly was called to meet on March 1, 1972, for the first session since the election. Premier Moores had already obtained an opinion from the Lieutenant-Governor that, if the two parties were tied in seats, he would have to dissolve the Assembly for a new election because neither side could appoint a Speaker and be able to govern. But, if either side had even a one-seat advantage, that party could appoint a Speaker and still govern, because the Speaker votes to break ties. As the members gathered, the forty-two seats were split twenty-one–twenty, with one vacancy. Our problem was, the twenty-one were Liberals!

Unless we did something right away, the Moores government would fall in the first vote in the Assembly. And Lieutenant-Governor Harnum would refuse to dissolve the Assembly. Because the Liberals had the larger number of seats, he would call on Ed Roberts to form a government. Even if Roberts found he couldn't maintain a stable government with such a slender margin, the Liberals would control the government going into an election, a not-inconsiderable advantage the way politics is played in Newfoundland. Were the Liberals about to ooze back into office despite the 52 per cent popular vote for the first Conservative government in the history of Newfoundland?

Let's not pussyfoot around this. I believed we were justified in doing WHATEVER HAD TO BE DONE to prevent the sleazy, discredited, anti-democratic Liberal party from suborning their way back into power without an election. A way had to be found to foil such foul tactics – and Frank Moores, bless him, found the way.

When the members gathered to be sworn in on the morning of March 1, one member did not turn up. William Saunders, who had won Bay de Verde for the Liberals by twenty-one votes, was nowhere to be found. Apparently, he had advised Roberts, his leader, that he was too ill to attend.

In reality, Saunders had decided to resign his seat. He never gave a reason. It seemed like a very odd decision, because Saunders had been a member for some years and, if he had been sworn in and signed the register that day, he would have qualified for his legislative pension. By not showing up, he lost his pension. I don't know what Moores did. And I don't know what Saunders got, but I think it was at least $100,000. Some of my friends suspected that it was my brother who secretly raised the money for Frank to give to Saunders. As a businessman, Andrew would have known when it was prudent to change sides.

When Moores talked to Lieutenant-Governor Harnum that night, following the Speech from the Throne, he had Saunders's letter of resignation in his pocket. The letter was the key to dissolution. It left the parties tied twenty–twenty (with two vacancies), meaning neither side could appoint a Speaker and be able to govern. Harnum had no choice. He couldn't run to Smallwood for instructions. He had to grant Frank the dissolution we wanted, and we headed into another election.

I don't care what Moores did or what it cost to secure Saunders's resignation. I endorse it, I support it completely, I applaud it. When it came down to that vital moment, we had to be prepared to be as underhanded as Smallwood ever was. We had to meet the House of Assembly. And it looked as though, with all this jiggery-pokery, we might be defeated and the Liberals might take the government back. We had to prevent that! If it took $100,000, or even more, it was the right move. I was delighted with Moores. Frank was good at this kind of stuff. He did a great job! He was the right man in the right place!

∽

We'd read the public mood accurately, The people were fed up with Liberal shenanigans. The election of March 24, 1972, was a landslide for the Conservatives. The public clearly agreed with our campaign slogan: "The Time Is Now!"

One of our few concerns was that Frank Moores's marital problems might hurt our chances. Frank was a charmer; he loved the ladies and they loved him. When he was an MP in Ottawa, he met Janis Johnson, who was a good Tory, the daughter of a cabinet minister in Manitoba who later became lieutenant-governor of that province. Janis was working for the Conservative Association in Ottawa when Frank started an affair with her or she started one with him. But Frank had a wife and seven children back in Newfoundland, and his relationship with Janis became known. Following the first election, in October 1971, Dodie Moores filed a divorce action against Frank, citing adultery and mental cruelty. But she withdrew the action and campaigned with Frank during the second election. Later, they got divorced and Frank married Janis. After that marriage ended, Janis worked in Brian Mulroney's leadership campaign in 1983, and he appointed her to the Senate later on.

As it turned out, Frank's philandering didn't become an issue in the 1972 campaign, and it had no discernible effect on the way people voted, illustrating the profound changes that had taken place in Newfoundlanders' attitudes on social, moral, and religious issues since Confederation in 1949.

On election night, we won thirty-three seats to just nine for the Liberals. We took 60 per cent of the popular vote, to the Liberals' 37 per cent. Of the nine Liberals elected, only four, including Roberts, had served in a Smallwood cabinet. Tom Burgess was defeated in Labrador West. The ambitious little storekeeper Hughie Shea, who defected to the Liberals, ran fourth in a two-member riding. He was never again elected to public office in Newfoundland. Val Earle recaptured Fortune Bay, while Brian Peckford, who would be premier after Moores, made his debut in the district of Green Bay. In St. John's West, I spent a miserly $3,346 and polled 5,949 votes, to 2,209 for my Liberal opponent, Duncan Sharpe.

For the first time since 1949, Joey Smallwood was not a candidate for election to the House of Assembly. Although he would make one final, pathetic attempt to return to public life, he would never again hold power. The Smallwood era was truly over. Now we had to start undoing the damage he had done to Newfoundland.

7

THE RAPE OF
NEWFOUNDLAND

DOZENS UPON DOZENS of economic-development projects – some serious, many hare-brained
– were proposed during my years in provincial
politics in Newfoundland. Four major ones occupied a large part of my time and attention in
each of my three incarnations – as a member of
Joey Smallwood's Liberal cabinet from 1966 to
1968; in Opposition to Smallwood from the
time I quit his cabinet in 1968 until the defeat
of the Liberals in late 1971; and as a member of Frank Moores's
Progressive Conservative cabinet from 1972 to 1976.

In my first incarnation, I tried – with the help of Clyde Wells
– to protect the interests of the province from the rapacious
demands of charlatans who all too easily got Smallwood's ear. In
my second incarnation, I hammered away at the Liberal government, exposing Smallwood's malfeasance and his failure to
ensure that the province's interests were safeguarded. Finally, in
my third incarnation, I worked with my colleagues in the Tory

Courtesy Guy Badeaux (Bado), Le Droit

government to clean up the mess and salvage what we could for the people of Newfoundland.

I don't mean to tar all Liberals with the Smallwood brush. During the period I was in Opposition, two of Joey's ministers, Ed Roberts and Bill Rowe – the only ones who had any intelligence to speak of – did try to stand up to Smallwood and to stop some of his worst excesses. There wasn't much they could do, but, to give them credit, they used whatever influence they had – which is probably why Joey sabotaged Roberts later, after Ed succeeded him as leader of the Liberals.

The four big projects were:

- the scheme by John C. Doyle's Canadian Javelin Limited for a mammoth linerboard mill at Stephenville to produce corrugated paper for cardboard;
- the proposal by John Shaheen and his Newfoundland Pulp and Chemical Limited for a pulp and paper mill and a chemical plant at Come By Chance;
- Shaheen's grand dream of a 100,000-barrel-a-day oil refinery, also at Come By Chance;
- and the Brinco Limited development of the hydro-electric resources of Churchill Falls, on the Upper Churchill River in Labrador.

The four projects had several elements in common. First, they were all driven by Joey Smallwood's ego and his grandiose dreams for Newfoundland. He had to be bigger and grander than anyone who went before or who would come after. The great Sir Robert Bond, one of our pre-Confederation premiers, initiated the first pulp and paper mill; another, the great Sir Richard Squires, promoted the second mill. The great Joey Smallwood was determined to outdo them. He was going to have not only a third great mill, but a fourth great mill, and, who knows, there might be a fifth great mill as well.

Second, in all four instances the negotiations were conducted by Joey personally. The cabinet was usually informed after the fact, if at all; the House of Assembly was kept completely in the dark, of course.

Third, all four involved venality on Smallwood's part. He accepted expensive gifts and lavish trips from Doyle and Shaheen, and he secretly speculated in Brinco shares while he was negotiating the Churchill Falls deal.

Fourth, all four projects cost Newfoundlanders dearly. The province sank more than $300 million into the linerboard scheme before bailing out and selling the mill to Abitibi-Price, now Abitibi-Consolidated, which is doing quite nicely, helped by the tax losses they acquired in the transaction. All Newfoundland has to show for Shaheen's paper mill and chemical company is an abandoned, uncompleted building in Come By Chance; it cost our taxpayers $4.4 million. As for Shaheen's oil refinery, it eventually went into operation, but only after the Newfoundland government had lost $78.8 million, and creditors in Japan were forced into bankruptcy. The refinery went broke and was mothballed for ten years; it's owned and operated today by Vitol Holdings and employs four hundred people. Finally, Churchill Falls proved to be a terrific deal for Brinco, a godsend for the province of Quebec, and a humiliation for Newfoundland, which receives a pittance for the electricity generated at mighty Churchill Falls. It is a terrible deal, a colossal giveaway. Newfoundland got rooked. Quebec refuses to renegotiate the contract price it pays for our power. The Supreme Court of Canada rejected Newfoundland's suit to reopen the deal. And the federal government, cowering in fear of Quebec, doesn't have the guts to intercede to secure justice for Newfoundlanders.

I could write a whole book, a series of books, about these shameful deals and about how the Newfoundland people were exploited, but I shall try to restrain myself.

JOHN CHRISTOPHER DOYLE

The important thing to remember about John C. Doyle was not that he was charming and personable, brilliant and cultured, a

linguist and oenophile, and a concert-calibre pianist and organ-
ist – he was all of those things, I suppose – but that he was a
crook. This was the big difference between him and John
Shaheen. Shaheen was a glib promoter, too, and a name-
dropper, and he had Joey completely in his pocket, but, as far as
I know, he wasn't a crook. Shaheen's problem was he didn't have
much money. Doyle was an evil genius, a seductive slug of a
man. He appeared to be crooked and always gave the impression
of being devious. He had no scruples at all. I always kept clear of
him. People had to be very careful with him, because he was the
type who was forever trying to get something on others. If
someone went to Montreal on business, Doyle would fix him up
with a woman. But he'd probably have someone photograph
what went on with the woman. He was that type. There was
nothing he wouldn't stoop to.

Doyle was deep into stock manipulation, constantly selling
shares of this or that, running the price up, and ripping off the
shareholders of Canadian Javelin. Javelin was operated for his
private benefit and the benefit of his pals. He was perpetually
under attack by the Securities and Exchange Commission in the
United States, repeatedly being sued in the courts, litigating
case after case – and surviving. He was heavily involved in
Quebec Liberal politics and was well connected with Liberal
senator Sarto Fournier, who was one of his directors. The federal
Liberals were always protective of Doyle, and some of their
lawyers in Quebec worked for Doyle and his companies. It took
me years in the House of Commons in Ottawa before we finally
got the government to move to collect the taxes he owed and to
break his control over Canadian Javelin. Later, he skipped bail
in Canada and fled to Panama, a fugitive from Canadian and
American justice.

When I was in Smallwood's cabinet, we set up a committee of
four ministers to negotiate with Doyle and Shaheen to try to
build some protection for Newfoundland taxpayers into the
financing agreements we had with the two promoters. But Doyle
thought he could buy everybody off. He would pay for things for

Smallwood or give him gifts and take him on trips. It was a very cosy arrangement.

In 1972, when the RCMP raided Doyle's apartment in Montreal, they found a list of payments to be made by Doyle. They included $375,000 to a Mr. J.R. Smallwood, of St. John's, and $375,000 to a Mr. L.R. Curtis, also of St. John's. Although there was no proof that these payments were actually made, the list was consistent with testimony given by a witness at an inquiry held by the federal Restrictive Trade Practices Commission to the effect that Doyle had instructed him to make sure that his friends Joey Smallwood and Leslie Curtis, who'd been Smallwood's attorney general, were looked after.

In my opinion, the relationship between Smallwood and Doyle was one of the most tawdry stories in twentieth-century provincial politics. It began after the United States–based Iron Ore Company (IOC) decided to relinquish to the Newfoundland government certain mineral rights it had been given in Labrador back in the 1930s. There's not much doubt that IOC made a mistake. The concessions it gave back around Wabush Lake were valuable. A high-rolling stock promoter and developer from Chicago, Doyle showed up in Newfoundland in 1953. He didn't know anything about mining, but, seeing the possibilities at Wabush Lake, he got the concessions from the Smallwood government for his company, Canadian Javelin. Then he negotiated a deal with a bunch of Canadian, Italian, and U.S. steel companies to set up a consortium to operate the concessions. They paid Canadian Javelin so much per ton of iron ore taken out. Doyle did very well.

Pretty soon Doyle learned that Smallwood was wild about getting another pulp and paper mill for Newfoundland. Labrador has huge stands of spruce wood. So Doyle conceived the idea of using Labrador wood for linerboard. He couldn't put the mill in Labrador because ice prevented shipping out the linerboard during about six months of the year, so the mill became a great project for Stephenville, on the west coast of the island. The wood was to be cut in Labrador. Originally, the logs were to be converted to wood chips there and carried by two 65,000-ton ships to Stephenville. This was supposed to make the whole thing economical. Then Joey announced that they couldn't put the wood-chip plant in Labrador after all; it had to be in Stephenville. This meant the wood was going to have to come down from Labrador in the form of logs and be carried from Goose Bay to Stephenville in smaller ships. The only thing that a lay person could understand was that this was going to be risky. But the Newfoundland government gave Doyle a guarantee of $53 million to do it.

As we learned later, the reason for changing the wood-chip mill from Labrador to Stephenville on the island of Newfoundland was because the federal government refused to spend twenty million dollars to dredge and extend the harbours at Goose Bay and Stephenville for the larger ships. It wouldn't do this because it wasn't satisfied that the project was feasible. The original plan was for Javelin to harvest 850,000 cords of pulp wood annually at Melville, in Labrador, with 550,000 cords to go to the mill at Stephenville, and 300,000 cords for export. This turned out to be impossible to accomplish.

It wasn't until a year after the Smallwood government had begun to guarantee funds that it appointed auditors to monitor Doyle's books. When the project ran out of money in May 1971, the Liberals began making secret loans and advances to Javelin. In June, $9 million was guaranteed and advanced; in October, the government made a direct loan of $6 million. Even though they were defeated by Moores's Conservatives in the election that month, Smallwood and his Liberals clung to power. On November 19, three weeks after being rejected at the polls, the Smallwood government guaranteed a further $7.8 million, and, on December 16, a final loan of $1.2 million was made. By the time our Conservative administration took office in January 1972, a total of $24 million had been advanced secretly, with $9 million of this coming after the Liberals' election defeat.

We next learned that, with the Javelin group of companies already owing the government $24 million, the Smallwood cabinet passed an order-in-council on December 10, 1971, to guarantee a loan of 100 million Deutschmarks, or $30 million Canadian, to Javelin. The order-in-council authorized the Minister of Economic Development – Smallwood – to negotiate and conclude a back-up agreement between Javelin and its affiliates and the government, the terms of which were to receive the prior approval of the cabinet. Either deliberately or carelessly, Smallwood turned the guarantee, signed by himself, over to Doyle, making it possible for him to borrow the money with the government's backing before any agreement was made as to what would happen to the funds. I don't know of a more serious act of negligence or malfeasance ever committed by any Canadian premier.

The Javelin linerboard situation was the most serious immediate problem facing the new Moores government. The mill, which Doyle had estimated in 1967 would cost $75 million, was now expected to cost in excess of $122 million, with the government's guarantees rising from $53 million to at least $110 million. Smallwood had agreed to more than double the guarantees without advising the public or the House of Assembly!

Our first decision as a government was that the linerboard mill must be completed. The province had too much invested to allow construction to halt. I was named chairman of a cabinet committee created to supervise the project, as well as chairman of a second committee to deal with Shaheen's Come By Chance refinery.

In March, less than two months after taking office, we served notice of defaults by Canadian Javelin under a trust deed between Javelin and the province of Newfoundland. Its subsidiaries, Javelin Forest and Javelin Paper, were insolvent and could not meet their obligations. They had not spent all of the money guaranteed by the government on construction of the mill and ancillary facilities, as they were pledged to. Instead, they had spent money on such things as equipping and furnishing an apartment for Doyle, and offshore payments to Javelin Export Limited in the Bahamas. And two million dollars was used to repay an alleged bank loan from the Union Bank of Panama to Javelin. This "bank" had the same telex number as Canadian Javelin in Panama and occupied the same premises. It had been formed by Doyle and two others and was not registered with the banking commission in Panama. Three weeks later, I announced that the government would take over and complete the linerboard project, including the related woodlands operation in Labrador.

We established a Crown corporation, Labrador Linerboard Limited, to manage the mill and auxiliary functions. The legislation authorized the payment of up to $5 million to Canadian Javelin for their equity in the project. It also authorized the government to assume the project's debts and to spend up to $50 million to complete the mill. We had an estimate that it would cost $44.6 million to take the mill into operation, bringing the total cost to $159.4 million, including initial working capital of $21 million.

The project had never been feasible, and was certainly not feasible when we took it over. With the horrendous cost of bringing wood from Labrador, and without an assured supply of wood on the island of Newfoundland, the issue now was basic economic problems, not mismanagement.

In September 1976, when I resigned as chairman of Labrador Linerboard, the Crown corporation was losing one hundred dollars on every ton of linerboard it produced. The subsidies required to keep it operating were becoming more than the province could afford. In 1979, it was decided to close the mill. The government later transferred all the assets at Stephenville to the Abitibi-Price Company, which uses the mill to manufacture newsprint.

During my negotiations to take over Canadian Javelin, the company asked foolishly to be compensated for two suspicious items. The first was $650,000 for two buildings on the former Harmon U.S. Air Force Base at Stephenville. The Smallwood government had agreed in 1970 to sell the two very large concrete structures, valued by the province at $8 million, to Canadian Javelin for $250,000. But Canadian Javelin didn't pay a cent until a month after the 1971 provincial election, and then just $100,000. When I asked why Javelin wanted $650,000 for the buildings for which they had paid only $100,000, I was told that "some third party" had received $550,000 worth of Javelin shares in connection with the transaction – in other words, a bribe. I refused to pay Javelin more than $100,000. We later discovered that $550,000 in Javelin shares had been issued as fully paid, although no payment had been made, to Engineering Services Limited, a company wholly owned by Oliver L. (Al) Vardy, former deputy minister of Economic Development and right-hand man to Joey Smallwood from 1949 to 1972!

The second suspicious transaction was uncovered when I was requested to repay a $3.997-million investment by Canadian Javelin in a fictitious timber concession in Labrador. This was an elaborate scheme to divert nearly $4 million from the linerboard project, with Canadian Javelin paying the money to a mysterious offshore company called Société Transshipping of Liechtenstein. The owner of Société Transshipping was not publicly known, but it was certainly John C. Doyle or an agent acting on his behalf.

I continued to press for federal intervention in the Canadian Javelin mess after I went to Ottawa in 1976 as the member of Parliament for St. John's West. In 1977, the Liberal government directed the Restrictive Trade Practices Commission to investigate Canadian Javelin, or Javelin International Limited, as it was then known. The investigator, Frederick Sparling, director of the corporations branch in the Department of Consumer and Corporate Affairs, did a first-rate job. He found a variety of frauds by Doyle and his accomplices against Javelin and its shareholders. Smallwood was represented at the inquiry by counsel who cross-examined witnesses and presented argument on his behalf, but he refused to testify. The Supreme Court of Canada held that Smallwood had no exemption from the duty to give evidence simply by virtue of his status as a former premier and minister. Sparling, however, decided not to wait while the courts dealt with the issue, and went ahead with his report without testimony from Smallwood.

There were other investigations into the linerboard scandal. The RCMP searched at least two dozen homes and businesses in four provinces, Smallwood's home, Al Vardy's apartment, and residences of Canadian Javelin executives in Montreal, including Doyle's apartment. In December 1973, Doyle was arrested in Montreal and charged with two counts of fraud involving $540,000, and two counts of breach of public trust. Vardy was charged with fraud, and accepting bribes totalling $218,200.

Vardy was also separately charged with two counts of fraud, two counts of accepting a bribe, and one count of breach of public trust alleging that, between 1957 and 1968, he had defrauded the Newfoundland government of $135,000 by taking kickbacks on printing orders. In May 1976, Vardy's accomplice, Jack L. Goodson, pleaded guilty to two charges of bribing Vardy with commissions on sales of printing materials to the provincial government.

Doyle spent the weekend in jail, then was released on $75,000 bail. He left Canada and fled to Panama, where he still lives. Vardy was already in Panama City at the time he was charged. He was arrested in Panama during 1974, but was freed by habeas corpus as he passed through the United States. He stayed there and died at his residence in Florida in 1980.

JOHN M. SHAHEEN

John Shaheen, a maverick American oilman of Lebanese descent, first appeared on the Newfoundland scene in May 1960, when Joey Smallwood announced that an oil refinery would be established at Holyrood, on Conception Bay, by Golden Eagle Refining Company of Canada. This was a small refinery, with a capacity of just fifteen thousand barrels a day, and there were no government loans or guarantees, although Smallwood did agree that Golden Eagle would be the exclusive supplier of petroleum products to the provincial government for the next twenty years. Shaheen was a promoter of this project; his company, Shaheen Natural Resources, built the refinery for Golden Eagle. The refinery operated until 1983; in 1984, it was dismantled by Ultramar.

Small provinces such as Newfoundland are desperately vulnerable to promoters like Shaheen and Doyle. Exxon or British Petroleum or any of the other major oil companies, for example, aren't interested in esoteric ventures or high-risk projects in out-of-the-way places like Newfoundland. Since they've got their huge established businesses, they don't need to go to provincial governments for financing. If they have a good prospect, they can finance it themselves. It's people who haven't got the financial resources, but who have imaginations like Shaheen's, who have to look around for money. They know there's no use going to Ontario or Alberta. They're not going to get any help there, but in Newfoundland or Nova Scotia they might.

We have provincial politicians who want to develop their provincial economies. They have huge problems such as unemployment, education, social services, and transportation. They need to create jobs and economic growth. They want to be re-elected. So this is where promoters go looking for help. This situation is not limited to Atlantic Canada. It's the same throughout the world.

In my experience, successful promoters have two things when they come calling on a small province. They have good credit cards so that they can entertain and act as though they've got hundreds of millions, and they hire the best law firms around so they can intimidate anyone who wants to probe their activities or be critical of their schemes. They would sue the pants off anyone who asked too many questions. That was the technique of both Doyle and Shaheen.

Every promoter in the world headed for Newfoundland because the word was out about how gullible Smallwood was. He wanted development. He didn't care what it cost. He didn't want feasibility studies. He hated the word "feasibility." He didn't want anyone to be in a position to say, "It can't be done, sir."

Smallwood was like Play-Doh in the hands of Shaheen. Shaheen was smooth, he knew how to flatter and to hold out hope for great things, and he seemed to know everybody who mattered. He hired Richard Nixon as his lawyer after Nixon was defeated in the California gubernatorial race and before he became president. Shaheen was a great name-dropper, and, when he said Richard Nixon was his lawyer, this got him quite a distance with people like Joey. On one occasion, Joey was in the Soviet Union with Shaheen; later, Smallwood recounted with great pride how he had met Nixon in Moscow after Nixon had that kitchen debate with Nikita Khrushchev. Shaheen had been in the Office of Strategic Services (OSS) during the Second World War, and William Casey, then the director of the Central Intelligence Agency (CIA), was another one of his acquaintances. Shaheen was forever talking about the people he knew to show how well connected he was. He had a story that the Seven Sisters, the seven big international oil companies, were out to screw him. According to Shaheen, they regarded him as a major threat, and a lot of his problems were caused by the nefarious influence of the Seven Sisters. It was nonsense, of course. The majors wouldn't even have noticed this little gnat Shaheen buzzing around trying to establish a refinery at some place called Come By Chance. But Smallwood bought the line.

Shaheen knew how to work the system. He was able to get the Export Credit Guarantee Department (ECGD) in the United Kingdom to guarantee financing for some of his promotions because they wanted to sell British equipment out here. With the ECGD behind him, investment bankers in London would put up the money.

Like Doyle, it didn't take Shaheen long to figure out that what Smallwood wanted the most in the world was a third pulp and paper mill for the province. So Shaheen first approached Joey with a plan for a third mill, plus a chemical plant at Come By

Chance, at the head of Placentia Bay, on the Avalon Peninsula. It was to be called Newfoundland Pulp and Chemical. The problem with the idea was that Newfoundland had insufficient wood for the two mills that were already here, much less a third mill. The trees on the eastern part of the island are very small and grow slowly. But that wasn't going to stop Smallwood.

With the 1966 provincial election coming up, Joey needed to make it convincing that the third mill was indeed going to go ahead. So he guaranteed loans of five million dollars to Newfoundland Pulp and Chemical, and they started construction on a building at Come By Chance. Smallwood was able to say the project was under way. Construction stopped after the election, and nothing further was done; you can still see the remains of the building at Come By Chance. The loans guaranteed to Shaheen were absorbed by the taxpayers, naturally.

By this time, Shaheen had transferred his affection from pulp and paper to petrochemicals. He would build a magnificent, world-scale oil refinery at Come By Chance. It was an ideal location. Come By Chance has an excellent, ice-free, deep-water harbour in good proximity to world shipping routes. Joey was just as enthusiastic about a refinery as he had been about a paper mill, because he thought it was going to bring a glamorous, high-wage industry to Newfoundland, with all kinds of exciting things to be manufactured. He started visualizing Newfoundland as a strategic place in the world for a huge petrochemical industry. And on and on it went.

In his original announcement in April 1967, Smallwood informed the House of Assembly that this 100,000-barrel-a-day refinery would cost ninety-seven million dollars and that the government had agreed to advance a loan of thirty million dollars to help set it up. Smallwood and Shaheen thought they had a way to finance the project. Crown corporations didn't pay any corporation tax at that time, so they worked out a scheme whereby the refinery would be owned by a Newfoundland Crown corporation that would lease it to Shaheen. This tax-avoidance device had been used previously in Newfoundland for much smaller projects, but the refinery project was very large and very complex. It would actually involve three provincial Crown corporations. One, Provincial Building Company, would build the refinery, contracting with a Shaheen company, Newfoundland Refining Company (NRC), to supervise the construction. The second, Provincial Refining Company, would be the operator; it would contract with NRC to manage the plant. The third, Provincial Holding Company, would own Provincial Refining Company; it would be sold to NRC at the end of fifteen years for two thousand dollars so long as the construction loans were repaid.

In the meantime, the money that would otherwise have to be paid in corporation taxes to the federal government could be used to meet the capital cost and other expenses of the refinery, including payments to Shaheen's NRC. NRC would supervise construction, manage the refinery, and act as sole sales agent for generous fees, including 5.1 per cent on gross sales, and a management fee of 27.5 per cent of the net profits of the refinery. The fee for supervising the construction would be the equivalent of their salary costs plus 100 per cent. In addition, the oil refinery would not be subject to provincial taxes during construction; no royalties would be paid to the provincial government; electrical power would be supplied to the refinery at a price of 2.5 mills per kilowatt hour, which was far less than the cost of producing the power; and the province agreed to construct, or arrange to have the federal government construct, the necessary wharf at Come By Chance for unloading crude and loading refined oil products. This wharf eventually cost the Government of Canada twenty-three million dollars. Once the money borrowed by the province to build the refinery was repaid, Shaheen would be able to buy the whole operation for two thousand dollars. It was the sweetheart deal to end all sweetheart deals!

Understandably, the federal government was extremely upset about Crown corporations being used as a blatant tax-avoidance device to establish an oil refinery that, if it were really feasible, would generate a tremendous cash flow and profits. As a result, Ottawa announced it was amending the Income Tax Act and regulations to close this loophole. And it did not agree easily to construct the wharf. In the end, the government's agreement was contingent upon the cost being repaid through wharfage charges and user fees.

I got involved in this mess when I was in Smallwood's cabinet, and three of us – Clyde Wells, Alex Hickman, and I – tried to amend Joey's deal with Shaheen to build in at least some minimal protection for the taxpayers of Newfoundland. Our cabinet committee was not formed to negotiate an agreement with Shaheen. It had already been negotiated by Smallwood himself. But there was a real risk to the government of Newfoundland. Apart from the fact that we were to lend thirty million dollars to help cover construction costs, the project was to be owned by one provincial Crown corporation and to be operated by another. While the government itself might not be legally responsible for the obligations of the Crown corporations, if we failed to ensure that they met their financial obligations, the credit of the province would be badly damaged.

The agreement was completely one-sided and, as far as Clyde and Alex and I could see, of little economic benefit to Newfoundland. After months of intense work, we succeeded in obtaining a few small improvements. Shaheen didn't like that, and he went to Joey to demand even more. Having no money to get the refinery off the ground, he told Smallwood the province would have to guarantee interim financing or the project would collapse. It was Joey's insistence that we give Shaheen his interim financing that prompted Wells and me to resign from the cabinet.

After Clyde and I were gone, there was no one left to stand up to Shaheen, and Joey did pretty much what he wanted. Two years later, in 1970, he put Newfoundland's credit at peril when he gave letters of comfort to the U.K. Export Credit Guarantee Department and to Kleinwort-Benson, the English financiers who were raising the loans for the refinery, assuring them that the Newfoundland government would stand behind all the financing. He did this without authority from the House of Assembly and without informing the public.

By the time Frank Moores and the Conservatives took office in January 1972 – with me as Minister of Finance, Minister of Economic Development, and head of the Treasury Board – the Come By Chance complex was 60 per cent completed and scheduled to begin the first stage of production in March 1973. The construction cost was $155 million, in addition to the $5 million in interim or bridge financing provided by Smallwood when Wells and I quit the cabinet. Another $15 million to $20 million would have to be found to complete the refinery. This was to cover Canadian customs duties and sales taxes not included in the original contract price, currency fluctuations, pollution equipment, and changes made in the plans as they went along. The Moores cabinet took the position that all this additional financing had to be arranged by the Shaheen interests.*

When the refinery was finally ready for its grand opening, Shaheen did it up in a style never seen in Newfoundland before, or since. An ordinary business tycoon would have an official opening and invite people to attend the happy event. He might even fly a few of them to Come By Chance for the occasion. But not Shaheen. At a cost of $97,000 a day, he chartered the Cunard luxury liner *Queen Elizabeth II* for a seven-day round-trip cruise from New York to Come By Chance, inviting executives and principals of major oil, shipping, and finance companies, together with politicians from Newfoundland, Nova Scotia, and Ottawa. He paid everyone's transportation to New York, plus all the food and booze on board, plus a party for a thousand guests at Come By Chance. The total tab had to be in the neighbourhood of $1 million. It was a spectacular event, with lots of media coverage.

---

* Details of the Come By Chance refinery project are spelled out in my 1973 Budget Speech as Minister of Finance to the Newfoundland House of Assembly.

Jane and I went to New York and joined the cruise. Smallwood was on board, too. I wasn't at all keen on being there, but Jane told me I had to go. She was really annoyed with me. She told me she was sick and tired of my opposing all these things, and here was something interesting to do, and I was refusing to go. She'd had enough of that, so I had to go on this ship of fools. It was the last place I wanted to be. By the time we got to Come By Chance, the weather was terrible, just terrible, with high winds and freezing rain. Shaheen had big tents set up, with food and drink for all his guests and the local people who worked on the plant. As we came ashore from the QE II, we could see streams of locals coming out of the tents, carrying hams, roasts of pork, lobsters, and God knows what else. They'd looted the tents and were carrying their booty home. It was a fantastic shambles!

The refinery didn't last long. Shaheen had contracted to buy his crude oil at the prevailing world price. Just as they were getting into operation, there was a crisis in the Middle East. In the space of a few weeks, the world price went from around one dollar a barrel to eight dollars, ten dollars, twelve dollars a barrel. Shaheen was stuck with that contract, so now one million barrels of oil on a VLCC (Very Large Cargo Carrier) tanker, instead of costing one million, would cost as much as twelve million. Their cash flow couldn't handle it.

When the refinery went into receivership in 1976, its total debt exceeded $500 million, making it the largest bankruptcy in Canadian history to that time. The province was owed $42 million on a second mortgage agreement, and the federal government $24 million in secured debt and $16.5 million in preferred debt. One of Shaheen's big offshore creditors, the Japanese Ataka Trading Company, lost $244.5 million and also went into bankruptcy. When the list of Shaheen's creditors was published, the Cunard company was on it. Shaheen hadn't paid them for the QE II.

It would have been a good deal worse for Newfoundland but for the fact that our new Conservative government had succeeded in negotiating an arrangement with Shaheen and his associates in 1973. Under the new arrangement, the parties involved in the original oil-refinery agreement undertook not to hold the provincial government responsible for the indebtedness of its Crown corporations in return for an agreement to establish a second, even larger, oil refinery at Come By Chance with a capacity of 300,000 barrels a day.

I was damned unhappy about this second refinery. I'd been in Florida, and Shaheen – he knew better than to come near me with his schemes – got to Frank Moores and charmed him. Frank had no previous background with these people. Shaheen got hold of Frank and made a dramatic new proposal for a second refinery. When I got home, it wasn't going to be just one refinery, but two refineries at Come By Chance!

This second refinery, to our great good fortune, was never built, although the amendments to the existing refinery deal did go into effect, saving the province from any further liability other than the loss of money lent directly to the project.

The refinery was mothballed for ten years, until 1986, when it was reactivated by an American company, Cumberland Farms Incorporated, which operated it under the name of Newfoundland Processing Limited until 1994, when it was taken over by Vitol Holdings, a major crude-oil trader in world markets. It's still operating today, employing four hundred Newfoundlanders.

CHURCHILL FALLS

Of the four economic-development projects that bedevilled Newfoundland politics and occupied much of my time, especially in the later years, Churchill Falls is in many ways the saddest tale. The hydro-electric potential of the mighty Churchill River in Labrador is Newfoundland's greatest natural resource. But Newfoundland receives almost no benefit from it. In the worst public-policy mistake Canada has ever known, Joey Smallwood agreed to sell virtually all the electricity produced on the Upper Churchill to Hydro-Québec at a low, fixed price for sixty-five years with not even any adjustment for inflation.

Newfoundland's dilemma stems from two facts. There is no cheap way to get electricity that is generated in Labrador to the island of Newfoundland, where the bulk of the population is. A cable across the bottom of the Strait of Belle Isle would be destroyed by scouring icebergs. A cable tunnel dug under the strait would be the answer. But it would be prohibitively expensive unless the federal government picked up much of the cost or provided the financing, which Ottawa has not been disposed to do.

Given this first fact, Newfoundland is trapped by the second. The only way it can derive economic benefit from the hydroelectric development of the Churchill River is to sell the power it can't use itself to someone else. Given the geography of Eastern Canada, there's only one "someone else" – Quebec. Quebec, up to 1997, was not willing to allow Newfoundland to build transmission lines across Quebec's territory to carry Labrador power to market in Ontario or the United States. If Newfoundland wanted to sell its electricity, it had to sell it to Quebec at a price Quebec was prepared to pay. Quebec would use what it needs for itself and sell the surplus elsewhere at the highest price it could get.

I've been told that the profit from the sale of Churchill Falls electricity adds $800 million per year to Hydro-Québec's bottom line. Newfoundland's economic rent from the development is a mere $10 million to $12 million a year in tax revenue – and even this minuscule amount is taken away in a dollar-for-dollar reduction of equalization payments by the federal government.

Quebec gets rich, relatively speaking, while Newfoundland – the owner of the resource – gets nothing. How could this outrage have happened?

The answer, as was so often the case, begins and ends with Joey Smallwood.

From the time of Confederation in 1949, and perhaps earlier, Smallwood had a grand vision of harnessing the rivers of Labrador, especially Newfoundland's own Niagara, the Hamilton River. Blessed with as much gall as imagination, Joey had the

name of the Hamilton changed to the Churchill River. He
went to England and managed to get in to see Sir Winston
Churchill, to whom he described his vision of the economic
boom waiting for Newfoundland with the development of the
resources of Labrador, including abundant supplies of cheap
electricity. Churchill sent Joey to Europe's greatest bankers, the
Rothschilds, who embraced his vision and set up a great consortium, a latter-day East India Company. They called it the British
Newfoundland Corporation, or Brinco, as it became known.

The rape of Newfoundland did not occur overnight. It took
fifteen years from the time Brinco was formed to negotiate the
agreement that was reached among Newfoundland, Quebec,
and Brinco in 1968. It took another year to translate the
agreement into legal language. Throughout this period, all of
Newfoundland's negotiating was done by Premier Smallwood
himself. He carried all the details in his head. There were no
documents. All the decisions were made by him, although occasionally he brought his cabinet up to date.

The Upper Churchill Hydro Project was approaching completion when the Conservative government took over in January
1972.* Five months later, it was officially opened by Prime
Minister Pierre Trudeau and Premier Frank Moores in the presence of hundreds of dignitaries, including Joey Smallwood.
Eight days after that, I revealed to the House of Assembly for
the first time the full dimensions of the economic disgrace that
Churchill Falls meant for Newfoundland.†

While it was true that the Upper Churchill project was a great
engineering and construction feat, unfortunately it was not and
never would be a major revenue producer for Newfoundland, nor

---

* See Philip Smith's book, *Brinco: The Story of Churchill Falls* (Toronto:
McClelland & Stewart, 1975). Smith tells the story of the Upper Churchill
River development from Brinco's point of view, but it is nonetheless an accu-
rate history.

† I commend to readers my speech of June 23, 1972, in the *Newfoundland
Record of Debates*.

a source of energy for industrial development in Newfoundland or Labrador. The revenues that had been so much talked of by Smallwood were to come from three main areas. The first was a fifty-cent tax on each horsepower produced at Churchill Falls each year. The second was an 8 per cent rental charge on the pre-tax income of the operating entity, Churchill Falls Labrador Corporation Limited (CFLCO). The third was Newfoundland's share of the Canadian corporation tax. In addition, as a shareholder of Churchill Falls, we might receive dividends. The Newfoundland government had purchased 775,998 shares of CFLCO – 9.2 per cent of the shares – at approximately eighteen dollars per share. The cost to the province was about fourteen million dollars, but interest on the money the province had borrowed to buy the shares would outweigh any dividends.

Newfoundland had the right to take back 300,000 megawatts of electricity; in fact, it wanted to exercise that right in order to supply electricity to the Iron Ore Company for an extension of its operations at Labrador City. But Newfoundland would have to give three years' notice of its intention to recall power. And it would have to pay the same price as Quebec to repurchase the electricity.

Adding to these frightful disappointments, we learned that, for every dollar of revenue received from the Upper Churchill project, the province would lose a dollar in tax equalization transfers from the Government of Canada under the equalization formula. As if this weren't bad enough, we discovered that, while the Public Utilities Income Tax Transfer Act (PUITTA) provided that Ottawa would rebate to the provinces 95 per cent of the federal corporation tax collected from privately owned public utilities, the Smallwood government had agreed to turn over one-half of our rebate (47.5 per cent) to CFLCO. To illustrate the point, if Newfoundland received ten million dollars as its share of the Canadian corporation tax paid by Brinco, it would lose ten million dollars in equalization. In addition, Newfoundland would be out the 47.5 per cent of the federal rebate that it passed on to Brinco. It's incredible, but the

Newfoundland government actually loses money overall on the Upper Churchill!

It's a terrible tragedy. We sit here in Newfoundland with the seat out of our pants, while Quebec makes hundreds of millions of dollars a year from our resource. It's not Quebec's fault for taking candy from a baby. It's our own fault. Our government did it. Smallwood did it, and it can't be corrected unilaterally.

Having learned all this, it was obvious to the Moores government that, if the Lower Churchill River was to be developed, the conditions would have to be very different from those on the Upper Churchill. The potential of the Upper Churchill is 5,225 megawatts. The Lower Churchill's is less, about 2,500 megawatts. In 1966–67, the House of Assembly had approved legislation authorizing the government to enter into a lease on the Lower Churchill on the same appalling terms and conditions as on the Upper Churchill. It was our good fortune that the lease had never been executed, leaving us free to negotiate new terms.

After we got in, the people from Brinco came down to propose that they go ahead with the Lower Churchill on the same terms as the Upper Churchill. As they saw it, this development at Gull Island on the Lower Churchill would produce 1,800 megawatts, or roughly one-third of the output of Churchill Falls. Brinco felt that Quebec was still the only possible customer for this power and proposed a development to include the construction of two transmission lines to the Hydro-Québec delivery point with a tie-line to Churchill Falls. The cost of the development was estimated at $550 million, and the mill rate for the power would probably have to be six or seven mills, more than double the Churchill Falls rate.

One of the characteristics of the Brinco people was arrogance. Bill Mulholland, later chairman of the Bank of Montreal, was in charge of things for Brinco. I told them to get lost. We were never going to do it on the same terms, because by this time we had it analysed and we knew what Quebec was making. We would let the river water run to the sea for the rest of the millennium unless there was a better arrangement than that. I told them we'd get back to them and tell them the conditions under which we'd do it.

When we set out our eighteen conditions, Brinco said they couldn't possibly do it.* They said our conditions would boost the price to twelve mills. The meeting was a failure. But we were in the position where we had hydro resources in Labrador that we couldn't develop because Brinco owned the water rights under the legislation Smallwood had approved. So we decided we would take over Brinco. We'd nationalize Brinco and get the resources back, which is what we set out to do.

Frank Moores went to London to meet with Sir Val Duncan of Rio Tinto–Zinc Corporation Limited, Brinco's largest shareholder. Meanwhile, I went to Montreal to advise Mulholland we were offering $6.75 a share for all of Rio Tinto–Zinc's shares of Brinco and would make the same offer available to all other shareholders. I told Mulholland that, if our offer was not accepted, we would enact legislation to nationalize the company.

Duncan and Moores and their advisers flew the next day to Montreal, where the negotiations began. The public reaction in Newfoundland appeared to be excellent, and I advised Moores to take a strong line so that Brinco would realize we meant business. Duncan offered to sell Brinco's water rights in Labrador, but said they would not consider selling their Brinco shares. The meeting did not go well for us because of a weak opening by Moores and the arrogant attitude adopted by Duncan. Rather than taking the firm position I had urged, Frank waffled throughout the meeting. During the lunch break, our group worked to stiffen the Premier's spine. He did take a tougher stance when the meeting resumed, and Duncan agreed to negotiate the sale of the shares. He suggested a price of $8.70 a share, putting Brinco's value at $210 million.

---

* The Moores government's conditions for the development of the Lower Churchill River and the issuance of a lease are spelled out in my Budget Speech of March 30, 1973, in the House of Assembly.

But, at the next meeting, Duncan, determined to dominate, was extremely offensive. At one point Mulholland passed Duncan a note and one of our officials saw what it said: "Moores' hands are shaking." That evening, we stiffened Frank's resolve again, persuading him to give Brinco until the next afternoon to accept our offer or face takeover legislation.

There was more backsliding by Moores in ensuing days as the two sides traded offers and counter-offers. We introduced the takeover legislation, and the Rio Tinto–Zinc group came to St. John's to negotiate further. In the end, we abandoned our attempt to acquire Brinco. We went after what we really wanted – Brinco's control of CFLCO, the operating company, plus the water rights in Labrador. We got both for $160 million, but only after I made it clear I would resign if the price was any higher.

However, the inept way that the negotiations were conducted on the Newfoundland side resulted in our paying ten million dollars more than we should have paid for CFLCO and the water rights. I was coming to feel that the stress and strain of dealing with the weak and irresolute leadership of Moores was almost as bad as the stress and strain of dealing with the dictatorial and autocratic leadership of Smallwood. My main consolation was that I had a great deal more influence in the Moores administration than in the Smallwood one.

The Brinco negotiations were intensely frustrating for me and brought me close to resignation. I considered it seriously on several occasions, but resignation was not to be carried out lightly. I had taken this extreme step once and would likely not retain credibility if I had to resign from a second government, no matter how justified the step might be.

I don't know why Frank kept waffling. I wasn't impressed by Sir Val Duncan or Bill Mulholland, or any of them. I always think I'm just as good as the people I'm dealing with, just as smart, just as intelligent – maybe smarter and more intelligent. If I have the same information they have, they're no better than I am. I don't think Frank had that same self-confidence, because, whenever we came face to face with them, he back-pedalled. They could talk him out of whatever position we were urging him to take. Frank is not unintelligent, but he wants to be liked.

The Moores government's takeover of CFLCO and the water rights in Labrador and its plan to develop power at Gull Island were ultimately frustrated by our inability to get the federal government's assistance to build a tunnel and transmission lines under the Strait of Belle Isle. The development of the power potential of the Lower Churchill River still waits.

In retrospect, there's no doubt that the Upper Churchill development should have been carried out without Brinco. It should have been carried out as a joint venture of the provinces of Newfoundland and Quebec, with the proceeds being shared equally between the two provinces. We now know this precise proposal was made to Joey Smallwood by René Lévesque, then Quebec's Energy minister. It was cavalierly dismissed by Smallwood because of his relationship with Brinco and those who had formed Brinco. We now know, thanks to Fabian O'Dea's royal commission into the Newfoundland liquor-lease scandal, that Smallwood was speculating in Brinco stock during the period he was negotiating the Churchill Falls agreement. We have no way of knowing how his conflict of interest may have influenced him in the negotiations. But we do know that he violated the trust of the Newfoundland people.

8

REFORMING
NEWFOUNDLAND'S
GOVERNMENT

Courtesy Sue Dewar, Ottawa Sun

FRANK MOORES WAS a complete contrast to
Joey Smallwood. Frank was the chairman of
the board. Discussion and debate were encouraged in cabinet. Frank was an engaging,
friendly, effusive personality who was more
than happy to delegate authority to others. He
was content to let me run the government in
most day-to-day matters. Although I enjoyed
the freedom and authority, I was still number two. I never considered myself an intimate of Frank's, but, for the most part, we
got along well.

Moores always enjoyed the good life, the high life, and this
didn't change by one iota when he became premier. He loved
travel, fine restaurants, salmon fishing, partridge hunting,
women, booze, late nights, and as little work as possible. In the
summer, people would say Frank had gone up river to spawn. He
was a great fisherman and, with access to government helicopters, he wouldn't be seen from the middle of June until the

end of the summer. He'd be fishing at Long Harbour or in Labrador or someplace else.

People said government was a game to Frank; winning the premiership was just another conquest, like a new woman, and, once he'd gotten the prize, he wasn't really smitten with the job. He was criticized for being a playboy, for his easygoing, fun-loving ways. Although he was too easily taken in by smooth-talking promoters and sometimes lacked the resolve to stand firm in tough negotiations, easygoing Frank was a refreshing change after the dictatorial Smallwood.

And the government Moores led was very much a reform government. We had to be reformers. We had no alternative. After twenty-three years of autocratic rule by the Smallwood Liberals, there was an urgent need for reform on all fronts. We had a comfortable majority behind us in the House of Assembly, and we went to work quickly to restore democracy to the province.

The first thing we did was to eliminate the arbitrary power that the government and its agencies, under Smallwood, had exercised over ordinary citizens. We wanted to establish the principle that citizens were free to criticize the government without having to fear that they would lose their livelihood or suffer other retribution at the hands of a vengeful administration. The tendering system for the awarding of government contracts was reformed. The all-powerful Newfoundland Liquor Commission was scrapped and replaced by two bodies: the Newfoundland Liquor Corporation, to administer the sale of alcoholic products, and the Liquor Licensing Authority, to license brewers' agents and establishments to sell liquor and wine. We took the politics out of the system by setting up an independent appeal board.

We increased the government's accountability by modernizing the rules of the Assembly. We introduced a daily oral Question Period, something Ottawa and most other provinces had had for many, many years. Specific times were set aside for consideration of departmental spending estimates. We streamlined the cabinet by establishing a planning and priorities committee of senior ministers, with groups of ministers assigned to formulate policy in the three key areas of resource development, social programs, and government services.

Remembering only too well the way Smallwood had accused me of conflict of interest when I left his cabinet in 1968, I took particular pleasure in writing and introducing Newfoundland's first conflict-of-interest code. Newfoundland was the first Canadian province to enact such a code. Its central principle was the requirement that elected members, cabinet ministers, and senior civil servants disclose any potential conflicts of interest upon assuming employment with the government or on election to the Assembly. The legislation did not require members or civil servants to divest themselves of private holdings, but they did have to report the holdings to the Office of the Auditor General in a disclosure statement, a copy of which could be obtained by any member of the public. Thereafter, members, ministers, and public servants were prohibited from taking part in any decision or action relating to their private interests.

Failure to comply could result in a fine or imprisonment. The disclosure statement had to be renewed annually and had to include interests held by spouses and minor children. All real estate holdings had to be disclosed, as did all shares of corporations and other investments that might pose a conflict of interest. Members of the House of Assembly were barred from voting, or even speaking, on matters in which they had a financial or other interest. Assembly members and provincial employees were forbidden to use for their personal gain any information obtained on the job, unless such information was available to the public generally.

If this law had been in effect when Premier Smallwood was borrowing money from the Bank of Montreal, the province's banker, to purchase shares in Brinco while he was negotiating with Brinco over Churchill Falls, he could have been charged. In all likelihood, he would have been convicted and incarcerated. My legislation made it clear that the premier and other cabinet ministers could not participate in any government decision affecting a company in which they held shares. Nor could they negotiate the development of resources by companies in which they had an interest. In my view, this legislation was more effective and far fairer than the current, confusing federal conflict-of-interest legislation.

Unlike the federal legislation, Newfoundland's didn't recognize blind trusts. A blind trust is useless when dealing with private companies. For example, when Don Jamieson was in Trudeau's cabinet, he owned 49 per cent of Newfoundland Broadcasting, which was federally regulated. He put his holdings in a blind trust. But how could the trust be blind? Jamieson knew he owned 49 per cent of Newfoundland Broadcasting. Everybody who worked at Newfoundland Broadcasting knew he was one of the owners. Everyone at the regulatory agency, the Canadian Radio-television and Telecommunications Commission, knew he was an owner. The only ones who didn't know were the people, because the contents of blind trusts were not made public. So how could Jamieson's putting his 49 per cent of Newfoundland Broadcasting into a blind trust possibly solve anything? It was just nonsense.

Probably the greatest achievement of the Moores administration was to put honesty back into government. Government business was conducted in an open manner, which was new. Wild schemes for economic development ceased. Proposals were properly analysed, which meant that most of them got thrown out. Of course, this is not something a politician could be elected on. He wouldn't get a single vote for telling people that the government had rejected a hundred schemes that would have wasted their money.

As we soon learned, nobody cared about conflict of interest, except the newspapers. The general public wasn't concerned. They either didn't believe these things were going on during the Smallwood years, or they assumed all governments thrived on influence-peddling. The main effect of our legislation seemed to be to make everyone feel free to criticize the Moores government, and they did. They no longer had to fear they would lose their tavern licence or their fishing loan if they attacked the administration. They knew they wouldn't be punished. They felt they were entitled to attack the government.

The whole program of industrial development was brought under control. A proper regime was prepared for the development of offshore oil and gas. The Moores government put together a first-class regime for the offshore and cancelled permits to Shaheen and John C. Doyle to explore huge areas out there that they had done nothing to earn. We put together a legal case that offshore petroleum and minerals, just like underland resources, were the property of the provinces, an argument we ultimately lost in the Supreme Court of Canada.

During my four years in the Moores administration, I was Minister of Finance and President of the Treasury Board from January 1972 until the cabinet shuffle of October 1974. I was Minister of Economic Development from January to July 1972, when I relinquished that post because it was not practical for one person to do all three jobs.

In my first Budget Speech, I announced the elimination of the Parents' Subsidy Program to save the province $3.2 million annually. This subsidy program, known as the "mother's allowance," had been instituted by Smallwood for political reasons and involved an *annual* payment of $20 for each child attending school. The subsidy program was no longer necessary, if it ever was, because the federal government had instituted a new family income security plan. This plan raised the total amount paid out to Newfoundland parents for their children, in school or out, from $19.1 million annually to $37.6 million. The average Newfoundland child started to receive $14.60 *per month*, up from $7.01 per month. Despite this improvement, a tremendous furore arose over the elimination of the $20 annual "mother's allowance." For years, I was portrayed as the greatest mother-stabber in the history of Newfoundland. The experience taught me how difficult it is to take away any government program or benefit once it is put in place.

Not that a Finance minister expects to win popularity. In my second Budget, I pushed total government spending to $674.525 million, a record for the province, even though I had cut back programs and done everything I could to hold down expenditures. And in my third Budget, I had to increase provincial income taxes and raise the retail sales tax from 7 to 8 per cent to pay for the spending.

In September 1974, Moores planned a major cabinet shuffle which involved my leaving both Finance and Treasury Board. His suggestion, a shrewd one, was that I take over the Fisheries portfolio and chair the cabinet's resource committee. I also became minister responsible for intergovernmental affairs, a new position, in charge of our relationship with the federal and other provincial governments. In the same shuffle, Brian Peckford entered the cabinet as Minister of Municipal Affairs and Housing.

The Fisheries portfolio gave me an opportunity to visit outport communities throughout Newfoundland, and the exposure was very valuable to me personally and politically. My opposite number in Ottawa was Romeo LeBlanc, with whom I had a pleasant and positive relationship and who many years later became Canada's first Acadian governor general. The fishery is clearly within federal constitutional jurisdiction, but provinces have a legitimate role to play in licensing and regulating fish plants and fish processing. The provinces can also supplement financial support to fishermen and fish-plant workers and assist with the construction and equipping of fishing vessels.

As the provincial Fisheries minister, I learned a great deal that would stand me in good stead later when, with fish stocks declining at an alarming rate, I became Minister of Fisheries and Oceans in Ottawa.

I also had to handle a burgeoning scandal arising from a federal–provincial program to deal with the losses incurred by fishermen along the northeast coast of Newfoundland when Arctic ice unexpectedly swept back to shore in the spring of 1974, destroying traps, nets, and other fishing gear. The two governments agreed to compensate fishermen for lost gear based on the individual fisherman swearing an affidavit as to his loss, supported by affidavits from businessmen, merchants, or others confirming the value of the equipment lost. The inevitable result of this loose system was wholesale fraud, with hundreds of fishermen collecting compensation for gear never lost and perhaps never owned. They had no compunction about swearing false affidavits, nor did the merchants with whom they shared the proceeds of the fraud. For me, it was a discouraging example of the ordinary person's ability to rationalize dishonest conduct when it comes to parting governments from public money.

Sixty or 70 per cent of my time in these years was spent trying to clean up the mess Smallwood had left us with John C. Doyle's Canadian Javelin linerboard mill at Stephenville, John Shaheen's oil refinery at Come By Chance, and Brinco's hydro development at Churchill Falls in Labrador. We had to get a grip on these projects and bring them under our control. It was difficult because nobody, except Joey, knew for certain what was going on. The files were in poor condition and Smallwood had taken a lot of them when he left. So everything had to be reconstructed.

Along the way, we appointed a royal commission to get to the bottom of the scandal of the liquor stores leased by the Newfoundland Liquor Commission. That's how we found out that Smallwood was one of the secret owners of the stores and that he was borrowing money from the Bank of Montreal to speculate in Brinco stock. One of those involved with him in this venal activity was his chief henchman and deputy minister Oliver L. (Al) Vardy. And we discovered that Vardy had another little scam going. Vardy had his own tuna-fishing yacht, *Altuna*, with its own captain and crew, whose salaries were charged to the government. He had *Altuna* built in Nova Scotia and paid for by the Newfoundland Department of Tourism. It was a beautiful sports-fishing boat with twin engines and a flying bridge. Supposedly, it took people out to sea to promote tourism. But it was really for Al and his friends and his girlfriend. Frank Moores took over *Altuna* and changed its name to *The Rowdyman*, but he was never much interested in it. Eventually, the boat was sold to a real-estate developer.

For one dollar a year, I had a first-class chartered accountant and businessman, Peter Gardiner, who taught at Memorial University, to help me bring some order to the chaos, which we eventually did. I worked like a Trojan. With other ministers, such as Bill Doody, I looked after everything of any consequence. Frank was the front man.

His relationship with Shaheen made me uneasy. And I had good cause. In January 1973, I went to Florida for a week's holiday. While I was there, Moores and Shaheen negotiated an agreement for an additional oil refinery. I talked to Moores twice that week by phone. He told me he was having discussions with Shaheen, but he gave me no reason to believe that any deal was imminent. When I returned to St. John's, I was astounded to learn that agreements had already been signed with Shaheen under which the government of Newfoundland had committed itself to providing a loan of $78.5 million to help finance a $300-million refinery with a capacity of 300,000 barrels a day – three times the size of Shaheen's troubled first refinery.

I was furious! At the time, I was Minister of Finance, President of the Treasury Board, and chairman of the cabinet committee dealing with Shaheen and his Come By Chance project. And no one had told me that our government was entertaining the absurd notion that it commit $78.5 million to a project for which there was no demonstrable need, promoted by a hustler who had yet to deliver on any of his promises to Newfoundland.

I took five days to study the agreements, then wrote two letters to Moores. I told him I was reassessing my place in his administration. I said that, unless he gave me his assurance that this sort of thing would not happen again – and unless these agreements were improved – I could not accept collective responsibility as a member of the cabinet for this deal. My second letter outlined changes that would have to be made for me to support the agreements.

Frank did not really attempt to defend what had happened, but was his usual sweet and reasonable self. I made it clear that I did not think his administration would have any chance of re-election if it continued the way it was going. As we talked, Moores suggested he would most likely resign in the next two or three years and not contest another election. I said that was complete bull. It reminded me of Joey's ploy of pretending that his retirement was imminent. When Janis Johnson, Frank's wife, came in, he asked her to give him a true and honest answer to a question he was going to ask. She said she would. He asked whether she had ever heard him say he would most likely be resigning in the next two or three years. She paused, then said she had never heard him say any such thing. It was an amusing moment.

After intense renegotiations with Shaheen, an agreement was arrived at that I could live with. It seems academic now. The second refinery never went ahead once the original refinery went bankrupt.

This was not the end of my woes with Moores, however. In 1976, when I was Minister of Mines and Energy, I again had to threaten to resign. This time the issue was hydro rates, which were my responsibility as Energy minister. I was out of the province when, without advising me, and without a full cabinet meeting on the subject, Moores announced a three-month freeze on a cabinet-approved increase in the wholesale price of electricity. The effect of this increase would have been to raise prices 14 per cent at the retail level. The issue wasn't whether the increase should have gone ahead. The issue was whether the premier, without reference to the responsible minister, should have unilaterally reversed a cabinet decision. Again, I wrote to Moores. I advised him I would not remain in the cabinet if this continued. I got his undertaking that it would not happen again. But I decided the time had come to look for other options in public life.

∾

It is a paradox of the democratic system that providing good administration, solving problems, and avoiding costly mistakes do not impress the electorate. The practice of good government is not spectacular. Seeing nothing spectacular, the public concludes that the people in power are not doing anything. Smallwood's bread-and-circuses approach is the way to make people believe their government is active and accomplishing great things.

Despite the tremendous efforts of the Moores government to save the province from complete disaster in the linerboard and oil-refinery projects, despite our efforts to gain something for Newfoundlanders from hydro development in Labrador, despite reform in such areas as the liquor laws, and despite the introduction of conflict-of-interest legislation and many other solid but unspectacular achievements, there was no doubt that the public was seized with a belief that we weren't "doing anything."

Thus it was with some trepidation that we faced the prospect of a general election. Moores began working on grass-roots organizational details in early 1975, and I travelled throughout the fishing districts in a pre-election campaign. Frank finally called the election for September 16, 1975.

This election was the last hurrah of Joey Smallwood. The Newfoundland Liberal party had spent most of 1974 self-destructing. Ed Roberts, then thirty-four, had been elected leader in 1972 and lost the general election that year. When his leadership came up for review in 1974, he was challenged not only by Roger Simmons and Steve Neary, both Assembly members, but also by Smallwood. Much to Joey's chagrin, Roberts led him, 337 votes to 305, on the first ballot, and beat him handily on the second. But Joey did not accept defeat gracefully. "Newfoundland is full of hundreds upon hundreds of people I made but they won't support me," he said. "But when they smell victory for me, I'll need steel coat tails."

Afterward, Joey did the Liberal party grievous harm when he formed his own Liberal Reform Party, with himself as leader. He was seventy-four when he announced "the rebirth of Liberalism" in Newfoundland. Liberal Reform fielded twenty-eight candidates, and they hurt the Liberals badly. We also took some lumps. With the number of seats increased from forty-two to fifty-one, the Conservatives elected thirty members, to sixteen for Roberts's Liberals, four for Smallwood's Liberal Reform, and one independent Liberal.

Joey himself was elected in Twillingate and he sat in Opposition in the Assembly until 1977, when he resigned his seat. The Liberal Reform Party disappeared then as its other members went home to the Liberal party.

Although we were re-elected – thanks, in part, to the votes that Smallwood's candidates stole from the Liberals – we lost five cabinet ministers. My usually comfortable majority in St. John's West shrank alarmingly; I was re-elected by just 437 votes. The public was trying to tell us something, but I was starting to hear voices coming from another direction.

∾

In February 1976, delegates from across Canada gathered in Ottawa as the federal Progressive Conservatives chose a successor to Robert Stanfield. Unlike Smallwood at the Liberal convention that had picked Pierre Trudeau eight years earlier, Frank Moores made no attempt to whip all Newfoundland delegates behind the candidate of his choice. While Moores supported Brian Mulroney, and Brian Peckford went with Joe Clark, I backed Flora MacDonald. Others in our caucus supported other candidates. I voted for Flora until she withdrew, then supported Joe Clark until he was elected on the fourth ballot, forcing Mulroney out after the third ballot and defeating Claude Wagner on the fourth.

The choice of Joe Clark struck me as strange, since he was virtually unknown to Canadians at that time. But Joe proved to be a decent, hard-working, and capable person who suffered image problems as a result of his unimpressive personal appearance and his marriage to a feminist who insisted on using her own name.

Throughout 1976, public antipathy mounted towards Trudeau and the Liberals. It was an opportune time for me to move to federal politics. My decision to do so was supported strongly by Jane, who was aware of the frustrations I suffered in the Moores government. Jane had never liked the atmosphere of Newfoundland politics and the savage personal attacks that were a constant feature of it. My commitment to provincial politics had been complete and unrelenting since my resignation from the Smallwood cabinet in 1968. I had put everything I had into the struggle to rid Newfoundland of the Smallwood administration and to deal with the problems it had left behind.

By this time, however, I knew I'd gone as far as I could in Newfoundland politics, and, frankly, I was tired of playing second fiddle. For all practical purposes, I was running the Moores government, working my butt off, and getting no appreciation from Frank for doing his work. And I was sick of being compromised by Frank when I was away and he felt like cutting a deal with John Shaheen or some other wheeler-dealer. That sort of thing made it easy for me to leave.

I was interested in national politics and national issues. The opportunity was waiting to be seized. Conservative Walter Carter had resigned as the MP for St. John's West, the federal counterpart of my provincial seat, in August 1975, to run in our provincial election. But with the Liberal government's popularity drooping, Trudeau kept putting off the St. John's West by-election.

Clark was keen to have me run in St. John's West, assuring me I would have an important role to play in his caucus and in the government if the Tories won the next general election. Over the summer of 1976, I discussed the situation with Moores. He agreed it would be a logical move for me, and one he would support. Given the strains between us, he was probably relieved to see me go. On August 11, I announced my candidacy. I resigned from the Newfoundland House of Assembly on September 8 – ten years to the day from my first election. The by-election finally took place on October 18, 1976, Trudeau's fifty-seventh birthday. I was determined to give him no cause to celebrate!

9

ON TO OTTAWA

Courtesy Donato, Toronto Sun

THE 1976 FEDERAL by-election in St. John's West was hard-fought, but it was fun – more fun, I thought to myself, than I'd had for the last few years in Newfoundland. Joe Clark came down to campaign for me and we had a terrific meeting at Witless Bay, where Joe – with encouragement from Jim McGrath, the MP for St. John's East, and me – confirmed the Conservatives' new policy on offshore oil and mineral rights. A Conservative government, he declared, would negotiate a deal with provincial governments to establish that jurisdiction over the offshore belonged to the provinces, not Ottawa.

This was a popular position in Newfoundland, of course, and the crowd in Witless Bay was suitably enthusiastic. Clark, however, suffered from having his speech sandwiched between mine and McGrath's. We both delivered the kind of florid oratory that Newfoundlanders love. Juliette O'Neill of the Canadian Press reported that I "stole the spotlight from federal Progressive Conservative leader Joe Clark . . . during a speech littered with wisecracks, insults and threats to the federal Liberal government." I was starting to work up my repertoire of Pierre put-downs, referring that evening to Prime Minister Trudeau as "Pierre the Petulant" and "Pierre the Perturbed."

The by-election campaign took an unexpected turn when abortion emerged as the major issue. Although rural St. John's West was traditionally Roman Catholic, none of the three candidates was Catholic, and none of us agreed with the Church stand against abortion. In a television debate, the Liberal, New Democrat, and I all took the position that abortion was an issue that should be left to a woman and her doctor. This so upset Catholic leaders that, at Mass on the Saturday evening and Sunday before the by-election on Monday, all three of us were denounced from pulpits throughout St. John's West. This concerned me more than it did my two opponents because the Catholic vote in eastern Newfoundland had been heavily Tory since 1949, suggesting that, if the Catholics were upset, it would be to my disadvantage more than to the Liberal and NDP candidates'.

The voting results established two things: the abortion issue was not as potent as I had feared, and the Liberals were even more unpopular than I thought. I won with 11,719 votes, to 8,597 for New Democrat Thomas Mayo, while Liberal Robert Innes trailed badly with 3,971.

I was sworn into the House of Commons with Jean Pigott, who had won a by-election for the Tories in Ottawa–Carleton on the same day. The fun I had experienced in the campaign continued. I felt liberated, transported from the cares and woes of Government to the freedom of those in Opposition, whose highest purpose is to demolish the government in order to replace it.

Politics may be the same game everywhere, but I found the demands of federal politics quite different. As a provincial politician, I'd always represented an urban district, which didn't require too much attention between elections. Although the name of my new federal riding was also St. John's West, it was much larger and more diverse. It took in part of the capital, the city of Mount Pearl, plus a large rural expanse out along Placentia and St. Mary's bays and along the southern shore of the Avalon Peninsula, where one-third of my constituents lived. For the first time, I had to go into outports to solicit the votes of fishermen and fish-plant workers. I also had to be prepared to meet the rigorous demands that rural constituents place on their elected member.

My friends noticed the change in me as I made the transition from provincial to federal politics. Paradoxically, perhaps, I became much more of a grass-roots politician. I started to pay closer attention to local issues than I'd had to when I was in the provincial House. In the outports of Newfoundland, life revolves around government cheques – unemployment insurance, old-age pensions, guaranteed income supplements, family allowances, disability pensions, social assistance of other sorts, plus loans and subsidies to fishermen. I fought to keep every fish-processing plant in St. John's West in operation. And I made sure that my riding got its fair share – more than its fair share, actually – of federal largesse for such things as wharves and harbours.

I believe I'm a compassionate man. I feel for people who work hard and who struggle just to keep their head above water. I've always identified more with the underdog, with the working people in the outports of Newfoundland and across Canada, than with the merchants of Water Street or the barons of Bay Street. I'm a fiscal conservative – I believe the country has to pay its way – but, on social and human issues, I consider myself to be an intelligent liberal. I stress the word "intelligent" – to distinguish myself from the brothel-creepers of the Liberal Party of Canada, who have done so much to divide our country and spend it into penury.

I got to know the people in the smaller communities of St. John's West. I had someone helping me in every village, keeping an eye on things, whether it was in Patrick's Cove, Point Lance, Bay Bulls, or Trepassey. I responded to every letter I got. If someone wanted to see me in person, even after I became a federal cabinet minister, I found the time. No detail was too small, no complaint too trivial, to command the attention of the honourable member for St. John's West. Besides, I loved touring the district. I loved getting in the car and driving from village to village, listening to the people, taking notes, and making sure their problems got taken care of.

Like any good Newfoundland politician, I understood that asphalt is one of the essential ingredients of democracy. I've been accused of being responsible for the paving of every road in St. John's West – not to mention every driveway. I don't know if this is strictly true. There may have been a few Liberal polls that we missed – inadvertently, of course – but I take the accusation as a compliment. Whether it was the paving machines or my performance as their MP, I did very well in St. John's West over the years. The only places we couldn't seem to win were Arnold's Cove and Come By Chance, but I never stopped trying to get them on side.

My main man on the ground was Bill Welsh, who ran my constituency office and generally looked after the riding for me. Bill's favourite expression was "I got 'em all stamped up." The effete élites, the snobs, the literati of Toronto and navel-absorbed places like that wouldn't know what Bill meant. What he meant was, he'd been to a fishing village and made sure everybody had their unemployment-insurance stamps up to date – and, if not, he'd organize a works project to get them more stamps – so they wouldn't have any problem collecting UI when the fishing season was over. Bill knew which men and women had worked enough weeks to qualify for benefits and which ones hadn't. He made sure everyone was able to take the maximum legal advantage of the UI system.

Back when I was in Opposition in Newfoundland, I'd stood up against Joey Smallwood's flagrant abuse of the patronage system. But what I did as an MP was different. I am a realistic man and I recognized the reality of the situation in a poor province like Newfoundland, with the highest unemployment in the country, where so many of the jobs are seasonal and where a bad season in the fishery – which used to employ 25 per cent of the provincial labour force – is beyond any individual's control, yet can wipe a family out financially.

I am against the *abuse* of patronage. I am not against the *use* of patronage. There is a difference. I am certainly not against patronage if it means appointing fine, upstanding, *qualified* Progressive Conservatives to every available job on the federal bench or on the Citizenship Court or on the boards of directors of Canadian National or the Bank of Canada – or to any other position within the federal government's purview. In Newfoundland, it's not a contradiction to preach the virtues of free enterprise and less government while accepting every scrap of patronage possible from the government. Come to think of it, I guess it's not a contradiction on Bay Street, either.

∾

As my career in federal politics began, my wife, Jane, still had one major decision to make. Would she move with me to Ottawa, returning to Newfoundland on some weekends and during vacations, or would she stay behind in Newfoundland to look after our Dandie Dinmont dog, Brigand? Our three children were all at university or living away from home. Only this dearly beloved animal remained to be cared for. Would Jane stay at home with Brigand or come to Ottawa with John? It was a toss-up, but finally Jane chose John over Brigand, and after Christmas 1976 we moved to Ottawa to start our new life in national politics.

I had no idea what a jungle I was getting into. The House of Commons was a zoo. The Conservative caucus was a circus. John Diefenbaker was still there, and nobody knew when he was going to embarrass the leader. He spent several years shafting Robert Stanfield, then he started on Joe Clark. Jack Horner, the big buck from Alberta, was still in the Tory caucus. Everybody in the caucus was scared to death of him and what he might or might not do. Claude Wagner, who was supposed to be Joe's

Quebec lieutenant, was unpredictable and lazy, and did nothing to assist. He was still sulking because Clark had defeated him for the leadership in 1976.

Poor old Joe had to try to run the Opposition with a caucus in this advanced state of disarray. Most of his Alberta MPs paid no attention to him; they tried to screw him every chance they got, and they wouldn't even let him decide what seat he was going to run in. It was hell for Joe.

As for me, there were some amusing moments. Not long after I was elected, Diefenbaker published one of the volumes of his memoirs. I bought a copy. I still haven't read it, but I figured I should buy a copy and get Dief to autograph it. In those days, Dief sat in the front row, next to Don Mazankowski, from Alberta, who later was Minister of Finance and Deputy Prime Minister under Brian Mulroney. The leader always had to be careful about who he put next to Diefenbaker. It had to be somebody acceptable to the old man. But he liked Maz and they got along well.

At the end of Question Period one day, I noticed Mazankowski had left his seat, so I went down and slid in beside Dief and I passed him the book and said: "Chief, would you sign this for me?" Dief got out his pen and started writing away, two or three lines. Wow, I thought, this was great. He hardly knows me and he's writing all these warm remarks about me. He handed the book back, and I read what he had written: "My dear Mazankowski, this is to a true and loyal colleague who has been with me through thick and thin for these many years . . . John G. Diefenbaker." I never bothered to tell him I wasn't Mazankowski.

∾

I didn't know Joe Clark well. I liked him as a person and he seemed like a decent fellow. I don't know what more he could have done, or whether he could have been bolder or stronger. His biggest weakness probably was his persona. He never managed to look like a leader, he didn't appear prime-ministerial. And he had to suffer the nasty prejudices of others because of Maureen

McTeer, his wife, who was her own woman, using her own name. It made certain people think of him as a wimp. Trudeau had a wife who was behaving very badly in those days, but it didn't harm him at all because he always looked as though he was the dominant partner in the marriage. Maureen made Joe look like a weakling. Say what you will, men don't think well of other men who don't appear to be in control of their personal relationships. It didn't help Joe one iota that he was a modern man who understood and sympathized with women's concerns.

But he was good in an organizational sense. He worked hard, and then he had the misfortune of not getting a majority in the election of 1979. Added to that misfortune was the fact that he proved to be less than a political genius. If he'd been a really shrewd political operator, a Mackenzie King type, devious and far-thinking, his minority government probably could have survived. Instead, he turned out to be just as foolish and misguided as the rest of us.

⁓

Although Clark didn't make any specific promises to me, I understood that he intended to give me a role to play in any government he formed. I also knew, of course, that my future position would depend on how well I performed in Opposition. He made me Energy critic to start with, but that changed when Jack Horner crossed the floor to the Liberals and was appointed Minister of Industry, Trade and Commerce.

That was an astonishing episode to me. There had been reports in the newspapers that Horner had been talking to Trudeau aide Jim Coutts about defecting. Horner came to our caucus meeting, and they were all so afraid of him that nobody would even question his right to be in the caucus while he was negotiating with Trudeau. I got fed up with this and moved that we expel Horner from caucus because of the disloyalty that had been reported in the papers, unless he was prepared to deny this was going on. Oh, you wouldn't have believed the fussing and the hand-wringing that greeted my motion! Everybody was shocked that I would dare to harass this wonderful man, Jack Horner. Of course, Horner did go to the Liberals, and twenty-four hours later he was a cabinet minister.

Clark asked me to become the Opposition critic for Industry, Trade and Commerce because I had no previous history with Horner; I could get after him, question him, attack him without reservation, and embarrass him whenever possible. Joe couldn't trust other MPs to do that. I confess I thoroughly enjoyed sand-bagging Big Jack, whom I accused of suffering from Horner-oids.

I found that humour, satire, whimsy, or otherwise poking fun at the government and its ministers would be reported widely in the press. One day, I learned of a million-dollar computer located in the East Block of the Parliament Buildings, which was said to be a highly sophisticated press-information retrieval system for the prime minister. As it was purchased and operated with public funds, all parties should have access to it, I proposed. I introduced a motion requesting that the Privy Council Office be "ordered to desist from bubbling up extensive baubles for the prime minister . . . so that no one would be tempted henceforth to bug the bauble or retrieve the prime minister." When France banned the importation of seal pelts after lobbying by Brigitte Bardot, I moved that Canada retaliate by banning the import of French champagne made from grapes "brutalized by human feet." Then I urged that Canada halt the import of *pâté de foie gras* produced as the result of cruelty to geese by overfeeding them until their livers burst, and that we officially endorse the "Save the French Goose Society."

I noted that Horner, when still a Tory, had made a colourful attack on Liberal Transport minister Otto Lang, declaring: "I shall see Otto Lang tarred and feathered and driven out of Saskatchewan. . . . I will pay for the oil and I will pluck the chickens." I put forward a motion asking Horner to advise the Commons whether, now that he had joined the Liberals, he was still prepared to pay for the oil and pluck the chickens, or whether he no longer desired such a sticky future for the Minister of Transport.

Noting that then Finance minister Jean Chrétien had given two seemingly contradictory answers to questions about the value of the Canadian dollar, I moved that the Commons unanimously resolve to award Chrétien the Baron Munchausen Award for the most extravagantly mendacious story heard in Parliament and that he have the length of his nose checked on an hourly basis in the hope he would escape the Pinocchio virus that at one time afflicted the hero of the famous Italian saga.

Although a general election was not called until 1979, a great many Liberal MPs were appointed to the judiciary, civil service, or Crown corporations. So I moved that, as the number of MPs was rapidly diminishing due to this frenzy of government appointments of unwanted Liberal MPs, as there was increasing nervousness among Liberal back-benchers and cabinet ministers about their prospects in the coming election, and as there was a very real danger that the House of Commons quorum of twenty might be threatened if the election was long postponed, therefore "either the Prime Minister call the election immediately, before this House becomes vacant by attrition, or that he cease and desist from further patronage appointments of members of Parliament who are now in danger of becoming an endangered species."

My best-known motion had to do with codfish and the seal hunt. I moved that,

> in view of the fact that the voiceless codfish, long forgotten by humane societies and by the world, but now at last recognized as the noble cod, is the subject of ecological and environmental as well as humane concern by a new organization founded in St. John's, Newfoundland, by Miller H. Ayre and known as Cod-Peace, of which Ayre is the cod-ordinator, and in view of the fact that the purpose of Cod-Peace is to protect the cod particularly against the

voracious, rapacious and unprovoked attacks of the savage
seal . . . [that] Cod-Peace be supported and encouraged by
all cod lovers of Canada and that the chief cod of Canada,
the Minister of Fisheries, make arrangements for the
support and protection of Cod-Peace and for arrangements
to be made for a National Yum Flipper Feast during the fes-
tival of the Easter Seal in late March, since the time is at
hand for all cod lovers of the world to arise since they have
nothing to lose but their cod-pieces.

The seal hunt was a deadly serious issue for Newfoundland, of
course. The hunt had been the object of savage and unjustified
attacks for the previous half-dozen years by organizations that
knew nothing and cared less about the facts, but knew they
could raise huge funds by alleging brutality in the killing of
baby seals. The seal hunt had an honoured place in the economic history of Newfoundland, providing essential income for
fishermen between fishing seasons. It was a dangerous occupa-
tion that had claimed the lives of hundreds of Newfoundlanders
over the centuries. Though the seal hunt was doomed by television and the propaganda campaigns of such organizations as the
Save the Animals Fund, a mighty effort was still under way in
Newfoundland to explain how the hunt was actually conducted.
Newfoundland MPs Jack Marshall and Bill Rompkey prepared a
petition to be presented to the Commons, asking for protection
for the hunt. I mailed the petition to every household in St. John's
West. Petitions signed by more than 28,000 Newfoundlanders
were tabled in the Commons in support of the hunt.

The Trudeau government was having difficulty hiding from
the public that it was not only arrogant but wasteful and extravagant. A prime example was Lang, the Transport minister, who
espoused the principle of user-pay concepts in connection with
the public use of transportation facilities, but who spent more
than $740,000 of taxpayers' money on flights in government air-
craft between 1973 and 1977. Newfoundland's Don Jamieson, a
man for whom I had considerable respect, found an expensive

way to send Christmas greetings to Canadian diplomatic personnel abroad when he was External Affairs minister. Instead of sending out government-issue Christmas cards, he had a twenty-five-minute movie, featuring himself, prepared, at a cost of $13,792.30, and sent to Canada's 110 diplomatic and consular posts around the world.

The ferreting-out of this kind of information – and there were many similar instances – is an effective way for an Opposition MP to damage the credibility of a government. That Jamieson was particularly sensitive to my exposés became apparent when I, alone among all the Newfoundland MPs, was not extended the courtesy of being allowed to invite five couples to a state banquet that he gave for the Queen when she visited St. John's. I accused him of petty vindictiveness and promised it would not dissuade me from continuing to make him as uncomfortable as possible.

And I did. I pursued the conflict of interest in which he found himself, as a cabinet minister, with 49 per cent ownership of Newfoundland Broadcasting Corporation, which had twenty-five television transmitters, six AM radio stations, and one FM radio station in Newfoundland. I submitted a brief to the Canadian Radio-television and Telecommunications Commission opposing a transfer of shares involving Jamieson's holdings. I appeared at a CRTC hearing in St. John's, suggesting that Jamieson resign as External Affairs minister unless he could clear up his conflict of interest. The CRTC eventually imposed some conditions on Newfoundland Broadcasting and expressed "concerns about the involvement in broadcasting, however indirectly, of a minister of the Crown."

During these years, I pursued other issues that reflected badly on the Liberals. I launched several campaigns aimed at John C. Doyle and Canadian Javelin. I presented motions in the Commons and followed up in correspondence with cabinet ministers and Prime Minister Trudeau himself. As a result of my pressure, the Restrictive Trade Practices Commission ordered an inquiry into fraud allegations involving Doyle and Canadian Javelin.

I showed the Commons that Doyle owed the government of Canada $4.5 million in back taxes and penalties from 1950 to 1954. Judgements had been given against Doyle in 1970, but he had dragged the case through the courts for years without paying a cent. He had lost before the Income Tax Appeal Board and before the Exchequer Court of Canada. His appeal to the Supreme Court of Canada had been pending for seven years, with the Department of National Revenue failing to force the appeal to proceed or to ask the Court to dismiss it. Every year, Doyle applied to the Supreme Court to have his case taken off the list – and National Revenue concurred. He had not been required, as the ordinary taxpayer was, to post a bond or pay the taxes while his case was appealed. Instead, he was permitted to turn a block of Javelin shares over to Revenue Canada as security. The shares were worth only a fraction of the money owed. In addition, Canadian Javelin had paid Doyle hundreds of thousands of dollars through Javelin Export Limited, a company incorporated in the Bahamas. Liberal senator Sarto Fournier, a former mayor of Montreal, was chairman of Canadian Javelin's board, which Doyle controlled. It was clear Doyle had received preferential treatment from Revenue Canada over a period of twenty-seven years, while ordinary taxpayers were pursued relentlessly and forced to pay whatever they allegedly owed to the government.

Eventually, I succeeded in rousing the interest of the press, and this forced the government to act. It initiated court action in Quebec to recover $1.4 million that Javelin had paid to Doyle since 1965. I charged repeatedly that this matter was "the greatest scandal in the history of the Canadian tax system."

In its statement of claim, the government averred that, on October 6, 1964 – at a time when Doyle owed Revenue Canada $4,734,646.29 – a letter of demand had been served on Canadian Javelin requiring the company to pay to the government any money it would otherwise pay to Doyle. The company ignored this legal demand, and no action was taken for thirteen years, until I forced the government to act. Would an ordinary taxpayer have been treated so leniently? As I told the Commons, Revenue Canada was hounding one of my constituents for $250, which he did not have, while Doyle was being permitted to owe millions for more than twenty-five years. I said my constituent's reply to the tax collectors in the future would be: "I have no money, own no oil, why not treat me like J.C. Doyle?" Trudeau made a weak defence of the government's handling of the Doyle affair, but behind the scenes he did take steps to ensure that this long miscarriage of justice was brought to an end.

∽

It was during this period that I suffered my first real health scare. I flew back to St. John's from Ottawa one night and went to bed. I woke up during the night when I tried to roll over and couldn't. My arm was paralysed. My doctor told me it was caused by a narrowing of the artery leading from the heart, so I had an angiogram done in Toronto, where they put dye in a vein in my leg to determine the state of my arteries. I was in hospital for a couple of days. I was lucky. They didn't have to operate, but I have to be careful with my diet and take an aspirin every day to thin my blood.

∽

Thinking on your feet is essential in the Commons Question Period. Many MPs can't manage it, but I seemed to have the knack, and I earned a reputation of being a quick man with a one-liner. One day, when I was accused of always having my foot in my mouth, I responded: "I would sooner have a foot in my mouth than a forked tongue." During a debate on currency devaluation, I said: "I think the honourable parliamentary assistant said that I called him a liar earlier today. If I called him a liar, what I meant to say was that he was a Liberal trying to stay in power. That is really what I meant. I know there is very little difference."

In Calgary, I attacked Trudeau for practising "Kung Fu federalism," adding there was "nothing to fear except Pierre himself" as part of a more serious suggestion that the issue of the next election would be the kind of federalism Canadians wanted. In Brampton, Ontario, I suggested that the issue was not "Joe Who?" but "Pierre Why?" I said Liberal Energy minister Alastair Gillespie suffered from the natural gas he was supposed to regulate, Trudeau seemed like a giant because he had surrounded himself with pygmies, and our Tory theme song for the coming election would be "We're coming to take you away, ha ha."

The result of all this speaking activity was that I gained a great deal of attention, most of it positive, from the national media. But there is a danger. It's often difficult to draw the right line between a serious discussion of public issues and entertaining an audience. In my experience, keeping the audience interested and entertained often involved making statements that I wished I hadn't made when I saw them in print the next day.

It happened in Thompson, Manitoba, at a Tory nominating meeting where I spoke from notes but without a full script. Premier Sterling Lyon's Conservative government had introduced a restraint program to reduce the provincial deficit, including cutbacks in the number of civil-service jobs. During the course of my forty-minute speech, I made the point that the federal Conservatives also intended to restrain expenditures and stop the growth of the public service. I should have stopped there. But I went on to add, gratuitously: "We will make Sterling Lyon look like a pussycat."

It was a stupid thing to say. Lyon's meat-cleaver approach to restraint was highly controversial, and my offhand comment made headlines. It took me much time and effort, through letters to newspapers and motions in the Commons, to reassure the public that, although we were committed to shrinking the number of government employees, we had no intention of doing it in a way that would make a Lyon look like a pussycat.

Early in 1979, Frank Moores announced that he intended to retire from political life. Within days, I announced that I would not be a candidate for the provincial leadership of the party. I had really made this decision two and a half years earlier, when I left to enter federal politics. As it was, the Newfoundland Conservatives fielded three strong candidates, Brian Peckford, William Doody, and Leo Barry. Peckford won on the third ballot, and later that spring led the Tories to a general-election victory, winning thirty-three seats, to nineteen for the Liberals. I had no regrets. My future was in Ottawa and, by the time Moores announced his retirement, we were on the brink of a federal general election – at last!

∾

Joe Clark weathered his difficulties; worked to have the caucus members devote their energies to useful work, such as the development of policy; met with the Conservative premiers in Kingston, Ontario, to produce an agreement on a Tory approach to federal–provincial relations; and took a number of other constructive steps. The public's mood, which had shifted back to the Liberals following the election of René Lévesque's Parti Québécois in late 1976, swung against them again in 1977 and 1978. The administration was drifting, and Trudeau didn't seem to care. His low point came in October 1978 when the Conservatives won twelve of fifteen by-elections.

With his government approaching the five-year mark, Trudeau called the national election for May 22, 1979. My efforts were confined primarily to Newfoundland, either in St. John's West or in the five ridings that did not have a Conservative MP. I made several campaign visits outside the province, but did not take part in any major campaign tours in any other part of Canada.

The national campaign was tightly controlled by three people: the leader; his campaign manager, Lowell Murray; and his pollster, Allan Gregg. Our basic issue was simple: the Canadian public was tired of Pierre Trudeau and wanted a change. Their overwhelming desire to get rid of Trudeau outweighed their doubts about Joe Clark. But did Clark know where Canada should be headed? And, if so, could he take Canada in that direction? These were difficult questions.

Our biggest problem was all the promises we were making – 211 of them – in our platform. We were most vulnerable on the economic front, where the party's many policies lacked coordination and consistency because of the philosophical differences among three heavyweights. Sinclair Stevens, a foe of the ever-increasing size of the federal deficit, wanted substantial reductions in government expenditures, while Jim Gillies and Robert de Cotret advocated a substantial tax cut to stimulate the economy and generate new government revenues. When all the Conservative economic policies were reviewed, there was no doubt that there would be a short-term increase, not a decrease, in the federal deficit, and so a "stimulative deficit" was the phrase used to explain this. In addition to new spending programs, we undermined our approach to deficit reduction with a major promise to permit the partial deduction from income tax of mortgage interest and property taxes. We estimated that this program would cost the government at least $400 million in lost revenue in the first year, and $1.6 billion annually four years later, when the deductions came into full operation. To add to our problems, the party pledged to cut personal income taxes by $2 billion for low- and moderate-income Canadians.

These promises would come back to haunt us. For the moment, however, victory was at hand, and it was sweet. The Conservatives won a plurality of seats, while the Liberals, still awesome in Quebec, took a plurality of the popular vote. We elected 136 members, the Liberals 114, and the New Democrats 26, with 6 Créditistes elected in Quebec (one of them, Richard Janelle, from Lotbinière, joined our caucus shortly before the opening of Parliament). With Liberal James Jerome carrying on as Speaker, we had a minority government that could survive only as long as the 5 remaining Créditistes, at least, voted with us.

The results in Newfoundland were not quite so sweet. Despite Clark's undertaking to make offshore oil and gas the property of the coastal provinces, we won only St. John's East and St. John's West. The Liberals took four seats, and the NDP one. My plurality in St. John's West was a healthy one, as I won 17,236 votes, compared with 10,024 for Liberal Patrick O'Flaherty and 9,033 for Thomas Mayo of the NDP.

The conjunction of the national Tory victory, followed one month later by Peckford's election triumph,* combined with my appointment as Minister of Finance for Canada, was a high point of my political life. Unfortunately, high points in politics are usually quickly followed by disappointments. We found that out, painfully, as our new government plunged unheedingly into governing – and into defeat.[†]

---

* Riding the momentum of Clark's federal victory, Peckford called the Newfoundland election for June 18, 1979. Perhaps the best political rally I was ever involved in was the one Peckford held in the late days of that provincial campaign at the CLB Armoury in St. John's. For serious students of the political mayhem in Newfoundland in that era, I recommend Robert Payne's *Ayatollahs and Turkey Trots: Political Rhetoric in the New Newfoundland – Crosbie, Jamieson and Peckford* (St. John's: Breakwater Books, 1980).
† For a painfully thorough chronicle of these unhappy months, see Jeffrey Simpson, *Discipline of Power: The Conservative Interlude and the Liberal Restoration* (Toronto: Personal Library, 1980).

10

THE CLARK INTERLUDE:
TIME ENOUGH TO CONCEIVE,
BUT NOT TO DELIVER

ON JUNE 4, 1979, one day before his fortieth birthday, Joe Clark was sworn in as Canada's sixteenth prime minister. I was forty-eight years old when I took the oath of office as Canada's thirty-second Minister of Finance. I was nearing the mid-point of my political life. It had been thirteen years since I joined Joey Smallwood's cabinet in Newfoundland; it would be fourteen years before I would voluntarily return to private life.

Those fourteen years – in government with Clark (for a mere 259 days), back in Opposition, running for the Tory leadership, and returning to government with Brian Mulroney – were hard years and exciting years, years of accomplishment, and years of frustration.

The frustrations began in the early weeks of the Clark administration as our party, out of power since Lester Pearson had defeated John Diefenbaker sixteen years earlier, tried to come to terms with the election results. We had won a plurality of the seats in the House of Commons, 136 of 282 – leaving us 6 seats short of a majority. But the Liberals, rolling up huge majorities across Quebec, had won a plurality of the national popular vote, with 39.8 per cent to our 35.6 per cent. The public had wanted to get rid of Pierre Trudeau and the Liberals, but they were not ready to leap into bed with Joe Clark and the Tories.

Out of inexperience and hubris, Clark made two foolish and reckless mistakes that ultimately sealed our government's doom. He decided to govern as though we had a majority, a decision that was as arrogant as it was presumptuous. However, it was a decision I agreed with at the time. And Clark decided that we had to keep all our election promises, however ill-advised or idiotic they were – a decision with which I did not agree. Although these two fundamental mistakes were the responsibility of Clark, as prime minister, and of his inner circle of political advisers, I cannot avoid some of the blame. I shared the cabinet's conviction that, if the Opposition parties were so foolhardy as to bring down our new administration in Parliament, the Canadian people would punish them at the polls.

∾

As Finance minister, I was a member of Clark's inner cabinet, which included David MacDonald, Secretary of State, from Prince Edward Island; Sinclair Stevens, President of the Treasury Board; Walter Baker, House leader and Privy Council president; Bill Jarvis, Minister of State for Federal–Provincial Relations; Flora MacDonald, Secretary of State for External Affairs; Robert de Cotret (who was appointed to the Senate when he lost his seat in the election), Minister of Industry, Trade and Commerce; Ray Hnatyshyn, Minister of Energy (and later Governor General), from Saskatchewan; John Fraser, Postmaster General and Environment minister, from British Columbia; and Roch LaSalle, Minister of Supply and Services, and Senator Jacques Flynn, Minister of Justice, both from Quebec.

Only two Conservative MPs had been elected in Quebec. Only two members of the inner cabinet, Jacques Flynn and I, had ever served in a cabinet. With the appointment of Jim McGrath as Minister of Fisheries and Oceans, Newfoundland, which had elected only two Tories, had both of them in the new cabinet. McGrath and I quickly became known as Mr. Fish and Mr. Chips – he had the fish and I had the chips, or money.

My deputy minister in Finance, William Hood, had been appointed to that position a few months before I became minister. He was orderly, able, analytical, and competent, and I was well satisfied to have him. Many members of our caucus, however, felt that the government had allowed itself to be taken over by the civil service and was not making sufficient changes at the top. In our system, the appointment of deputy ministers is the prerogative of the prime minister, who may or may not bother to ask for the advice of the ministers concerned. Clark decided to replace Hood, appointing in his place Grant Reuber, whose résumé included a doctorate in economics from Harvard, chairmanship of the economics department at the University of Western Ontario, and of the Ontario Economic Council, and the position of chief economist of the Bank of Montreal. Reuber was a brilliant choice, fitting in well from the beginning.

Three days after I was sworn in, I was interviewed by Roy MacGregor of *Maclean's*, and I told him that I had already been Minister of Finance once and barely survived, and didn't expect to survive long this time. I told him that I had hoped for the Energy portfolio, but that, when Clark offered Finance, I accepted. "I didn't campaign for it. I didn't ask for it. I didn't want it, but I'm very proud to have been offered the job. Since I've no further political ambitions, I'm ready for the scrap heap – whenever it comes." He thought I was exaggerating, and so did I!

Columnist Allan Fotheringham was content to recycle certain stereotypes about me, writing that I was a consummate actor who dressed as if the Salvation Army was my tailor. "He goes around dressed like an unmade bed and talking like an out-of-work butcher. All the time his mind is doing nip-ups, curve balls, fandangos and madrigals. He is about as slow as Bernard Baruch." Fotheringham suggested that Clark had given me the navigator's chair on the *Titanic*.

∾

As Finance minister, I wanted to prepare a Budget that would be sensible and would lead the country towards economic recovery and fiscal health without unduly damaging the party's popularity. I found I had to manoeuvre my way around the inconsistent, ill-conceived promises with which we had littered the campaign trail. The bulk of them totally unnecessary to win the election, the Tories' 1979 election promises were a truly breathtaking array:

- Mortgage interest payments and property taxes would be made deductible from income tax.
- Income taxes would be cut by up to three hundred dollars a year for low- and middle-income people.
- A tax credit of up to five thousand dollars a year would be granted to small-business investors.
- Sixty thousand civil service jobs would be eliminated through attrition.
- Canada would be made self-sufficient in energy by 1990.
- We would expand the grain-handling capacity of the country by 50 per cent by 1985.
- We would move the Canadian embassy in Israel from Tel Aviv to Jerusalem.
- There would be a free vote in Parliament on capital punishment.
- We would introduce a Freedom of Information Act.
- We would abolish compulsory retirement at age sixty-five in areas of federal jurisdiction.
- Petro-Canada and Loto-Canada would be dismantled.
- Housewives would be permitted to contribute to the Canada Pension Plan.

- There would be a referendum in the Yukon to determine whether the territory would become a province.
- We would put a "fresh face on federalism" by giving coastal provinces jurisdiction over offshore resources.
- Provinces would be given increased jurisdiction in communications, fisheries, and culture.
- The armed forces would be expanded and re-equipped.
- Unemployment insurance would be cut back.
- We would reduce the federal advertising budget by $50 million and cut spending on outside consultants by $250 million a year.
- The capital-gains tax would be eliminated on the sale of publicly traded shares in Canadian-owned companies.
- We would give tax credits of up to $125 million a year to corporations for research and development.

Whew!

The press, of course, made a great fuss about us keeping our promises. And Joe and the people around him developed a fetish about them. It was insane. We wanted to reduce the deficit, yet we were going to lower taxes and introduce a mortgage-interest deduction. It was totally inconsistent. The mortgage deduction would have wrecked the Treasury. Apart from the cost to the federal government, we would have lost an additional one billion dollars because we would have had to reimburse the provinces for their losses as a result of the deduction. Ottawa collects the income tax for the provinces, so, if we allowed mortgage interest as a deduction from income, it would have applied to the provincial share of the income tax as well to the federal share.

Just after we took office, I went to the cabinet with a recommendation that we drop this scheme, but I couldn't get anywhere. I then suggested that we make it a tax credit, not a deduction from taxable income, because a tax credit would need to come only from the federal share of income-tax revenue. It didn't have to affect the provinces. By not having to reimburse the provinces, we would lessen the fiscal damage by $1 billion.

Clark agreed to a tax credit of up to $1,250 for mortgage interest and $250 for property taxes, with a maximum credit of $375 in the first year. The credit would cost the Government of Canada as much as the deductibility scheme, but, by removing the impact on provincial revenues, we would forgo "only" about $1.5 billion in tax revenue, instead of losing $2.5 billion.

At the end of September, I unveiled the new mortgage interest program to give Canadian homeowners tax credits of up to $375 in 1979, rising in annual increments to $1,500 by 1982. The cost to the federal Treasury would be $575 million for the 1979–80 fiscal year, and $2.3 billion when fully phased in. The legislation was opposed by the Opposition and had not passed when the government was defeated in December. So the scheme never went into effect. This was the one salutary aspect of our election defeat in February 1980.

My chief concern at the time was inflation, and I made it clear, in cabinet and in press interviews, that I was worried about the effect of the stimulative tax cuts we had promised. I had no alternative but to try to straddle, to obfuscate, and to manoeuvre my way as well as I could through this minefield of inconsistent, irrational promises.

In a speech in Guelph, Ontario, during the election, Joe Clark had said: "We also intend as a national government to move this nation towards lower interest rates." The problem was, rates were going in the opposite direction. Not long after we took office, the Bank of Canada, for which I, as Finance minister, was responsible, decided to raise the bank rate – the rate it charges to lend money to the chartered banks – to a record 11.75 per cent, a signal to the banks to raise their rates for business and consumer loans. The bank rate had gone from 7.5 per cent at the start of 1978 to 11.25 per cent by January 1979 as the Bank of Canada tried to combat inflationary pressure, to attract foreign capital, and to sustain the level of the Canadian dollar in the exchange markets.

In Opposition, the Conservatives, led by Jim Gillies, a Toronto MP, had been vocal critics of the increases. Now, as the bank rate reached 11.75 per cent, Gillies was installed in Clark's office as the prime minister's chief economic adviser. The rate kept going up, reaching 14 per cent by late October 1979. With each increase, chartered banks and other lending institutions raised their interest rates until they hit a staggering 18 per cent.

My discussions with officials in the Finance department and with Gerald Bouey, the Governor of the Bank of Canada, convinced me that there was no realistic alternative to interest-rate increases. The Canadian economy needed strict fiscal and monetary discipline if we were to bring down inflation (then running at around 9 per cent), to reverse an ever-worsening current-account deficit and to restore investor confidence in Canada. Like every other politician, I disliked high interest rates, but as a Finance minister I knew they were a necessary evil. They were the result of conditions that had been allowed to develop over the previous ten years of Liberal maladministration. I had no intention of intervening to forbid Bouey to take the actions he believed were necessary for the economic health and future of Canada. If I or the government did intervene, Bouey, if he had any backbone, would resign. The result would be financial chaos and grave damage to Canada in world money markets.

When they are in Opposition, politicians always attack governments, even when governments have no option but to take certain actions in the national interest. Later, when the Opposition party comes to power, it finds it must carry out the very actions it denounced. During our 259 days in power, the Liberals attacked each bank-rate increase as though it was an act of deliberate cruelty. They knew we were doing exactly the same thing that they'd been forced to do. After the Liberals were re-elected in 1980, interest rates went above 21 per cent. And, of course, we denounced them.

As Minister of Finance, I couldn't blame Conservative MPs for their hatred of interest-rate increases; I knew how much flak they were taking from their constituents. Alvin Hamilton, the Tories' elder statesman on the Prairies, led a caucus revolt against escalating interest rates, condemning my policies in the media and attacking me in caucus. I felt increasing pressure from the Prime Minister's Office to do something. I asked Clark to send Jim Gillies to join me at one of my weekly Friday meetings with Bouey, and I encouraged Gillies to put every conceivable argument to Bouey which might indicate that the bank-rate policy of the Bank of Canada was wrong and should be reversed. Gillies was unable to present a single compelling argument. Thereafter, I heard no more from the PMO about bank-rate increases.

∾

Apart from the economic promises that I had to circumnavigate, the two election pledges that caused us the most damage were Clark's bizarre plan to move the Canadian embassy in Israel from Tel Aviv to Jerusalem – a transparently cynical attempt to woo the Jewish vote in Toronto – and the unpopular proposal to privatize Petro-Canada, the Crown-owned oil company. The Jerusalem issue disappeared after former Tory leader Bob Stanfield reported to Clark on the political realities of the Middle East. The Petro-Canada issue continued to bedevil us, both in Parliament, where the Opposition parties attacked us fiercely, and in the country, where the public never warmed to our privatization plan. They felt that having a Crown corporation in the oil and gas business was essential in a time of recurring energy crises. Although I, Energy minister Hnatyshyn, and most of the rest of the inner cabinet wanted to leave Petro-Canada alone, Clark stubbornly insisted that we keep his election promise.

He was afraid that a change of policy would be seen as further evidence of weak leadership. I believed that it never hurt politicians to admit they were wrong occasionally, as long as they explained clearly why they had to change their policy. The privatization of Petro-Canada was initiated some years later by the Mulroney Conservative government. It was eventually completed by the Liberals. By then, it had general public support, proving that in politics, like love, timing is everything!

∾

Near the end of August, the inner cabinet met for four days at Jasper, Alberta. We talked at great length about the fight between Ontario and Alberta over domestic oil and gas prices. The domestic Canadian price for crude oil that summer was $13.75 per barrel, or $11.00 below world levels, and for many reasons this gap had to be narrowed. Ontario, led by the Conservative government of William Davis, wanted any increased revenues from higher prices to be set aside to cushion consumers and to finance new energy projects in Canada. Alberta, led by another Tory premier, Peter Lougheed, wanted the full world price. He opposed any consumer protection, arguing that Alberta had already subsidized lower Canadian oil and gas prices to the tune of many billions of dollars, and now the increased revenues should flow directly to the producing provinces.

The pricing of oil and gas was one of the most difficult issues the Clark government faced. With Conservative governments in a majority of the provinces, we thought a speedy agreement could be reached on a new energy policy. But as negotiations with Alberta dragged on, our political position was undermined by the public perception in Ontario that we were caving in to Alberta. Premier Davis waged a deliberate campaign to discredit our federal energy policy in order to protect the popularity of his own provincial party in Ontario. Rather than prepare his people for the higher oil and natural gas prices that had to come, Davis told Ontarians that any increase in oil prices would be disastrous.

So we struggled with Lougheed for months while being systematically undermined by Davis. Meanwhile, the Canadian public simply refused to believe there was an energy crisis or any need for prices to rise. They couldn't accept that the Canadian price for oil was only one-half the world price and, because Canada wasn't self-sufficient in oil, couldn't continue at that level. And why should they accept it, when the premier of the largest province, a respected Conservative, was telling them there was no need to pay more? Unless the two Tory premiers made a special effort to be reasonable, the outcome of the dispute was bound to be political humiliation for the first Tory prime minister since Diefenbaker.

Clark, Hnatyshyn, Gillies, and I met with Lougheed and several Alberta ministers in Montreal on Thanksgiving Day. The meeting was a disaster. There was no sense that we were all members of the same political party seeking a solution to a common problem. There were no pleasantries and no collegiality. Lougheed laid down the Alberta position and told us to take it or leave it. We left it.

Lougheed was so obdurate and imperious that I used to refer to him as "Ayatollah" or "Emperor Bokassa II." He was far more formidable than Bill Davis in appearance, intellect, and pugnacity. He looked good on television, sounded as though he knew what he was talking about, and gave the impression that he could stand up to any other premier or prime minister. He didn't give an inch. Hnatyshyn was a nice fellow, but appeared ineffectual against both those hard-nosed and aggressive regional potentates.

The lesson to be learned from the energy-price negotiations in 1979 was clear. In federal–provincial relations, premiers will always pursue their own political self-interest, no matter how damaging it may be to the national interest or to the party in power in Ottawa – even if it's their own party. In the final analysis, the only rules that apply in federal–provincial relations are the rules of the jungle.

We also fought in the inner cabinet over ways to reduce federal spending. Sinc Stevens, the President of the Treasury Board, wanted government-spending increases held to an average of 5 per cent – four points below the inflation rate of 9 per cent – and he proposed major cuts in politically sensitive programs. I thought that would be Draconian, and argued for a 9 per cent increase – in other words, no real growth. The inner cabinet opted for 9 per cent, but also confirmed that a reduction in the deficit would be the prime object of our economic policy. I had no option but to raise taxes.

∾

A cabinet minister's life is very different from the life of an Opposition MP, as I soon discovered. Cabinet ministers have many opportunities to attend meetings abroad, where they enjoy all the pomp and hospitality that host countries lay on for visiting dignitaries. In our first few weeks in office, I attended the annual meeting of the Organization for Economic Cooperation and Development, in Paris, and the Group of Seven summit meeting of presidents and prime ministers, in Tokyo. Later, I led the Canadian delegation to the annual meeting of the International Monetary Fund and the World Bank. For the first time in the history of the IMF, they met in a Communist country, Yugoslavia.

On the way to the IMF meeting, I visited Washington to meet financial officials there. I was then to take the Concorde for a quick flight to London, expecting to arrive around nine o'clock that evening and be in good shape to attend meetings in London the following morning and deliver a major financial address. The flight left Washington on time, but, before we were halfway across the Atlantic, some of the dials in the cockpit acted up and the captain decided to turn back to New York. After a four-hour wait, we resumed our flight, landing in London at 8:00 A.M., meaning I had to proceed with the day's business with no rest at all. I flew to Dublin next day to meet the Minister of Finance and Deputy Prime Minister of Ireland. Afterward, my hosts drove me to the airport in a large black limousine, and I was taken aback to see people waving, genuflecting, and making the sign of the cross. Thinking this a pleasant bit of overreaction to a visiting Finance minister, I asked the driver what was going on. "Well, sir, sure and they thinks you're the Pope," he replied. Pope John Paul was to visit Dublin for the first time the next day, and the people thought the jet-lagged Protestant in the back seat of this gleaming limousine must be His Holiness! The moment was particularly poignant for me because, back in the 1920s, my grandfather, Sir John Crosbie, who was a staunch Mason and Orangeman, had been involved in a heated argument with a local Roman Catholic editor, Sir P.T. McGrath. The gist of his blunt advice to McGrath was conveyed in a startling headline in the *St. John's Evening Herald*: "Sir John Crosbie Says Pope Can Kiss His A ———.."

Jane and I attended a meeting of Commonwealth Finance ministers in Malta, where an uncle of mine by marriage had commanded the Royal Navy hospital during years of intensive bombings in the Second World War. On our return through London, we visited Paul Martin, Sr., Canada's high commissioner to Britain and father of the Minister of Finance in Jean Chrétien's Liberal government. Our pleasure at seeing Martin and our enjoyment of the superb restaurant he took us to on the Thames River were strained, however, by the delicate condition of our innards. Jane and I had picked up the trots in our travels and, while our distinguished host held forth with many sage observations, his guests spent the meal rushing to the washroom.

∾

When Parliament convened in the fall of 1979, I tried to continue to use humour as a weapon against my opponents. When I was attacked for appearing to enjoy myself, I replied, "One must be very lugubrious if one is to be Minister of Finance in this House. From now on 'lugubriousness' is the order of the day." When Bob Rae, the New Democratic Party Finance critic (who later became premier of Ontario) recited some of the NDP's oft-repeated complaints about unemployment being too high and about the need for tax cuts and subsidies, I observed, "There's no hope for the NDP. It's a wonder they have any hands left. They're always wringing their hands in distress." One day, Svend Robinson, an NDP member from Vancouver, asked me what I meant by a "small developer." "How big is small?" he asked. I replied, "How big is small? How small is big? How big is little? How little is big? The honourable member's guess is as good as mine. . . . I know down in Newfoundland we have a lot of small developers. We do not have too many big ones. But we are not as big as British Columbia. We are little. Where British Columbia is big, we are little, where it is great, we are small. What is small? What is great? The small is greater than the big, in my opinion, in the province of Newfoundland." For once, Robinson was at a loss for words.

One weekend, Pierre Trudeau turned up at a discothèque in New York with a girl named Linda when he was supposed to be attending a Liberal policy seminar in Vancouver. He'd told the seminar organizers he had a cold and couldn't go. So I christened the Liberals "Disco Daddy and the Has-Beens." I suggested to the Canadian Tax Foundation, "You won't believe this, but there's a move afoot to move our interest rates to Jerusalem." And I declared that, as a Newfie, I was proud to be Canada's first "ethnic" Finance minister.

∽

The main outlines of my first (and last) Budget, in particular energy policy and oil pricing, were discussed by the inner cabinet, as was the need for increased revenue if the deficit was to be reduced from the previous year. An excise tax was the only way to obtain revenue, to encourage conservation in the use of oil products, and to move Canada away from dependence on imported oil and towards energy self-sufficiency. An excise tax of thirty cents a gallon on all transportation fuels was discussed, but there was vociferous opposition, led by Sinclair Stevens. No one in the inner cabinet seriously suggested that the Opposition might precipitate an election by defeating the Budget, because Trudeau had announced his intention to resign as Liberal leader and there was to be a convention in 1980 to elect his successor.

To our later regret, we paid little attention to the November

Gallup poll, which was published on December 3, just eight days before Budget day. It showed a steep drop in Conservative popularity. Our support had held at 36 per cent during the summer and early fall, but the November poll put us at 28 per cent, nineteen points behind the Liberals. We were in deep trouble.

We'd become increasingly unpopular because of our perceived lack of leadership, our difficulties in settling the Petro-Canada policy, our flip-flop on moving the embassy in Israel, our seeming failure to keep election promises, our inability to negotiate an agreement on petroleum policy and pricing with Alberta and Ontario, and the unrelenting attacks on us by the Conservative premiers of those two provinces.

I didn't know it at the time, but the Conservative party had done no polling of its own since August. The responsibility for this omission lay with the leader and his political advisers – Lowell Murray, now a senator, and Bill Neville, then chief of staff in the PMO. Worse, we'd made no effort to snuggle up to the Créditistes, believing we could wipe them out in the next election and elect some Tories in Quebec. Looking back, if I'd been the leader of a minority government, I would have put a higher premium on survival. I would have counted carefully, cuddled up to the Créditistes and kept them very happy, but Joe mistakenly assumed that the Liberals wouldn't risk another election. He insisted that we act as though we had a majority. It was a fatal error. In honesty, however, I never suggested at the time that I thought Joe's strategy was a mistake. I was part of it.

I never thought about whether we should postpone the Budget vote scheduled for December 13. These kinds of things were determined by the prime minister. That's why he was the leader. That's why he had an extensive staff of political geniuses to advise him. Obviously, there was nothing to stop me from going to Joe and saying, "You can't do this" or "You mustn't do that." But I didn't object. I thought the same way Joe did.

⌦

There's a hoary parliamentary tradition that the Minister of Finance must buy and wear a new pair of shoes when he presents his Budget Speech. On Budget day, Tuesday, December 11, 1979, I appeared in the Commons in a new pair of grey and black sealskin mukluks made by an aboriginal woman in Happy Valley–Goose Bay, Labrador. I thought it would add a bit of interest to the occasion if I wore something other than the conventional black wing-tips. Besides, the mukluks demonstrated support for the seal hunt and for Newfoundland.

I brought down the Budget I thought was right for the time. "Part of the reason for our disappointing economic performance during the past decade has been the failure of governments, particularly the federal government, to face up to economic reality and to make the most of the country's opportunities," I said in my Budget Speech. ". . . This I and my colleagues are determined to do, even if it means risking some unpopularity, hopefully short-term. We are committed to the proposition that in the longer run good economics is good sense and thus good politics."[*]

By raising new revenues and holding government spending to a no-real-growth increase of 9 per cent, we would reduce the federal deficit from $11.2 billion in 1979–80 to $9 billion dollars by 1983–84. The national-account deficit was to be reduced from $9.4 billion in 1979–80 to $4.4 billion in 1983–84, in part through higher energy prices designed to induce conservation and to cut oil imports in half.

The highlights of the Budget included:

- an immediate increase in the excise tax on gasoline of four cents per litre, or eighteen cents per gallon, to raise $535 million in 1979–80 and $2.45 billion by 1983–84;
- a rise in energy prices of $4 per barrel in 1980, and $4.50 per barrel each year thereafter until 1983, with a review

---

[*] For an excellent account of the problems of controlling spending and of the workings of the Department of Finance, see Donald J. Savoie's *The Politics of Public Spending in Canada* (Toronto: University of Toronto Press, 1990).

mechanism to keep Canadian prices at 85 per cent of the
world price;

• a new federal tax to take back one-half of the revenues
generated by an oil-price increase above $2 per barrel (but no
agreement had been reached with Alberta on the exact
nature of the tax or how the money would be spent);

• creation of a federal–provincial energy bank to which
Ottawa would contribute part of the revenues from this tax,
the proceeds to be invested in energy-related projects across
Canada;

• an energy tax credit of up to $80 per adult and $30 per
child, weighted so that those families with incomes below
$21,380 in 1980 would receive the full credit and those with
incomes above $21,380 would receive less;

• increases in taxes on cigarettes, beer, and wine;

• a 5 per cent surtax on federal income tax paid by corporations;

• a new common-stock investment plan allowing taxpayers to
defer capital-gains taxes on shares of Canadian corporations.

The excise tax on transportation fuels was increased from
seven cents per gallon, which the Liberals had imposed several
years earlier, to twenty-five cents per gallon to raise an additional
$2.1 billion in a full year.

The Budget could be made to appear to be tough medicine,
although any objective analysis showed it to be more progressive
than regressive in its effect on individuals. It also had measures
that were politically attractive to our back-benchers. For
example, I allowed as deductible the salary of a wife working
in her husband's small business. This reform survived and is in
effect today. I helped farmers to avoid some capital-gains tax on
the sale of their farm by allowing them to invest up to $100,000
of the proceeds in a Registered Retirement Savings Plan. There
were other tax changes to help small business.

If the Liberals and the NDP together voted against the Budget
– and if they brought out all their MPs – the government would

need the votes of the five Créditistes to survive. Fabien Roy, the Créditiste leader, told reporters that he didn't like the Budget, especially not the excise tax. He didn't say how the Créditistes would vote on the non-confidence motion that had been moved by Bob Rae of the NDP.

The reaction of the business and financial community to my Budget was very positive. The reaction of the media was positive as well. The Toronto *Globe and Mail*'s Report on Business made me its Man of the Year. But the general public was far more negative because of the eighteen-cent-a-gallon increase in excise tax on transportation fuels.

Many months later, *Canadian Taxation*, a journal of tax policy. published a perceptive article by Andrew Doman, an economic analyst based in Ottawa. In it, Doman concluded that my Budget was more progressive than any Budget introduced by Liberal governments over the previous ten years. His analysis suggested that my Budget would have produced an important shift of the tax burden from the poor and lower-middle-income earners to middle- and upper-income earners. Alas, Doman's analysis was too late to help the author of the Budget. Politics is not about reality but about perception.

∾

On Wednesday, December 12, the day after I presented my Budget, it became apparent that the government was likely to be defeated. The Liberals and New Democrats were preparing to bring out all their members. The Créditistes said they would abstain from the vote. The Conservatives were missing several MPs, who were either sick, legitimately away from Ottawa, or sulking. We could have postponed the Budget vote to give time for all our members to return to Ottawa and for a few Liberals to develop cold feet. This would also have given us an opportunity to negotiate with the Créditistes. But Clark and his political advisers were determined to show that his government was firm and decisive. Like Clark and his advisers, I believed we would win if an election was forced, and I made no move to have the vote delayed. No serious attempt was made to work out a deal with the Créditistes. Roy had indicated that his party would vote with the Conservatives only if the government agreed to commit all the revenue from the excise-tax increase to the government of Quebec or to energy projects in Quebec. This we could not do.

On Thursday, December 13, Jane and I went to dinner at the home of friends who once lived in Newfoundland. I told them I had to be back in the Commons by 9:30 for a vote, and they were astounded to learn that the government would likely be defeated. Minutes before the vote, Clark spoke to our caucus in the Government lobby, saying we were ready for an election and would win a majority government. With one exception, all NDP and Liberal MPs – 139 of them – were present and voted for Rae's non-confidence motion. No Créditistes voted, and all 133 Conservatives present voted against. The government fell, and Clark announced he would see the Governor General in the morning. Jane summed our plight up perfectly: "The operation was a success, but the doctor died."

∽

I approached the election campaign with gusto, confident that the Canadian people would vindicate us. I thought we'd hand the Liberals the defeat of the century. This view was widely held among Conservatives, and it was not until the results of polling, both private and public, started to come in during January that I realized we were likely to be defeated. I believe the result of the February 18, 1980, election convinced all practising politicians that the road to success does not lie in debating the real issues facing the country or the difficult measures a new government might have to introduce. The public wants to be gulled, lulled, and fooled by its politicians. It doesn't want to be asked to approve of tough measures before a government introduces them. The public prefers to look down on politicians as untrustworthy, sneaky, devious, and selfish, and doesn't accept attempts to be honest during election campaigns.

∽

At the time I brought down the Budget and in the days follow-ing, I was suffering from a kidney stone. I had never had one before and didn't realize what lay in store for me when this stone began to move through the kidney and out through the urinary tract. I returned to St. John's for Christmas with Jane and our family, and immediately afterward we went to Puerto Rico for six days' holidays before the election campaign began in earnest. When I returned to St. John's, the stone became active. I had either to wait for the stone to discharge itself or opt for surgery. As anyone who has had a kidney stone knows, the pain is inde-scribable and only endurable with the help of strong painkillers. I had to go on the national campaign trail, so I decided on surgery. To my great relief, thirty minutes before the operation, the stone passed.

∽

The campaign managers decided that I should campaign across the country as the author of the defeated Budget that had pre-cipitated the election. I was more than willing. For five weeks, I lived a frenzied existence, stumping the country, giving fifty-nine speeches at public meetings and campaign events. At the same time, Joe Clark carried on a magnificent and courageous campaign in every part of the country.

In trying to explain why Canada had to have higher prices for oil products and why we needed increased excise taxes to encourage energy conservation, I told a story of two St. John's grocers in the 1930s who both sold potatoes. When a customer went into Leo Healey's to ask the price of potatoes, he was told $4 a gallon. He protested this high price and told Healey that, at W.J. Murphy's, potatoes were only $3.50 a gallon. Well, Healey said, "Why don't you go down to Murphy's and get your potatoes there?" The customer replied that Murphy was out of potatoes. "Well," said Healey, "when I'm all out of potatoes I sell them at $3 a gallon." The point of my story was that, once we were out of oil in Canada, it wouldn't matter what price we sold it for, there would be no oil.

I think we might have won if it hadn't been for the beating we took from Lougheed and Davis. I secretly got a kick out of observing from the sidelines as Trudeau savaged the Alberta government over the next four years. They deserved it. They deserved the National Energy Program that he shoved down their throats. They brought it on themselves because they wouldn't give Clark any help, not one jot or tittle of assistance. I never saw such selfish characters. Between Lougheed and Davis, our chance for re-election was wrecked.

The basic strategy of the Liberal campaign was described six months after the election by their Toronto pollster, Martin Goldfarb, to an American audience in New York. He said the Liberals adopted a strategy of "low-bridging" Trudeau by keeping him out of sight during the election. Their goal was to make sure that Clark was the issue and to keep the electorate focused on fear and doubt. In Goldfarb's view, "You win elections on dreams and fears. This one was a fear election. We had to create over time what the people had already sensed, that Mr. Clark was inept."

Goldfarb's view was that Clark's broken promises were non-issues and would not affect voting behaviour. The fundamental issue, he said, was that people perceived Clark to be incompetent. They were embarrassed by his performance and his mannerisms. The Liberal strategy was to hammer away at his alleged inability to lead and to think. Goldfarb said Bill Davis's aggressive criticism of the Budget had legitimized the Liberal attack on it. "Davis created the fear. The task of the Liberals was to maintain it and feed it."

On February 18, the Canadian public validated this cynical Liberal strategy. The Liberals elected a majority government with 146 MPs, to our 103, the NDP's 32, and 1 independent. The Créditistes were wiped out.

∾

Although I had a solid victory in St. John's West, I was angry, very angry, on election night as I heard Trudeau welcome Canadians to the 1980s. The arrogance of him! The Liberals assumed that the 1980s were going to be another Liberal decade. I'd had quite a bit to drink and I was raging away in the CBC studio in St. John's. I wanted to blame the Canadian people. They were so stupid, they'd let the Liberals steal the government from us! I was starting to say this kind of stuff on the air, but luckily my uncle Bill Crosbie raced over to the studio and got me out of there. I don't know what kind of a disaster I would have gotten myself into if he hadn't dragged me out. If I'd gone on record with it all, I wouldn't have been able to run for the Tory leadership a few years later – that's for sure.

11

BACK IN THE TRENCHES

THE 1980s WAS probably the most exciting, dramatic, and unpredictable decade in Canadian political history. It was a roller-coaster. The decade opened with the humil-iation of Joe Clark, his minority government, and the entire Progressive Conservative party. It ended with the Tories ascendant – in power with our second consecutive major-ity government – while the Liberals, in won-drous disarray, tore themselves apart over their leadership. In the intervening years, Canadians witnessed a referendum in Quebec on sovereignty-association; patriation of the Con-stitution; the introduction of a National Energy Program that amounted to confiscation of provincial resources; the ballooning of inflation, interest rates, and the deficit to historic highs; the ousting of Clark from the Conservative leadership and the ascen-sion of Brian Mulroney; the retirement of Pierre Trudeau and the return of John Turner; the election of a Tory government with the largest majority in Canadian history; the negotiation of a

Courtesy Terry Mosher (Aislin), Montreal Gazette

185

historic free-trade agreement with the United States; and the political demise of Turner, once the brightest young star in the Canadian political firmament.

Although Parliament is not always at the heart of the political action in this country, it was throughout the 1980s. It was the engine of Tory revenge. We Conservatives – so devastated, so bitter, so angry when the decade began – used every weapon at our disposal in the House of Commons to tear down the revivified Trudeau Liberal government. Day by day, week by week, we ripped them apart. It was exhilarating! It was the most spectacular piece of political demolition Canada had ever seen, and it took us only four years to do it.

It was open warfare from that wretched moment on election night 1980, when Trudeau had the effrontery to go on national television and welcome Canadians to the 1980s. Having been a Liberal, I'm not partial to them. They believe only in power. They have no principles whatever, and the biggest mistake Tories ever make is to trust Liberals. We should never let our guard down. We must stomp on the Grits at every opportunity. They actually think they're the natural governors of Canada. If they don't control the Commons, they'll use the undemocratic, appointed Senate to thwart the will of the elected government and the Commons. They have no scruples and no honour. There's nothing a Liberal won't do to get his or her way.

I know these people only too well. I spent several agonizing years trying to reform and to democratize the Liberal Party of Newfoundland. This was in the years when the Great Democrat Himself, Pierre Elliott Trudeau, was newly ensconced on his Ottawa throne. But neither he nor any of his courtesans gave a damn about democracy or our struggle to unseat the dictator Smallwood. Not once did I receive the slightest breath of support, encouragement, or understanding from Trudeau; the national Liberal party; Don Jamieson, who was Newfoundland's representative in the Trudeau cabinet; or any person acting on their behalf. Not a word, not a letter, not a phone call. Trudeau

Right: Election night, October 28, 1971, in front of our St. John's home. *Below*: Winning the Tory nomination for St. John's West in June 1971 at Canon Stirling Auditorium, on stage with backers, from left to right: Bill Eaton, Jane, Dodie Moores, Frank Moores, me, Jim McGrath.

With Flora MacDonald and Joe Clark at the Tokyo Summit in June 1979.

PC caucus meeting, with David Crombie and John Diefenbaker.

Top: With staff at Finance, from left to right: Ross Reid, Robert Parker, Claudy Maillie Kyles (later married to the journalist Charles Lynch), Marie Dowden, and Peter Burn. *Right*: With Ross Reid, July 1979, on our way to my first press conference as Minister of Finance in the Clark government. Reid served at the time as my executive assistant.

Peter Bregg

United Press Canada

Above: The famous
Budget mukluks,
December 1979.
Left: Budget night,
outside the House
of Commons, with
Joe Clark.

In opposition, in the House of Commons, 1984.

Caucus meeting, 1984. Among those present are David Crombie, Howard Crosby, Lloyd Crouse, and Perrin Beatty.

The Tory leadership convention, June 1984: John Laschinger, Bob Wenman, and me in discussion at the Ottawa Civic Centre.

The Crosbie blimp threatens to fly out of control.

Listening as the results are announced, from left to right: Senator Bill Doody,
Brian Peckford, me, Jane, daughter Beth.

preached participatory democracy. Participatory *hypocrisy* is what it was.

The only help I and my supporters received from federal Liberals came from three independent-thinking senators, Eric Cook and Ches Carter from Newfoundland, and Dan Lang from Toronto. The rest didn't care a fig about corruption or one-man rule. If they'd cared enough to support Liberal reform, they could have saved Newfoundlanders from the worst excesses of the Smallwood era. I blame the Trudeau Liberals for failing to prevent the waste of at least $400 million of Newfoundlanders' money.

Knowing the Liberals as I did, I wasn't going to give them an inch, I wasn't going to give them the benefit of the doubt, ever, when Parliament resumed after the 1980 election. I feared they would be in power for two or three terms – eight or twelve years. But I also thought we had a fighting chance of turfing them out again in four years' time.

Improbable though it seemed, they were far more arrogant than they'd ever been before. Romeo LeBlanc, who went back in as Minister of Fisheries and Oceans, opened his first meeting with department officials with these words: "As I was saying when we were so rudely interrupted . . ." Their presumption was stupefying and, of course, they thought the Tories were complete dummies from whom they had nothing to fear. So they proceeded to make a whole series of disastrous mistakes in Finance and Energy and in the constitutional field, and these errors gave us ammunition.

∾

We called a final cabinet meeting to approve the mechanics of handing power back to the Liberals. It was a painful, emotional meeting. All of us in the cabinet room had had great expectations just nine months earlier, and all of our hopes had been dashed. In his final remarks to us, Joe broke down in tears. Jim McGrath saved the day by singing, "For He's a Jolly Good

Fellow." We all joined in to show Joe our affection and respect for him, and for the wonderful battle he had put up in the campaign.

But Joe was resilient and clever. Before long, he dropped Walter Baker, who'd been our House leader in government. Walter was popular, a pleasant fellow. Everybody liked him, but he was too nice. He was outmanoeuvred by Allan MacEachen of the Liberals and Stanley Knowles of the New Democratic Party. In his place, Clark appointed Erik Nielsen, the MP for Yukon, as House leader and his right-hand man. Erik was a formidable piece of work who'd been around a long time and was trusted by the caucus. He was exactly what we needed – resourceful; cool, calm, and collected; a pillar. He was also tough, unbending, disciplined, a hard worker, humourless, articulate, controlled, driven, unsentimental, and guided by an overwhelming fetish about the need to be "loyal" to the leader of the party, no matter what.

The Grits and the NDP hated Erik, and Erik hated them with a passion. Erik would split a Liberal from stem to gudgeon. He'd put the dirk right in, down at the base of the backbone, and he'd take it right up to the neck, without so much as a grimace. Some people were repelled by him, but I wasn't. He could be relied on to do any job he was assigned. The job Joe gave him was to make us into a fighting force and to mount an unremitting and ferocious Opposition. If Erik succeeded, Tory MPs would be fully engaged with the real enemy and be diverted from the internal struggle over leadership. So the appointment was a shrewd move on Joe's part.

Nielsen's appointment meant there would be no compromise and little civility until the next election. Normal parliamentary courtesies gave way to total war. Conservative MPs no longer "paired" with the Liberal ministers, so cabinet members had to stay close to Ottawa whenever there was a chance that a vote might be held.

Erik went into attack mode when a parliamentary delegation travelled to France on a Canadian Forces transport aircraft to attend meetings in Strasbourg, at NATO in Brussels, and at the headquarters of the Organization for Economic Cooperation and

Development in Paris. I and three other Conservative MPs were on the trip, along with two New Democrats, six Liberal MPs, and several senators. The group went from Strasbourg to Brussels to Paris, then back to Strasbourg, before returning home following a planned weekend off. Nielsen called us when we got back to Strasbourg, directing us to return to Ottawa without alerting the rest of the group. With any luck, the Liberals might be caught unawares and be defeated in a vote on Friday afternoon. The Tory Four slipped out of our hotel at 6:00 A.M. on Friday and caught a commercial flight to Paris, then to Montreal. We were met at Mirabel Airport and whisked to Ottawa, arriving with an hour to spare. By this time, of course, the Liberal MPs in Strasbourg had discovered we were missing, but there was no way they could get back in time for the vote. Although we didn't defeat the Liberals that day, we made it close, and we forced their whip to track down ministers and MPs who had fanned out across Canada and order them back to the capital.

∾

In the six-week period between the time the Liberals were sworn back in and the opening of Parliament, Jane and I visited China as guests of the People's Republic. It was Jane's first trip to China, but my second. I had been there as a member of the Moores cabinet in Newfoundland to attend a Canadian trade show in Beijing in 1972. With friends Al and Marjorie Mercer of St. John's, we spent three weeks visiting ancient sites, communes, manufacturing plants, and hospitals. The Chinese have their own ideas about protocol, so Jane and I were driven around in a limousine while Al and Marjorie followed behind in a small car.

Because the Chinese authorities made all the travel arrangements, no one in Canada knew where we would be. When we got to Chonqing, we stayed in a huge hotel built by the Soviets, and discovered that a Canadian, Rod Stewart, the author of a book on Norman Bethune, the Canadian doctor made famous in China by Mao, was living at the hotel with his wife and daughters while teaching for a year at a Chinese school. Jane and I attended a theatrical production that evening. Later, back at the hotel, I went to bed with a cold while Jane visited the Stewarts. At six o'clock the next morning, the telephone rang in our room. I stumbled out of bed to answer: "Hello." I was amazed to hear Barbara Frum, then host of CBC radio's *As It Happens*, say "Hello" to me. Barbara recognized my voice and said, "My God, it's John Crosbie." I replied, "Yes, Barbara, how are you?" At this point the telephone operator cut us off because she realized she had connected Barbara to the wrong room. She was calling Rod Stewart, but the hotel operator had put her through to our room by mistake. The CBC has often played the tape to illustrate how a billion-to-one coincidence can happen.

While in Wuhan, I sent a postcard to Allan MacEachen, the new Liberal Finance minister. My message was simple: "Wish you were here!" I signed it from Jane and me and the Gang of Four. He never acknowledged its receipt. He has no sense of humour, which is why I nicknamed him "the Celtic Sphinx."

∾

I spent a great deal of my time crossing swords and wits with the Celtic Sphinx. Clark asked me to be Finance critic in his shadow cabinet, and, just one week after the new Parliament opened, the Liberals made their first major error when MacEachen, while speaking in the Throne Speech debate, introduced a Budget. A "mini-budget," he called it. MacEachen's action was breathtakingly offensive. He was bringing down a Budget without a formal Budget Speech or the requisite six-day Budget debate – and without affording the Opposition critics their traditional right of reply or allowing them to present non-confidence motions.

This blatant denial of the rights of Parliament touched off a savage procedural battle and created a poisonous atmosphere that would hang over the Commons for the next four years. It brought our caucus to life and started me on the way back up in Ottawa. What's more, MacEachen's so-called mini-budget contained virtually every item that had been in my ill-fated December 1979 Budget, except for two: the eighteen-cent increase in the excise tax on a gallon of gasoline, and our prohibitively costly mortgage-deductibility plan. It included a major jump in energy prices through a "blended" price for oil products that would shift a $1-billion burden to consumers from the federal Treasury. Although Trudeau had promised in the election that "we will hold the line on government expenditure growth to under the rate of growth of GNP," MacEachen forecast a negative rate of growth in the gross national product, yet announced that spending would rise by 13.7 per cent. This was well in excess of my Budget's 9 per cent. He projected a $14.2-billion deficit, nearly $4 billion greater than mine. It would be the largest deficit in Canadian history to that time, and the Liberals would not permit Parliament to debate it! Is it any wonder that I accused MacEachen of being as "slippery as a cod tongue in a barrel of cod's liver"?

Among the new tax changes presented by MacEachen was a different method of collecting the tax on gasoline and diesel fuel. He changed it from a tax of so many cents per litre or gallon to a percentage tax (9 per cent) on the selling price of gasoline and diesel fuels. This meant the tax would go up automatically every time fuel prices went up, without the necessity of obtaining parliamentary approval for a tax increase.

Later on, MacEachen introduced what he called "the first Budget of this new decade." This Budget launched the National Energy Program, which resulted in a major confrontation between Alberta and Ottawa. When I replied to MacEachen for our party, my speech lasted two hours and fifteen minutes. Columnist Charles Lynch described it as one of the most stirring oratorical performances heard in the Commons since John Diefenbaker's heyday. He kidded my accent by quoting me as saying that MacEachen's "boojit" had "no goots and no goomption," that MacEachen had "bloofed" the Canadian people, and that the interest on the national debt had reached "a stupenduss figger." I called Energy minister Marc Lalonde a "plucked goose, flying along, cooked" and said MacEachen "has not got the courage of a castrated lemming."

MacEachen's next Budget was even worse. He decided to cut several billion dollars from federal transfers to the provinces. He proposed 150 separate tax changes. As the Department of Finance had not been given time to work out the technical details, most of the hundreds of interest groups affected found mistakes that would create injustices or hardships. With the economy moving into recession, investors needed encouragement, yet MacEachen cut incentives, outraging business across the country. The private sector was unrelenting in its attacks on the Budget as up to twenty thousand letters a day poured into Ottawa.

We kept the pressure on in the Commons until MacEachen was forced to back down and to keep backing down. Christina McCall and Stephen Clarkson described what happened in the second volume of *Trudeau and Our Times*: "Over the next two months in a slow-motion series of provisional exemptions, delays in implementation, clarifications, grandfathering of existing practices, and amendments to proposed measures – he [MacEachen] withdrew from his budget the bulk of the proposed 'loopholectomies,' until nothing remained either of that document's reformist thrust or of the Liberals' Restoration momentum."*

The *Ottawa Citizen*, which was normally Liberal, declared the Celtic Sphinx to be "perhaps the worst finance minister of all time." Trudeau must have agreed, because he replaced MacEachen with a much more formidable Finance minister, Marc Lalonde. Lalonde managed economic problems more capably, but he did the country serious damage, bringing down budgets with deficits in excess of thirty billion dollars, seriously exacerbating the debt problem that still bedevils Canada today.

We pursued the government on all fronts, exploiting every

---

* (Toronto: McClelland & Stewart, 1994), p. 240.

opening we could find. I went after Trudeau for his arrogance in awarding the contract to design the new Canadian embassy in Washington to his buddy Arthur Erickson, despite the fact that Erickson hadn't even made the short list of finalists in a competition staged by a government-appointed selection committee.

We put Justice minister Jean Chrétien's feet to the fire after Clark asked him whether the government was considering making a unilateral reference to the Supreme Court of Canada for a ruling as to whether Ottawa or Newfoundland owned the mineral resources of the Newfoundland continental shelf. With interest building in the Hibernia offshore oil field, the province had already referred a similar question to the Newfoundland Court of Appeal. Chrétien told Clark that "no decision has been made at this time." Asked again, he gave the same answer. We soon learned, however, that a decision to refer the matter to the Supreme Court had in fact been made by the Trudeau cabinet that very day, several hours *before* Chrétien denied it in the Commons. The following morning, Chrétien flew to St. John's to make the official announcement.

Although it was clear that Chrétien had misled the Commons, Trudeau tried to wriggle out of it by saying the previous day's cabinet decision had been "conditional" and it did not become effective until an order-in-council was enacted the next morning. Trudeau was a party to Chrétien's deception and obviously didn't care about ministers' obligation to be truthful in Parliament.

In Newfoundland, Premier Brian Peckford and the Tory MHAs reacted by wearing black armbands and declaring a day of mourning. They accused Ottawa of being arbitrary, highhanded, and insulting to the Newfoundland Court of Appeal, which was already considering the issue.

I rose in the Commons on a question of privilege to accuse Chrétien of misleading Parliament. I caused a great uproar when I said Chrétien was "an outright liar who deceives the members of this House." After a long procedural argument, in the course of which I refused to withdraw my unparliamentary language, I was "named" by the Speaker. On a vote of 116 to 99, I was expelled from the Commons for the day.

With the battering they were taking, the Liberals sank lower and lower in the opinion polls, and Clark set up a travelling task force to collect complaints in public hearings from coast to coast. We paralysed the Commons for two weeks by keeping the division bells ringing when we refused to vote on a huge legislative package, an omnibus bill, to write the Liberals' energy program into law. Unemployment figures set postwar records, the deficit continued to rise, inflation passed 12 per cent, and international confidence in the Canadian dollar collapsed, causing it to fall to 76.8 cents U.S.

The Liberals responded to these problems by inventing a new economic scheme, their "Six and Five" program. Increases in wages and benefits would be limited to 6 per cent in the first year, and 5 per cent in the second. Meanwhile, I travelled across the country, speaking to Conservatives and other community groups. I made hay from the fact that the Liberals had allowed fourteen increases in energy prices in the first fifteen months of the new Trudeau government, with ten of these increases being the result of raising the federal tax. I had wanted to raise the excise tax on gasoline by a modest eighteen cents a gallon in my 1979 Budget. Since the return of the Liberals, the price of gasoline in St. John's had risen by seventy-three cents a gallon! I suggested that Trudeau, MacEachen, Lalonde, and Industry minister Herb Gray should be known as "the Four Horsemen of the Economic Apocalypse," although they represented only one end of the horse – and "that is not the head."

My speeches and the articles I wrote were not all quips and wisecracks. I advanced thoughtful suggestions to remedy the country's economic ills. In Washington, I spoke to 350 members of the Tax Executives Institute, telling them that the degree of foreign ownership in the oil and gas industry in Canada had to be reduced from its 70 per cent level. I made it clear that Canadians did not intend to be drawers of water and hewers of

wood for the United States. And I suggested that Canada establish a royal commission to review our relationship with the
United States, including the possibility of free trade or a common
market with it and Mexico. Perhaps Trudeau was listening,
because, not long after, he appointed former Liberal cabinet
minister Donald S. Macdonald to chair the Royal Commission
on the Economic Union and Development Prospects for
Canada, which later, during the Mulroney administration,
recommended that Canada negotiate a free-trade agreement
with the United States.

Even though I usually had something serious and worthwhile
to say, I found it fun to comment, in response to a rumour that
Trudeau might become secretary general of the United Nations,
"This is wonderful news for Canada, but I wouldn't wish it on
the world." Or to comment on Lalonde's appointment as
Minister of Finance: "When the Canadian economy needed a
blood transfusion, it wasn't sensible for the Prime Minister to
put Count Dracula in charge." However, because I used humour
to lighten my serious comments, I could always count on some
lazy lout of a reporter calling me a buffoon.

∾

While our war with the Liberals was raging in Parliament and
across the country, the universe was unfolding on two other
fronts – the Constitution of Canada and the leadership of the
Progressive Conservative party.

The Parti Québécois referendum in the spring of 1980 asked
Quebecers whether they wanted to separate from Canada by
way of negotiating some form of sovereignty-association with
Ottawa. Just under 60 per cent voted No. The Trudeau government's response to the referendum was to propose the patriation
of the Constitution with an amending formula and the
entrenchment of a bill of rights limited to basic democratic
rights and minority-language protection. Chrétien, as Justice
minister, spent that summer negotiating with the provinces and

threatening to act unilaterally if there was no agreement. A meeting between the premiers and the prime minister was held in Ottawa, but the process broke down as a result of a leaked federal document prepared by Michael Kirby of Trudeau's office that indicated that the Government of Canada was dealing in poor faith. When the conference failed, the Trudeau government acted unilaterally. Eight of the provinces, all but Ontario and New Brunswick, totally opposed its actions.

Speaking at my alma mater, Dalhousie University Law School, I warned that, although our party might not be upset if Trudeau moved the Constitution from a "cubby hole in Westminster to a cubby hole in Ottawa," if he attempted to impose an amending formula or constitutional changes affecting the powers of the provinces we would fight them in Parliament, in the streets, and on the beaches. The Liberals not only did that in their constitutional resolution, but brought in a closure motion to choke off debate. The foul atmosphere in the Commons was illustrated by an exchange when I was questioning Trudeau about a meeting with Ed Broadbent, the leader of the NDP, who was supporting the Liberal constitutional package. "We know that the Prime Minister and the leader of the New Democratic Party are heart to heart, brain to brain, toe to toe and nose to nose and we know where the leader of the New Democratic Party's nose is," I told the Commons. In response, Trudeau suggested that I "check Hansard if his [Crosbie's] brains are not constantly in the area that he suggested somebody else's nose is."

In my speech on the closure motion, I said that I had not expected closure after only twenty-four hours of debate, with just 46 out of 279 sitting members having spoken. It took God six days to make the world, but it would take Trudeau only twenty-four hours of debate to remake Canada. The NDP joined us in opposing closure, but, after a day of fierce debate, insults, and the singing of "O Canada" by Tory MPs, the debate was cut off and the resolution passed. The constitutional battle continued throughout 1980 and 1981. The new Constitution, with its amending formula and its Charter of Rights and Freedoms, finally became the law of Canada in 1982, with the Charter introducing concepts that greatly increased the powers of Canadian judges and limited the powers of Parliament and the provincial legislatures.

∾

Historian W.L. Morton observed that "one of the blessings of Canadian life is that there is no Canadian way of life, much less two, but a unity under the crown admitting of a thousand diversities." I agree with that. Although cultural diversity may have been a primary factor in the selection of a federation rather than a legislative union for Canada, the principal reasons for maintaining a federal structure in modern Canada are the imperatives of geography, of vast spaces, of huge changing landscapes, the dictates of topography, and the different ways of growing up and making a living on a diversified continent. There is no one Canadian way of life.

We cannot keep all Canadians feeling part of the whole without maintaining a flexible federal structure and a strong and effective private sector. A centrally directed, increasingly state-owned and -planned economy is not compatible with the varied aspirations of Canadians living in a country with great resources and where great initiative and enterprise are required.

The Trudeau approach failed to take account of the fact that there has been, and should continue to be, an ebb and flow of powers between the two levels of government to meet the changing needs and desires of Canadians. Canadians want a central government acting for all of Canada, not a government acting for central Canada. I believe that, while we desired union in Newfoundland, we did not desire uniformity, and that this is true of all regions of Canada.

I approach constitutional issues believing in these principles and remembering what Sir John A. Macdonald said: "Whatever you do, adhere to the Union. . . . We are a great country and shall become one of the greatest in the universe if we preserve it. We shall sink into insignificance and adversity if we suffer it to be broken." It's these words of Sir John A.'s that the people of Quebec and of Canada must remember if we are to overcome our constitutional impasse. Canada without Quebec will sink into insignificance and adversity, as will Quebec without Canada.

It's not necessary that each province have exactly the same constitutional and legislative powers as every other province. The concept of asymmetrical federalism doesn't frighten me. If it's necessary to provide some special status, powers, or legislative jurisdiction for Quebec because of its size, numbers, language, or culture, so be it – so long as the same kind of legislative jurisdiction or power is available to others if they need it. Federal systems can be very diverse. We should adopt the federal system that suits our needs. It's not the country that must adapt itself to some particular constitution or constitutional rule, but the constitution that must adapt itself to the needs of the country and its people.

∽

Jane and I visited South Africa at the invitation of the South Africa Foundation, an independent business organization. The foundation made no attempt to propagandize on behalf of the National Party government or the apartheid system still in effect then. I checked with Clark before accepting the invitation, and he said it was up to me as a private individual to decide whether to go. I anticipated the trip would attract criticism, as there were, and are, interest groups in Canada who want to control where Canadian public figures go, what they do, and whom they meet. They equate a visit to a particular country with support for the country's government or social or economic system. This is nonsense. If we refuse to visit countries of which we do not approve, we would have very few countries to visit. Our visit to Red China did not mean I supported communism. My visit to Chile did not signal approval for the Pinochet dictatorship.

Jane and I had a fascinating time in South Africa, meeting with blacks, coloureds, whites, municipal officials, businessmen, academics, and others, and I returned much better informed about the situation there. But, when I got back, the professional left-wingers created a flap over the trip. In Canada, the concept of "political correctness" colours almost every issue. I decided never to let myself be imprisoned by the wardens and guardians of the penitentiary of political correctness.

∾

It was obvious from our very first post-election caucus meeting that Joe Clark was on trial. His trial dragged on longer than O.J. Simpson's, starting with our first post-election caucus in 1980 and not ending until the leadership convention three and a half years later that chose Brian Mulroney.

Caucus members admired Joe for being courageous, hard-working, decent, and approachable, but the general attitude was that, unless events showed he could win an election, we could not afford to have him continue as leader. The party needed to project an image of electability, and, unless Joe could change his public image, he would be doomed. I intended to support him loyally in whatever tasks he assigned to me. If an opening occurred, I was prepared to try for the leadership myself, but, in the meantime, I decided to do or say nothing that would hurt Joe.

Most of our MPs were watching and waiting. Many Conservatives were angered by Joe's failure to seize the patronage opportunities available to us during our 259 days in power. He wanted to set up some new kind of patronage system, to make sure that the most worthy types were appointed first. I managed to get just two appointments for Newfoundland; I got Alex Hickman made Chief Justice of the trial division of the Supreme Court of Newfoundland, and Bill Doody appointed to the Senate. Most of us had no use for Clark's new system. Parties are nuts if they don't appoint their own people to patronage jobs – jobs that are outside the civil service. They get no credit for not appointing them. As long as our people are qualified, what criticism can there be?

Although my relations with Joe were good throughout this period, I was getting a lot of exposure and favourable publicity as Finance critic, and Joe decided it was time to lower my profile. So when he shuffled his shadow cabinet, he made me External Affairs critic. If you're in Opposition, External Affairs, or Foreign Affairs as they call it now, is zilch. Question Period is fuelled by domestic issues, and the External Affairs critic is seldom in the thick of combat. But I didn't make any fuss. I figured the change would give me a chance to broaden my experience for a future leadership campaign.

The pressure on Joe mounted following the Tories' 1981 general meeting in Ottawa, where, as the party constitution required, delegates were asked to vote by secret ballot on whether they wanted to hold a leadership convention. The opposition to Clark wasn't organized at all, and his opponents stayed mainly underground. Very few delegates indicated by way of buttons, banners, or public statements that they favoured a leadership review. The Clark machine was in charge of preparations and propaganda for the meeting, and Clark himself was in the limelight, delivering several major speeches. Despite that, 714 delegates, or 33.6 per cent, voted in favour of a leadership review, and 1,409, or 66.4 per cent, were against. I voted against a review, but the vote showed that Clark was vulnerable. He knew it. At our next caucus meeting, Joe promised he would support a leadership review if he did not do appreciably better at the next general meeting, to be held in 1983 in Winnipeg.

I started to think seriously about running for the leadership and discussed my situation quietly with long-time supporters Frank Ryan and Basil Dobbin in Newfoundland. Both were successful Newfoundland businessmen, and Ryan had considerable experience in managing election campaigns. I knew and liked John Laschinger of Toronto, a former national director of the

Conservative party, who at the time was assistant deputy minister of Tourism and Recreation in the Ontario government. I first met "Lasch" in the fall of 1976 when he helped to organize the Tory by-election campaigns for Jean Pigott in Ottawa–Carleton and for me in St. John's West. In 1979, Laschinger managed Brian Peckford's successful campaign for the leadership of the Newfoundland Tories. He also directed Peckford's winning provincial election campaigns in 1979 and 1982.

Dobbin, Ryan, Laschinger, Jane, and I met on St. Patrick's Day, in 1981, at our home on Circular Road in St. John's to review the situation and consider whether I could be a viable leadership candidate. We were not a group of starry-eyed romantics, but experienced and pragmatic businessmen and political professionals. We recognized that there were at least four major obstacles to my winning the national leadership:

- I couldn't speak or understand French.
- It was my Budget in 1979 that had led to the downfall of the Clark government.
- I was new to the federal Tories, having arrived on the national scene only in 1976 (I hadn't even met such party luminaries as Hugh Segal!).
- I was from a region other than Ontario or Quebec, where most of the votes are.

We decided there was a reasonable chance of overcoming these obstacles. We agreed that everything we did would have to be done surreptitiously, and we made it a cardinal principle that I would take no steps to undermine Clark. But we would be ready when a convention was called.

We decided that my first step must be to ensure that I had the support of key Newfoundland Conservatives and that I could raise the money I would need for a national campaign. I asked Laschinger to be my campaign manager and to start assembling an organization.

By the middle of 1981, we had assembled a national strategy group that met quarterly until the leadership convention two years later. We wanted the campaign to be fun, so we came up with a bunch of silly titles. Lasch was named the "Toronto Codfather," with Dobbin and Ryan being the "Fishermen" out to make a financial catch. Each one thousand dollars raised was a "ton of fish." Chester Burtt, who had worked with Laschinger before, came to work in my parliamentary office. Rob Parker and Jean Pigott, both MPs who had been defeated in 1979, were part of the team. Parker had helped me in my 1969 campaign to lead the Newfoundland Liberal party and had worked for me during the Clark administration. Jean was a successful Ottawa business-woman and a key recruit who had formerly supported Clark. Jim Good of St. John's, a reformed news reporter, became my policy coordinator. The group also included Bob Wenman, MP for Fraser Valley West; Fred King, MP for Okanagan–Similkameen; Lorne Greenaway, MP for Cariboo–Chilcotin, all in British Columbia; and Jack Murta, MP for Lisgar in Manitoba. Jack left us later to join the Mulroney campaign because he felt, rightly as it turned out, that not speaking French was too great a disadvantage.

The lack of French was the only obstacle I could not over-come. Even though I had weekly language lessons in Ottawa and took French immersion in Quebec, I could not acquire any facility in the language unless I devoted full time to it, which I couldn't do with my heavy tour schedule. Not learning French was a risk I had to take.

I soon had an elaborate speaking schedule designed to enable me to hit the regions where most of the convention delegates would come from. We gathered lists of delegates to past party meetings, of party workers, of people who had corresponded with me. The names were stored in databanks, broken down into such categories as issues that interested them, and their opinion of me. We set up a national network to add new names, along with a sophisticated correspondence system through which copies of speeches and other material were sent to target groups. Directed by Laschinger, my small group produced a complete strategic plan for a leadership campaign, including what to do in the first hours, days, and weeks following the convention call. A campaign budget was prepared, work began on policy papers, and a list of hard-core supporters was created that soon exceeded six hundred Tories.

A typical meeting during this two-year pre-campaign period was held in August 1981 in the Ottawa boardroom of Morrison Lamothe Incorporated, the bakery company controlled by Jean Pigott's family. At this meeting, we updated our strategy and decided to concentrate on personal appearances in British Columbia, Ontario, and the Atlantic provinces. We decided on a maximum of one speech per week in the autumn. We analysed the situation in each province, deciding to ignore Alberta because it was solidly behind Clark. We adopted a communications plan in which I set aside time to telephone former candidates or potential delegates. We set plans for a direct-mail fund-raising campaign. We analysed a Goldfarb survey on Canadian views. We discussed policy positions on the role of government in the economy and on the role of both working women and stay-at-home moms. Reviewing speaking invitations, province by province, we chose some and rejected others. I had carried out thirty-nine speaking engagements outside Parliament in 1980, and fifty-five were scheduled for 1981. These ninety-four speeches covered all provinces except Saskatchewan – 18 per cent in the West, 50 per cent in Ontario, 6 per cent in Quebec, and 27 per cent in Atlantic Canada.

Meanwhile, Wenman looked out for my interests in the caucus, while Elmer MacKay, from Nova Scotia, did the same thing for Brian Mulroney, and Chris Speyer, from Ontario, represented David Crombie, the former Toronto mayor and current MP for Rosedale. They kept in touch informally so that each camp knew what the others were thinking. Frank Moores, the former Newfoundland premier, was working hard to undermine Clark and to raise money for Mulroney. Patrick MacAdam, one of Brian's old college cronies, was secretly working for him out of the Parliament Hill office of Gordon Towers, a sympathetic MP from Alberta whom Mulroney later appointed lieutenant-governor of that province. Only a minority of caucus members still wanted Clark as leader. A Gallup poll showed us with a fifteen-point lead over the Liberals, but it didn't help Joe at all. The more likely it seemed that we could win the next election, the greater the pressure grew to get rid of him, lest he blow our chances.

Our internal tensions erupted in a major battle at a weekly caucus meeting when Erik Nielsen, with Clark absent, delivered a strong "loyalty to the chief" speech and attacked other MPs for not being as faithful to Clark as he thought they should be. Nielsen named Speyer, MacKay, John Gamble, and myself as examples. There was a two-hour battle royal in which many caucus members who had not previously declared their views expressed support for a leadership review. I made a speech attacking Nielsen. I'd been through this loyalty-to-the-leader business in Newfoundland, and I wasn't going to accept lectures on loyalty from Erik Nielsen or anyone else ever again.

Mulroney appeared, for a time, to back off in his campaign to undermine Clark. But the apparent truce was exposed as phony when Jean-Yves Lortie, Mulroney's backstage organizer in Quebec, deposited $35,000 at party headquarters in Ottawa to cover the travel costs of 175 Quebec delegates to the party convention to be held in Winnipeg in January 1983. Delegates were required to pay the first $200 of their travel costs, while the party paid the balance. Lortie's cheque covered the first $200 for each of these obviously anti-Clark delegates.

Jane and I went to Winnipeg for the 1983 Tory convention with our "Codfather" team of Dobbin, Ryan, Laschinger, and Jean Pigott. This time, I voted for review. The results were almost identical to those at the general meeting in Ottawa two years earlier. A total of 1,607, or 66.9 per cent, voted No to a leadership convention, while 795, or 33.1 per cent, voted in favour. Joe had wanted a clear mandate; he received the support of a majority of the delegates, but that mandate fell far short of the ringing endorsement he needed. He announced that he would recommend to the party's executive that they call a leadership convention at the earliest possible time – and he would be a candidate to succeed himself.

After three years of recriminations, infighting, and clandestine campaigning, the leadership race had officially begun. And I'd already been running secretly for two years.

In Pursuit of
Leadership (ii)

THE PROGRESSIVE CONSERVATIVE party embarked on its great adventure in January 1983 when Joe Clark took to the stage of the Winnipeg Convention Centre to call on the party to convene a leadership convention as soon as possible. Bitterly disappointed by the fact that one-third of the delegates in Winnipeg had voted for leadership review, Clark announced he would step down as leader and would be a candidate to succeed himself at the convention.

My advisers decided to get me out of Winnipeg as quickly as possible. This was no time to be cornered by inquisitive reporters. An incautious comment might antagonize anyone who had voted against leadership review. It was certainly not the time to be seen to be lusting after Joe's job.

A good friend, supporter, and fund-raiser, Bob Foster, of Capital Canada Limited, in Toronto, had a chartered aircraft standing by. Leaving in the twin-engine, propeller-driven plane first thing the next morning, we had a long, cramped flight to

Toronto that was made bearable by a few drinks. Over a fine, merry dinner that evening at Foster's home, we analysed how to proceed to win the leadership.

We saw no reason not to continue along the path Jane and I had been following since our initial meeting with Frank Ryan, Basil Dobbin, and John Laschinger on St. Patrick's Day in 1981. The campaign I had been clandestinely waging for nearly two years was ready to go public. But first my campaign manager, John Laschinger, felt it would be prudent to test my standing in the party. He commissioned Market Opinion Research (MOR) to conduct a poll of delegates who had been at the Winnipeg meeting. Many of the same people were bound to be delegates again when the leadership convention was held in Ottawa in June. MOR found that 39 per cent of those polled would give their support on the first ballot to Clark, 21 per cent to Alberta premier Peter Lougheed, 18 per cent to Ontario premier Bill Davis, 11 per cent to Brian Mulroney, and 3 per cent to me, with the remaining 8 per cent scattered among other candidates.

Why, one might wonder, would John Crosbie – who came from the "wrong" end of Canada, who was the father of the 1979 Budget that brought down Clark's government, and who was hopeless in French – persist in running in the face of a poll that put his support at a lowly 3 per cent?

In *Leaders & Lesser Mortals: Backroom Politics in Canada*, a book that Laschinger co-authored with Geoffrey Stevens, the authors posed that precise question. They suggested the answer was partly ego, partly stubbornness, partly the love of a good fight, and partly the fact that I knew I had to run, and run strongly, to consolidate a power base in the party for whatever the future might bring.* All that's true, as far as it goes. But my primary reason for running was this: I thought I was the best person to lead the party and to win the next general election. If you think you are the best man or woman available for a position, you should go after it, no matter how heavy the odds may

---

* (Toronto: Key Porter Books, 1992), p. 103.

seem to be against you. And if you don't think you are the best person – if you don't think you're the greatest – you shouldn't be in the game.

This is why I found it so deplorable in the winter of 1993 when the leading lights of the Tory party, some of whom had been in the cabinet of Brian Mulroney for nine years, decided not to run for the leadership to succeed him. It was simply because Kim Campbell was far ahead in the polls, was the media darling *du jour*, and was the one to whom all the smart money was pledged. If they thought themselves to be the best available candidate, as some of them did, they should have run instead of running away. As the leadership campaign progressed and Campbell's inexperience and lack of political savvy became obvious to even the most myopic pundits, her star began to lose its brightness in the media firmament. Her colleagues who had been too timid to run would have had a fair chance of winning the convention, as Jean Charest demonstrated.

Michael Wilson shouldn't have run in 1983. He was barely known then. When he should have run was in 1993 against Campbell; he was a major figure in the party then. The same applies to Perrin Beatty and others. But they were all scaredy-cats; they turned tail just because the polls showed Campbell to be popular at that moment. It was a discouraging spectacle to see them flocking to her side.

Although the 3 per cent finding by MOR was not encouraging, I had been under no illusions that the party rank and file were panting impatiently for an opportunity to place their crown on my greying head. And 3 per cent was not really as bleak as it seemed, because some of the prospective candidates would obviously not run, and neither Lougheed nor Davis did. As it turned out, I did better than just about everyone expected. I received 21 per cent of the vote on the first ballot, and lasted three ballots before Mulroney moved ahead of Clark to win on the fourth. If it hadn't been for my lack of French, I believe I'd have won.

∾

When Conservative MPs returned to Ottawa from Winnipeg, Clark resigned as leader of the Opposition. On Joe's recommendation, the caucus named Erik Nielsen, the House leader, to lead the Opposition until the convention. Nielsen decided that any member of the shadow cabinet who wanted to contest the leadership would be relieved of his critic's responsibility; subsequently I and Wilson and David Crombie left the shadow cabinet. I made my candidacy official at the end of a luncheon speech to the Canadian Club in Toronto on March 21. As Mulroney was making his announcement the same day in Ottawa, we arranged to make them at different times. Mulroney had turned forty-four the day before his announcement. I was fifty-two, and in a few days I would mark my thirty-fourth anniversary as a Canadian. I had been in public life for eighteen years.

In the selection of delegates, I was badly outgunned by both Clark and Mulroney. I had made a point of getting Newfoundland premier Brian Peckford on my side and was able to influence the choice of delegates in my home province. My sons, Ches and Michael, were elected as youth delegates, along with my cousin Paul Crosbie. My wife, Jane, was to be an ex-officio voting delegate from Newfoundland, while I, as an MP, was an official delegate.

With the exception of Jim McGrath, the MP for St. John's East, who supported Clark, every delegate who was active in public life in Newfoundland supported me. McGrath, who was Fisheries minister in the Clark government and later became lieutenant-governor of Newfoundland, was a paranoid type; he had never wanted me as the member for St. John's West because he saw me as a threat to his ambitions, which I suppose I was. According to surveys done by Patrick Martin, Allan Gregg, and George Perlin for their book, *Contenders: The Tory Quest for Power*, 94 per cent of the Newfoundland delegates to the leadership convention voted for me.[*]

---

[*] (Scarborough, Ont.: Prentice-Hall, 1983).

It was obviously in my interest to do everything within my power – or within the power of my friends – to maximize the number of delegates that Newfoundland would send to the convention. Normally, Newfoundland, the second-smallest of the provinces, sent about a hundred delegates to Tory national meetings. But Laschinger – the man was a genius! – found a loophole. The student Conservative club at any recognized post-secondary institution in Canada was entitled to send three voting delegates, so Laschinger said, Why not arrange to have more post-secondary institutes given official recognition and create more Conservative clubs? With the assistance of the Tory government of Newfoundland, we were able to identify twenty-one such institutions, including the Newfoundland Flying School!

One of my supporters, Lynn Verge, who was the province's Education minister (she later became Tory leader), conferred instant post-secondary status on all twenty-one, and we created Conservative clubs at each one. We organized founding meetings, wrote club constitutions, and held delegate-selection meetings. I don't know whether it was technically vote fraud, but, if it was, it was an ingenious vote fraud, and in a good cause.

Sixty-three applications for delegate status were delivered to party headquarters in Ottawa. Headquarters was suspicious, but what could they do? After much hemming and hawing, the party accepted the *bona fides* of eighteen of the twenty-one new institutions, giving me an additional fifty-four votes at the convention. As Laschinger joked, the Newfoundland Flying School unfortunately crashed on take-off; it was not deemed to be a legitimate post-secondary institution.

If I had been able to replicate my Newfoundland organizational successes across the country, I'd have won on the first ballot. But I didn't have the people or the organization in the other provinces to field slates of delegates committed to me and have them elected. I encouraged my friends and supporters in various parts of the country to make their own efforts to get elected as delegates, but other than that I had to wait until delegates were chosen, then try to win them to my side.

Quebec became the bloody battleground between the Clark and Mulroney organizations as they fielded slates and packed meetings in every corner of the province. Their methods produced great criticism from the media and the general public, but these tactics are used in every party when candidates are fortunate enough to have the organizational strength to try to control the delegate-selection process.

∾

All my life I have been a believer in free trade with the United States. My father campaigned for economic union with the United States at the time of Newfoundland's referendum on Confederation with Canada. As a teenager at the time, I supported Dad's campaign, and ever since I have held firmly to the view that free trade makes every bit as much sense for all of Canada as it made for Newfoundland in the late 1940s. I made free trade the policy centre-piece of my leadership campaign, packaged in a twenty-seven-page document, *Agenda for Action*, that we mailed to all delegates.

I felt it was very much in the interest of Canada to cease our anti–foreign investor, anti–private sector, anti-American rhetoric and establish a new partnership with the United States through a free-trade agreement. In my view, Canada had to open its borders to more U.S. investment in order to grow, while economic nationalism would doom our people to a dubious and diminishing economic future.

These opinions made Laschinger and some of my other advisers nervous. They warned me that free trade was a sensitive issue in Ontario; they didn't want me to talk about it at all. In response to their concerns, I started to use the term "freer" trade, rather than "free" trade, although the terms meant the same thing as far as I was concerned.

My proposal for a new economic partnership with the United States was a positive move for my campaign because it showed me as a candidate who wasn't afraid to give serious thought to

Canada's economic problems and how to overcome them. The Tory campaign slogan used to defeat Sir Wilfrid Laurier's Liberals in the 1911 Reciprocity election had been "No truck nor trade with the Yankees." In a *Maclean's* interview, I explained: "That was nearly 100 years ago and conditions have changed. We already have the truck and trade – we need it on a safer and sounder basis."

The issue helped to set me apart from Clark and Mulroney, whose brands of pragmatic Toryism were very similar to mine. Mulroney warned that "opening the flood gates" by embracing free trade with the Americans would endanger Canada's economic and political sovereignty. "The implications of free trade with the U.S. strike at the heart of Canadian sovereignty," he said. Although he favoured a close, productive relationship with the United States, "that does not, however, include free trade." Clark took the same general position as Mulroney. Two years later, however, both converted to the free-trade cause and adopted my policy.

∾

It's always difficult to know whether delegates are really going to vote for you. Most people don't like to offend a candidate who asks for support, and will often indicate support when in fact they have no use for him or are committed to some other candidate. As I made the rounds of members of the Tory caucus, I went to see George Hees, who had been a leading light in the Diefenbaker cabinet and was still a vigorous MP. George greeted me effusively, pumping my hand with exuberance, and sitting me down so that he could devote his full attention to everything I said. When I told George that I was going to be a candidate for the leadership, he expressed great enthusiasm and much pleasure. I told George what a great fellow he was, what a magnificent contribution he had made to our party, and how much he was looked up to by all who knew him – and I asked for his support.

I couldn't have asked for a more heart-warming response. George clapped me enthusiastically on the back and volunteered that I had all the qualifications, background, intelligence, and experience necessary to be a first-class leader of the Progressive Conservative party and prime minister of Canada. I floated happily from his office and reported to my campaign staff that I thought we could put George Hees down as a supporter. The very next day, the media reported who in the caucus were supporting Brian Mulroney – and leading the list was George Hees!

It's the hallmark of a good politician to make people believe that he agrees with them. An experienced and wily politician does not lie. If you listen carefully to every word spoken, you will notice that at no time does he actually promise to do what you want him to do. But, if the politician is adept at his trade, you will leave him believing you have his support, his interest, his attention and affection. That's the way it was with Hees. I lost none of my affection and admiration for him even when I discovered he had been committed to Mulroney from the beginning.

∾

We set up the Crosbie national campaign headquarters in a pair of large rooms on the eleventh floor of an office building at the edge of the Byward Market in Ottawa's Lower Town. In addition, we had full-time offices in St. John's, Moncton, Montreal, and Toronto. Laschinger was campaign manager; Basil Dobbin, of St. John's, was national fund-raising chairman; Chester Burtt, campaign secretary; Diana Crosbie (no relation to me), from Toronto, press secretary; Paul Scrivener, tour director; and Steve Denison and Peter Doucet, youth co-chairmen. Frank Ryan headed my Newfoundland campaign, supported by Mac Lemessurier as provincial campaign chairman.

At headquarters in Ottawa, there was always a group of volunteers stuffing envelopes – 45,000 envelopes by convention time. Computers churned out individual letters to suit each delegate, eventually printing 30,000 of them. Scrivener planned my travel itinerary around meals, making sure I had three square meals a day, including plenty of red meat. I travelled with a black briefing book, updated each week with the names and details of the delegates I would meet. I had a detailed itinerary with the names of local drivers, campaign contacts, members of editorial boards, and people I should recognize or remember. The tour organization reviewed requests for meetings and visits and chose communities accessible to a reasonable number of delegates. The criteria were a one-hour drive for an Ontario delegate, or two hours in the Prairies. Food was provided for meetings, with a cash bar.

In early May, the leadership candidates met in an ill-tempered televised debate in Toronto where seven contenders addressed a crowd of 2,300, many of them openly hostile to Clark. Clark was booed when he spoke in French. All those in the audience were given a survey sheet and asked to phone in their preference among the candidates. Of the 561 responses, Clark led with 30 per cent; Mulroney had 17 per cent; I got 16 per cent; David Crombie 13 per cent; Michael Wilson, who was from Toronto, 11 per cent; Edmonton's Peter Pocklington 10 per cent; and John Gamble, an extreme right-winger from outside Toronto, 3 per cent. More significant, the survey found that I was the second choice of 36 per cent, compared with 19 per cent for Mulroney and just 4 per cent for Clark.

∾

The most dangerous enemy of a politician is bone-numbing exhaustion. And while federal general election campaigns in those days lasted fifty-odd days, leadership campaigns go on for many months. Candidates lose control of their lives. They're on the campaign trail six days a week, meeting delegates, speaking at party functions, raising money, and so on. If they're lucky, they get one day a week at home, and that "day off" is usually given over to staff meetings and strategy sessions.

My leadership campaign was three months in its most active phase. I travelled constantly throughout Canada, concentrating on the areas where we felt I had the best potential, and meeting as many delegates or potential delegates as was humanly possible. Jane often came with me and was a tower of strength. She was very popular, easy to meet and to talk to, enthusiastic, sincere, and a beautiful woman, to boot. My constant companion on the campaign trail was Ross Reid of St. John's, who'd been my executive assistant when I was a cabinet minister in the Moores government, moved with me to Ottawa when I became an MP, and worked with me while I was Minister of Finance in the Clark administration.

The week of May 15 was a typical, busy week. It started with Sunday morning off in Ottawa, followed by strategy and tour meetings in the afternoon, and a flight to Vancouver in the evening. On Monday, at 6:45 A.M., Ross got me up to attend a breakfast meeting at 7:35 A.M. in Surrey for 200 delegates and guests. I made a speech and took questions. I met and spoke personally to everyone at the breakfast. At 10:45 A.M., we flew to Victoria for a speech at noon to a Chamber of Commerce luncheon, followed at 1:30 P.M. by a private meeting with delegates from the Victoria area. I attended a fund-raising reception, where, at 5:45, I spoke to 200 people. At 7:50, we had a reception for delegates at our hotel in Victoria and I made a speech to the 130 people attending. I packed it in for the day at 10:00 P.M.

On Tuesday, Ross roused me at 5:00 A.M. for a 7:30 flight to Prince Rupert in northern B.C. At 10:15 A.M., we toured the port facilities in Prince Rupert, and at 11:35 I had a private meeting with delegates who would be going to the convention. At noon, we had lunch with the delegates and I spoke. At 2:00, we flew to Smithers, a small town in the interior, where, at 3:05 P.M., we had a reception for delegates and a speech. At 4:15 P.M., we flew from Smithers to Prince George, where I attended a 6:15 reception for delegates and made another speech. Next followed a community dinner attended by 450 people, where I spoke again. I was a basket case by the time I finally reached my hotel room at 9:30 P.M.

On Wednesday, I was up at 5:00 A.M. again to fly to Kamloops at 6:00 A.M. to speak to 350 people at a Chamber of Commerce breakfast at 7:30. At 8:45 A.M., I had a private meeting with delegates, and at 10:00 I flew to Kelowna. It was a small private plane, and strong winds in the mountains made the flight extremely rough. At noon, I spoke to a Kelowna Chamber of Commerce luncheon, and at 1:30 P.M. met privately with delegates. At 2:30, we flew to Penticton for a reception for delegates and a speech at 3:30 P.M. We left Penticton at 5:20 P.M. to fly to Cranbrook, eating aboard the aircraft. At Cranbrook at 7:30 P.M., 300 people came to a reception to hear me speak. We left Cranbrook at 9:40 P.M. to fly over the Rockies to Calgary. I got to bed in Calgary around 11:30.

On Thursday, I slept in until 8:30 A.M. and, following breakfast, I made telephone calls to delegates until 11:15, when I met with the local Conservative youth group. At noon, we had lunch and a speech followed by questions and answers and, at 1:20 P.M., by a press conference. At 2:05, I flew to Edmonton, where at 3:45 P.M. I met with Premier Lougheed and his Alberta caucus, making a short speech to them and fielding questions. Following this, I had a private meeting with fellow candidate Peter Pocklington. I liked him and I wanted to see if there was any possibility of his supporting me at the convention. At 6:30 P.M., I held a reception for delegates at the Edmonton Club. This was followed by a dinner for delegates at 7:30, with a speech and question-and-answer session. I was back to the hotel at 10:00 P.M.

On Friday morning, I made an unscheduled visit to a hospital in Edmonton. On the flight from Calgary to Edmonton the day before, I had suddenly experienced a severe attack of hemorrhoids and, by the time we reached Edmonton, I could barely walk. I also found it too painful to sit. I had gotten through my meetings with Lougheed, the Alberta caucus, and Pocklington, plus the reception and dinner for delegates, but my performance was less than sparkling and I could not very well explain my deep-seated problem! As I couldn't campaign without walking and sitting, I had no choice but to undergo emergency surgery.

Ross Reid took me to a hospital, where I attempted to look inconspicuous while waiting for the doctor – or as inconspicuous as a prominent candidate for national leadership can look while trying to hide behind a newspaper in a public waiting-room, grimacing in pain. The surgeon performed a minor operation to give me immediate relief, and he gave me a sanitary napkin to control the bleeding. He was a fine man with a sense of humour who commented that this was the "closest he had ever been to the centre of power." He had my cheque framed as a memento of my visit.

Ross and I left the hospital quickly, and I hobbled off to meet two Edmonton businessmen who wanted to have a look at me before deciding whether they were going to contribute to my campaign. That done, we flew to Ottawa. I hadn't missed a single campaign engagement!

My campaign received a huge boost when I appeared on the cover of the May 23 issue of *Maclean's* with an article headed: "Crosbie: The Tory to Watch." There was a page on Jane – "No Plain Jane, But a Feisty Lady" – which presented a most positive, attractive, and altogether accurate picture of my wife. The reporter, Susan Riley, caught the essence of Jane, then fifty-two: "As she has done for all her 30 years of married life, Jane Crosbie was putting first things first – 'helping my husband.' Impeccably dressed and unfeignedly pleasant she confidently stroked delegates, cracked irreverent jokes with them and smiled steadily as her husband endlessly repeated the same hotel room speech. But she is not mere decoration: Jane Crosbie's a curiously spirited woman with views of her own."

∾

As my campaign prospects improved and as the news media started commenting that I was the candidate with the best chance of upsetting Joe Clark, the fundamental weakness of my candidacy – my lack of French – moved more and more to the fore. My campaign was going exceptionally well everywhere except in Quebec. My inability to address French-speaking Quebecers in their own language became a real obstacle; it also hurt me in the eyes of non-French delegates who were highly sensitive to the fact that the region of the greatest weakness for the Tories was Quebec. Of all the candidates, Brian Mulroney gave the most promise of increasing the party's ability to win seats in Quebec, seats we had to have if we wanted to elect a majority government.

I knew from the outset that my lack of French was going to be a problem, but there wasn't much I could do about it. I studied French in high school in Ontario, although I wasn't much good at it. I took French lessons twice a week when I went to Ottawa as an MP. On one occasion, I went to language school at St. Jean in Quebec. But I couldn't have fooled anyone into thinking I was proficient in French and, once I became a leadership candidate, I didn't have time to do anything about it. Rather than butcher the language, I stayed away from expressing myself in French, other than a few scripted words in a prepared speech.

If someone is going to try to lead a political party in Canada, obviously it is preferable that he or she be able to communicate with French-speaking people, who comprise one-third of our population. However, I didn't think that unilingualism was an absolute block. We'd had a number of prime ministers who were not fluently bilingual, including Lester Pearson and John Diefenbaker. If I'd thought it was an absolute bar to becoming leader, I wouldn't have run. In the course of our leadership campaign, Pierre Trudeau was asked whether he felt a politician needed to be bilingual to lead the country. "I wouldn't make it an absolute rule," Trudeau replied, adding that a prime minister has a head start if he speaks both languages, "but a lot depends on his openness to the 'French fact' in his personal and political life." I agreed with that.

I have a theory. Even if I'd made myself proficient in French, I don't think it would have mattered when it came to a general election. If a leader is not from Quebec, he is not going to have much influence there. People are not going to vote for him because he is fluent in French. If they were, Clark, who worked exceptionally hard to develop his facility in French, would have won a reasonable number of seats in Quebec. But in the 1980 election, we won exactly one seat there. Politics is a folk thing in Quebec. They move together. And as long as the leader is a Quebecer they trust, they'll go with him. If I'd been leader at the time of the 1984 election, and if I spoke just as good French as Mulroney, I couldn't have done what he did – win fifty-eight of the seventy-five seats in the province, because I was from Newfoundland, not Quebec. The history of Canadian politics over the last three decades shows the Conservative party can get a majority only if it has a Quebec leader – not a French-speaking leader, a leader from Quebec.

The herd instinct in the news media just makes matters worse. They think like this: *Crosbie doesn't have French, so that's his weakness. At every opportunity, we'll stress that Crosbie doesn't speak French. We'll ask him all sorts of questions in French. At every press conference, we'll make sure that he gets asked a number of questions in French so we can see him get embarrassed again. Here's a little irritation, a wound. Let's make it gangrenous, let's really do a job on Crosbie's little cut.* That's the attitude of the press. In my case it was language. With somebody else, it's something different – Joe Clark's mannerisms, for example. It's the way the sheep in the Ottawa Press Gallery work.

I refused to feel guilty about not having French. At a campaign stop in Montebello, in western Quebec, I said, "I'm not going to be defensive. There are 19.5 million Canadians who are unilingual and I'll be damned if we should be thrown on the scrap heap because we're not bilingual." I went on to say that, if Quebec voted Conservative, it would not be because our leader spoke French but because the public were fed up with the

Liberals. Even so, Mulroney had a very effective argument when he maintained that there were seventy-five seats in Quebec and another twenty-odd in other provinces where French-speaking voters either were in a majority or were a very powerful influence. This wasn't an issue just in Quebec; it was an even bigger issue with delegates or party members outside Quebec who had seen the Tories lose repeatedly, basically because we couldn't get seats in Quebec. They'd come to the conclusion that the party had to have a leader who spoke French if they were to have a chance to win in Quebec.

In *Contenders*, the authors concluded that

> for a few weeks in the spring of 1983 the leadership of the Progressive Conservative party was within John Crosbie's grasp. . . . This paradoxical character from Newfoundland had waged the most remarkable campaign of all the contenders. He had made a Newfie jokester prime ministerial; a former Liberal, one of the most respected Conservatives and a shy introvert the most popular candidate of the race. Yet the very qualities which took him to the top were also the ones that pushed him over. . . . He was a long-ball hitter who couldn't check his swing.[*]

They were right. In the last week of May, I made a final campaign tour in Quebec. It was a terrible mistake. It was a trip I didn't need to make, because I wasn't going to win any delegates there even if, by some miracle, I could suddenly spout fluent French. It was a trip I shouldn't have made, because it exposed my campaign to needless risk.

The place where I failed to check my swing was the lobby of the Holiday Inn in Longueuil. Arriving by campaign bus from Quebec City, I had foolishly agreed to hold an informal scrum for a crush of eager reporters. The previous day in Quebec City, reporters had zeroed in on my lack of French, so I should have

---

[*] Ibid., p. 103.

known what to expect in Longueuil. I was surrounded by reporters firing questions. As in Quebec City, they concentrated on my lack of French. I was tired, frustrated, and angry about this constant harping on my French. I said, "I am not some kind of criminal, I'm just an ordinary Canadian who has been in politics for a long time and has a lot to offer. Just because I'm not fluent in the French language doesn't mean a disaster is going to occur. . . . There are 20 million of us who are unilingual English or French. . . . I don't think that the 3.7 million who are bilingual should suddenly think themselves some kind of aristocracy and only leaders can come from their small group."

I said I understood many of the problems of Quebec and could talk to the people of Quebec, but a reporter then asked how I could do that if I spoke only English. My angry reply killed my leadership hopes. "I cannot talk to the Chinese people in their own language either. . . . I can't talk to the German people in their own language. Does that mean that there should be no relationships between China and Canada or Canada and Germany or whatever? . . . There are many different languages." At last, the reporters had what they'd been waiting and working for. They knew that my goose was nicely cooked. And so did I as soon as I saw the newspaper headline: "For Crosbie, French Is Not More Important than Chinese or German."

My two principal opponents made good use of my gaffe, and I couldn't blame them. Mulroney, for example, thought my remarks "preposterous" and asked Albertans to consider whether they would vote for a unilingual francophone. He said Tory delegates had to ask themselves whether they thought they could take a chance on Crosbie, given my lack of French and what appeared to be insensitivity to the importance of French.

∽

Although my unchecked swing in the lobby of the Longueuil Holiday Inn took the momentum out of my candidacy, the campaign continued, and in early June my organizers from

Newfoundland moved to Ottawa to prepare for the convention. Soon we had 150 full-time workers operating out of 600 square metres of rented office space. We had an additional 750 square metres of warehouse space to store materials. By convention time, our full-time workers would be supplemented by 600 volunteers. There were thirteen hospitality suites to be set up at Ottawa hotels, and information booths to be erected and staffed at the airport, train station, hotels, and the Ottawa Civic Centre, where the convention would take place. Entertainment had to be provided, and a number of "Screech-Ins" arranged around and about Ottawa. We ordered 6,000 one-ounce bottles of Screech from the Newfoundland Board of Liquor Control. A 5-metre by 20-metre mobile warehouse was stationed outside the Civic Centre for the material we would use on the convention floor. Donors had provided twenty-five to thirty vehicles, including a large bus, mini-buses, trucks, and cars. Each day during the convention the *Crosbie Express*, our campaign newspaper, was distributed to every hotel room where delegates were registered.

Money suddenly became a problem. At the start of the last week of the campaign, I met with my campaign committee and was agreeably surprised to learn that, while we had estimated the cost of the campaign at about $750,000, we had actually collected in excess of $900,000. If we kept to our budget, we should have money in hand at the end of convention week. This fantasy didn't last long. We laboured under the delusion that we had cast-iron spending controls in place, but the events of the last week of the campaign and the convention blew away all attempts to control expenses. With more than 1,500 Crosbie volunteers, delegates, friends, constituents, observers, and hangers-on in Ottawa for the convention, expenditures soared so far out of control that our initial budget of $750,000 went to $950,000, to $1.2 million, to a final tally of $1.85 million. We ended up raising $1.3 million, leaving a debt of $500,000.

I'd decided after running up a huge debt in the 1969 Liberal leadership in Newfoundland that I'd never put my own money into a campaign again, and I didn't. My fund-raisers, Bob Foster in Toronto, and Frank Ryan and Basil Dobbin in St. John's, did an extraordinary job for me both before and after the convention. At one point, Basil arranged a breakfast meeting at the Château Laurier hotel in Ottawa with Robert Campeau, the big developer who subsequently lost his shirt in the department-store business in the United States. Dobbin, Ryan, Campeau, and I had a fine buffet breakfast, and, although Campeau had always been a Liberal, he knew the political winds were changing, and he got into the swing of it, banging on the table, making the dishes dance as he denounced Trudeau. After a half-hour, Basil walked Campeau to the elevator, saying to him: "You know, Bob, all of this costs money." "Yeah, how much are you looking for?" he asked. "Ten thousand dollars. That would be an appropriate donation. You're going to be here in Ottawa and you're going to need some access when the regime changes," Dobbin told him. Campeau seemed shocked. "That's an incredible amount of money. You can't be serious. I just had one small breakfast," he objected. He asked if Dobbin had a private place where they could go. He took him to a room in the hotel, where Campeau reached in his pocket and pulled out a cheque already written for ten thousand dollars. We've always suspected he had four or five cheques in his pockets for various amounts and, of course, we wondered if we'd asked for enough.

After the convention, we had to face the debt. Some of the bills were unpaid for a year, and some of the creditors were good enough to accept considerably less than payment in full to settle their accounts. If it hadn't been for the fact that my campaign had impressed many people who wanted to help, I might never have been able to clear off the debt. The winner of a leadership convention can always find contributors eager to help with his post-convention debts. If all else fails, the party will look after them. A loser is on his own.

We did some innovative things. John Leckie, a business associate of Basil's, hosted a fund-raising dinner for me at his home in Calgary. We arranged to have Mulroney, as the newly elected leader, come out for the dinner, and we charged $5,000 a head.

Thirteen people came, enabling us to reduce the debt by $65,000. We put on another fund-raiser at the Hotel Newfoundland in St. John's, drawing 700 or 800 people at $140 a head. In Toronto, we rented Roy Thomson Hall for an event. The big attraction there was actress Shannon Tweed, who was *Playboy* magazine's Playmate of the Year. Shannon is from Dildo, Newfoundland, where her father had a mink farm. She auctioned off the seal-skin mukluks that I'd worn when reading my 1979 Budget in the House of Commons. An insurance agent paid $8,000 for the mukluks, taking another bite out the debt. This chap was a friend of Dobbin's, and he gave the mukluks back to Basil, who donated them to the Bata Shoe Museum in Toronto.

∾

The leadership convention is a blur in my memory. Candidates are under so much pressure that they lose track of what they're doing and why they're doing it. I felt caught in an irresistible current; it was as though I spent the entire week trying to walk up a down escalator. All I knew was that Jane and I had to look positive and pleasant at all times, regardless of how we actually felt. We met many fine people; we also met some fools and some knaves – and we had to treat them all with the same deference and respect.

The big event at the convention was the candidates' speeches. It proved to be my finest hour in the campaign, and one of the finest of my political life. I like to speak off the cuff or from notes, but neither is possible at a leadership convention, where the times for demonstrations and speeches are very strictly con-trolled. Laschinger insisted that I use a text and follow it faith-fully. Everything was rehearsed and timed to the second.

The Civic Centre was jammed to the rafters and badly over-heated. As Jane and I walked into the arena behind our band and our cheering supporters, we were preceded by a huge Crosbie balloon with my picture on the side and a little motor at the back. Like a small Goodyear blimp, it was supposed to float down the Civic Centre in a slow, stately fashion while we made our way to the stage. But the heat must have affected the balloon's gas or its controls, because the thing went berserk, soaring up and bouncing off the ceiling, then coming down and attacking the spectators. In the confusion, I missed the turn to the stage and Jane had to pull me back on course.

Once I started my speech, I could tell right away that it was going to be, as the *Toronto Star* described it the next morning, a "barn-burner." Politicians learn to read crowd reactions. Are they listening or are they not listening? Do they agree or do they not agree? Are they applauding in Mulroney's section as well as in my own? As I proceeded, I could feel the enthusiasm swelling from all parts of the arena. When I reached the French section of my speech – "Je suis canadien et je suis fier . . ." I began – I tackled the language issue directly, promising that by the next election I would be able to speak to Canadians in both languages.

Clark and Mulroney had been emphasizing Quebec as an issue. They had many signs proclaiming "Mulroney equals le Québec" and "Clark plus Quebec equals Canada." So I took that a step further, telling the convention: "Crosbie plus Newfoundland, Nova Scotia, Prince Edward Island, New Brunswick, Quebec, Ontario, Manitoba, Saskatchewan, Alberta, British Columbia, the Yukon, and the Northwest Territories equals Canada." In other words, there was more for them to consider than just Quebec. As I stepped back a pace from the podium to gauge the effect, I saw that all around the arena delegates were applauding, and many were standing. At some point, I threw my arms in the air in a gesture of triumph or defiance, and this colour picture dominated the front page of the *Toronto Star* the next day.

My speech could not have gone any better than it did. None of the other candidates' speeches was great, and none roused the crowd like mine did. It created excitement in my campaign and generated some momentum going into the voting the next day.

But no speech, however wonderful, could overcome the fact that the party wanted a leader who could win Quebec and I couldn't speak French. The balloting reflected this reality.

∾

Saturday, June 11, 1983, was the day of decision in Ottawa. It was a sweltering day, and the Civic Centre was even hotter than the atmosphere outside. It was jam-packed with thousands of delegates and others, full of excitement, music, cheering, partisan songs and chants. It was complete bedlam. We knew that Clark would lead on the first ballot. We also knew I was a more popular second choice than Mulroney. If the principal objective of the delegates was to replace Joe Clark, I would have to be close to Mulroney on the first ballot – within 150 votes, Laschinger estimated. Only if I was that close would I be able to attract enough votes to carry the "Anyone But Clark" banner on to victory. On ballot No. 1 the result was:

Clark, Joe	1,091
Mulroney, Brian	874
Crosbie, John	639
Wilson, Michael	144
Crombie, David	116
Pocklington, Peter	102
Gamble, John	17
Fraser, Neil	5

I was 235 votes behind Mulroney, who himself was 217 votes behind Clark. We knew that Joe's total was unlikely to move upward. Anyone who still wanted him as leader wanted him on the first ballot. It appeared unlikely that I could overtake Mulroney, but we thought it was not impossible. Clark had received roughly 37 per cent of the votes cast on the first ballot, and, as later research by the authors of *Contenders* would show,

Joe had drawn support from all regions, but his greatest strength came from the party establishment. For example, 45 per cent of the ex-officio delegates, people automatically granted a vote because of their official status within the party, had opted for Clark on the first ballot. Of the 874 first-ballot votes for Mulroney, 45 per cent were from Quebec. At this point, the crucial question for the Conservative party seemed to be: Could they trust Mulroney?

By the time of the second ballot, Pocklington and Wilson had dropped off and endorsed Mulroney, calculating that he had a better chance than I did to stop Clark. John Gamble and Neil Fraser had dropped from the ballot and had given their support, for what it was worth, to me. David Crombie had stayed in the race. The result of the second ballot was:

Clark, Joe	1,085
Mulroney, Brian	1,021
Crosbie, John	781
Crombie, David	67

Wilson and Pocklington couldn't deliver their delegates to Mulroney. Half of Pocklington's supporters came to me, as did 35 per cent of Wilson's; only 49 per cent of the Wilson vote went with him to Mulroney. Clark dropped six votes, but confounded the experts by holding just about all his first-ballot vote. Brian Mulroney's vote had increased by 147, while mine went up 142, so I was still in contention at 781. Crombie would now be dropped from the ballot.

In between the first and second ballots, John Laschinger had come across three friendly Western MPs, Bill McKnight, Don Mazankowski, and Jake Epp, who had supported Clark, but were depressed by his showing on the first ballot. They didn't believe he could now defeat Mulroney. They felt that someone had to stop Mulroney and proposed to Laschinger that, if Clark's vote did not increase significantly on the second ballot, to well over

1,100, and if mine did increase, they would come as a group to me on the third ballot and bring as many supporters with them as they could. Meanwhile, Ross Reid had met David Small of the Clark organization, who proposed that, if the Crosbie vote or their vote fell off, while the other rose significantly, there would be the makings of a third-ballot deal. Although my vote rose significantly on the second ballot, Clark's had held. He was still in first place and would not consider coming to me now.

The third-ballot result was:

Clark, Joe	1,058
Mulroney, Brian	1,036
Crosbie, John	858

Joe had dropped another 27 votes, but Mulroney had increased by only 15, while I, picking up the Crombie delegates, had gone up by 77. Mulroney was now just 22 votes behind Clark, but I was the candidate with the momentum.

After each ballot, there was a time period in which candidates were permitted to withdraw before the composition of the next ballot was announced. Laschinger now met with the three Clark MPs from the West, and with Clark's chief strategist, Lowell Murray, to see whether Clark would now withdraw to leave me to face Mulroney on the final ballot. But no deal could be made. Murray took the position that Clark would be on the fourth ballot and the issue was closed. Lasch told the Clark representatives that they were stalled and our people preferred Mulroney by two to one over Clark. We could not deliver their votes to Joe even if I personally endorsed him. But Joe could deliver to me. The proposition was starkly simple: Clark could lose to me or he could lose to Mulroney. Murray believed there was nothing to decide. The former prime minister of Canada was still running first on the ballot in a campaign to retain his leadership and could not withdraw in favour of a third-place candidate, no matter what. As well, with my lack of French, this might be seen as an attack on French Canada.

One final effort was made to convince Clark himself to withdraw in my favour when Brian Peckford went to Clark at his seat in the stands to plead with him to withdraw. Millions saw it on national television. Joe shook his head, while Maureen McTeer was more graphic, telling the Newfoundland premier, "Fuck off, you nerd."

I didn't think so at the time, but looking back I believe Clark made the right decision. He might or might not have been able to deliver enough of his delegates to enable me to defeat Mulroney, but the consequences for the Tory party in Quebec would have been dire. Then there was his own pride and dignity to consider. How could Clark endorse a unilingual anglophone to become leader of the party when one of his own greatest accomplishments as leader had been his understanding of Quebec and his attempt to open up Quebec for our party?

The 858 delegates who had voted for me would decide the issue. As low man, I was off the ballot, and I walked with Jane, my children, Ches, Michael, and Beth, and other close advisers to a private room to decide what step to take. I had already made my decision the evening before that in this situation I would not endorse any candidate. I knew that, left on their own, most of my delegates would choose Mulroney. Although I didn't think that the Conservatives could elect a majority government with Joe, I didn't want to damage him any further. I owed it to Clark to let the delegates decide for themselves. Meeting in a small dressing-room with the key members of my campaign team, I told them Clark had given me the highest honour he could bestow by making me his Minister of Finance. He hadn't proved to be a leader who could win, but the leadership process was taking care of that, and I wasn't going to be the one to put the final nail in his coffin. I said if I didn't do anything, Mulroney was going to become leader, and that was the way it should be.

Ballot four gave the inevitable result:

Mulroney, Brian	1,584
Clark, Joe	1,325

In 1983, the Conservatives were looking for a winner. Brian Mulroney looked as though he could be that winner, as he proved to be.

∽

The aftermath of a leadership contest is shattering not just for the losing candidate, but for his wife and family, and the supporters who worked long and hard for him. I broke down when I tried to speak for a final time to the people who had supported me so loyally and worked for me so tirelessly. I couldn't finish what I was trying to say, and Jane had to finish for me.

When Jane and I returned to St. John's a few days after the convention, Prince Charles and Princess Diana were there on the Royal Yacht *Britannia*. The yacht was tied alongside the apron on the north side of St. John's Harbour, and we were invited, with hundreds of others, to a reception on board the vessel. Thousands of people were crowding the waterfront to get a glimpse of the royal couple and their guests. When Jim McGrath, the St. John's East MP who had supported Clark, went up the gang-plank, the crowd booed. But when Jane and I started up, there was tremendous cheering. We will never forget the cheers and applause of our fellow Newfoundlanders. It was inspiring.

∽

A few days after the convention, I had another lesson, as though I needed it, in how churlish and destructive the news media could be. I was sandbagged by a *Toronto Star* reporter who wanted to know whether I was going to take French lessons, as I had promised in my speech at the leadership convention. Having succeeded in upsetting me with that line of questioning, the lout asked me about Clark's decision not to withdraw after the second ballot and throw his support to me. I was exhausted by the gruelling campaign and the convention, down in the mouth about the result, and I took the bait. "We didn't count on the ardent stupidity of Joe Clark," I said, adding that Maureen had "put her foot down decisively on any suggestion of Clark coming to me or that he permit some of his people to come to me."

These were foolish, unfair, ungracious remarks and did not reflect my considered opinion of what had happened. They got wide publicity, of course. But Clark displayed his usual decent qualities when he commented: "We're all tired and I think Jane should take John away on a holiday."

It was an exceptionally gracious response from a defeated leader as he – and I – witnessed the dawning of the era of his conqueror, Brian Mulroney.

13

LEADERS I HAVE KNOWN

MANY PROGRESSIVE CONSERVATIVES – most of them, probably – had serious misgivings about Brian Mulroney. We'd heard all the stories. We'd seen the way he'd used drifters and homeless people to pack delegate-selection meetings, and we'd noted unhappily all the fawning cronies who hung around him, flattering him, waiting for scraps from the banquet tables of the state.

I'd known Brian years earlier, when I was in the Newfoundland cabinet and he was president of the Iron Ore Company of Canada. He would come to Newfoundland fairly regularly to deal with our government. He wasn't my type – too smooth, too suave, too much the mover and shaker. He wasn't someone I would naturally cotton to, and I was on guard whenever I met him. I didn't trust him. I didn't support him when he ran for the leadership the first time in 1976. The people around him struck me as "fixer" types, and there's not much those types won't stoop to if they think it's to their advantage. Frank Moores supported Brian in 1976 and again in 1983. Frank's a hail-fellow-well-met type and he had much more natural affinity for Mulroney than I did.

But I had no complaints or problems with Mulroney as Tory leader. He was a good leader; he worked hard at it; he thought ahead; he listened to people, or appeared to listen to them. Whenever I needed something from him, he was forthcoming. He backed me completely on the Hibernia offshore oil project, which couldn't have gone ahead without his support, and he brought in the Atlantic Canada Opportunities Agency (ACOA), which is a wonderful thing for the Atlantic region. When the fishery was in crisis, he supported me to get hundreds of millions of dollars from the cabinet at a time when we were trying to reduce the deficit.

We had no major differences on ideological matters. Mulroney was no right-wing Conservative. He believed in the private sector, as I did, but on social issues he was on the left, as I was. Like me, Mulroney was a red Tory. He supported extending human-rights legislation to protect gays and lesbians, and he was pro-choice on abortion. If anything, he was probably a bit more liberal than I was.

I'm not sure how pragmatic Mulroney was when it came to the private sector, however. One thing you learn in politics is not to put too much trust in the business community. No matter what you do or what policies you adopt – and they may be policies business really wants – business people will always fail you when a controversy develops. They won't back you up. When it comes down to a gut fight, they disappear, leaving you stranded. I don't know whether Mulroney understood that, but the only time I've seen business be of any use to a political party was in the 1988 free-trade election, when for the first time they left the sidelines and made a real effort on a controversial issue. They were helpful because they weren't regarded as being partisan. But, by and large, the business community won't take stands on public issues.

The public developed a perception of Mulroney and our government as being self-serving, and even corrupt. I wish I knew how all that started. Some of it must have begun with the crony-ism around Mulroney. His friends and associates looked like a gang of conspirators planning to raid the public treasury. They had a sinister appearance. Of course, a lot of them were from Quebec, and Quebec politics had a certain aura about it. They've got a different approach there. All kinds of things go on in Quebec politics that the rest of us think are corrupt and improper.

Some of this went back to the mid-1970s and all the manoeu-vring that went on around Claude Wagner when he was being courted to run for the Tories, and the questions about whether Wagner had a secret trust fund that Mulroney had helped to set up. Some of the Mulroney people were engaged in tawdry inci-dents in those days; then, after the Mulroney government was elected, we had a series of incidents where Quebec MPs were caught trying to use their influence illicitly. There are a few bad apples in every barrel, but every now and then some Quebec MP would be charged with improperly using his office budget, or something like that. This reinforced the negative image of Mulroney and the government.

Then there's the fact that Mulroney started out as a working man's son and he obviously came to enjoy the good life. He liked good clothes, good food, and having multi-millionaire friends. Mila, his wife, liked these things, too, and she loved shopping.

So what?

Canadians have an inferiority complex. They hate people who look successful. They turn up their nose at the smell of success. We're 100 per cent different from Americans. In the United States, if people have done well, the public expects them to look like they've done well. Down there, if men are big spenders and own a thousand suits or pairs of Gucci loafers, or if women have got five thousand dresses and spend thousands of dollars shop-ping in all the best places, they're celebrities. Americans love celebrities. Canadians don't like celebrities, we don't trust them, they make us nervous, we look down on them. If a leader has a pair of Gucci shoes, there must be something wrong. He must have gotten his money somewhere he shouldn't have gotten it.

All of these niggling things gave Mulroney an image that alien-ated the Canadian people. It wrecked his name and reputation, and brought him low in the public's estimation.

Anyone who knows Brian and Mila well knows they are a warm, personable, thoroughly admirable couple. They were the first ones to call if there was a death in your family. Or if you were sick, they were always the first ones to get in touch or send you something. Mila was always pleasant and easy to talk to. She liked Jane. If Jane and Mila were going somewhere on a bus excursion with other Tory women, Mila would want Jane to sit with her. We had a good relationship with them, but our fami-lies weren't that close. It was only in the last two or three years in Ottawa that we had much to do with the Mulroneys on a personal basis.

They were friendly and decent people with a lovely family. Their three children were magnificent, well brought up and well mannered. But the public couldn't see all of this. They got a very different impression from the media.

Brian was tremendous in personal relations; he always kept in touch with the caucus. He had a certain number of MPs to lunch every week. He always gave the impression to his minis-ters and his MPs that he was interested in their views on all aspects of government and politics. He was also very good at sending notes of congratulations. In my files I have a short note dated November 20, 1987, on the stationery of the prime minis-ter, stating: "Dear John, I have been working at home, but was able to watch your superb performance in the House a few minutes ago." It was always pleasant to receive such a note and to know that the prime minister noticed your efforts.

∾

I liked Pierre Trudeau, too. I liked him as a person and I liked his attitude. He had intelligence and character. I voted for him at the Liberal leadership convention in 1968 when I was still a Grit and a member of the Smallwood cabinet in Newfoundland. I often disagreed with Trudeau's policies and actions, but I always admired him as a man. I thought he handled the break-up of his marriage with great dignity.

He wasn't one to run around scared of his own shadow. I hate people who go around looking woeful, apologetic, afraid to defend themselves. They're a bunch of sheep in Ottawa these days. They don't even dare to defend their parliamentary pensions or their other perks. I've got no patience with that. I'm a disciple of Shakespeare's King Lear, who says, "I have done the state some service and they know it" – and if they don't know it, they should know it.

While many Tories had a visceral dislike of Trudeau, I admired him for his style, his intellect, and his don't-give-a-damn approach. He wasn't forever watching every word he uttered lest he offend someone, especially in the media. He had a healthy frankness and a willingness to engage in battle with anyone.

Of course, I like a bit of arrogance, and Trudeau had that. I might attack it in public, but I admired it in private. His intelligence and mental agility made him fun to tangle with in the Commons. I knew if I put a question to him, I'd get a pretty darned good answer. I had to be on my toes, ready to respond with a supplementary question. He was a worthy adversary. Duelling with him was always risky, but it was very tempting.

On one occasion, I was questioning Trudeau about a conflict of interest involving one of his ministers, suggesting there was a conspiracy of sleaze in his government. When Ed Broadbent, the leader of the New Democratic Party, followed with another question, Trudeau replied that there was a time-honoured test for these issues: "Quad semper, quad ubique, quad ab omnibus." This roughly translates from the Latin as "What has been accepted by everyone, everywhere, everytime." I shouted that this was "the Jesuit coming out" in Trudeau. He responded that he knew his observation had been beyond the grasp of the honourable member for St. John's West. So I lapsed into Latin, too – "Res ipsa loquitur," which, as every lawyer knows, means "The thing speaks for itself." Opposition MPs gave me a hearty cheer for my quick thinking. "Now I will turn to Greek," Trudeau said, not to be outdone. "Ta zoa etrekhē." He added, "And that applies to him" – meaning me. Trudeau's Greek translated as "The animals are running," referring to the Opposition. The only Greek I knew was the school motto of my old school, St. Andrew's College, in Aurora, Ontario. So I replied, "Andrezesthe krateousthe," which translated as "Could ye like men be strong." There was considerable consternation in the Commons and applause on both sides. I was lucky that these Latin and Greek phrases, the only ones I knew, were appropriate for the occasion. "Insults in Greek and Latin Pepper House Conflict Row," head-lined the Toronto *Globe and Mail*.

When my daughter, Beth, was to be married in the fall of 1983, I thought it would be a nice touch if the prime minister sent his congratulations and best wishes to the bride and groom. Following Question Period one day, I asked Trudeau if he would do this for me. He was pleasant and willing, and had his legislative assistant ensure that his telegram arrived to be read with other messages at the wedding ceremony.

I liked Jean Chrétien, too, even though I got suspended from the Commons for a day for calling him a liar when he was Minister of Justice. In that particular instance, he stretched the truth a bit, but that had nothing to do with whether I liked him. Chrétien was a completely different type. He wasn't an intellectual. He read nothing. When he was Finance minister, he didn't read any of the reports or departmental documents. He always depended on somebody giving him a verbal briefing. He worked from intuition, or whatever it was. He wasn't my type, nor Trudeau's, but Chrétien enjoyed life, he had a good personality – a bit of a rough diamond, but a decent fellow.

You had to take Chrétien as you found him. History will judge his performance as prime minister, but I thought he did an extremely poor job when he was the Opposition leader. He was worse than poor; he was absolutely hopeless. His worst characteristics were illustrated by his speech in the Commons during the lead-up to the 1991 Gulf War. Chrétien had just returned to

Parliament as the newly elected Liberal leader, replacing John Turner, and tensions were building in the Persian Gulf. In his first speech as Opposition leader, Chrétien insisted that Canadian troops should be withdrawn immediately if hostilities broke out. He argued that, once the United Nations trade embargo became a blockade or an act of war, Canada should not support it. In effect, he was suggesting that Canada support the U.N. until the going got tough and then pull out. It was a ridiculous and seemingly cowardly position. To Chrétien's credit, he reversed his position when hostilities began in earnest later the same week. He then said it was the duty of all Canadians to stand united in those circumstances, which, of course, it was.

The same debate produced one of John Turner's finest hours. After losing two elections to us, Turner had resigned as Liberal leader and was getting ready to leave public life. While Chrétien sat there with a stony face, Turner made an unexpected speech on the Persian Gulf crisis in which he completely supported our government's action in backing the U.N. when Iraq invaded Kuwait. He repudiated his new leader's position. Turner's clinching argument was: "The whole history and tradition of commitment of the party to which I have belonged for 35 years has been in support of the U.N." That's the best speech Turner made in the Commons in the years after he came back into politics as Liberal leader in 1984.

I'd been an admirer of his when he was in the Trudeau cabinet. He had ability, a good appearance, and a lot on the ball, and I thought he was very capable. But I can never forget his intellectual dishonesty on the Canada–U.S. Free Trade Agreement. Turner had no valid reason for being against free trade. I also couldn't accept the way he set Sheila Copps and the rest of his "Rat Pack" loose; he allowed them all the running room they wanted. He encouraged their tactics and exhibited no standards in setting the moral tone of the Opposition. Instead of leading, he ran behind, encouraging the Rats. There was no authenticity to anything he did as Opposition leader, and no sincerity, because he didn't believe in the positions he took. Except for that one fine speech on the Persian Gulf. It was a very good speech because he was finally saying something he believed in.

∾

Counting Chrétien, who came to power in the election in which I retired, I knew six prime ministers in my seventeen years in Ottawa, the others being Trudeau, Clark, Turner, Mulroney, and finally Kim Campbell in 1993. Campbell, the neophyte, was the oddest, most improbable of the lot.

Obviously, there is no such creature as the ideal leader. But if there was, he or she would combine the best qualities of Pierre Trudeau, Joe Clark, and Brian Mulroney, with elements from a few of the provincial premiers I have known thrown into the mix. Thus the ideal leader would project an image of being as intellectually tough, remote, devil-may-care, and inscrutable as Trudeau was. He or she would have the determination and fortitude of Clark in the face of adversity. And Mulroney's knack for human relations – his ability to keep in touch with the members of the caucus and cabinet, to make them all believe that he cared about them and valued their opinions, and his willingness to spend endless long hours on the telephone checking with people throughout the country.

To this combination, the ideal leader might add the iron will of Peter Lougheed, the common touch of Ralph Klein, the ruthlessness of Brian Peckford, the aura of unflappable confidence of Bill Davis, the ability of Clyde Wells to comprehend and articulate complicated issues, and the media savvy of Brian Tobin. A leader who had all these attributes would be unbeatable – assuming, of course, that he or she was fluent in French!

14

WELCOME TO THE
HEAVYWEIGHT DIVISION

BRIAN MULRONEY WASTED no time in putting his own stamp on the Conservative leadership that he captured in June 1983. He was quick and he was shrewd. He moved to pre-empt any internal opposition from diehard Joe Clark supporters by publicly inviting Erik Nielsen, who had been Joe's loyal lieutenant and enforcer, to play the same role for him. He asked Nielsen to carry on as leader of the Opposition until he could win a seat, which Erik was most pleased to do. At a special caucus meeting, Mulroney made a fine, conciliatory speech that produced great enthusiasm among all the Tory MPs. Elmer MacKay, one of his earliest supporters, resigned his seat in Nova Scotia and, just four days after winning the leadership, Mulroney announced he would be a candidate in the by-election in Central Nova.

He made sure the candidates he defeated for the leadership were on side. On the morning after the balloting, a member of Mulroney's entourage called John Laschinger, my campaign manager, to ask if I would meet Brian that afternoon at the

Château Laurier, where he was staying. We talked for ten or fifteen minutes. He said all the right things – about the high regard in which he held me, about how he hoped I would continue in politics, about the important role he wanted me to play. The press was buzzing all over the hotel, of course, and Mulroney went out and told them what a "national treasure" I was. For my part, I wasn't committing myself to running in the next election. I told the press I would make up my mind over the summer, which is what I did. I went home to Newfoundland, where I spent much of the summer organizing our daughter's wedding in the fall, as a father should.

I felt I had a continuing obligation to the people of Newfoundland who had supported me so enthusiastically. I wanted to help my province, and I wanted to do whatever I could do to assist Brian Peckford and the Progressive Conservative Party of Newfoundland. So I decided to stay in politics to make sure that any policies adopted in Ottawa served the interests of my native isle.

The same day that he met me at the Château Laurier, Mulroney also held private sessions with the other candidates, including Clark. Their relationship was very awkward for both Mulroney and Clark. They didn't get along, and everyone could see it. They had been friends in earlier days and, in a sense, had grown up together in the Conservative party. As young men, they worked together in Davie Fulton's campaign for the national Tory leadership in 1967, and afterward both served the new leader, Robert Stanfield – Clark in the leader's office in Ottawa and Mulroney in Montreal as a key Quebec volunteer organizer and strategist.

Brian, however, never got over losing the 1976 leadership convention to Clark, whom he regarded as his inferior, intellectually and politically. In the years following that convention, Mulroney and his acolytes tried assiduously to undermine Clark by planting doubts about his leadership through their contacts in the news media and in the party. This effort became quite intense following our defeat in the 1980 election. At one point, Peter White, one of Brian's principal henchmen, tried to win support among Tory MPs for a nasty scheme in which the Conservative caucus would have voted non-confidence in Joe's leadership, and then humiliated him by forcing him and Maureen and their daughter, Catherine, to move out of Stornoway, the official residence of the leader of the Opposition.

Although the 1983 convention finally gave Mulroney the leadership he craved, it didn't solve his problem with Clark. As much as he wished to, Brian couldn't simply dump Joe, because of the large number of Clark loyalists who continued to hold influential positions in the party, especially in Ontario. Some of these Clark people were quite fanatical; I still come across them at Conservative gatherings today.

I know from things Mulroney said to me at the time that he didn't want Clark, that he would have been much happier if Joe had just disappeared. He would have liked to appoint him ambassador to Afghanistan or high commissioner to some other place even more remote from Ottawa. But Joe didn't want that. He has a lot of pride. He's a warrior. He accepted his defeat, maintained his dignity, and went on. I always got on well with Joe and I thought he served the government well as Minister of External Affairs, and later on the Constitution.

Mulroney won the by-election in a landslide in August and came back to Ottawa in September to name his shadow cabinet. I was back as Finance critic. I knew I would be in the thick of the fray in Parliament until we got a chance to take on the Grits in a general election in a year or so.

᛫

Mulroney spent the first year of his leadership preparing the caucus and the party for the election that eventually was called on July 9 for September 4, 1984. During this time, he led the party in Parliament and in the country in the same firm, decisive manner he had demonstrated in his initial days as leader. He had little difficulty in keeping the caucus under tight control. Because we all realized that we had an excellent chance of winning and forming a majority government, we accepted much stricter caucus discipline than we were accustomed to. Our MPs knew they were, in effect, auditioning for the next cabinet.

Brian was sure-footed in dealing with issues that the Tories might have stumbled over in the past. He supported the linguistic rights of the French-speaking minority in Manitoba, and the enforcement of the principle of universality in medicare through strict new standards incorporated in the new Canada Health Act that was introduced by Liberal Health minister Monique Bégin.

At the end of February 1984, Pierre Trudeau took his celebrated walk in the snow, in the course of which, he said, he decided to retire as Liberal leader and prime minister. There's nothing like a leadership race to generate publicity and push a party up in the polls. By the time the Liberal convention opened in June with seven cabinet ministers in the running, they had climbed ten points in the Gallup poll to pull ahead of us for the first time in three years. Lady Luck shone on the Conservatives, however, when John Turner defeated the more popular Jean Chrétien. As Liberal party president Iona Campagnolo indiscreetly, but accurately, told the crowded convention hall, Turner was first in the balloting, but Chrétien was first in Liberal hearts. Within days of being sworn in as prime minister, Turner went to see the governor general and the dramatic 1984 election was on.

For the Tories, the 1984 campaign was very much the Brian and Mila Show. Campaign strategy and organization were tightly managed by Mulroney's cronies from Quebec, and by Norman Atkins, Harry Near, pollster Allan Gregg, and other cogs from Ontario's Big Blue Machine. These characters were paranoid, obsessed with control, and they clearly viewed me as a wild thing who might throw their closely scripted, highly orchestrated, leader-focused campaign off track with a single quip or retort. Like other senior members of the caucus, I was cut off from personal access to Mulroney. The only time any of us saw him was if he spent a few hours campaigning in our constituency before being marched off to his next stop.

While Brian and Mila, and their staffs, advisers, gurus, sched-
ulers, strategists, security people, and media handlers, flew high
overhead, I campaigned on the ground in a tour of the nation's
boondocks as the party tried to exploit my popularity at the
grass-roots level without letting me near the major media
centres. In the end, I logged more miles than any Conservative
other than the leader. I campaigned deep into rural and small-
town Canada. With a single aide, Jim Good, I made major swings
through northern Manitoba and Saskatchewan, northern and
southwestern Ontario, and Atlantic Canada.

In Saskatchewan, we travelled through Regina, Saskatoon,
Moose Jaw, and North Battleford, then on to Prince Albert,
where, in a motel room in John Diefenbaker's political home
town, Jim and I watched the television debate that changed the
course of the election. Mulroney challenged Turner to defend
all the patronage appointments that he had made at Trudeau's
behest to the public service, diplomatic corps, and judiciary on
the eve of the election call. The debate produced that defining
moment when Mulroney looked Turner in the eye and said, "Sir,
you had an option," telling the Prime Minister he could have
refused to make the appointments. While Mulroney basked in
the glory of his debate triumph, Jim and I hit the road again, to
Manitoba – Thompson, Gimli, and Winnipeg.

They let us make one visit to Toronto. But, when we got
there, we were joined by a full-time party organizer named Rob
Peacock, who later confessed he had been assigned by the
master-builders of the Mulroney campaign to make sure I did
not commit any verbal indiscretions or otherwise depart from
the agenda and script they had so thoughtfully written for me.

At every stop in my travels through the boonies, solicitous
local organizers would ask Jim what I needed to ensure my perfect
comfort in my hotel room. Jim's answer was always the right one:
a bottle of Scotch, preferably Ballantine's. And the bottle was
always there. Being of Scottish descent, it was not my inclination
to leave partly consumed bottles of good Scotch behind when I
left town. Before long, I had accumulated an impressive number

of bottles, which I carted with me in a soft-sided suitcase. As we were leaving Calgary one day, the inevitable happened. A local campaign worker was carrying my special suitcase across the tarmac to a private plane that would carry me to Ontario, when the handle snapped. The bag fell to the pavement with the loud crash of broken glass. Poor Jim Good was petrified that a photographer would get a picture of a certain prominent national politician on the tarmac, perhaps in tears, as he tried desperately to salvage the unbroken bottles in his precious trove. Luckily for us, there was no photographer in the immediate vicinity.

The rest is history. On September 4, 1984, the Mulroney Tories recorded the greatest electoral victory in Canadian history, winning 211 of the 282 seats in the Commons. The Liberals, the giants who had towered over the political landscape since 1935, were lucky to survive as the official Opposition, with 40 seats. The New Democrats did better than they expected, winning 30 seats, and one independent was elected. In Newfoundland we picked up 2 seats, giving us 4 of 7, and we came close in the other 3. The humiliation we had suffered in the 1980 election had been avenged!

∾

The first and most daunting chore facing a new prime minister is to pick a cabinet. This is not as simple as the public thinks. If it were just a matter of naming the thirty or forty most intelligent, most capable, or best-qualified members of caucus, cabinet-building would be a breeze. Instead, the prime minister has to construct a delicately balanced edifice, weighing such important considerations as language, region, province, sex, stature in the party, age, length of service, ideology, interests, religion, and whether an individual represents a rural, urban, or suburban constituency. Then there are intangibles. Any PM will like some of his MPs better than others. He will want to reward as many as possible of those who supported him when he ran for the leadership by appointing them to a cabinet post. He may also desire – prime ministers being human – to punish others who lacked the foresight to support him, but he will administer such retribution with caution. Prudence will dictate that he invite a few of his erstwhile enemies into the cabinet, where he can keep them under surveillance, rather than leave them on the outside, where they might stir up trouble unobserved.

With 211 members to choose from, Brian was faced with an embarrassment of riches. We all waited for The Call. As I had been Minister of Finance in the Clark administration, Opposition Finance critic for the previous year, and had a considerable following in the national party, I was sure I would be in the new cabinet. I also knew it was extremely unlikely that both Jim McGrath of St. John's East and I would be called. Although McGrath had been Fisheries minister in the Clark government and had more years in Parliament than I did, he had blotted his copybook badly with Mulroney. Jim had supported Brian against Clark for the leadership in 1976, but in 1983 he turned around and supported Joe instead. Jim said it was a matter of loyalty to Clark, who had made him a cabinet minister. But Mulroney was not the type who would quickly forget McGrath's "treachery." He would have forgiven him if Jim had supported me, because he understood the politics of these things – if you're from Newfoundland, you're expected to support the local boy. Although Brian left McGrath out of his cabinet, he was very fair to him later, offering him the choice of a Senate seat or appointment as lieutenant-governor of Newfoundland. For some odd reason, McGrath chose to be lieutenant-governor, a five-year appointment, in preference to a Senate seat until age seventy-five. Later, when Jim and his wife separated, Mulroney found a federal job for Margaret McGrath.

The Call for me came on the morning of September 12, eight days after the election. Fred Doucet, an early friend and supporter of Mulroney's, called to say Brian wanted to see me at 10:00 A.M. but to wait for another phone call, which eventually came at noon. I was asked to go to the Château Laurier and, when I got there, I was taken to a room, where I waited for another hour while Mulroney talked to someone else. Other putative ministers were secreted in other rooms in the hotel. The whole exercise was conducted in a cloak-and-dagger atmosphere. Doucet made it plain to me that I was not to pass on to anyone anything that might be said to me by "The Boss" during our meeting. Any would-be minister who leaked information would be eliminated from consideration.

When I was ushered into Mulroney's presence, he offered me Minister of Justice and Attorney General. I was surprised but not disappointed. I'd thought it possible that I might be made Minister of Finance again, but I wasn't really expecting it. A Finance minister works very closely with the prime minister, he has to have the complete confidence of the prime minister, and he has to know the PM will always back him up. My relationship with Mulroney wasn't that close, and the crowd around him didn't trust me enough. They thought I was too independent.

I didn't particularly care what job I got as long as it was an important and interesting portfolio. I wouldn't have been interested in Health and Welfare, but Justice was fine. My years in politics and government in Newfoundland and Ottawa had shown me that one's portfolio was less crucial than being a member of the inner cabinet – the Priorities and Planning Committee, or "P & P" as it was known – and a member of other pivotal cabinet committees.

Mulroney told me I would be a member of Priorities and Planning. With forty people in the full cabinet, ministers who are not on P & P have little opportunity to influence anything outside their own departments. Mulroney said I had done brilliantly as Finance minister for Clark and as Finance critic in Opposition, but a clean slate and new team were needed in that area. For Finance, he chose Michael Wilson, who had been an investment dealer in Toronto before entering politics and was well liked on Bay Street.

As Minister of Justice, Mulroney said, I would be in charge of the preparations for the constitutional conference that had to be held in 1985 on aboriginal issues. He told me he wanted

to abolish the Senate, and he wanted me to improve communications between the government and the party. We talked about
several issues involving the Department of Justice, including
constitutional change, divorce reform, Criminal Code amendments, and the appointment of more women judges.

Justice was important and it was going to be interesting. The
entire body of federal legislation had to be reviewed to make
sure it was in harmony with the new Canadian Charter of
Rights and Freedoms. And I knew I would be called on to deal
with a number of highly contentious issues, including abortion
and the rights of gays and lesbians.

I was pleased, but then I did something stupid. Disregarding
Fred Doucet's warning, I telephoned Allan Lawrence. Lawrence
had been attorney general of Ontario, narrowly lost the
Conservative leadership there to Bill Davis, got elected to the
federal House, was solicitor general in Clark's government, then
Justice critic in Opposition. If anyone had a right to expect to be
Mulroney's Minister of Justice, it was Lawrence. But I was getting
the job he wanted; in fact, he didn't get in the cabinet at all.
Making matters worse, Al had supported me for the leadership.
I couldn't leave him sitting out there, waiting for a phone call
that would never come. Out of friendship, so that he wouldn't
have to read it in the papers, I called him to say I'd been invited
to be Minister of Justice. I told him I'd been warned not to tell
anyone. So what did Lawrence do? He picked up the phone and
called Mulroney's office and raised hell about me, not him,
getting the Justice portfolio. Properly, I got a dressing-down
from Doucet over that, but they didn't rescind my appointment.

∾

Many of my problems with the Prime Minister's Office in the
next few years stemmed from my great belief in the principles of
cabinet government. I believe that a cabinet minister is responsible for everything that goes on in his (or her) portfolio.
Subject to the mandate given to him by the prime minister, a

minister should be allowed to run his department as he sees fit. If he is not performing adequately, the prime minister may remove him. I also believe in the collegiality of cabinet; every member bears a share of the collective responsibility for the decisions and actions of the cabinet as a whole. This traditional view of British-style, decentralized cabinet government did not coincide with the American style of centralized "executive government" favoured by Mulroney and practised, zealously, by his cohorts in the PMO. They believed that all power flowed from the centre, from the office of the prime minister, and that the PMO could and should be directly involved in all activities of the government, with or without reference to the minister responsible. They regarded cabinet ministers as impotent appendages.

The leader in today's cabinet system isn't merely the "first among equals." Television, scientific polling, and modern communications have exalted him. The prime minister is pre-eminent. He's at the centre of the spider's web of power. He has his own staff to provide him with political intelligence, the Privy Council Office to oversee operations, and the Treasury Board staff to help him control government spending. The officials of the Department of Finance are at his beck and call for advice on all fiscal and economic matters. He has the power to delay or delete any item on the cabinet agenda. If he has the energy, the will, and the interest, he can control everything of any significance that happens in his administration. No mere cabinet minister can hope to compete with the influence of the prime minister.

I knew that. But I was determined to control everything that happened in my own portfolio and to use my influence in all matters affecting Newfoundland and Atlantic Canada. I was also determined to exert influence on matters of special interest to me in the government generally.

The cabinet committees on which a minister served were important, but there were far too many of them (eleven in all), far too many meetings, and far too much time wasted (twenty hours in some weeks). In addition to Priorities and Planning, I was on the Security and Intelligence Committee; the Special Committee of Council; the Legislation and House Planning Committee; and the Privatization, Regulatory Affairs, and Operations Committee. When a special subcommittee on trade negotiations was established, I was a member. Later on, I was vice-chairman of both the Economic and Regional Development Committee and the Privatization, Regulatory Affairs, and Operations Committee, and a member of the Foreign and Defence Policy Committee, the subcommittee on trade negotiations, and the Federal–Provincial Relations Committee. I had more than enough to keep me and my excellent staff extremely busy in Ottawa and in my ministerial and constituency offices in St. John's.

∾

An enormous amount of my time in the first two years of the Mulroney administration was taken up attending meetings of the Program Review Task Force, or Nielsen Task Force, as it was known. Headed by Deputy Prime Minister Erik Nielsen, the members other than me were Finance minister Wilson and Treasury Board president Robert de Cotret. Our mandate was to review all federal government programs with a view to improving their delivery, making them more accessible, and reducing waste and duplication. I'm not sure why Mulroney put me on the task force, but it may have been because of my previous experience in both provincial and federal governments.

It was a bizarre exercise, a joint public–private sector effort. Nielsen enlisted Darcy McKeough, then chief executive officer of Union Gas Company, and before that Treasurer of Ontario, to head up a private-sector advisory committee that analysed the work done by joint public–private teams examining the departments and programs of government. Any such exercise is very sensitive politically because, whenever it is suggested that a program or service be eliminated, there is a chorus of opposition from groups that benefit from it. To make matters worse, Erik insisted, against my advice, that the review be made public as we went along. The inevitable result was the government came under instant siege whenever the task force threatened a program that was important to some particular pressure group.

The exercise was flawed in other ways. For one thing, the task force brought out its recommendations without reference to the ministers whose programs would be affected. In one memorable fiasco, Nielsen decided to virtually eliminate the Department of Indian Affairs without consulting the minister, David Crombie, let alone the Native people. Crombie never really recovered his confidence in the Mulroney administration, of which he was an increasingly isolated member.

A more fundamental flaw was the reasoning behind the task force's creation: that the elected leaders of the government couldn't trust the bureaucracy to do a proper review of the programs they administered, so we had to bring in selected officials from other departments, plus people from outside, to do these studies. The minister was not involved, his deputy minister was almost completely excluded, and other departmental officials were kept pretty much in the dark other than to respond to requests for information.

The exercise offended me because I thought it was improper and wrong-headed for a bunch of outsiders to go mucking around in a minister's department. The proper course would have been to call on the minister responsible to lead a review of his department's programs. What's more, the task force soon became a symbol to the public of the opaque and sinister "hidden agenda" of the Tory government; our lack of faith in the bureaucracy; and, ultimately, of our amateurish, inept approach to governing.

The Canadian public believes that Conservatives have no hearts, or, at best, are black-hearted accountants who wish only to save money and create misery, compared with Liberals and socialists, who are all heart and generosity. Therefore, it's difficult for a Tory government to achieve major expenditure restraints or to reduce the deficit. The public seems to think that, if Liberals or New Democrats propose restraint, such a step must be necessary because they would never suggest it unless they were absolutely forced to. Restraint is presumed to be contrary to the dictates of their sensitive souls. By the same token, the public seems to think that Tories initiate spending cuts because they are vindictive by nature and enjoy inflicting pain on ordinary Canadians. This, in part, explains why the Chrétien Liberal administration had such an easy time of it when they instituted spending cuts after they were elected in 1993. Those who decry the failure of the Conservative government from 1984 to 1993 to eliminate the deficit and to solve our fiscal problems should review the political environment within which the Mulroney government had to operate.

Although the Nielsen Task Force exercise produced a few recommendations that we implemented, its labour, and mine, largely went for naught. We produced a report that ran to twenty-one volumes, with hundreds of recommendations. I can't imagine there is a single Canadian, aside from the task-force members, who's actually read the whole thing.

∾

Our inexperience hurt us from the beginning. Most of our ministers lacked any background in federal or provincial governments, other than eight months with Joe Clark in 1979–80. The caucus was composed of many first-time MPs, with a large new contingent from Quebec who had their own agenda. There were too many cabinet committees, and often no clear government agenda. Nielsen appeared to have a great deal of power, to be ascendent, and to be in total charge of dealing with political emergencies that other ministers were in the dark about. The Prime Minister's Office employed too many people who were inexperienced in government, close to Mulroney and loyal to him, but distrustful of ministers. They constantly attempted to micro-manage the government and to subvert ministerial authority. They often spoke in the name of the prime minister without any authority to do so.

In the first two years of the Mulroney administration, the PMO staff made continuous efforts to subvert Joe Clark, whom they did not trust, despite his splendid acceptance of defeat in the leadership convention and his loyalty to Mulroney's leadership. They kept trying to control loose cannons like me, and to intimidate other ministers. To this was added Mulroney's mistake in selecting John Bosley, the MP for Toronto's Don Valley West, as Speaker of the Commons. John was an able and articulate member, first elected in 1979, but he was totally ineffective as Speaker. He was unable to maintain order and decorum, and to secure the respect of members. Opposition MPs were forever being allowed to breach the rules to the degree that Question Period became a circus of sensational, usually untrue, allegations against the government or government MPs, as Bosley permitted the Liberal "Rat Pack" of Brian Tobin, John Nunziata, Sheila Copps, and Don Boudria to dominate the Opposition side of the Commons.

∾

At the beginning of his administration, Mulroney made a fundamental mistake. He decided that he would not appoint regional ministers to be responsible for advising on patronage matters and for acting, in effect, as federal ambassadors to their home provinces. Instead, Nielsen, as deputy prime minister, devised an elaborate system of provincial action committees to recommend who should get governor-in-council positions. All this accomplished was to undercut the authority of the local minister. It made no sense to have a dozen or more party activists fighting and arguing over who should be made a director of the Canada Post Corporation from Newfoundland or Prince Edward Island. Nielsen and the others insisted that it would be better if the prime minister and his officials were free to deal directly with provincial governments and with federal activities in each province.

Within two years, Mulroney changed the system because, without a strong regional minister as its spokesman and defender, the government was vulnerable to the incessant attacks of self-serving premiers who were only too happy to blame everything under the sun on the federal government. The prime minister has neither the time nor the knowledge to involve himself in the local controversies that erupt every day in one or more of the provinces. He must have a regional minister to represent the government in each province, to answer allegations and charges, and to take the offensive against the provincial satraps.

In his book *Regional Ministers: Power and Influence in the Canadian Cabinet*, Herman Bakvis describes how, despite the explicit efforts of Prime Minister Mulroney to suppress the regional proclivities of ministers, within two years his government resurrected the Liberal practice of formally designating a "political minister" for each province and created a new set of regional agencies, such as the Atlantic Canada Opportunities Agency (ACOA), to enhance the standing of ministers and of the government in the regions of Canada. Bakvis concluded that "ministers such as Donald Mazankowski and John Crosbie possessed more influence than did comparable ministers under the Liberals; and they were able to exercise that influence in terrains extending beyond their own province."[*]

With the return of regional ministers, the government created an alphabet soup of regional funding agencies: ACOA; FED-NOR (Northern Ontario Development Board); and WDO (Western Diversification Strategy Office). Senator Lowell Murray was made responsible for ACOA, and I reported for the agency to the Commons. As I explained to the Commons when I introduced the ACOA legislation, "one of the issues . . . of program

---

[*] Published by the University of Toronto Press, Toronto, in 1991, this book is an excellent study of regional influences and the role of regional ministers in the Canadian government.

delivery, is who gets the credit for it. We want to be sure that the federal government is going to get credit for the programs involved in the spending of 100 per cent federal money or 75 per cent federal money." The provincial advisory committees on appointments were dismantled. Control over patronage went back to where it belonged: to the federal political minister for each province.

∞

Mulroney's ostensible reason for not appointing regional ministers at the outset was that he wanted to get away from the confrontation that had scarred federal–provincial relations during the years that Pierre Trudeau's Liberals were in power. Another, more compelling reason was the determination of Mulroney and his original coterie to control everything they could – to control all federal programs and operations in the regions, to control patronage everywhere, and to control their own cabinet ministers. The last thing Mulroney and his intimates such as Fred Doucet and Peter White wanted was to have strong political ministers who knew more about the needs of their regions than the control freaks in the PMO did.

There was great tension between the staff of the PMO and ministers and their staffs in the early years of the Mulroney regime. The people in the PMO were dedicated to the proposition that the prime minister must be preserved and protected at all costs, and ministers were there to serve that purpose. Ministers were replaceable, but not the prime minister. Ministers were regarded as likely not to be competent, to be continually getting themselves into trouble. They were judged on the basis of whether they did what the PMO thought they should do, and whether they thought the way the PMO thought they should think.

The staff of the PMO treated the staffs of ordinary ministers as aristocrats used to treat servants – they were there, but they weren't there. The PMO people were arrogant, heavy-handed, seldom thoughtful, and not particularly insightful.

Telephone calls often came from members of the prime minister's staff to ministers or to ministerial staffs, suggesting that Mulroney would like a certain matter handled in a certain way. When I was Transport minister, we got calls from the Prime Minister's Office about the awarding of a multimillion-dollar contract to develop Terminal Three at Pearson International Airport in Toronto. Don Matthews, a friend and supporter of Mulroney's, was with one of the consortiums chasing the contract. Matthews and his group were complaining to the PMO that they hadn't been treated fairly. The contract went to another consortium, headed by Toronto developers Huang and Danczkay, as recommended by a committee of civil servants that I had put in charge of the project. I simply told the PMO to forget it. I told them everything had been done properly and there was going to be no change.

Ministers never knew whether these little operatives in the PMO were really speaking for the prime minister or just for themselves or their friends. I gave instructions to my staff that requests from the PMO were not to be acted on. They were to be referred to me. As I have never been in the habit of taking orders from power-sniffers on anyone's staff, and have always prided myself on my independence, my practice was to ignore these calls unless I was certain that they actually reflected what the Prime Minister wanted done. Otherwise, I advised these would-be caesars that I would be pleased to do whatever it was the Prime Minister wanted if he would kindly speak to me personally about the matter. I don't remember a single instance in nine years where the Prime Minister ever requested or directed me to take an action that I had indicated to his staff I didn't want to take.

In the early stages, the Prime Minister's Office was an unmitigated disaster. Mulroney's style was very personalized. He had a sizeable ego and responded to flattery. He surrounded himself with cronies and loyalists whom he liked to play off, one against another. His first chief of staff, Bernard Roy, a lawyer and Mulroney supporter from Montreal, was there because Brian trusted him, not because he was competent at sensitive political work. A decent-enough fellow and a person of character, he was devoid of political instinct and he never did understand how the system worked. Fred Doucet, a senior adviser, was another old Mulroney friend. He was like a character out of a Dickens novel – prolix and entirely Mulroney's man. Later, he caused Mulroney image problems when he opened the most lucrative lobbying firm in Ottawa, using the contacts he had made while he was in the PMO.

Pat MacAdam, Mulroney's special assistant for caucus liaison, had been Brian's eyes and ears in Ottawa since 1976. Peter White, the special assistant for appointments and staffing, was a distant type with whom I had nearly as many problems as I did with Doucet. Some of the others in the PMO were able people, including Bill Pristanski; Jocelyne Côté-O'Hara; Lee Richardson (later a Calgary MP); Charles McMillan, the senior policy adviser; Geoff Norquay, policy development; Ian Anderson, communications director; and Bill Fox, press secretary – even though Fox once misspoke himself, describing me as a "congenital idiot" when I did something that angered the PMO.

It was only when Mulroney reached beyond the ranks of his friends and cronies to bring Derek Burney from External Affairs to head up his staff that the PMO started to function in a tight, organized, disciplined way. Burney was his own man. He wasn't into flattering the PM or playing power games. He was a no-nonsense type of person who knew how to delegate authority and how to react if persons to whom authority was delegated didn't measure up. Derek brought what the PMO had needed – a firm hand setting the agenda, delegating the workload, liaising with ministers, and creating an atmosphere where we could all work towards common objectives. Burney respected cabinet ministers and understood their importance in the system. He was a good man to work with. So was Stanley Hartt, who came in when Burney left.

~

The poor relationship between ministers and the early PMO was illustrated by a seemingly innocuous episode that occurred in December 1985, when, as Justice minister, I brought to the P & P Committee recommendations for the appointment of twenty-nine lawyers as Queen's Counsel. They were to be announced on December 31, as was the custom. Twelve of the prospective QCs were employed by the Department of Justice, and seventeen were in private practice but had acted for the government at one time or another. P & P approved all twenty-nine, including Lyall Knott of Vancouver. The necessary orders-in-council were signed by the Prime Minister on December 18. There then followed a series of extraordinary events illustrating the kind of power and authority that officials of the PMO thought they could wield.

Two days later, I was in St. John's when I was notified that Pat Carney, a cabinet minister from British Columbia, had advised the Privy Council Office that she thought the appointment of Knott should be revoked. He had been her campaign manager and she was worried that it might look like some sort of personal reward. I telephoned Pat to explain how decisions about QCs were made and why I had recommended Knott. She agreed the appointment should proceed. My office then confirmed with the PCO that the full list should proceed to the Governor General for signature.

I heard nothing further until December 26, when Knott telephoned from Vancouver to inform me that Peter White of the PMO had contacted him suggesting that his QC should not go forward because it might cause problems in British Columbia. I explained to Knott that the cabinet had approved his appointment and there would be no change. I had not been contacted about any change and did not agree with any change. I suggested he contact White and advise him of my position. White could call me if he wanted to pursue the matter further.

On December 30, when my office checked with the Privy Council Office to make sure all the documents were in order and signed, they discovered an order had been given by White to the

PCO to delete Knott from the list, suggesting his name had not been approved by the cabinet. As a result, the PCO was holding all of the appointments until the next cabinet meeting in January because they didn't think they could delete only one name from the list. Since a member of the prime minister's staff was now changing cabinet decisions without any reference to the minister responsible, obviously the PMO thought ministers didn't count and could safely be ignored. White's office had even phoned my officials to delete the Knott name from my press release without asking me. If I put up with this, I would be without authority in my own department.

I decided that Knott would be a QC or I would be an ex-minister. Either I would be allowed to exercise the authority of a minister or I would resign. I telephoned Mulroney at his country residence at Harrington Lake. He confirmed that Knott was to receive his QC and that the total list would be announced on December 31. Knott did get his QC, but, if I hadn't called the Prime Minister, there would have been no federal QCs that New Year's Eve.

Two weeks later, I wrote an angry letter to Mulroney in which I pulled no punches. It was not tolerable, I wrote, that officials of the PMO should feel that they had the authority to ignore ministers and give orders and directions directly to officials in a minister's department. It was not tolerable that they should feel free to change cabinet decisions. And I said I intended to have no further interference in my department. Mulroney never replied, but I experienced no further attempts by the PMO to interfere with my direction of any department of which I was the minister.

∽

I got myself in trouble with the Prime Minister's Office about a year after we took office. The Minister of Fisheries, John Fraser, had resigned over the release of tainted canned tuna, and this, together with other issues and contradictions at the time, made it seem as though our government was stumbling in the dark. On an open-line radio show in St. John's, the host, Bill Rowe, asserted that the PMO must be staffed "by a bunch of dolts." His assertion coincided with my perception, but I couldn't say that on air. So I hedged:

> Well, that's another possible interpretation. I wouldn't say it's staffed by dolts, but perhaps they're not as, perhaps you could say they aren't as astute politically or as politically intuitive as they should be and there is something lacking in the system there, smelling out political danger. For example, when that tuna business first came to the attention of anyone in the PMO, if they were astute political types, they would smell the danger. There's something dangerous about it. This is something we'd better check on. You know, any suggestion that tainted tuna has gone to the public should have, you know, that should have alerted them immediately and they should have followed it up immediately and done something then. So perhaps there is something to that.

I couldn't say any less than that because the truth was the tainted-tuna business had been completely mishandled by the PMO, and the minister had been needlessly sacrificed. However, I was quickly reminded that honesty is not highly valued in Canadian politics. My remarks received great publicity, and most of the questioning in the Commons the next day was directed at me. This went on for several days because, with Bosley as Speaker, there weren't any rules to govern Question Period. Someone in the PMO then leaked a story that I had been "blasted" by Mulroney for publicly criticizing his aides over their handling of the rancid-tuna affair. "You might say the PM read him the riot act," an unnamed PMO spokesman told the press. In fact, the cabinet did have a discussion about the series of events bedevilling the government and about the need to avoid making comments that could further add to the government's woes. But I wasn't "blasted" by Mulroney.

The following day, I was invited to a reception held by the Tory women's caucus to open an art show and auction off one of the paintings. I told the audience, "As you know, in the last couple of days I've had a bit of foot trouble. Erik Nielsen was good enough to ask me what was the matter. Had I bitten too deeply?" When I auctioned the painting entitled *Naissance de la Nuit*, I said, "This painting is just about as perfect and as flawless as the Prime Minister's Office. I hope this is being recorded. I don't want anyone to report tomorrow that I said the Prime Minister's Office is like the birth of night. I'm sure that they'll say that I said the Prime Minister's Office was a nightmare."

∾

My greatest clash with the PMO came over, of all things, St. Pierre and Miquelon. It happened because, with the Newfoundland government engaged in a series of confrontations with Ottawa, the PMO and the Department of External Affairs masterminded the greatest public-relations disaster ever between Canada and Newfoundland. I was plunged into one of the worst crises of my career, and the two governments into a virtual civil war. It would never have happened if the PMO and External Affairs hadn't been so insensitive and arrogant. It never would have happened if the PMO had had any respect for the rights and capabilities of cabinet ministers.

At the centre of these upsetting events were St. Pierre and Miquelon, the two tiny islands owned by France about 20 kilometres off Newfoundland. Because of these islands, the French have had certain fishing rights in the area ever since the Treaty of Paris ended the Seven Years War in 1763. So the French fishing issue was not a new one. Matters got more complicated in 1977, when Canada declared a 200-mile economic zone, which was accepted by most of the international community.

France, however, claimed a 200-mile economic zone around St. Pierre and Miquelon, with the result that there was a large disputed area off the south coast of Newfoundland where it was unclear which country had the right to control fishing or to exploit possible undersea mineral resources.

The Mulroney government was anxious to resolve the issue because Brian and his ambassador in Paris, Lucien Bouchard, wanted to demonstrate good relations with France, in part to counter Quebec's attempts to cosy up to France. But the negotiations were complicated by an agreement that the Trudeau government had entered into with France in 1972 that now governed fishing relations between the two countries. The 1972 treaty gave the French Metropolitan fishing fleet the right to send ten trawlers to fish in the Gulf of St. Lawrence until the end of 1986. Under the terms of the treaty, St. Pierre and Miquelon could also send fishing vessels into the Gulf. The treaty did not specify any quotas for French fishermen, but if the two countries did not agree on the amount of fish France could take, the French had the right to go to international arbitration. In addition, the treaty gave French fishermen the right in perpetuity to take fish within Canada's 200-mile zone; again, France had the right to go to arbitration to determine a quota. This one-sided and stupid treaty had no termination date. It would bind Canada forever unless Paris and Ottawa agreed to terminate it.

Brian Peckford's government in St. John's had already made the northern cod a major issue; it did not want France to be allowed to take a single northern cod, regardless of treaty obligations. With the cod stocks declining, it was clearly in Canada's interest to have the boundaries of the economic zones resolved so that the fishery could be administered properly and the fish stocks preserved. Canada wanted to have the boundary dispute referred to international arbitration. But France would not agree to that unless it received generous quotas for fish, including northern cod, within Canadian waters until the arbitration decision.

The negotiations were of intense interest to the Newfoundland fishing industry, to fishermen and their union, and to the provincial government. All of these groups were worried that Ottawa would "give away" too many Newfoundland fish at the expense of our local fishery in order to win an amicable settlement with France. The various groups had been fully consulted as the negotiations continued through 1986, and they supplied experts who attended the talks as observers.

The Canada–France negotiations broke down during meetings in Ottawa in mid-January 1987. The French negotiators returned to Paris, but, unknown to me, External Affairs renewed contacts with the French. They suggested to the Prime Minister's Office that a deal could be made in which France would agree to arbitration if Canada agreed to "significantly increase" France's fishery quotas in Canadian waters after 1987. External Affairs and the PMO wanted negotiators sent to Paris immediately, but they were anxious to exclude the Newfoundland government, representatives of the fishing industry, and officials from the federal Department of Fisheries and Oceans because the French didn't want them there.

Although I was Newfoundland's representative in the cabinet, I was not consulted about any of these proposals or discussions. When I heard about plans for the trip to Paris, I immediately contacted External Affairs minister Joe Clark, who said he knew nothing about it, but would check. He told me later the proposed trip had been cancelled. But the following morning, I discovered through Fisheries department sources that the group had in fact gone to Paris.

Fred Doucet was the PMO official quarterbacking this operation. When I spoke to him and expressed my alarm, he assured me that the representatives of the province and the industry groups were not invited to Paris because it was a technical meeting involving the drafting of language. Doucet also told me that the two Canadian negotiators were not empowered to sign any agreement binding on Canada. Any agreement reached would have to be approved by the Canadian cabinet. These deliberate misrepresentations and falsehoods were made to me by Doucet on a Friday.

On Monday morning, I learned to my consternation that a binding agreement had been signed over the weekend in Paris. In it, Canada had given France an annual quota of northern cod during the arbitration period.

There was outrage in Newfoundland. It was the kind of ammunition Peckford needed to demolish the standing of the federal government in our province. The deceit, stupidity, and ham-handedness of the PMO and External Affairs had delivered me, as the regional political minister, into his hands. Just about everyone in Newfoundland supported Peckford in his opposition to the Paris agreement. I had to spend most of 1987 fighting a vicious civil war with Peckford's government. He went on province-wide TV to attack the agreement, and I had to go on TV and radio to respond. The provincial government sent a pamphlet to every household, giving their version of events. I had to respond with a brochure explaining exactly what had happened, what had been agreed at Paris, and how we would be conducting matters in the future. Peckford even managed to convene a meeting of seven other premiers in Toronto to discuss the matter; at the end of it, they issued a statement chastising the federal government for being beastly to Newfoundland.

I pointed out to Mulroney that we had handed Peckford an issue on which he could ride to glory with every patriotic Newfoundlander cheering him on. I thought it was an issue that could cost us all four of our federal seats in Newfoundland, including mine.

I was ready to resign. In a lengthy letter to Mulroney, I set out all my complaints – about not being consulted, about being deceived and lied to by Doucet, about the exclusion of Newfoundland observers from the negotiations, about an agreement being signed without proper cabinet authorization. I said we owed the people of Newfoundland an apology – and, in fact,

Don Mazankowski, as deputy prime minister, did make a public apology on behalf of the federal government.

In a meeting with me and the three other Tory MPs from Newfoundland, Mulroney agreed to one of my essential requests – that I was to be fully involved with the External Affairs minister and the Minister of Fisheries in all further negotiations. He also agreed to state publicly that he particularly valued my advice on all matters affecting the Newfoundland fishery and on all matters involving the people of Newfoundland and Labrador, and that no final agreement would be reached with France without my concurrence and without the support of the Newfoundland MPs in the federal caucus.

I told Mulroney, and he agreed, that, if Newfoundlanders continued to have the impression that only Peckford and his government truly represented their interests, then we were finished as a political force there. I said Ottawa could not properly protect itself in Newfoundland unless I had the authority to deal with Peckford in the certain knowledge that the Prime Minister had delegated authority in these matters to me. I shortly received an extremely satisfactory, supportive letter from Mulroney, affirming my role and authority, which we released to the press. In it, he stated that "Canadian interests, not relations with France, are the paramount consideration."

Mulroney knew I'd been at the point of resignation. He gave me his support when I needed it most, and my relationship with him grew more positive from that time on.

I returned to Newfoundland, where I addressed a Tory luncheon and launched my counter-attack against Peckford. I told the Premier that political brothers don't call one another liars and traitors, regardless of their disagreements on policy. In addition, I reminded him that the Conservative government in Ottawa had given Newfoundland jurisdiction over the offshore riches of Hibernia. If he wanted to make war on me, I would fight him from the fish stages to the street corners of St. John's. I agreed that what had happened had been inexcusable, but that future negotiations would be conducted in an entirely different manner, with me in charge.

Author/journalist Michael Harris summed up the Battle of St. Pierre and Miquelon in the *St. John's Express*: "Whether the fish deal stands or is scrapped, this is the bottom line: Nobody in Ottawa, including Fred Doucet, can humiliate John Crosbie without dire consequences for the federal government. Nobody in Newfoundland is going to get a better deal from Ottawa by giving a raw deal to the man with no more cheeks to turn."

Harris concluded, "Keep your gloves up, Messieurs Peckford and Doucet. Welcome to the heavyweight division."

15

REFORMER JOHN

ONE BIG DIFFERENCE between being a minister of the Crown and an ordinary member of Parliament is the security that surrounds cabinet ministers. When I was appointed Minister of Justice and Attorney General in 1984, Jane got a call from the Mounties saying that officers were being dispatched to make a security inspection of our residence. Our "residence" at that time was a rented flat on the second floor of a house in the Glebe, in south-central Ottawa. In due course, a security system was installed on the doors and windows, and a panic button was mounted on the wall by the head of our bed. I don't know what would have happened if we'd ever hit the bedroom button by accident, but thankfully that never happened.

I did occasionally have trouble, however, with the security system on the door when I would arrive home late and activate the alarm. When that happened, the police would telephone to check, and I was supposed to answer with a code name to reassure them that I was safe and well. Of course, I could never remember the silly code name, so the next thing I knew the police would be at the door. One time, the alarm somehow went off by itself at 2:00 A.M. Jane and I were awakened by a call from the police asking us to make sure our premises were secure. We looked outside to find the lawn already covered with Mounties, and two members of the SWAT team poised at the front door, ready to break it down.

As a cabinet minister, I also had a car and chauffeur. Our driver was a wonderful man named Roy Pantelone. Roy had been my driver, in fact, when I was Joe Clark's Finance minister. Before that, he'd driven for Jean Chrétien and, when the Clark government was defeated in 1980, he went back to Chrétien. I got him back again in 1984. For some reason, the Minister of Justice is deemed by the security people to be especially important or vulnerable. Roy had been trained in security driving manoeuvres, and he would frighten me half to death by practising these manoeuvres on the way to Parliament Hill in the morning. As Minister of Justice, I also rated two bulletproof vests, which were kept in the trunk of the car. It was never clear whom the two vests were for – for Roy and me, but not Jane, for Jane and me, but not Roy, or for Jane and Roy, but not me? It was also not clear to me what practical use bulletproof vests in the trunk would be in the event of a terrorist attack. Would the hitmen be willing to wait while we stopped the car, got out, opened the trunk, and pulled on the vests? In any event, we never had occasion to use them, and I was amused to note that, when Brian Mulroney moved me from Justice to Transport in 1986, the two vests mysteriously disappeared from the car trunk. I would spend another seven years as a cabinet minister, but I never rated a bulletproof vest again, not even during Desert Storm in 1991, when Mulroney made me a member of his "War Cabinet."

∾

Justice has long been regarded as a plum portfolio in the federal cabinet, and in recent decades it's also been something of a stepping-stone to greater things. Pierre Trudeau used Justice as a springboard – or perhaps a trampoline – to launch himself into the leadership of the Liberal party and, simultaneously, the office of prime minister. Both John Turner and Chrétien had highly successful, and visible, careers as Justice ministers before becoming Liberal leader. More recently, Justice got the credit – or blame – for giving Kim Campbell's career the momentum that catapulted her into the Progressive Conservative leadership.

I wasn't looking for a catapult to anything, but I was pleased by Mulroney's invitation to take on Justice. There were many interesting challenges, controversial issues, and important changes to be made to the legal system that would benefit millions of Canadians, changes that wouldn't cost much money. That was a significant consideration at a time when our new government was trying to reduce the deficit left by the Liberals. All the job required was the political determination to tackle reforms and the willingness to risk abuse while doing it. I have never lacked determination, and no one has ever accused me of shying away from controversy. As far as I'm concerned, controversy and abuse go with the territory for anyone who wants to make his mark in public life.

I'm proud of my record as Justice minister. I tackled some of the toughest and most sensitive questions that governments must deal with – divorce, pornography, sexual exploitation of children, prostitution and street soliciting, abortion, aboriginal rights, the role of women in the armed forces, legal protection of the mentally ill, prosecution of war criminals, rights of gays and lesbians, and even that old chestnut, Senate reform.

My twenty-two months as Justice minister were busy, varied, and happy. Determined to be an activist minister, I took on more issues, introduced more legislation (nineteen bills), and got more of them (sixteen bills) through Parliament than my Liberal predecessors had attempted or accomplished during the previous

four and a half years (during which just eleven Justice department bills were passed).

When Mulroney shuffled the cabinet in 1986, he asked me to
take on another department – Transport – that also required ener-
getic, reform-minded leadership. The huge, unwieldy Transport
department was on the cusp of a revolution. My task was to pilot
a new National Transportation Act through public hearings and
through Parliament, then to preside over the deregulation of
the entire transportation system. This assignment presented a
kaleidoscope of issues – from the scrapping of the Crow's Nest
Pass freight rates to the privatization of Air Canada, from a
sober consideration of the future of the St. Lawrence Seaway to
an angry confrontation over the closing of Canadian National's
repair shops in Moncton, New Brunswick.

∾

I was faced with an immediate challenge when I arrived at
Justice. In just seven months' time, Section 15, the equality-
rights section of the Canadian Charter of Rights and Freedoms,
was scheduled to come into force. The entire body of federal
law would have to be made to conform to Section 15 as of
April 17, 1985, but the Trudeau administration had done
nothing to prepare for the day. I introduced legislation to
amend fifty acts and published a discussion paper, *Equality Issues
and Federal Law*, which identified significant economic and
social issues that might be affected by Section 15. These
included eligibility for unemployment-insurance benefits,
mandatory retirement, and the treatment of the mentally
handicapped by the criminal law system. The most controversial issues were referred to the equality-rights subcommittee of
the Commons Justice and Legal Affairs Committee. Chaired
enthusiastically by Patrick Boyer, the Tory MP for Toronto's
Etobicoke–Lakeshore, the subcommittee held public hearings
and brought in eighty-five recommendations.

After months of briefing, wheedling, and cajoling cabinet ministers and caucus members – many of whom did not share my enthusiasm for reform – I announced the government's response to the Boyer subcommittee report. In a paper entitled *Towards Equality*, we unveiled a policy that still seems progressive today. We scrapped mandatory retirement at age sixty-five in areas under federal jurisdiction. We prohibited discrimination against homosexuals in employment in the federal sector, including the Royal Canadian Mounted Police and the Canadian Forces. And we expanded the role of women in the armed forces to include combat duty, with commanders retaining the discretion to keep women out of the front lines if military effectiveness required it. Because these initiatives all involved areas of exclusive federal jurisdiction, we were able to act unilaterally.

I proposed an amendment to Canadian human-rights legislation that would have further extended protection against discrimination for gays and lesbians. The amendment would have given sexual orientation or preference the same status as race or religion for human-rights purposes. For example, a landlord would not have been able to refuse to rent an apartment to people just because they were gay.

Not surprisingly, this initiative caused an unholy row in the Conservative caucus. Alex Kindy, a troglodyte MP from Calgary East, announced he would fight the issue in caucus and in the country, and would vote against it in the Commons. Kindy later crossed the floor to the Liberals, who never worried much about the ideological *bona fides* of defectors who came their way. Another right-wing Tory back-bencher, Dan McKenzie from Manitoba, advised the news media that a majority of caucus members were totally opposed to my proposals to advance the rights of homosexuals and to widen the roles for women in the military. He predicted that my amendment would never pass the Commons.

Mulroney deserves considerable credit for standing up to the reactionaries and fundamentalists in our caucus. Whenever human rights were at issue, the Prime Minister would support a "liberal" as opposed to a "conservative" approach.

The Prime Minister's support, however, didn't make it any easier for me at the Conservative national conference in Montreal in 1986. I had to plead for understanding and compassion in the face of vociferous attacks by delegates who were angry about legal protection for gays and lesbians, and were upset that the government had not come through with a promised free vote in the Commons on capital punishment. I argued that the test for our government had to be the test of tolerance: How well do we tolerate that which we don't necessarily like? I explained that the human-rights legislation, when amended to bar discrimination on the ground of sexual orientation, would not give homosexuals any greater rights than other Canadians. It would simply give them the same protection as heterosexuals.

I wish I could report that my impeccable reasoning, compelling oratory, and generous sprinkling of humour carried the day in Montreal, but this would not be factually correct. The Tory crowd reserved their greatest applause for a young minister of the Fundamentalist Christian Assembly Church in Abbotsford, B.C., who argued that homosexuality is something that is learned, and Ottawa should not condone it. He saw a serious danger to Canadian children in pedophilia in the gay community. He said he had children and he wanted to protect them. Those were, and are, the views of many Canadians, and they illustrate why it was so difficult to change the law.

If I'd stayed in Justice, I would have pushed my human-rights amendment through Parliament, but I was shifted to Transport before action was taken. Ray Hnatyshyn, who succeeded me as Justice minister, didn't want to go to battle for gay rights, so the impetus for that particular reform fizzled out. Years later, Jean Chrétien's Liberals promised to bar discrimination on the ground of sexual orientation, but they found the same thing we'd found – fierce opposition within their own caucus. It was ten years after my attempt before the Chrétien government was finally able to secure parliamentary approval for a sexual-orientation amendment.

There was an amusing footnote to the saga – amusing to me, at least. The president of the Vancouver Gay Rights League telephoned to inform me that I had been selected the league's Man of the Year for 1986. They also made me an honorary member of their organization. Luckily, I managed to keep this good news from the attention of my colleagues in the Conservative caucus!

Another challenge waiting for me when I became Minister of Justice was to formulate a policy on pornography and the sexual abuse of children. We had two federally commissioned reports on these matters – Toronto sociologist Robin Badgley's report on child sexual abuse, followed by a report on pornography and prostitution from a commission chaired by Vancouver lawyer Paul Frazer.

I proposed a reform package that was based, in part, on these two studies. As with the sexual-orientation amendment, there was no way I could please everybody. The public demanded and expected Draconian measures against people who sexually prey on children. My task was made more difficult by the fact that these expectations had been fuelled by the campaign rhetoric of many of our own caucus members. The legislation I introduced called for a maximum ten-year prison term for anyone convicted of touching a young person under fourteen years of age for sexual purposes or inviting the touch of a young person. I also proposed a ten-year sentence for anyone who produced or distributed pornography depicting young people under eighteen years of age, adults who appeared to be under eighteen, or adults dressed in children's clothing. Anyone who solicited or procured the sexual services of prostitutes under age eighteen would face five years behind bars, while those who lived off the avails of juvenile prostitutes would be liable to a sentence of up to fourteen years. At a news conference, I said that the new amendments were designed to illustrate the abhorrence Canadians felt towards such conduct and were a statement that those abuses were unacceptable and would not be tolerated.

In addition, my legislation proposed to amend the Criminal Code to define pornography as "any visual matters showing vaginal, anal or oral intercourse, ejaculation, sexually violent behaviour, bestiality, incest, necrophilia, masturbation or other sexual activity." The proposed definition of pornography also covered visual depictions of sexual acts, including real or simulated physical harm, degrading scenes such as one person urinating on another, or violent sexual behaviour. Written material would be censored only if it encouraged, condoned, or presented as normal any child sexual activity or child sexual abuse. My target was visual pornography rather than written material, which I did not consider needed to be prohibited.

My proposals were intended to replace the obscure obscenity provisions in the Criminal Code. To obtain a conviction under that law required proof of "undue exploitation" of sex, or sex linked with crime, horror, cruelty, or violence. This ambiguous definition left it to the judiciary to decide what constituted "undue exploitation," and Canadian courts were following the U.S. example in concluding that exploitation was undue when it exceeded contemporary community standards. This led to different views by different judges, since the standard was subjective, not objective.

The line between what is pornographic and what is not is a fine one. It was only when I was offered a selection of material purchased in Toronto and looked at these magazines myself that I could appreciate the real need to control the distribution of hard-core pornography. I alarmed Karen Mosher, my special adviser on these issues, when I took one of these pornographic publications, devoted to bondage, to the Commons to review its contents during Question Period. Karen was afraid I'd be in trouble if I was caught looking at such disgusting material in the hallowed halls of Parliament, but she wasn't in a position to exercise censorship over me and I did take the magazine with me.

I also introduced a tough new law on soliciting aimed at reclaiming the streets of Canada's major cities for the use of law-abiding citizens. This was a particularly hot issue in large urban areas such as Vancouver and Toronto, where women residents of certain neighbourhoods were often harassed by prowling males who mistook them for prostitutes.

On a visit to Vancouver, I attended a dinner party with Brian Smith, then the Attorney General of British Columbia. Smith suggested that he and I go out with the police on an after-dinner patrol so that he could show me, firsthand, the nuisance caused by street prostitution. When Brian called the local police station to ask for a police car to take us on a patrol, however, the officer in charge refused to believe he was the attorney general. He hung up on him several times. Finally, after verifying that we were indeed the provincial attorney general and the federal Justice minister and that we really did want to go on a hooker patrol, they sent a car. But, to Brian's great disappointment, we drove through a supposedly afflicted neighbourhood at 1:00 A.M. without spotting more than one or two cold and forlorn-looking prostitutes who weren't being a nuisance to anyone.

We did amend the Criminal Code, however. The Supreme Court of Canada had interpreted the previous provisions as meaning that a street prostitute had to be "pressing and persistent" in his or her offer of sex for sale, making it virtually impossible to get a conviction. My amendments made it illegal "for the purpose of engaging in prostitution or obtaining the services of a prostitute" to stop, or attempt to stop, a motor vehicle, or to impede pedestrians.

Generally speaking, human-rights and anti-porn groups responded favourably to the bills to combat child sexual abuse, while the new definition of pornography was felt to be vague and confusing. The National Action Committee on the Status of Women and the Canadian Coalition against Media Pornography attacked the definition as too broad, alleging it would improperly ban material showing explicit sexual activity between equal and consenting adults, making it censorship of the worst kind. As Louise Dulude said on behalf of the National Action Committee on the Status of Women, "It really is extremely puritan and totally unacceptable."

In my considered view, it's the National Action Committee that's totally unacceptable. NAC was the most strident and menacing lobby group I ever came across. In the early years of the Mulroney government, we met annually with them at their request, ostensibly to have a dialogue on government policy. But NAC consistently behaved in an abominable and uncivilized manner. They didn't want a dialogue; all they wanted was a chance to abuse government ministers. A NAC member would ask a question, and, when a minister stood to answer, they would hiss and boo, shake their fists, grimace, and shout the minister down. After several years of that kind of behaviour, the cabinet refused to meet with them any more. We finally recognized NAC for what they were: rude, belligerent, ignorant, and interested only in trying to intimidate the government. They're the sort of group that gives lobbying and lobbyists a bad name.

My reform package suffered a mixed fate. The provisions dealing with the sexual exploitation of children were passed. So was the new law on soliciting. But the pornography measures languished after I left Justice. Hnatyshyn reintroduced the bill, with some modifications, but it was never enacted.

∾

A reform of which I was particularly proud was the new divorce legislation. My aim was to make it easier and quicker for Canadian couples to divorce in the event of a marriage breakdown and to make it much more difficult for spouses to default on support payments. The legislation permitted no-fault divorces after one year of separation rather than after three years. Marriage breakdown would be the sole grounds for divorce. But my proposal still allowed for an immediate divorce where adultery or physical or mental cruelty was proved by one of the marriage partners. The bill also provided that certain government information banks be opened to locate children who had been illegally taken by one parent, or to find spouses who had defaulted on their support payments. Finally, legislation permitted the

federal government to garnishee income-tax refunds, unemployment-insurance benefits, and the Old Age Security and Canada
Pension Plan payments of spouses who defaulted on support payments. I noted that about one billion dollars in federal assistance was going each year to support women and children who
were left impoverished following a marriage break-up. An estimated 60 per cent of support orders were breached by spouses
who did not pay at all, or paid late, or paid too little. With more
than sixty thousand divorces every year in Canada, we had to
accept the fact that marriage breakdown was an unfortunate part
of modern life. My goal was not to make divorce easier, but to
make the consequences of divorce easier to handle. This divorce
reform was a significant advance for women in Canada, and a
major change in family law.

∾

Abortion is an issue that plagues every Minister of Justice. We
spent months on it during my years in the Mulroney administration, knowing that whatever we did would infuriate roughly
half of the Conservative caucus and create even more public
tumult than gay and lesbian rights. I staked out my pro-choice
position in the 1976 by-election, in which I was first elected to
Parliament, and I have not wavered from it. In my opinion, abortion is a question to be decided by a woman and her doctor, and
the state shouldn't get involved.

After the Supreme Court of Canada threw out the old abortion provision in the Criminal Code, the government came under
great pressure to come up with a replacement law. After many
tiresome months of negotiating with anti-abortion members of
the caucus, the cabinet finally came up with a compromise position that would have put abortion back in the Criminal Code
but would not seriously have impeded a woman who wanted an
abortion in the early months of her pregnancy.

I was long gone from the Justice portfolio by this time, but
Kim Campbell got the measure through the Commons, a few

Conservative members voting against it. Then we were shang-
haied in the Senate by several of our own senators. It was
another example of the untrustworthiness of people who consider themselves to be feminists or supporters of women's rights.
One of them was Frank Moores's ex-wife, Senator Janis Johnson,
from Manitoba, who voted against the compromise because she
didn't want any impediments at all to abortion.

Another was Pat Carney, who was ungrateful to the prime
minister and forgetful of her former cabinet colleagues who had
spent months working out a necessary compromise on this emotional issue. Pat owed Mulroney everything; despite her difficult
personality, he'd made her a cabinet minister, and later he
appointed her to the Senate. She pretended that she wasn't
going to be present for the abortion vote, then she came back
to Ottawa and hid until the vote was called. Senator Norman
Atkins, the campaign manager from Ontario, was a third sabo-
teur. Three or four of them unexpectedly voted against the bill,
and it failed on a tie vote, leaving the country with no abortion
law at all. In theory, any woman can have an abortion for any
reason; it's not illegal. But she has to find a place that will
perform the procedure. Most hospitals in the Atlantic provinces
won't do abortions.

∾

Lest anyone think I'm a bleeding-heart liberal because of my
views on divorce, abortion, and gay rights, let me point out that
I can be a hard-liner when it comes to making sure that murderers feel the full weight of the justice system. As Justice minister,
I had to deal with the celebrated extradition case of Joseph
Kindler, an American who had been convicted in Pennsylvania
of murdering a friend who planned to testify against him in a
criminal case. After beating his friend to death with a baseball
bat, Kindler tried to dispose of the body by weighting it and
dumping it in a river. Following his conviction, but before he

was sentenced, Kindler escaped from jail and fled to Canada, where he was apprehended. The U.S. government asked for Kindler to be extradited to Pennsylvania so that he could be sentenced and the process completed.

Canadian legislation gives the Minister of Justice discretion to refuse to extradite a fugitive to a jurisdiction that has the death penalty for the crime in question. Pennsylvania law provided for capital punishment for murder. Therefore, I had the authority to deny extradition or to impose a restriction that Canada would extradite Kindler only if the Americans agreed to waive the death penalty in his case.

Kindler's lawyers made exhaustive submissions, which I studied carefully. I reviewed the evidence at his trial. I considered his age, background, and family circumstances. I examined the procedure in Pennsylvania by which a jury weighs all the mitigating factors before voting for a death sentence. Finally, I considered the remedial avenues that would be open to Kindler, including an application for clemency in capital cases.

In the end, I decided that Canada should surrender Kindler without seeking any assurance that the death penalty would not be carried out. In my response to his lawyers, I noted that I was obliged to consider the Canadian public interest, including the need to avoid encouraging those who commit murder in a foreign state to seek haven in Canada. Kindler was eventually returned to Pennsylvania. As I write this, he is still waiting on death row.

I didn't consider it to be the business of Canada to try to impose our views on the justice system of another country. We have no right to judge whether that country should or should not execute murderers simply because we have abolished the death penalty here.

A similar case that received widespread publicity involved Charles Ng, who was arrested in 1985 in Calgary, where he was convicted of attempted murder and sentenced to four and a half years. Ng was wanted in connection with a series of grisly murders in California, where the death penalty was in force. He fought extradition, using the same arguments as Kindler. We extradited Ng, but his trial in California was delayed because of the bankruptcy of Orange County.

For some reason, Canadians have the view that the American system of justice is not as good as our system in Canada. They seem to feel that we should not return fugitives without laying down qualifications or conditions. I was totally unsympathetic to that point of view and had no intention of interfering with another country that operated according to the same basic legal system as we did. It's not up to Canadians to tell Americans whether they should have the death penalty for certain crimes, just as we would never accept any dictation from the United States on whether we should have capital punishment in Canada.

∿

I'd been Justice minister for only about a month when the Mulroney administration was rocked by an improbable political crisis. Richard Hatfield, the Tory premier of New Brunswick, was charged with possession of thirty-five grams of marijuana a month after the RCMP made a routine security check of his luggage as it was being put aboard an aircraft carrying the Queen on a tour of the province. My officials informed me of the investigation in New Brunswick and outlined how the matter was being dealt with. I wanted to make sure everything was handled in the proper manner and that any decision to lay charges would be made in the normal fashion, as if the person involved was not a prominent personality. If the RCMP recommended laying charges, and if the lawyers of the Attorney General's department agreed, then they would be laid.

Because it was obvious that the Opposition would hammer us with questions as soon as the incident became public, I felt I had to inform Mulroney that charges were going to be laid against Hatfield. Neither the prime minister nor the cabinet had any right to interfere in the decision to prosecute or not prosecute. But because of the political sensitivity of the matter, they did have the right to be notified when the decision was made so they would be ready to answer for the government.

I saw the Prime Minister, told him what had occurred, and advised him that charges would shortly be laid. He thanked me for the information and said he was sorry to hear the news, but he made no suggestion whatsoever that the case be handled any differently than it was being handled.

The Hatfield case created a political storm mainly because Solicitor General Elmer MacKay, who was responsible for the RCMP, foolishly agreed to meet privately with Hatfield at an Ottawa hotel between the time the marijuana was found and the time charges were laid. It was a fundamental error in judgement. Both the Liberals and the New Democrats demanded Elmer's resignation.

A few months later, Hatfield, who claimed the marijuana had been planted in an outside pouch of his suitcase by someone who wanted to embarrass him, was acquitted in provincial court in New Brunswick. But the affair did not end there. Within days of his acquittal, Southam News revealed that two former university students had signed affidavits alleging that, when they and two other students were invited to Hatfield's home in Fredericton four years earlier, they were offered marijuana and cocaine. Hatfield acknowledged that the young men had been in his house, but he flatly denied supplying them with drugs.

There was another uproar in the Commons as the Liberal "Rat Pack," led by John Nunziata, made wild allegations to the effect that our government was improperly protecting its friend Hatfield from prosecution. I didn't help myself when I told reporters following Hatfield's acquittal on the marijuana charge, "I know the man and I am a friend of his and I am glad he was found not guilty." This produced an outcry because, as minister, I technically had the final responsibility for deciding whether the acquittal should be appealed. In fact, these decisions are made by the lawyers in the department without reference to the minister. When reporters asked me whether I thought my comments were appropriate, I said: "I don't think I am expected to be inhuman just because I'm Minister of Justice or Attorney General. I'm simply stating that I, as one person, was pleased that a particular individual was found not guilty."

For Dick Hatfield, the affair spelled a tragic end to a splendid political career, not only in New Brunswick, but on the national scene, where he had always been a moderate and statesman-like voice in federal–provincial conferences on the Constitution, aboriginal affairs, and the economy. In the next provincial election, his Conservatives lost every one of their seats, Hatfield's among them.

∾

Every newly elected government has illusions of doing something about that most infuriating of institutions, the Senate of Canada. In the end, they all give up in frustration and despair.

Brian Mulroney was not immune to the fix-the-Senate syndrome. When he offered me the Justice portfolio, he told me he wanted to abolish the Upper House. His passion for abolition, however, soon evolved into a more modest ambition – to reform the Senate.

Our immediate problem with the Senate was its membership. The Liberals had been in office so long, and had appointed so many Grits to the Red Chamber, that they thought they owned the place, which, in effect, they did. They held 72 of the 104 seats; the Tories had just 25, with 3 independents, 1 independent Liberal, and 3 vacancies. Although we had just won the largest number of Commons seats in Canadian history (211) and enjoyed an overwhelming public mandate, the Grits, as arrogant as ever, thought they could thwart the public will and maintain control of the government through their huge majority in the Senate.

Liberal senators began harassing the government by failing to pass legislation sent from the Commons. A bill to authorize the government to borrow $19.3 billion to service the national debt, most of it incurred by wastrel Liberal regimes, was kept buried in a Senate committee for more than two months. It was clear the harassment was going to get worse, and I thought the sooner we met the problem head-on, the better. Although I personally felt the Upper House should be abolished because it no longer performed any useful function, I told the press that it might be possible to reform it in some way that would make it more in tune with our democracy. Of the options open to us, I said, the government would prefer to pass legislation restricting the power of the Senate to delay government measures, but we recognized that the senators, not being inclined to self-evisceration, would surely baulk at approving such legislation. But if we couldn't get the senators to fall on their swords, perhaps we could pull out their teeth.

So rather than proceed by legislation, in May 1985 I introduced a resolution to reform the Senate by amending the Constitution of Canada. My resolution set a thirty-day limit on the length of time that the Senate could hold up money bills from the House of Commons, and a forty-five-day limit for all other Commons bills. It also gutted the power of the Senate to amend bills from the Commons by giving MPs fifteen days to accept or reject any changes made by senators. If the Commons took no action, the original legislation, minus the Senate amendments, would come into force. "If the Liberal cabal in the Senate can reject or delay unduly legislation of the House, then the people of Canada are not choosing who governs them," I told the Commons as I opened the debate on the constitutional resolution.

An amendment to the Constitution requires the approval of the Commons and seven provinces with at least 50 per cent of the population. (The Senate can only delay constitutional amendments for 180 days; it cannot kill them.) I secured the consent of eight provinces by promising that we would convene a constitutional conference before the end of 1987 on the subject of more fundamental Senate reform. Manitoba's New Democratic Party government would not agree to my amendment, and Quebec's Parti Québécois government was boycotting all constitutional matters. But I had the other eight lined up.

Several circumstances conspired to cause my constitutional amendment to be stillborn. Frank Miller lost the provincial election in Ontario, and the Tories were replaced by David Peterson's Liberals. The Liberal majority in the Senate, seeing my constitutional juggernaut coming their way, began to give our government a modicum of cooperation on bills. And Mulroney's support for the steps I was taking evaporated once the Senate finally passed the borrowing legislation it had been delaying. The Prime Minister felt we were already engaged in enough battles on other fronts. Despite my urging, we failed to give the Senate resolution priority in the Commons, and it died.

That was a major mistake. Although Peterson might not have given us Ontario's support, there was a chance Robert Bourassa would if he brought the Liberals back to power in Quebec later in the year, as he in fact did. If we'd completed what we started in the spring of 1985, we would have saved ourselves a great deal of grief later, including the stalemate that developed in 1988 when the Liberals in the Senate would not pass the legislation to implement the Canada–U.S. Free Trade Agreement. It took the election of 1988, which produced another Conservative majority, to make the Senate see the light.

Outright abolition of the Senate became more difficult when some premiers embraced the wacky notion of a "Triple-E" Senate. "Triple-E" meant a Senate whose members would be *elected*; that would have *equal representation* from each province; and that would be *effective*, with powers comparable to those of the House of Commons. Politics is full of bad ideas, and the Triple-E Senate, beloved of some Western premiers and Newfoundland's Clyde Wells, was one of the worst. It would have been a disaster – a prescription for deadlock between the two Houses of Parliament.

∾

One of the priority tasks Mulroney gave me when he made me Minister of Justice was to assist him in preparing the federal position for a First Ministers' Conference on Aboriginal Affairs to be held by April 1985. This was an entirely new area for me. I convened a meeting in Ottawa with the representatives of the various aboriginal groups to discuss the agenda for the confer- ence. I was taken with their ability, articulateness, oratorical skills, and their immense sense of grievance arising from our past dealings with their people. At this initial meeting, I proposed a mechanism for entrenching agreements on Native rights in the Constitution. This was to include recognition of the right of aboriginal peoples to self-government.

Saskatchewan and Alberta, both provinces with large Native populations, were extremely reluctant to entrench the right of aboriginal self-government in the Constitution without knowing what the concept meant or what its implications would be. Nova Scotia and Ontario felt the same way. I sympathized with their position, but Mulroney had been anxious to move ahead. The lack of definition is still the big problem today; it's impossi- ble to know what self-government will mean until detailed agreements can be reached with the various Native groups.

When the first ministers' conference opened in April 1985, Mulroney put forward the strongest support Ottawa had ever offered for Native self-government. But the objections of the three most westerly provinces were summed up by British Columbia premier William Bennett: "We feel we must define, then sign – not the reverse." Near the end of the conference, Mulroney put forward a compromise draft amendment suggested by Premier Grant Devine of Saskatchewan recognizing the prin- ciple of Native self-government but removing any reference to a constitutional obligation on the part of the provinces to negoti- ate terms. It appeared that seven provinces would accept this, the bare minimum required for a constitutional amendment. While the Métis National Council and the Native Council of Canada agreed they could live with the revised amendment, the compromise was dealt a fatal blow when the Assembly of First Nations, representing Canada's status Indians, flatly rejected it, as did representatives of the Inuit.

The proposal was never revived successfully. The issue of aboriginal self-government still remains to be dealt with.

∾

In June 1986, with our government's popularity in steep decline, Mulroney shuffled his cabinet, firing six ministers, reassigning twenty-one, and bringing in eight new faces. The most important change was the move of Don Mazankowski from the Transport department to the position of deputy prime minister and leader in the House of Commons. The Prime Minister, learning from his previous mistake in not creating regional ministers, appointed political ministers for each province. I was made the political minister for Newfoundland. I was also now the Minister of Transport, and the transportation system was about to go through a reformation of deregulation and privatization.

Just a month before the shuffle, Mazankowski had proposed a new National Transportation Act. There would be a new agency to replace the Canadian Transport Commission; increased competition for business between different transportation modes; lower costs for air, truck, and rail users in densely populated areas; and the possibility of higher costs or subsidies in more remote areas. The government had also been considering the sale of Air Canada to private investors, and the introduction of user fees for the coast guard and other federal navigation services. A parliamentary committee was studying the future prospects of the St. Lawrence Seaway, and we had to reorganize the movement of Western grain to our ports.

Both Canadian National and Canadian Pacific had immense problems dealing with the costs of thousands of kilometres of unnecessary rail lines that they had been prevented by the government from abandoning. And CN, finding it no longer needed its repair shops in Moncton, decided to close them.

I went to Moncton with five other cabinet ministers from Atlantic Canada, plus Monique Vezina, the Minister of Supply and Services, for a two-day conference with Atlantic Tory MPs to consider economic conditions in the region. CN had managed to interest Canadian General Electric in purchasing the Moncton shops for use in their manufacturing operations. The SOS (Save Our Shops) Committee wanted Ottawa to block the sale to CGE because CGE would employ only 303 workers, instead of 437, as CN had. A mass demonstration of support for the CN workers was held near the hotel where we were meeting.

I responded to questions, and, before long, my attempt to level with the people of Moncton led me into a new foot-in-mouth controversy. "Are you saying that we should direct CN not to attempt to compete, not to be more effective than their opposition in trucking and water transportation or in the other railways?" I asked. "They have to function as productively and efficiently as they can." I said we wanted to help workers who would lose their jobs when CN disposed of its Moncton shops. This was why we were trying to bring in CGE or other enterprises.

I said it was unfortunate there was an "imbalance" in the economic advantages from one part of Canada to another. "Certainly, a person living in Southern Ontario has a big advantage over a resident of Cape Breton." But I emphasized that Atlantic Canada could only be considered a "have not" region when compared with other parts of Canada, parts of the United States, or other industrialized countries.

I would have been okay if I'd stopped there. But I continued, saying that the comparison changed when Atlantic Canadians are measured against people in the third world. "We are not a 'have not' area when compared to Bangladesh, we are not a 'have not' area compared to Haiti and we are certainly not a 'have not' area compared to Jamaica," I said, adding that anyone living in the Atlantic provinces was 1,000 per cent luckier and better off than they would be in one of those third-world nations. "We shouldn't always be looking at Southern Ontario. It's very healthy occasionally to look at Haiti or Sri Lanka . . . and then we're very 'have' when we do that."

I wasn't putting down the concerns of the Atlantic provinces. I wasn't trying to lecture. It wasn't a dumb statement. But people across Atlantic Canada went berserk when they saw incomplete reports of these comments in the news media. It was reported that I had advised Atlantic Canadians to consider themselves lucky compared to Haitians, Sri Lankans, Bangladeshis, and Jamaicans, and this infuriated the people of the region.

Mayor Elsie Wayne of Saint John, New Brunswick (and later a Tory MP), led the attack, followed by the deputy mayor of Fredericton, who declared that his town certainly wasn't Haiti. Jim McLeod, the deputy mayor of Sydney, Nova Scotia, suggested I confine my remarks to Newfoundland. Liberal MP Russell MacLellan from Cape Breton said I had sunk "to a new low for insulting Maritimers." Another Cape Breton Liberal MP, Dave Dingwall, announced: "I'm calling for the prime minister to ask for the resignation of John Crosbie." Even Nova Scotia premier John Buchanan, a Tory, felt obliged to be insulted – "Quite frankly, I think it was one of the most outrageous statements that I've heard in a long while."

Comment in the news media and on open-line shows was in the same vein. The *Halifax Chronicle-Herald* denounced my "remarkably condescending sentiments." I did get support from Harry Bruce in *Atlantic Insight* magazine. "John Crosbie was right to suggest Atlantic Canadians are better off than Haitians or Sri Lankans, but if you're a politician in Canada it pays not to be right but to be pussyfooting, mealymouthed, or a spouter of the obvious," Bruce wrote. "But Crosbie, poor Crosbie, he actually uttered something that had a touch of thought, something that was as true as Romeo's love for Juliet, and the outcry was such that you'd have thought he was Benedict Arnold, Vidkun Quisling and Tokyo Rose all rolled into one. What exactly was the treason he committed against his fellow Atlantic Canadians?" Bruce repeated what I had actually said, commenting:

Now I felt this was salutary stuff. Indeed, I had often thought, thank God, I don't live in a country where they shoot journalists who speak their minds, or the official

penalty for getting drunk is death by stoning. . . . We complain like crazy in this country about the boring, bland,
two-faced and utterly empty yak-yak that passes for political discourse. But the truth is that those who dare to speak
in something other than the prescribed puffed-wheat prose
tend to get themselves into trouble. . . . We constantly
bellyache about the wimpish platitude-spouters who make
our politics so tedious. But the moment John Crosbie says
anything remotely interesting we go after him the way
piranha fish go for a bleeding pig in a Brazilian river.

Bruce's column was a vivid contrast to the inane, unthinking
comments of most of the media. Is it any wonder that we can't
have a decent political debate in Canada on issues, when even
such harmless but truthful statements as mine in Moncton can
arouse such ill-will and venom?

Kim Campbell found herself at the centre of a similar uproar
during the 1993 federal election when she declared that an election campaign was neither the time nor the occasion for an in-
depth discussion of social policy. She had a valid point. There
doesn't seem to be any occasion in Canada when a sensible
public debate can be held on important public issues. Canadian
politicians all participate in a conspiracy of silence when it
comes to discussing serious issues, because their experience tells
them that whatever they say will be twisted by the media and
misunderstood by the public.

∾

The massive deficits we inherited from the Liberals plagued the
entire Mulroney administration. Deficits can't be wiped out
overnight, and Finance minister Michael Wilson's first Budget
in 1985 projected a deficit of $33.8 billion on spending of $105
billion. For the first few days, the Budget seemed to be well
received, but backlashes against budgets are often slow to build.

In this case, there was a crescendo of protest that spread across the country against, in particular, Wilson's decision to cut back inflation-related pension increases. The storm centred on our proposal to partly dismantle the indexing system that insulated the buying power of Old Age Security and family allowances. Wilson proposed that, in future, indexing would offset only inflation that exceeded 3 per cent annually. This de-indexing would not apply to the Guaranteed Income Supplement paid to the neediest 1.3 million pensioners, but it would partially expose basic Old Age Security to the inroads of inflation. Canada's 2.6 million old-age pensioners stood to lose a total of $1,500 to $2,300 apiece over the following five years.

The indexation of tax brackets and social benefits during the previous twelve years had been a major contributor to the national deficit. By cutting back on indexing, we were lessening the risk that inflation would return to the levels of the 1970s. But we were accused of favouring business and the rich at the expense of the poor. The outrage generated in support of pensioners was especially difficult to handle. We had a choice of backing off or alienating elderly Canadians, who accounted for nearly 20 per cent of the electorate. Soon Mulroney, feeling the heat, conceded, at an Israel bond dinner, that the Budget contained "imperfections." The Prime Minister was harassed and harangued by pensioners when he entered or left the Parliament Buildings. All Tory caucus members felt the heat in Ottawa and at home.

We had gone into this controversy unprepared. But now that we had taken a stand on indexing, I believed we would do ourselves great damage if we reversed our position. It would send the wrong signal. It would weaken our determination and undermine future efforts to restrain spending. At the cabinet Priorities and Planning Committee, I argued against any change in the Budget's proposal for de-indexing. Robert de Cotret, Marcel Masse, Erik Nielsen, and Sinclair Stevens agreed with me. Joe Clark, Flora MacDonald, and others urged that we surrender on the issue and restore full indexing. When Wilson failed to hang tough, the cautious won the day. Mulroney concluded that we could not defend the Budget with respect to the elderly poor, so it was decided to throw in the towel and restore indexing. It became clear to me then that our administration lacked the necessary political will to slash spending and bring the national debt under control.

∾

From time to time, my role as regional minister for Newfoundland clashed with my stance as one of the leading deficit-cutters in the Mulroney cabinet. Unemployment insurance was the classic case in point. UI was considered by many Canadians to be vitally important. It was also a highly controversial program because it was no longer an insurance program, but rather an income-support program for rural areas of the country. Many Canadians believed it weakened the national work ethic. Less than a year after the Mulroney government came to office, we appointed Claude Forget, an economic consultant, to conduct an inquiry into all aspects of the UI program. At the time, the annual cost of unemployment insurance was $11.5 billion.

UI is of incalculable significance in Newfoundland and throughout Atlantic Canada. Fishermen's unemployment insurance is immensely important and, coupled with the UI coverage given workers in seasonal fish plants around the province, it has established a basic income in rural Newfoundland that makes it a desirable and comfortable place to live.

In its report in November 1986, the Forget Commission recommended sweeping changes that would involve cutting three billion dollars a year from UI. The proposed cuts targeted benefits for two categories of workers: seasonal workers, and the so-called ten-and-forty-syndrome workers. The latter were those who work for only enough weeks to qualify for unemployment insurance, then live on UI benefits. Year in and year out, they work for the minimum ten weeks, then collect UI for the maximum forty weeks.

The report recommended major changes to the ways that self-employed fishermen benefited from the UI program. Fishermen had been subject to special rules and were largely funded from general revenue. The commission suggested that these benefits be phased out over five years, and that fishermen be treated like other workers. The commission also recommended that "regionally extended benefits" under UI should be progressively abolished. It proposed only one entrance requirement, one benefit phase, and one maximum duration of regular benefits.

Atlantic Canada would have been harder hit by these changes than any other part of Canada. Newfoundlanders alone would have lost $300 million to $400 million a year. The Mulroney government was soon on the defensive, and ministers from slow-growth regions and areas dependent on the fishery were under heavy pressure to reassure their constituents. My position was a simple one. I had not campaigned on the basis that I would change the UI system to reduce the benefits that were so crucial to my constituents. I could not be expected to be elected in St. John's West, then go to Ottawa and acquiesce in measures that would reduce the income of most of my rural constituents by 40 to 50 per cent. I had to oppose proposals that would have such dire results for them. "Forget in English spells forget, so let us all forget Forget," I told the people of Newfoundland.

The Forget report was politically unacceptable; it was quietly shelved, and UI continued to function basically as it had since the early 1970s. Although I believed the UI system needed fundamental changes, I am not ashamed of the fact that I did everything I could to prevent those changes when the Forget report appeared. A foolish consistency, as Ralph Waldo Emerson said, is the hobgoblin of small minds. I was elected to represent the people of my riding and my province; if I did not stand up for their vital interests, I did not deserve their support.

16

THE GLOBAL VILLAGE IDIOTS

I'VE ALWAYS BEEN a news junkie, and never more so than in my years in Brian Mulroney's cabinet. Every day for those nine years, I read the Montreal *Gazette*, *Ottawa Citizen*, *Ottawa Sun*, Toronto *Globe and Mail*, and *Toronto Star*. I didn't read every word, but I looked at every page and knew what was in them. One of the advantages of having a driver was that I could get a lot of reading done in the car. I also read the *St. John's Evening Telegram*, and I'd take time during the week to go through the Robinson and Blackmore community papers from Newfoundland. Plus there were clipping services with stories from newspapers across the country and transcripts of what was said on radio and television newscasts. I had to keep up with all of this stuff.

Like everyone else in Ottawa, I started the day with CBC radio news, usually while I was shaving. In the evening, I'd listen to the radio news at ten o'clock on CBC as well as the national newscasts on the various television networks. I had a TV set in my office, which I used mainly to watch what was happening in the House of Commons.

We've had television in the Commons for twenty years now, and it has been a mixed blessing. TV has allowed millions of Canadians to see their MPs at work, but it has also delivered a thoroughly distorted view of how members discharge their responsibilities. Question Period has always been the public focus of the parliamentary day; that's the time when constituents and schoolchildren crowd into the Commons galleries to see Parliament in action. Television loves Question Period because it's when the Opposition goes after the Government on the issues of the day. TV doesn't know what to do with the rest of the Commons day because there's not enough "action" for the medium's liking. The Commons is not really a forum for cut-and-thrust debate. Most of the day is given over to a series of set-piece speeches, often long and tedious, sometimes thoughtful and provocative, on subjects of varying complexity and public interest.

What television has done is to elevate Question Period from being the focus of the parliamentary day to being, in the public's mind, the *entire* parliamentary day. It's the only part of the daily proceedings to which television reporters pay any attention, and their weak-minded print colleagues follow along like the sheep most of them are.

Question Period is a forum for the Opposition. By concentrating on it to the exclusion of almost everything else, the news media encourage bad parliamentary manners, enhance trivial exchanges, and exaggerate the significance of attacks on the Government, many of which are wholly spurious. Day after day, Canadians are given the impression that the government is on the defensive, in disarray, on the retreat. They don't learn anything about the substance of the government's programs. Is it any wonder that the Canadian people come to the conclusion that the government must be in trouble? No matter how wise its policies, the government starts to slip in the opinion polls. Before long, panic sets in, and the government adopts short-term fixes designed to regain points in the polls, rather than longer-term strategies to address the real needs of the nation.

As a believer in candour in politics, however, I will confess to a double standard. In Opposition, I took great delight in exploiting Question Period, and the media's fascination with it, to embarrass the Government. I knew if I came up with an issue and a few good lines, I would look like a conquering hero in the clips on the evening news, while whichever Liberal minister I had chosen to be my victim would come across as an evasive incompetent. It was mostly illusion, of course, not reality. But I don't think we could have demolished the Trudeau government in just four years, as we did between 1980 and 1984, if it hadn't been for television and TV's fixation with the theatre of Question Period.

Naturally, my perspective changed after we became the government, and my role went from launching attacks to fending them off. After nine years of repelling the slander and vilification of vicious little rodents like the Liberal Rat-Packers Copps, Tobin, Boudria, and Nunziata, I came to the considered conclusion that television in the Commons does more harm than good to the parliamentary process. It is far too late, of course, but Parliament would be a better place if the television cameras could be ripped out of the Commons chamber!

∽

The reporters and commentators of the news media are never shy about offering advice and criticism to politicians. I trust they won't object if I offer a few comments about their grubby little craft.

Let's start with the question of bias. The practice of journalism has altered significantly since I began my political journey in the 1960s. Prior to the 1960s, journalists were expected to be neutral in their treatment of public figures and public issues. Editors insisted that reporters keep their personal and political opinions out of their stories. There was no quicker way for a political reporter to find himself back on the police beat than to start mixing commentary with reportage. The right or power to express opinions was reserved for columnists and editorial writers, and their columns and editorials were clearly labelled as such. It was sort of like the health labels on today's cigarette packages – you could read that stuff at your peril.

Times have changed, for the worse. A casual examination of any newspaper today will reveal stories that claim to report on events, but that are actually replete with the biases and opinions of the reporter. Stories distributed by the Canadian Press, the national news-gathering collective, are filled these days with descriptive words and phrases that clearly indicate what the writer thinks about the events, views, or people he or she is describing – and what he or she thinks any right-minded person should think about them.

If someone in the news examines issues from a conservative point of view, that individual is almost invariably identified in journalists' stories as "right wing." The Fraser Institute of Vancouver is invariably described in news reports as "the right-wing Fraser Institute" whenever they issue a report or analysis. Yet organizations or individuals expressing views contrary to the Fraser Institute's are never described as being "left wing."

Anyone interested in the deficiencies of the media in Canada should read the book *Gotcha!* by George Bain, published in 1994.* Bain reports on a study in 1982 by Peter Snow, who was then a journalism professor at the University of Western Ontario. Snow surveyed 118 national-affairs journalists, and his results mirrored those in similar American studies. Forty-three per cent of the journalists surveyed said they belonged in the middle of the political spectrum, neither left nor right; 42 per cent put themselves to the left of centre; only 4 per cent felt they were right of centre. Yet in party terms, 37 per cent supported the New Democrats, 17 per cent the Liberals, and only 11 per cent the Conservatives. As Bain pointed out, it was clear from these figures that, while those responding had some difficulty in

---

* (Toronto: Key Porter Books).

defining where they thought the middle of the political spectrum lay, wherever it was they were not to the right of it.

In the years since I entered public life, journalists have come to see themselves as advocates or as adversaries in relation to established institutions, particularly the institutions of government. With some of the younger journalists, objectivity is no longer an ideal to pursue, but rather a term of opprobrium.

It is instructive to compare the national media's treatment of the Mulroney Conservative administration with their treatment of the Chrétien Liberal administration. The ferocity of the attacks by journalists on possible mistakes made by the Mulroney government is documented in Bain's book and is burned into the memory of everyone who was active in federal politics in the 1980s and 1990s. The media were in pit-bull mode throughout the Mulroney years; when Chrétien came to office, they turned into poodles.

No matter the enormity of Chrétien's mistakes and failings – of which his nearly fatal blundering in the 1995 Quebec referendum was merely the most obvious – the fourth estate turned a blind eye. Unlike the way the press treated Joe Clark's short-lived government, tarring and feathering us over every unkept promise, the media largely ignored the Liberals' failure to carry out most of the pledges they made in their 1993 "Red Book" of campaign promises. Chrétien and his ministers weren't grilled day after day about how they were going to square their election promises with their post-election actions in restricting unemployment-insurance benefits, reducing transfer payments to the provinces, cutting services to Canadians, privatizing Canadian National, and eviscerating the Department of Transport by transferring its most important functions to the private sector. These were all policies that the Liberals had opposed when we proposed them.

The only broken Liberal promise that caught the media's attention was the foolish and irresponsible promise to abolish the Goods and Services Tax. The GST, of course, was of such great interest to everyone in Canada that even the Liberal-leaning media couldn't ignore the Chrétien government's failure to keep its word.

~

I'm a good deal more concerned about the consistent left-wing bias of the reporters and commentators who write in our newspapers and broadcast on television and radio than I am about the ideological precepts of their proprietors. There was much alarm and horror expressed in 1996 when Conrad Black, a Canadian boy who became an international press baron, acquired a majority of the moribund Southam newspaper chain, meaning he controlled half of the daily newspapers in the country. The perennially befuddled Council of Canadians, led by Maude Barlow, our Canadian version of Spain's La Pasiónara, challenged the Southam acquisition in court on the ground that our country and its institutions were somehow endangered by having too many newspapers controlled by one person. We can be sure of one thing: Maude and her motley crew would not have challenged the takeover if the purchaser had been a socialist or a supporter of liberal causes. If the owner was Conrad Broadbent rather than Conrad Black, there wouldn't have been a whimper from our limpid left-wing media mediocrities about the foulness of the Southam purchase.

In actual fact, most newspaper owners have little influence on the contents of their papers. An occasional proprietor, like Black, may want to have his or her views reflected on the editorial page, but editorials are ineffectual. They don't sway public opinion. Public opinion is affected by the headings above the stories, by the way stories are phrased, by what is included and what is left out of stories, and by the bias or slant that the writers bring to their reportage.

The fact that Conrad Black is an intelligent, interested, vocal person who likes to write articles for publication in his own newspapers may distress left-wingers. But Black has a perfect right to put his ideological stamp on his newspaper properties. Some of us are glad he's doing it. We think it's about time that someone who is committed to the market economy provided some intelligent, creative thinking to counter-balance the dead weight of liberal thought that lumbers so many Canadian publications.

Most Canadian newspapers and television and radio stations are owned by anonymous people or corporations who are simply interested in operating a successful and money-making business enterprise. They can't be bothered with propagating their own views because their eye is on the bottom line, not on the editorial line. I believe Canadians – especially Canadian journalists – should be delighted when newspapers are acquired by an entrepreneur like Black who is not afraid to express his opinions and who cares as much about what his papers have to say as he does about how much money they make.

∾

The media have a lot to answer for. They put an almost unbearable pressure on political leaders. Television subjects leaders today to unrelenting scrutiny night and day. How the leader looks and what he or she says is immediately recorded, and is available for use at any time in the future, and in any context whatsoever. If a leader slips and falls down or tumbles off a stage, or has any similar sort of mishap, that embarrassing position will turn up in photographs and the impression will be circulated that he or she isn't smart enough to stay upright. What the media do best is reinforce preconceptions. The celebrated photograph of Conservative leader Bob Stanfield dropping a football in the 1974 federal election, even though he had successfully caught several other passes that day, made him appear hapless. But photographs or television footage of Pierre Trudeau doing somersaults off a diving-board confirmed an image of a young, dynamic, capable, and athletic leader. The media might productively ask themselves what catching footballs or performing fancy dives has to do with leading a complex, modern nation.

Intense media scrutiny makes it extremely difficult for today's political leaders to make the kind of compromises our leaders have historically had to make to hold their parties together, to implement sweeping national policies, to reconcile the differences of disaffected regions and provincial premiers, and to hold the country together in the face of the centrifugal forces of geography and culture. Every political leader has had to make compromises along the way. Today, however, these compromises, these shifts in policy and tactics, are recorded and revealed by the unforgiving, uncomprehending electronic web that surrounds leaders, elected members, and candidates.

It is no longer possible for a politician to pretend to be adopting one policy in one part of the country while embracing a different policy in another part of the country. It is no longer possible to say one thing in Quebec, for example, but something even slightly different in British Columbia. This can be a good thing to the extent that it discourages deception by political practitioners, but it can be a very bad thing when it prevents a leader from seeking a course that will be acceptable to most Canadians in most regions.

Freedom-of-information legislation adds to the woes of politicians, at least to those on the government side. This kind of legislation – and most jurisdictions now have it in one form or another – gives the media and other mischief-makers the ability to ferret out snippets of information with which to embarrass political leaders and to titillate the public. In the vast majority of instances, embarrassment and titillation are the only objects of access-to-information requests.

In earlier years, for example, no one cared about the travel or hotel expenses of prime ministers and cabinet ministers. It was accepted that they represented the country, and that the country had to ensure that its leaders travelled in style and occupied the best accommodations, because anything less would reflect negatively on the prestige and standing of their country. None of this matters any more. What is news these days is whether it cost five hundred or a thousand dollars a day for a hotel suite in Paris or

Tokyo. The prime minister and his entourage have no sooner left their beds in a foreign capital before applications arrive under freedom-of-information legislation for the earth-shattering details of their hotel bills. The purpose of the visit, the discussions that were held, and the agreements that were signed are less important to our media "watchdogs" than how much the prime minister spent to buy a mineral water from the mini-bar or to send his shirts to the hotel laundry. Is it any wonder there is no intelligent political discourse in this country?

∾

Media coverage, especially television coverage, produces some odd and contradictory effects. On the one hand, the coverage can be so intense, so relentless, and so repetitive that it causes political leaders to become overexposed very quickly. Seeing them too frequently and believing they know them too intimately, the public grow weary of their politicians, who burn out far sooner than they did in the days before television. Mackenzie King dominated federal politics for three decades; with his peculiarities, he wouldn't last more than one four-year term in the television age.

On the other hand, television overexposure seems to breed contempt without familiarity. I was struck by a Gallup poll in July 1988, nearly four years after the Mulroney government took office. Despite the exposure we'd had every day in the media, only 31 per cent of respondents could name a single cabinet minister. Thirty per cent had heard of my name somewhere (the same percentage had also heard of Joe Clark), but only 8 per cent could name me as a cabinet minister. That was better than Deputy Prime Minister Don Mazankowski, the most powerful member of the administration; only 5 per cent could name him. Five or 6 per cent thought Pierre Trudeau was a Mulroney cabinet minister.

The public's abysmal ignorance of political personalities and policies is compounded by the media's penchant for stereotyping public figures. I probably suffered more from this than most of my colleagues because I refused to act as though I'd been weaned on a pickle. I often tried to lace my remarks with humour – a few jokes, some one-liners, a little hyperbole. My audiences, both in the Commons and at my speeches in various parts of the country, enjoyed my remarks and had a few laughs. The media, however, wouldn't make the effort to listen to what I was saying or to understand what I was doing. Instead, they stereotyped me as a buffoon, an entertainer, a jokester who was incapable of taking serious matters seriously.

They also characterized me as a loose cannon because I refused to pussyfoot around issues and say only safe, predictable things. One of my passions in public life was an unwillingness to prevaricate or evade. I was committed to being honest and decisive in speech and action. It was the key to my public persona. Because I felt I had to stand up for what I believed, others concluded that I had an alarming tendency to say things that would be better left unsaid. My candour was particularly unsettling to the crowd around Brian Mulroney because it did not mesh with the image he cultivated of being a smooth, controlled, media-wary politician.

∾

I don't want to tar all media people with the same brush. There are some who are fair, unbiased observers, who understand the political process, and who see through the duplicity of many of their colleagues. Douglas Fisher, the political columnist for the *Sun* newspapers, was the best-informed, most impartial journalist in Ottawa. Another who could always be trusted to be sensible and intelligent was George Bain, who was based in Ottawa for many years, and later wrote columns from Nova Scotia. Fisher and Bain were seasoned, experienced observers. They understood better than others how the Mulroney government's policies were consciously and consistently misrepresented by the Ottawa press corps and their allies, the snivelling élitists among the cultural literati. Fisher and Bain didn't have to stoop to the dubious tactics of some of their younger colleagues, who seemed to feel they had to produce hyped-up, sensationalized stories in order to make a name for themselves.

When the media aren't stereotyping or distorting, they find time to demonstrate a breathtaking lack of principles or ethics. I was blind-sided by the media's lack of scruples shortly before the 1984 election campaign. I was on my way to a meeting of the Conservative shadow cabinet, carrying a large sheaf of documents relating to the pre-election promises made by Mulroney and the party. One of our priorities was to reduce the thirty-billion-dollar-plus deficit the Liberals had run up, but the Tory campaign promises were going to cost the Treasury several billion dollars. My staff and I had done a great deal of work on the fiscal framework and on costing out our promises. As I walked down the corridor to Mulroney's office, I didn't realize that the top document was a summary of the likely cost of the promises made to date. On my way into the meeting, I was surrounded by a scrum of at least thirty print, radio, and television reporters, and cameramen.

I stopped to answer questions. While I was looking at the faces of the journalists and responding to their questions, a female member of the pack got down on her knees in the crush and crouched by my side to read whatever she could decipher on the top sheet under my arm. If I'd thought there was any chance of such an unprincipled act, I would have buried the summary down in the pile. This reporter had quite a scoop, reporting, to our embarrassment, that the Tory promises were going to cost twenty billion dollars and pointing out how inconsistent this was with our pledge to reduce the deficit.

A similar thing happened to Marc Lalonde when he was the Liberals' Finance minister. He invited television cameras into his office for a pre-Budget "photo opportunity," and one of the cameramen filmed a page of the Budget as Lalonde was reading it. We were in Opposition then and we demanded Lalonde's resignation and generally made life miserable for him. He had to change his Budget before he read it because a page had "leaked." Lalonde was careless to hold his document where a camera could record it, but he was grossly negligent not to assume the worst of the news media.

It is revealing that no one in the press criticized either the cameraman in the Lalonde incident or the woman reporter who, in my view, stole the information about our election promises. Unfortunately, there is no code of conduct for the news media. Everything is permissible. Foul is fair. The media can use any dirty, dishonourable trick they like, and it's entirely acceptable, even commendable, in the judgement of their peers.

∾

Like a lot of ordinary Canadians, the news media are totally ambivalent, even hypocritical, about honesty in politics. They say they want honest politicians, but if they find one who actually says what he means, they turn on him. They patronize him, sneering that he may deserve high marks for candour, but none for common sense. It happened to me in the weeks before the 1984 election. When pestered by reporters in Ottawa about what programs we would cut to reduce the deficit if we were elected, I said I had no intention of telling them. "If we told you what we were going to do, you would never elect us," I said. That statement added to my notoriety. It may not have been politically helpful, but it was entirely truthful. No political party ever says in detail what they will do about government overspending, because the truth will cost them the support of voters.

The public, I'm convinced, don't want their politicians to tell them what they're really going to do. They've heard all the talk about deficits and spending cutbacks. They know that, when the election is over, there are going to be cuts. They know that whoever is elected will have no choice. But they don't want politicians telling them there will be cuts, making them face the issues, and forcing them to participate and to take responsibility for what will happen. They want the politicians to take all the responsibility. They want us to deceive them. Then, when we get elected and have to make cutbacks a few months later, the public can feel free to be outraged, to denounce deceitful politicians, and to claim we lied to them and cheated them.

The public doesn't want, won't accept, and will not support honest, forthright, and truthful politicians. They love to look down on politicians for not being truthful and straightforward. This is the underlying hypocrisy of Canadian politics and it is fed by the news media, who understand perfectly well that they are agents for the destruction of trust and candour in public life.

17

FREE TRADE

Courtesy Donato, Toronto Sun

IF THE PUNDITS ever stop kicking us around and give the historians a chance to write an objective account, they will proclaim the accomplishments of the Mulroney era. They will record that our greatest achievements lay in the field of trade. It's an incredible record. The historic free-trade agreement (FTA) with the United States. The North American Free Trade Agreement (NAFTA) with the United States and Mexico. And Canadian leadership in the international trade arena that led directly to the creation of a new World Trade Organization (WTO) to replace the old General Agreement on Tariffs and Trade (GATT).

These accomplishments were the result of inspired leadership by Prime Minister Mulroney, his willingness to risk extreme unpopularity in parts of Canada, and the hard work and negotiating skills of Canadian public servants. Canada is more dependent on foreign trade than any country in the world. The advances made by the Mulroney government will go a long way towards ensuring that Canada's economy will continue to grow, and its citizens to enjoy a rising standard of living well into the twenty-first century.

It was an exciting time to be in government, and I was in the middle of it when Mulroney, in a cabinet shuffle on March 31, 1988, shifted me from Transport to International Trade, where I succeeded Pat Carney. It was thirty-nine years to the day since Newfoundland had joined Confederation (thereby making me a Canadian) and forty years after my father, rejecting union with Canada, had led a movement in Newfoundland to create an economic union between Newfoundland and the United States. As International Trade minister, it fell to me to introduce the legislation to implement the Canada–U.S. Free Trade Agreement, to steer it through Parliament, to sell the agreement to the Canadian people, and to bring it into force. Along the way, we fought and won a general election on the issue, and faced down the Liberal-controlled Senate, which had cynically refused to pass the FTA legislation. Afterward, I was the lead minister for Canada in the early NAFTA negotiations, a sales-man for NAFTA across Canada, and minister responsible for our participation in the Uruguay Round of multilateral trade nego-tiations and for putting forward the proposal that resulted in the establishment of the WTO.

I don't know when Mulroney came to embrace free trade, but his support for the concept was revealed at his so-called Shamrock Summit with President Ronald Reagan in March 1985 in Quebec City, where the two leaders declared they would seek "a more secure climate for our mutual trade." We'd been in office for six months by then, and there had been no discussion in cabinet or in the Conservative caucus about pursuing a free-trade deal with the Americans. As far as any of us knew, Mulroney was still opposed to free trade, as he was during the 1983 Tory leadership campaign. But the Royal Commission on the Economic Union and Development Prospects for Canada, chaired by former Liberal

Finance minister Donald S. Macdonald, reported in 1985. It embraced the notion of free trade, and I think that probably helped to change Mulroney's thinking.

The reason that free trade was so controversial in parts of Canada, especially Ontario, was because of cultural ideology, not economic reasoning. Fears were fed by the little group of people that I call "the cultural literati," the encyclopedia pedlars like Mel Hurtig – people who were as nervous as virgin brides when it came to relations with the United States. But I could never see how securing our trade with the Americans – and thus ensuring our future prosperity – would endanger our independence. The province of Ontario was already selling 90 per cent of all its exports to the United States. They had the Canada–U.S. auto pact, which had turned Ontario's struggling automotive industry into an economic powerhouse, yet the Ontario government wouldn't support the free-trade agreement. Faint-hearted, they thought it would be easier for them politically if they opposed it.

Liking or disliking Americans was irrelevant. I don't care about them one way or the other. Some of them are fine, some are jerks. But I am not afraid of them and I'm not afraid to compete with them. I'm not concerned that they're going to dominate me intellectually or that somehow their culture is going to crush Canadian or Newfoundland culture. If the stuff our writers and other artists produce is any good, it will be appreciated. Our problem is a lot of our artistic output is mediocre; it's dull and boring, and people don't watch it, read it, or listen to it. But if the material we produce is interesting and of high quality, people will want it. Some of our artists don't have any confidence in themselves – that's why they want to be protected from American competition.

~

By the time I became Minister of International Trade, the agreement with the United States had been negotiated by a high-powered Canadian team headed by Simon Reisman, who was a former deputy minister of Finance. Mulroney had picked Simon for the job, and I was delighted with the choice. I'd known Reisman since I was Finance minister in the Newfoundland government. He was a man of towering ego when it came to publicity and dealing with the media. He assembled a brilliant team to conduct our negotiations.

It wasn't difficult to discern the dislike and rivalry between Reisman and Pat Carney, the minister to whom he reported. Pat was an economist and consultant by training, and a tough woman by nature. Like Reisman, she had a healthy ego. She was always outspoken, and sometimes cantankerous. She thought Simon was getting too much publicity, and she'd have knock-down fights with him in front of the cabinet committee to which the negotiators reported.

Carney was like that outside the cabinet, too. I remember an occasion while Pat was still Trade minister when we took the cabinet out to British Columbia, her province, for a meeting. A number of events were arranged while we were there. One of them was a meeting of the "500 Club," which was a transparent fund-raising gimmick. Individual Conservatives who donated one thousand dollars or more to the party got to be members of the so-called club, the idea being there would be only five hundred members, so it would be pretty exclusive and they would get special access to cabinet ministers. The party arranged a reception for the 500 Club in Vancouver, and all ministers were expected to attend. I was there, talking to Carney and to someone else, when one of her constituents approached her. This was in her own bailiwick, and the fellow was a big contributor to her campaign and to the party. She turned on him angrily and rudely. She told him not to bother her. She said she certainly wasn't going to talk to him about his problem at an affair like this, and she carried on talking to me and the other person. Pat sounded like a bad-tempered Irishwoman.

When she flew back and forth between Ottawa and Vancouver, if there wasn't a seat on the flight, she was reported likely to make a fuss at the counter and say she had to be given precedence because she was a cabinet minister. Inevitably, one of these altercations got reported in the newspapers when someone complained about being taken off a plane to make room for her. The airline later said it had acted independently in doing this. Pat liked to toss her weight around, which is the worst thing a politician can do. It's career-threatening.

She pursued me when I was Minister of Transport because she had a residence on one of the Gulf islands and she wanted me to change the commercial helicopter route between Vancouver and Victoria. The helicopters were flying over her residence and she and other residents didn't like the noise. I said I couldn't intervene to get helicopter routes changed. She was angry with me because I wouldn't protect her peace and quiet.

The Toronto *Globe and Mail* put it succinctly in its editorial comment on my appointment: "Patricia Carney's replacement by John Crosbie as trade minister reflects Miss Carney's temperamental incompatibility with charm, which is important to the selling of free trade. Mr. Crosbie certainly has the wit and vigour for that vital job."

∾

When the negotiators reached agreement on the free-trade deal in Washington, in October 1987, John Turner, the Liberal leader, denounced it immediately as a "sell-out." New Democratic Party leader Ed Broadbent warned that Canada could become part of the United States and, in his judgement, "within a quarter-century, we could be absorbed totally, lock, stock and barrel, if this is not stopped."

I thought the Opposition arguments were vacuous. They claimed we were giving away Canadian sovereignty, surrendering our independence, and creating a branch-plant mentality. The two Opposition parties and the labour movement consistently lied about the impact of the trade deal on Canada. They distorted and misrepresented its provisions. A simple lie, a simple exaggeration, or a simple allegation was far easier for ordinary people to follow than a complicated response explaining the truth. At every opportunity, I lashed back, saying the opponents of the FTA "don't think Canadians can hack it. They don't think Canadians can compete. They're subsidy seekers. They're security-blanket supplicants." In Ontario, I pointed out that, if Newfoundland could survive political and economic integration with mainland Canada without losing its distinctive culture, then Ontario and the rest of Canada could survive economic integration with the United States. In Newfoundland, we had not lost our culture, I said. "Here in Ontario, what culture are you going to lose?"

Premiers David Peterson of Ontario, Howard Pawley of Manitoba, and Joe Ghiz of Prince Edward Island also opposed the pact. Five premiers, led by Robert Bourassa of Quebec, endorsed it, while two, Brian Peckford of Newfoundland and John Buchanan of Nova Scotia, were at first uncertain. Only a small part of the agreement, involving less than 10 per cent of the trade between the countries, required provincial cooperation. The principal area was provincial control over the sale of beer, liquor, and wine.

The free-trade agreement amounted to a major change in the status quo, which made people nervous. When the opponents of change stated that the FTA was going to interfere with medicare, the social-security system, or pensions, the public was inclined to believe them. The fears of people dependent upon government are easy to arouse and hard to assuage, as the public tends to believe predictions of dire effects, no matter how far-fetched.

Within days of my appointment, I took on the alarmists in a speech to a Tory group in Ottawa. As always, I tried to speak plainly. I pointed out that "CBC-type snivellers" in Toronto were spreading alarm about the loss of Canada's cultural identity. I told my audience to beware of "the self-anointed fakirs and philosophers of Hogtown. That's where this alarmist reasoning comes from. The professional anti-Americans – envious, morally smug – that's who spreads this nonsense about our culture. We don't have to love them [the Americans] but we have to live with them."

Support of the provincial governments was not essential for the *approval* of the free-trade agreement. But it was important for the successful *implementation* of the FTA. I made every effort to persuade the provinces to agree to implement the parts of the free-trade agreement that fell under provincial jurisdiction. At the same time, I warned them that, regardless of their response, we were going to proceed, because the enabling legislation had to be passed by both Parliament and the U.S. Congress by the end of 1988 to permit the deal to take effect on January 1, 1989, as scheduled.

Ontario's Peterson, a Liberal, was my principal opponent. I considered him to be a gentleman and found him pleasant to deal with. Although we disagreed, our relationship was not at all acrimonious and, after some sparring, Ontario accepted the fact that we could legislate whatever was necessary to implement the agreement, even as it related to the sale of liquor, wine, and beer in the provinces. Ontario is the most civilized of the provinces, and the Peterson government, while vigorously opposing the signing of the FTA, calmly accepted the reality of it.

Two months after my appointment as International Trade minister, I tabled our FTA legislation in the Commons. The bill ran to 123 pages, with a long list of tariff changes. As the debate in Parliament proceeded, I hired my old leadership campaign manager, John Laschinger, to organize a sophisticated propaganda operation to sell free trade. We shipped more than thirteen million brochures and booklets across the country. When the Group of Seven industrial leaders met at their annual economic summit, they strongly welcomed the FTA. British prime minister Margaret Thatcher gave her enthusiastic personal endorsement when she addressed a joint session of Parliament in Ottawa. We staged seventeen seminars across Canada in the summer of 1988 to explain to business interests how they could boost exports to the U.S. market under free trade. We coordinated speeches at events ranging from Rotary Clubs to international gatherings anywhere in Canada.

At a seminar in Montreal, I was asked by reporters whether I had read the whole 194-page agreement, with its 2,106 clauses and 1,000 pages of tariff schedules. I told the truth. I said I hadn't read the whole thing and didn't need to read it, because I had a department full of people to read and to interpret the agreement for me. I was sure no member of the Commons or cabinet had read the FTA in its entirety. My simple admission of the obvious was pounced on by the Opposition. Indignant MPs called for my resignation. Liberal leader John Turner was so full of synthetic indignation that he could scarcely spit out his insults: "He has not read the document! What hypocrisy! What incompetence!"

I responded that I had once sold encyclopedias without reading everything in them, and vacuum cleaners without ever having vacuumed a house. I recited examples of parts of the FTA text that I had skipped over, including a complicated mathematical formula in the wheat-acreage reduction section wherein "$C = K - L/M$." When Liberal MP George Baker suggested I had never gotten past my Dick and Jane books at kindergarten, I replied that I was sorry to hear Baker's library had burned down. "He lost all two books, one of them before he finished colouring it. The other one was *Playboy*."

My problem in defending myself was that the Prime Minister, in a flight of trademark hyperbole, had not only insisted that I had read the agreement, but that he had read it, too, and so had every one of the seven world leaders who attended the G-7 economic summit in Toronto. For public consumption, I had to say that, if the Prime Minister said he'd read it, I believed him. But of course he hadn't read it. Of course, Margaret Thatcher and the rest of the G-7 leaders hadn't read it. Why would they? They're not that interested, and they haven't got the time. There wasn't one member of the Conservative cabinet, the Liberal Opposition, or the NDP Opposition that had read that whole agreement. I'd read more of it than any of them, and I understood it better. But the facts were irrelevant, it was the perception that mattered. So I was accused of another instance of Crosbie loose-cannonism. I could have lied when the question was asked in Montreal, or sloughed it off. Instead, I answered truthfully. There's a moral to this: A person cannot be truthful in politics. And that's a terrible thing. Mulroney never said a word to me about this controversy. He just sighed and set about to defend the government after another of my "outrages."

With the FTA debate in the Commons serving no useful purpose, we used our parliamentary majority to impose closure and to force the vote that approved the agreement on second reading, by 114 votes to 51. Turner, who had vowed to tear up the treaty if his party formed the next government, was vacationing at his cottage in northwestern Ontario and didn't even bother to turn up for the vote. Two weeks later, however, he announced that the Liberal majority in the Senate would not approve the free-trade legislation because the Conservatives had not had a free-trade plank in our 1984 election campaign. Liberal senators, Turner said, would not pass the bill unless we called and won a general election.

In September 1988, Mulroney called the election for November 21. It was obvious to me that the central and most important issue in the campaign would be free trade and the Senate's refusal to pass the legislation. But it wasn't that obvious to the Prime Minister and his handlers. Mulroney's strategists, slaves to their daily polling numbers, blithely pursued their campaign theme of "Managing Change," which, for banality, ranked up there with the Liberals' smugly disastrous 1972 slogan, "The Land Is Strong."

As in 1984, the Prime Minister's team, terrified of being sunk by a loose cannon, kept me on a leash. They allowed me to travel widely in the country, but only to rural areas where the national media would not follow. It was there, in small-town Canada, that I encountered the other election campaign, the one that the boys and girls in the cocoon around the leader weren't even aware existed. In every riding I visited, I found Tory candidates on the verge of panic. As they went from door to door, our candidates found the voters wanted one thing – answers. Answers to the lies the Grits and New Democrats were telling about the FTA.

Their favourite tactic was to suggest that the FTA would mean the end of medicare and most of our social-security programs. When I campaigned through Prince Edward Island, Pat Binns, our MP for Cardigan, showed me the virulent anti–free trade propaganda that was being handed out by Roman Catholic priests. (Binns lost his seat in the election; he later became premier of P.E.I.) The Liberals even spread their lies in my own backyard. Jean Payne, the Grit candidate in St. John's West, went around with a loud-speaker in front of the old folks' homes, shouting that, if the old people voted Tory, if they voted for Crosbie, they would lose their pensions because of free trade.

Everywhere I went, I found Tory candidates desperate for ammunition, for information they could use to counter the misinformation that was being spread by their opponents. But the political geniuses at campaign headquarters weren't interested in providing free-trade information. Stick to the script, they said. Follow the strategy. Stay the course. That's what our gurus said.

That's what they told me whenever I telephoned from the road to demand that the party come to the aid of the good men and women who were being clobbered by the anti–free trade rhetoric of their opponents. I remember sitting late one night in my underwear in a hotel room in Cape Breton, sipping Scotch, as I argued on the phone with Harry Near, one of Mulroney's top strategists (mere cabinet ministers weren't permitted to talk directly to the Prime Minister about the campaign). What was being done, I asked Near, to prepare our candidates for door-to-door combat on free trade? Where were the ads and the TV commercials? Where were the press hand-outs? Where were the messages from the leader? Always courteous, Near assured me there was no cause for concern. Allan Gregg's polling showed we were maintaining our lead. There was no need to panic, no reason to change strategy.

It took the leaders' debate on television to create the panic and provide the reason to change. Mulroney was blown away by

Turner, who made a direct frontal attack on free trade. Mulroney looked evasive, unsure of himself, and uncertain about his commitment to the FTA. Turner, by comparison, seemed genuine in his concerns about the evils of free trade, or so the pundits agreed. Overnight, free trade shot to the top of the list of voter concerns. The Liberals pulled even with the Conservatives in the polls, then moved ahead. With three weeks to go before the election, we found ourselves twenty points behind, with no free-trade commercials in the can and a campaign strategy that had crashed and burned.

Mulroney saved the day. He was brilliant. He broke free of the failed strategy and took control of the campaign. Because he didn't know enough about the details of the FTA, his chief of staff, Derek Burney, was put on the campaign plane to brief him about the sections of the agreement that had suddenly flared into election issues – the sections on resources and disputes resolution. Mulroney started to fight back, and he sent two of his senior ministers, Don Mazankowski and Michael Wilson, forth to publicly accuse the leading opponents of free trade of lying to the Canadian public. And Mulroney approved new television commercials, very nasty ones, that attacked Turner's credibility.

The campaign in the last three weeks became the free-trade election I had been anticipating for months. Our victory was not as huge as the one four years earlier; we won 171 seats, to 81 for the Liberals and 43 for the NDP. We lost six cabinet ministers, including Ray Hnatyshyn and Flora MacDonald. In Atlantic Canada, we lost seats, although I was declared re-elected in St. John's West fifteen minutes after the polls closed. At forty-nine, Mulroney had become the most successful Conservative prime minister since Sir Robert Borden, and the first leader of any party to win back-to-back majorities since Louis St. Laurent did it for the Liberals in 1949 and 1953.

The day after the election, Mulroney announced that Parliament would reconvene on December 12 to revive the trade legislation that had died in the Senate when the election was called. Liberal Senate leader Royce Frith confirmed that the Upper House would keep its promise to pass the legislation quickly now that we had won a fresh majority. The legislation passed both Houses in short order and we made our January 1, 1989, deadline.

Then began the detailed work of putting all the bits and pieces of the free-trade apparatus in place. I met with the new U.S. trade representative, Carla Hills, for the inaugural sitting of the Canada–U.S. Trade Commission, of which we were co-chairs. We created a select panel to discuss the auto pact, resolved a dispute over wine pricing in Ontario, and agreed on the terms of reference for joint working groups to tackle several tough issues. The only real irritant at the meeting was the continuing argument over Canadian standards for plywood. The U.S. plywood industry did not agree with the Canadian standards, which prevented the use of American-grade plywood in Canadian homes. The issue would take a year or more to sort out.

We're always complaining about the Americans, but we adopt the same kind of tactics when we have the opportunity. We had a regulation in British Columbia that prevented the sale of fresh salmon or raw herring to anyone other than Canadians. This was certainly protectionist. It was meant to protect Canadian fish processors and packers from U.S. competition, and the fishermen's union in Canada stupidly supported the regulation. Its members, the fishermen, would obviously be better off if American purchasers could compete with Canadian processors to buy their fish. But the Americans were not allowed to compete. We're just as protectionist as the Americans are.

The Americans are bully boys, everyone knows that. But they are bully boys with or without a free-trade agreement. With an agreement, we have a few better means of protecting ourselves. The more we can get world-trade rules codified, the better off we will be as the weaker partner in our relationship with the United States. Huge powers like the European Community and the United States can look after themselves. They can countervail, they can attack, they can block imports from other countries. As a middle power, it's in Canada's interest to have rules and a system for adjudicating disputes.

There are some fields where international agreements like the FTA and NAFTA don't help, because protectionist pressures are too powerful. In Canada, it's still the cultural industries and the supply-management/marketing-board system in agriculture. So the FTA wasn't a perfect agreement, but it was an improvement over what we'd had. Naturally, once the agreement was in place, its detractors tried to blame it for every plant closure and corporate takeover in Canada. The government countered this by publicizing every new or enlarged business in the country, whether actually related to the FTA or not.

∾

Just after the 1988 election, Canada hosted the mid-term meeting in Montreal of trade ministers from the 105 nations involved in the Uruguay Round of trade negotiations under the GATT. Mulroney opened the meeting and, as the host minister, I spoke after him. I used a story to illustrate the fact that, although the negotiations would be hard, I hoped that everyone would be reasonable and prepared to give a little in the interests of a settlement. I referred to a report I had come across of a dispatch sent by British prime minister George Canning to his ambassador at the Hague in the Netherlands in 1826. In it, Canning passed along some advice in verse about how to negotiate with the Dutch:

> In matters of Commerce the fault of the Dutch,
> is offering too little and asking too much.
> The French are with equal advantage content,
> so we clap on Dutch bottoms just 20 percent.

Canning was reminding his ambassador that the Dutch were hard negotiators. I thought the verse was amusing and innocuous. But one can never be too careful in diplomacy. I was informed that the Dutch trade minister, a woman, was very upset by what she considered to be my unprovoked attack on her country. To try to make amends, I sent her a bouquet of flowers, and they must have done the trick, because her ruffled feelings didn't seem to produce any lasting strain in the relations between our two countries.

At this time, Canada's chief trade negotiator was Sylvia Ostry, who was an economist and an outstanding authority on international trade. But Sylvia was also a chain-smoker, as was Arthur Dunkel, the director general of the GATT secretariat. I had to sit between Sylvia and Arthur during one of our all-night negotiating sessions in the Uruguay Round. As they puffed away on either side, I thought the second-hand smoke would kill me. I would have cheerfully agreed to anything – no concession would have been too great – just to get out of that room.

∾

One of the fringe benefits of being Minister of International Trade was the chance to travel widely in the world. Jane and I went to Japan for our first "working funeral." Emperor Hirohito had died, and we joined Governor General Jeanne Sauvé and her husband as Canada's official representatives at the funeral.

I also went to Australia to attend a ministerial meeting in Canberra of the Pacific Economic Cooperation Group, followed by a meeting in Japan of the Quadrilateral (known as "The Quad") trade ministers, representing the interests of fifteen countries (Canada, the United States, Japan, and the twelve members of the European Community) and a meeting in Thailand of the Cairns Group, composed of representatives of thirteen countries that were major exporters of agricultural goods. I led trade missions from Canada to Hong Kong and Korea, followed by visits to Germany and France.

Part of my job was to sell Canadian products, and I led a mission to Boston, where thirty Atlantic firms, eighteen of them from Newfoundland, showed off handicrafts, high-quality preserves, caribou meat, marine and fishing equipment, consulting and engineering services, shipping containers, knives, and women's work uniforms.

∽

I kept in careful touch with Carla Hills and Jaime Serra Puche, the Mexican trade minister, about possible discussions between the United States and Mexico on a new North American free-trade arrangement. There were many economic reasons why we should be involved in these discussions, the chief among them being my desire that Canada do everything it could to protect our gains in the free-trade agreement with the United States. I felt it was in Canada's interest to participate from the outset in these new trade talks, because, if we didn't get involved, we would lose the opportunity to exercise a direct influence on the negotiations. At no time was there ever any opposition that I was aware of from either Mexico or the George Bush administration in Washington to Canada's participation. In fact, the Mexicans were very keen on our participating because they felt it would help them to combat the economic might of the United States. As I pointed out at a trade meeting in Mexico, Canada and Mexico had nothing to fear since the only thing that stood between Mexico and Canada was some Hills and Bushes.

Hills and Serra Puche knew that Canadian participation in the negotiations would be a sensitive issue in Canada. Just how sensitive it was became apparent when I announced, on September 24, 1990, that our government intended to enter into three-way free-trade negotiations. A Gallup poll showed 44 per cent of Canadians opposed to the idea, and 39 per cent in favour. A Tory-dominated parliamentary committee recommended that Canada be involved in some way in the trilateral discussions. The business sector was in favour. Predictably, however, the Opposition parties, organized labour, and the familiar, dreary cast of small-minded economic nationalists who had fought tooth and nail against the FTA all came out against

Canadian involvement in what became the North American Free Trade Agreement. But they couldn't obscure the facts: with Canada, the United States, and Mexico, we would have a market of 350 million people and $6 trillion (U.S.) in annual economic output.

Liberals automatically opposed everything we did, so they opposed NAFTA. But they did it without any real conviction, because, unlike during the FTA debate, they were unable to whip up any anti-American hysteria. Once the Liberals assumed power under Jean Chrétien in 1993, they endorsed NAFTA enthusiastically and returned to their traditional stance of encouraging free-trade arrangements wherever in the world they could be entered into.

The trade unions and their political lackeys in the NDP were completely hypocritical. They tried to spread fear that Canadians would lose their jobs to low-wage Mexican workers. But there already were very few tariff barriers to Mexican goods entering Canada; 80 per cent of Mexico's exports to Canada came in duty-free. Besides, the NDP's position on NAFTA didn't square with its usual humanitarian concerns. The socialists have always been bleeding hearts, yet they didn't want to give Mexico a chance to improve its economy through freer access to the Canadian and American markets. *Cut them off*, the NDP said. *These Mexicans make lower wages than Canadian workers. Don't let struggling third-world workers compete with our comfortable Canadian workers. Don't give them a chance to better themselves economically. Don't let them enjoy a higher standard of living.*

In the United States, where there had been little or no opposition to the free-trade deal with Canada, NAFTA became a hot issue. The AFL-CIO decided to oppose it, ostensibly on the ground that American jobs would be threatened by low-wage imports. But the real reason was racial. To many working-class Americans, Mexicans are sinister, brown-skinned, Spanish-speaking, cruel, Pancho Villa–*bandido* types. Because many Americans look on Mexicans that way, it was easy to persuade them to be against NAFTA. In Canada, we're not afraid of

Mexicans. We don't live next door to them, like they do in Texas, and we're not afraid that they're going to come riding in here in their big sombreros to take away our women or our jobs. Of course, Mexicans aren't pouring into Canada as illegal immigrants. I think that explains the difference.

Once again, most of the provinces, including Quebec, supported our decision to join the North American talks. The Liberal government of Ontario was opposed, again. But the NAFTA negotiations were never as troublesome politically as the Canada–U.S. free-trade talks because they didn't rouse the same fears about domination by our huge neighbour next door.

When I was moved to Fisheries and Oceans in the April 1991 cabinet shuffle, Michael Wilson took over International Trade as well as the Department of Industry, and he concluded the NAFTA negotiations.

∾

While the negotiations for the Canada–U.S. Free Trade Agreement were winding down and the NAFTA negotiations were cranking up, the Uruguay Round negotiations for a new agreement under the GATT were going on, and on, and on. The GATT was so complicated, its issues so arcane, and its negotiations so protected that no one who had not made it a life's work could be expected to understand what was at issue. To my mind, anyone who could pick a path through the intricacies of the GATT was a genius.

The GATT, however, was at least as significant to Canada as the Canada–U.S. Free Trade Agreement. It was crucial that we, as a medium-sized country and middle power, secure our entry into other world markets, which we could not do unless there was an international organization such as the GATT to be a trade watchdog and to prevent our trading partners from setting up protectionist barriers. In the Uruguay Round, we were anxious to make sure that the European Community and the United States settled their differences over agricultural subsidies; to secure a further liberalization of trade in resource-based products; and to make a positive contribution to the harmonization of international-trade practices in the years ahead.

The Uruguay Round had been going for four years when, in March 1990, my young cousin Bill Crosbie, a lawyer who was working as an assistant to me on trade issues, prepared a memo for me on the role of the GATT after the Uruguay Round. Bill's thinking, reflecting the work that Canadian officials in External Affairs had been doing and the input they had received from trade experts around the world, was that we had to be concerned about more than just the details the negotiators were struggling with. We needed to look ahead, he suggested, to the institutional structure that the world community would require to administer the new rules that would emerge from the Uruguay Round. The GATT had many deficiencies, and Bill urged me to make it a Canadian initiative to replace the GATT with a new body, an international-trade organization, which we soon christened the World Trade Organization.

The following month I wrote to Arthur Dunkel, at the GATT; to Frans Andriessen, vice-president of the European Commission; and to Carla Hills, of the United States, and Taro Nakayama, of Japan, to propose the creation of the World Trade Organization. A few days later, I went to Switzerland to unveil this Canadian initiative at a press conference in Geneva, where the GATT was based.

The GATT was created in 1947 as a temporary secretariat to regulate international trade in goods; it was given few powers and, forty-three years later, it was still operating under a provisional agreement with a total staff of fewer than one hundred. After the Second World War, the industrial nations had proposed that there be an international-trade organization (ITO) to function alongside the International Monetary Fund and World Bank. This proposal for an ITO had fallen by the wayside when the U.S. Congress refused to ratify its charter, and by necessity the less ambitious GATT had taken its place. If the Uruguay Round succeeded and a whole new series of substantial rules was put in place covering services, intellectual property, and investment, the inadequate GATT structure would have to be replaced.

Without a World Trade Organization to monitor and regulate international trade, individual countries would continue to take matters into their own hands, make their own rules, and devise their own rewards and punishments. The superpowers could look after themselves, but Canada and most other smaller nations needed an effective multilateral trading system to help balance the scales, lay down common principles and rules, and ensure that both large and small nations lived up to their commitments.

My officials prepared a comprehensive reform package and a timetable for its approval and implementation. Our WTO would feature a better system of settling disputes – one that could impose binding settlements, rather than rely on consensus. It was obvious that international trade had become too big to be managed by seat-of-the-pants policy and supervision.

After Dunkel decided to support my initiative, I formally presented it at a meeting of trade ministers from twenty-eight GATT countries in Puerto Vallarta, Mexico. Carla Hills also endorsed the creation of the WTO, although our colleagues from Japan and the European Community were less enthusiastic initially. Once the Uruguay Round negotiations were successfully concluded, everyone agreed to create the World Trade Organization. Even the U.S. Congress ratified it. The WTO came into being at the end of 1993. It's a great achievement, a Canadian achievement. It was my initiative and I'm proud of its success.

∾

In May 1990, I went to a Quad meeting held in Napa, California. Some months earlier, Carla Hills had asked for my advice as to where the United States might arrange to hold the next meeting and, knowing she was from California, I suggested the Napa Valley would be ideal. I had an ulterior motive. My wife,

Jane, had a married sister in Napa, and her mother and several other sisters also lived nearby. At this meeting it was decided that the next one, to be hosted by Canada, would take place in St. John's. When the time came, we took the visiting trade ministers on a helicopter ride over St. John's and out along the southern part of the Avalon Peninsula so they could see moose and caribou, as well as the scenic outports that are strung along the Southern Shore. At the end of the tour, the helicopters landed at Beachy Cove, where I hosted a dinner for my guests at the magnificent home of our friends Craig Dobbin and Elaine Parsons on the cliffs looking across Conception Bay to Bell Island. The house is a real showplace, with a magnificent collection of Newfoundland and Canadian art.

At the meeting in St. John's, Hills properly singled out the Canadian system of supply management, or marketing boards, as an example of protectionist farm policy that all countries must dismantle if the Uruguay Round was to succeed. This was a very sensitive issue in Canada. We defended our own supply-management system while simultaneously battling for the elimination of agricultural subsidies in other countries, particularly members of the European Community. We didn't want any unfair interference with our sales of Canadian wheat and other agricultural products abroad, but we had a supply-management system that prevented any foreign country from selling milk, eggs, broilers, or products like these into Canada. It's a system in which dairy, poultry, and egg production in Canada is matched to domestic consumption, and the balance is maintained by restricting imports.

I argued that we intended to continue our supply-management system and denied that our refusal to change the system could precipitate the failure of the trade talks. The Japanese trade minister, Kabun Muto, continued to defend his country's import ban on rice.

The agricultural policy of most nations is not rational, but political, and a tribute to the power of farmers. Canada is no exception. We squander billions of dollars every year on a system that succeeds in two perverse endeavours at once. It raises food prices for consumers and it depresses the commodity prices paid to farmers.

In the early 1990s, it cost about $8.8 billion a year to subsidize Canadian farmers. Wheat farmers received about $2.4 billion of that, with dairy farmers receiving $2.2 billion, and beef growers $808 million. The support continued in the form of price-fixing and supply-rigging by the marketing boards, together with a thick wall of quotas and tariffs against competing imports.

The purpose of this supply-management system is to permit thirty thousand or forty thousand farmers to bleed the rest of the Canadian public and get prices for milk, butter, chickens, and hogs that are two or three times as high as they would otherwise be. The consumers are such suckers! They sit by and they never say a word. They aren't organized. They don't fight. The farmers are well organized, particularly the dairy farmers in Quebec. They've got every elected member from Quebec terrified that they'll be defeated if the supply-management system is tampered with in any way. And these Quebec dairy farmers are separatists. The executives of the groups representing the dairy farmers are all out campaigning for separation, while we, fools that we are, go nuts trying to keep the supply-management system intact to protect them. It's really amazing!

It's not much better in Newfoundland. We're not really an agricultural province and we barely have a farming industry. Yet our farmers are so well organized that we have a supply-management system in Newfoundland with huge subsidies to farmers from the provincial and federal governments – and nobody complains. It's a demonstration of how small numbers properly organized can dominate the scene.

If we took away the subsidies, the price-fixing, and the supply-rigging, the best of our Canadian farmers would compete successfully, and those who couldn't compete would go under, as they should. Look at Albania, Burma (now known as Myanmar), and North Korea: their economic systems are a shambles and they are neither productive nor competitive – but they have complete protection.

∾

As 1991 began, Jane and I went on a trade mission to Thailand, spending the New Year's holiday in Bangkok, which is one of the most delightful cities in South-East Asia. We went on to Vietnam, which I was the first Canadian cabinet minister to visit in many years. Hanoi was an entirely new experience for us. The Vietnamese people led a very difficult existence, yet their country was opening up to the world, and the state was beginning to ease its grip on every aspect of their lives. It was clear that Vietnam was poised for the same rapid economic growth and wealth creation that had been experienced earlier by other South-East Asian nations. I wanted Canada to be in at the beginning of Vietnam's economic rebirth so that we could exploit the trade and investment opportunities that would be created.

Unfortunately, after several days in Hanoi, I heard from Canada that my brother, Andrew, had died. Andrew had had lung cancer for some time and was battling the disease with great courage when we left St. John's. When I heard of his death, I flew immediately to Saigon, where I caught an Air France flight to Paris, then on to Toronto, and finally to St. John's. The trip took thirty-six hours, but I arrived in time to deliver the eulogy at the funeral.

Andrew and I had had our political differences, but, by and large, he had stuck with me and supported me. I admired him as the kind of adventurous businessman that Newfoundland must have if we are ever to pull ourselves out of our state of dependency. As the *St. John's Evening Telegram* put it in an editorial: "Driven by the belief that Newfoundland could be a better place, he dedicated his life and talents to building up the province and his native city."

Andrew had suffered serious business reversals at the beginning of the 1980s, primarily as a result of overexpansion at a time when interest rates soared past 20 per cent. He was into the Canadian Imperial Bank of Commerce and the Bank of Montreal for very large amounts, and he couldn't keep up with the interest. Crosbie Offshore was making a barrel of money working for oil companies like Mobil Oil, but he had to give the money he made there to the banks to keep them quiet on his other loans. When the bank took back one of the vessels operated by his Chimo Shipping, it was the beginning of the end. Andrew managed to keep all the balls in the air for another year or so, but eventually a lot of his businesses went into bankruptcy. He was too shrewd to lose everything, however. Andrew had family trusts, he was able to continue living on his estate, and his family didn't fare too badly when he died.

Andrew had been a tremendous drinker in his day, and this was very noticeable at the time of his business reverses. He'd go off drinking for three or four days at a stretch. We'd never see Andrew staggering around; but he could drink a couple of bottles of hard liquor a day and still walk a straight line. I always figured he was an alcoholic, because our father was. Andrew was a great admirer of our father, so if Dad had some kind of a fault, Andrew would have the same fault.

Andrew's death meant I was now the only surviving child of Ches and Jessie Crosbie. Our older sister, Joan, had died ten years earlier, when she fell down the basement stairs at our mother's house and broke her neck. Joan had a tragic life. She was an alcoholic and, after her second marriage broke up, she moved back in with Mom, which was where she was living when the accident happened.

∾

These were years of great achievement by the Mulroney government on trade matters, but they were also years of great controversy over domestic issues. Our agenda was too full and, inevitably, the government's popularity suffered. Everybody hated the Goods and Services Tax, and everybody got upset about the Meech Lake constitutional accord.

The Liberals, obviously having learned nothing from the showdown over the free-trade legislation two years earlier, were prepared to use their majority in the Senate to block the GST. For the first time in history, Mulroney resorted to a little-known constitutional provision that enabled him to pack the Senate by adding eight new seats to give us the votes we needed. In our view, democracy was at stake, but unfortunately this view was not shared by the public. The pollsters found Canadians to be more upset about the GST and by the Prime Minister's handling of the affair than they were about the powers of the appointed Senate.

If the government had succeeded on Meech Lake, I think we could have survived to win a third term. But too many things were coming at us too close together – and we'd spent so much of our political capital on free trade that we had none left for Meech Lake.

18

Pass the Tequila, Sheila

MY FRIEND AND cabinet colleague Barbara McDougall – who served with distinction in several portfolios in the Mulroney administration, including External Affairs – put her finger on my problem. "Mr. Crosbie," she said, commenting on one of my frequent scrapes with the forces of political correctness, "is a man who often says the wrong thing and does the right thing."

My penchant for saying the wrong thing at the wrong time got me in trouble more often than I care to recall during my nine years in the federal cabinet. I've lost track of the number of times that someone – an opportunistic Opposition MP, a strident special interest group, or a sanctimonious media commentator, among others – demanded that I resign or be fired. I'm sure Brian Mulroney would like to forget how frequently he was called on to defend me, apologize for me, or remonstrate with me for something I said that offended someone somewhere. Anyone following my adventures through the news media could

330

be excused for concluding that there wasn't an identifiable group in society that I had neglected to insult, from women to Afro-Canadians to vertically challenged Newfoundlanders. As the media saw it, John Crosbie was always a good story, especially when he said something they thought was stupid or ill-considered – or something they could twist to make it sound more outrageous than it was.

It is one of the paradoxes of my career that so many people, as Barbara McDougall suggested, heard the wrong things I said but failed to see the right things I did. I was not a troglodyte. I was not a reactionary or a right-winger. My record was among the most progressive, if not *the* most progressive, of any member of the Mulroney cabinet. I appointed more female judges than any previous Minister of Justice. I reformed Canada's divorce law to make it much easier for women to get out of unworkable marriages, and I changed the support system to assist women to track down deadbeat ex-spouses and to collect the financial support to which they and their children were legally entitled. I stopped discrimination against women in the armed forces, and I brought in legislation to prevent the exploitation of women and children by the pornography pedlars. I introduced a human-rights amendment to make it illegal to discriminate against a person on the basis of his or her sexual orientation. Although the amendment did not pass at the time, I was one of the first cabinet ministers who had the guts to publicly take up the cause of gays and lesbians. In addition, as the minister responsible for the Atlantic Canada Opportunities Agency, I supported the special needs of women in business, and I saw to it that qualified women were appointed to federal boards, agencies, and commissions. I doubled the number of Newfoundland women who held federal patronage positions; by 1993, 31 per cent of all such positions for Newfoundlanders were occupied by women.

My problem was that I refused to play the political-correctness game as it was practised by the obnoxious National Action Committee on the Status of Women and other interest groups that thought they had a monopoly on virtue, wisdom, and human decency. I was determined to be myself, to stand up for what I believed, and to say my piece the way I wanted to say it. A lot of people, some of them Conservatives, agreed with me until my words created a controversy, and then they ran for cover. I have little use for cowards and hypocrites.

As long as I have breath, I will not bow to the enforcers of thought and speech control. The arrogance of the politically correct censors, many of them professional feminists, was illustrated by the American black radical Angela Davis, who, when asked in 1971 why "PCers" would not even listen to other points of view, said: "How can there be an opposing argument to an issue which has only one correct side?"

∽

Sheila Copps was not a black American radical. She was a white Canadian Liberal, but that didn't stop her from bringing the same sort of arrogance, intolerance, and closed-mindedness to her career that Angela Davis brought to hers. Sheila was one of the leading champions of the constipating doctrine of political correctness in the House of Commons, which meant she spent an inordinate amount of her time and energy trying to score points at the expense of the Commons' most vigorous foe of political correctness – John C. Crosbie. I disagreed with almost everything Copps stood for, and I deplored her Rat Pack tactics, but she was a worthy antagonist and we had some celebrated clashes.

First elected to Parliament from Hamilton East in 1984, after three years in the Ontario legislature, Copps was an aggressive Opposition MP, pushy, loud, raucous, and well able to handle herself in debate. She attracted a great deal of attention one day when she hurdled a row of committee-room chairs in angry pursuit of my cabinet colleague Sinc Stevens. On another occasion, she called Mulroney a "slime bag" in the Commons. A charter member of the Liberals' Rat Pack in the Commons, she was one of the Press Gallery's favourite MPs.

Sheila's big problem was that, like so many others of her femi-nist ilk, she had no sense of humour. She displayed this deficiency one day in 1985 when she was harassing me noisily in the Commons, and I told her, "Just quiet down, baby." She could have taken my somewhat anachronistic instruction in the light-hearted vein in which I uttered it, but she chose instead to treat it as an insult to her personally, and to Canadian womanhood generally. The next year, at the tender age of thirty-four, she published her autobiography and called it *Nobody's Baby*. On the dust jacket, she proclaimed herself to be a spokeswoman for a new breed of politician and a new generation of women, "daring, dedicated and demanding of a new standard of public life." In the final paragraph in her book, Sheila stated: "Women are moving forward, in politics and in life. 'You've come a long way, baby,' as the saying goes. But until all of us are 'nobody's babies,' we won't have come nearly far enough."*

My staff bought me a copy of this seminal, if precocious, auto-biography and arranged for Copps to sign it. She did, with an inscription: "To John, from the bottom of my gritty heart, with no cod tongue in cheek or jowl, have a great Christmas with Jane and the family – as long as your good fortune doesn't proceed too far into the new year. Liberally, Sheila."

I had a run-in with Sheila during the 1988 federal election campaign. I was invited to debate free trade at Simon Fraser University in Vancouver. Michael Walker, an economist with the Fraser Institute, and I argued in support of the Canada–U.S. Free Trade Agreement, while Copps and a Saskatchewan farmer argued against. The gymnasium was packed with hundreds of eager students, all in a boisterous mood. As it happened, Sheila was late arriving, and after twenty minutes we started without her. I was the first speaker and, in my opening remarks, I explained that Sheila had been "delayed because of a mechani-cal breakdown in her broom."

---

* *Nobody's Baby: A Survival Guide to Politics* (Toronto: Deneau Publishers, 1986).

When she arrived and was told about my joke, she took great offence, even raising it later as a question of privilege in the Commons. The advocates of political correctness can't take a joke!

My most celebrated encounter with Copps occurred in early 1990. It made the CBC national television news for two nights running, which says something about the news judgement of television producers. I'd spent several days in Vancouver on government business, and Jane and I stayed at the Pan-Pacific Hotel. When we left the Pan-Pacific, I went to Victoria to speak at a Tory association fund-raiser. It was a thoroughly partisan crowd, and they expected me to flay some skin off the Liberals. Never being one to disappoint a friendly crowd, I spent some time satirizing the various candidates who were running at that time for the Liberal leadership to replace John Turner.

Poking fun at Jean Chrétien, I quoted the Frenchman Alexandre Leduc-Rollin, who said at the time of the Paris revolt of 1848: "There go the people. I must follow them for I am their leader." When I came to Sheila Copps, who was also a leadership candidate, I suddenly remembered Johnny Cash singing "Tequila, Sheila." The words of the chorus popped into my head and I said them: "Pass me the tequila, Sheila, and lie down and love me again." The audience laughed, taking this light-hearted remark in the spirit of good fun, as I had intended. At the end of my speech, I got an enthusiastic ovation. My cabinet colleague Mary Collins, the associate Defence minister, who had just been given additional responsibility for the status of women, thanked me, telling the crowd I had been "absolutely marvellous, as always."

I'm sure Mary regretted having said that when the feminist zealots and professional purveyors of political correctness went berserk. CBC had a camera crew at the meeting and taped my remarks, highlighting "Tequila, Sheila" on the national news. Jane and I didn't see the news that night, but we thought people looked at us oddly as we hurried to catch a flight back to Ottawa the next morning. At the airport in Ottawa, I was met by a pack of reporters and cameramen, all anxious to ask me about my

Victoria speech and get my response to all the usual censorious people who had been denouncing me while we flew back across the country.

"John's Joke Bombs," shouted the headline in the *Ottawa Sun*. The first paragraph stated: "An off-colour 'joke' hurled by Trade Minister John Crosbie at Liberal leadership hopeful Sheila Copps has outraged women, sparked demands for his resignation and left Crosbie wondering what all the fuss is about." The story went on to report that the National Action Committee on the Status of Women was outraged. Since this group was outraged at every action of the Tory government, even when the government did what NAC suggested, their "outrage" didn't strike me as news. A NAC spokesman, Janet Maher, sent Mulroney a letter demanding that I be fired and claiming that my "Tequila, Sheila" remark "is part of the same 'culture of misogyny' that led to the massacre of women in Montreal."

It seemed to me – and I think any fair-minded observer would agree – that to draw a connection between my joking reference to a Johnny Cash song and the actions of the man who had murdered fourteen women at the École Polytechnique in Montreal strained logic beyond the breaking-point.

Mulroney, under siege by the media, said that he would look into the affair. Copps, naturally, took full advantage, saying she didn't want an apology because she'd had her share of apologies from me and they hadn't yielded anything. My remark, she said, had been "typical Crosbie . . . the ongoing saga of the running mouth. . . . Maybe this is a Freudian cry for help to get him out of politics." For Copps to take advantage of the uproar was a perfectly natural part of the political process. But all the other professional feminists jumped on the bandwagon. New Democrat MP Lynn Hunter said her party would demand an official apology – "What that statement says is, 'Give a woman a couple of drinks, and . . .'" Mary Clancy, a Liberal MP from Halifax, demanded that I apologize to all Canadian women for my "unacceptable sexist comment." The affair, Clancy said, "just shows that from the backbenches to the senior levels of cabinet, this

Government has no commitment to gender equality." In a vain attempt to calm the hurricane of feminist fury, I issued a statement saying I had aimed no insult at Copps or anyone else and I regretted it if I had offended anyone.

Of the thousands of speeches I made in twenty-seven years in public life, the "Tequila, Sheila" speech in Victoria generated the most publicity and controversy. Depressingly, it appears to be the incident for which I am best remembered. I am still given bottles of tequila as a token of gratitude when I speak to groups around the country. The problem is, I'm a Scotch drinker.

Later, when I had a chance to obtain all the words to "Tequila, Sheila," I found they told quite a story. The Sheila of the song had a red satin dress and was invited to the hotel room of a gambler who lived on the Mexico–United States border. He'd just won a card game and had a great deal of gold. Hearing footsteps outside the room, he discovered the place was crawling with "damn *federales*." He believed that Sheila had tipped off the *federales* to his whereabouts. He couldn't make love to a squealer, so he suggested that Sheila remove her red dress and put on his clothes. He sent her out of the room into the hands of the *federales*, while he ran out the back and rode for the border. People who took the trouble to look up the lyrics became even more enraged with me.

Most of the nation's editorialists, ever willing to afflict the afflicted, wrote that they were shocked to their tiny cores. The *Ottawa Sun* lectured me: "Not funny, John Crosbie. Gratuitous, sexist, insulting and sleazy. But not funny." "The amazing amount of outrage whipped up by Crosbie's gaffe is not, as he suggested in his public apology, evidence of a slow news week," wrote the *Ottawa Citizen*. "What it does show is that many Canadian women feel oppressed, abused and victimized and that these feelings demand much more serious consideration." The Montreal *Gazette* was equally perturbed: "It is simply not acceptable for persons holding high public office to make remarks – 'humorous' or otherwise – that play on people's origin or on racial, religious or other stereotypes. . . . This particular joke was not even of the tiresome but familiar class of humour denigrating mothers-in-law, women drivers and so on. This joke played on dangerously dark stereotypes and fantasies."

In retrospect, "Tequila, Sheila" may have been in bad taste, but most of the press reaction was moralistic nonsense – an abject surrender to those who would censor people on the basis of what is deemed to be correct or incorrect to say. It didn't matter what I'd done for women. I had failed to adhere to the precepts of the fanatics who run the feminist movement. They didn't care whether I was sympathetic to women. They were only concerned with appearances.

A Conservative MP from Quebec wrote a letter to the Speaker of the Commons asking for an emergency debate on my remarks. Pressured from all sides, Mulroney termed my joke "unacceptable," but he said he would not fire me over it. "If you got rid of all the politicians that put their feet in their mouths, there wouldn't be a single person sitting in the House of Commons," the Prime Minister said.

The real beneficiary of the "Tequila, Sheila" flap was Copps herself; it gave her leadership campaign a needed boost. Female politicians like her try to have it both ways. Even though they are just as aggressive, ruthless, and insensitive as men, they trade on the fact that they are women, and seek public sympathy by levelling the allegation of sexism against any man who dares to ridicule them or poke fun at them. In an interview with Barbara Yaffe of the *Vancouver Sun*, Jane defended me, arguing sensibly that women cannot consider themselves liberated or equal until they learn to laugh at themselves and their sex. I also took some solace from a verse sent to me by an anonymous sympathizer:

John Crosbie asked his friend Sheila
For some love and a shot of Tequila.
Job-wise he was blessed, he made his request,
For Tequila to Sheila not Mila!

Some years later, when Sheila turned forty, her staff asked if I would send a humorous message to be read at her birthday celebration. I made up a rhyme and sent it off:

To Sheila on Her Fortieth

I regret that Ms. Sheila Copps
Always pops when she hears my bon motts,
Throws feminist fits at my sexist bits.
Gets very shrill if I mention the pill,
Gets very irate when I'm not acting straight,
When I pass the Tequila she isn't my Sheila,
She hollers and squealers.
So –
Let's switch to good Rye, and
Here's mud in your eye.
Happy Birthday Ms. Copps
From the guy from the Rocks.

∽

Jane and I have another reason – besides "Tequila, Sheila" – to remember that 1990 trip to Vancouver and Victoria. After we got back to Ottawa, I received a letter from Glen Silliphant, from Saskatchewan, to say that he had recently attended a home builders' convention in Vancouver at the Pan-Pacific. He'd sent a shirt to the hotel laundry but, when his laundry came back, the shirt had the name "Crosbie" printed on the collar. The night I was speaking in Victoria, he and his wife went to a ball in Vancouver. When they returned to their room, they flipped on the news and caught a close-up of me making my infamous speech. Mrs. Silliphant took one look and declared: "Mr. Crosbie is wearing your shirt!"

Glen suggested I check to see if the label said "Bellissimo." (It did.) He was not, he wrote, particularly concerned about the shirt and would not resort to any clichés about the government taking the shirt off the back of its citizens. He added that he would be pleased to let me keep his shirt for good luck, although he was not sure I'd want it after the uproar I'd created while wearing it.

I returned his shirt and wrote back saying that I was holding the shirt to blame for "Tequila, Sheila" – remarks I surely would not have uttered if I hadn't been imprisoned inside a strange shirt that had unbalanced my mental processes. (Meanwhile, the Pan-Pacific Hotel sent my shirt back to me.)

∾

My adventures in the swamp of political correctness weren't confined to brushes with Sheila Copps. A year or so before I left politics, I received a cheque for eight thousand dollars from the federal Department of the Secretary of State to deliver to an association in Newfoundland. The group was called the Newfoundland Association for the Short-Statured. I'd never heard of this group before, but two representatives came to my office in St. John's to pick up the cheque. They were what I'd always heard described as dwarfs or midgets. However, the terms "midget" and "dwarf" are no longer acceptable, hence the replacement term "short-statured." The same doublespeak applies to the "crippled" who are now "physically challenged" – and don't be so foolhardy as to call them "handicapped" – and to the formerly "mentally retarded" who are now "developmentally delayed," and so on.

Some time later, I noticed a Canadian Press report: "'Short-statured' activists are urging Newfoundland's sports groups to describe players without using the M-word. That word is 'midget,' a term linked to 'freak shows' and horror films by the short-statured people of Newfoundland. Members of the group, all under 4 foot 10 inches for reasons such as dwarfism, say players should be classed by age. In the opinion of John Dunn, who stands 4 foot 1 inch, 'midget' is a derogatory term. There's a stigma attached to the name."

The association was demanding that the Newfoundland Sports Federation change the name of midget hockey, the designation given to players aged sixteen and seventeen. The people who ran the minor-sports organizations were dumbfounded – and so was I. They thought they'd been doing tremendous things for youth over the years by organizing midget soccer, midget hockey, and other sports, and suddenly they were being attacked by dwarfs. What nonsense!

Remembrance Day or Armistice Day provides another illustration of the way we cower before the forces of political correctness. I couldn't get used to the disquieting spectacle of politicians wearing poppies in their lapel for a full month before November 11 and for a couple of weeks after. Frankly, they were afraid that if they took the wretched poppy off, people would think they weren't patriotic, didn't care about veterans, or didn't appreciate the sacrifice that our brave men made to save Canada for democracy.

I also remember the flap when I was given the second annual Colin M. Brown Freedom Medal by the National Citizens Coalition, which as far as most of the politically correct media were concerned was a right-wing group. There's a real double standard in Canada. If someone is a Liberal or a New Democrat, and some do-gooding association wants to give him or her an award for advancing feminist causes, for supporting gay or lesbian rights, or for watching the CBC religiously every day, well, that's just marvellous. There's not a word of criticism. But if a person is a Conservative and some presumed right-wing outfit wants to give him or her an award, that person is portrayed as fascist, as worse than Franco. He or she shouldn't accept the award. That's what happened with my National Citizens Coalition award. It was worth ten thousand dollars and, although I gave the money to charity, I was harshly criticized by Opposition MPs and by addled editorialists for accepting the award at all.

～

I suppose I should have learned, but I got in trouble again when I accepted an invitation to speak at a $150-a-plate fund-raiser for the provincial Conservative party in Prince Edward Island. In my remarks to the four hundred Tory supporters, I spoke about the economy of the Atlantic provinces and the improvements as a result of the policies of the Conservative government in Ottawa. I said the number of people living below the poverty line in Canada had decreased significantly since we took office, "and that includes 297,000 fewer children and 333,000 fewer adult women, if there are any." I went on: "Oh, God, I'm in trouble now," noting that there were 955,000 more women working than there were when we took office – "Is it any wonder we're in trouble with women?" I thought this was a pretty feeble attempt to kid feminists, who take themselves so seriously, and I didn't anticipate that anyone would find my words offensive. But I was wrong.

The leader of the P.E.I. party at the time was a woman, Pat Mella. She had invited me to be the guest speaker at their fund-raising dinner because she hoped to attract more people and to collect more funds. I had agreed to take time out from my other activities to assist her. The event was a great success; my speech was well received. But, the next morning, a local CBC commentator decided to make an issue of my remarks about women, and soon calls were pouring in from people who felt it would be politically correct to be upset about my speech. The provincial women's network called on me to apologize or resign. The P.E.I. Federation of Labour demanded that I apologize to all Islanders and to all women in Canada.

The CBC, declaring I was in trouble again, then looked for comment in Newfoundland. Tory MHA Lynn Verge, who later became the provincial leader, accommodated them by saying I should apologize. "I can't say I'm surprised, but I'm disappointed. You'd think by now John Crosbie would know better, but he seems to persist. He's not the only one and there's an audience out there for sexist remarks. That's why we have a women's movement."

Back in P.E.I., Mella went into contortions trying to distance herself from me. At first, she said she wasn't offended by my remarks and that she didn't think I meant them to be taken seriously. Then, with the fuss mounting, she went on television to say she regretted that she had not confronted me after the speech, but she said she did phone my office to convey her concern. "I said that the remark was offensive and it was seen as being offensive to women."

Mella went on to explain to the news media that I was known as a loose cannon and that she could not control what I said. She agreed with my critics that my comments perpetuated the kind of attitudes towards women that needed to be changed. Finally, Mella wrote a grovelling letter to Wayne Collins, the CBC commentator who had started the snowball rolling, in which she said, among other things, that "Mr. Crosbie can answer for himself and I feel no obligation whatsoever to defend him whether he is a member of my party or not."

I was amazed at this example of ingratitude and political cowardice on the part of our provincial leader. I had gone out of my way to help her to raise sixty thousand dollars, and she had joined with the censorious paragons of virtue who were attacking some incidental and harmless remarks. When I needed some assistance to defend myself, Mella had instead joined my opponents in heaping calumny on me. Mella's and Verge's conduct suggested that the rules of politics have changed. Feminism now takes precedence over party loyalty. Female politicians seem to believe that a special set of rules applies to them, and they never need to rally to the defence of members of their party if the issue involves women.

∞

One evening in October 1992, I had another experience that brought home to me the changes in politics over the past three decades. One of the principles when I entered politics was that, if politicians had a private conversation, it was confidential.

They didn't go out and quote each other or attack each other over what they'd said in private. However, with the new emphasis on the participation of women in politics, organized feminism, the rise of a huge number of special interest groups, and the new spirit of political correctness, anything could happen.

I was campaigning in Newfoundland for support for the Charlottetown constitutional accord. The National Action Committee on the Status of Women, headed by Judy Rebick, was campaigning vigorously against it. As I walked through St. John's airport, I saw Rebick. She waved and motioned for me to join her and two or three other women. They started to question me about why NAC or other women's groups were not represented at the constitutional bargaining table when all of the first ministers and representatives of Native groups were there. Knowing it was a private conversation, I spoke bluntly: "We can't have women represented at the bargaining table on the Constitution since, if we did, the next thing would be that we would have to have all of the other special interest groups, including the cripples and coloureds."

I would never have used "cripples and coloureds" in public, but instead would have employed such sanitized terminology as "physically challenged" and "Afro-Canadians." Neither Rebick nor her companions made any complaint about my choice of language. The next day, however, Rebick told a public forum in Halifax that I had said to her: "We can't have women representing themselves or the next thing you'll know we'll have to have the cripples and coloureds."

"I was horrified," Rebick said. "Sure, I guess he meant it as a joke, just as he meant 'Pass the Tequila, Sheila,' as a joke. But it was a racist, anti-disability, and sexist remark and it was showing contempt for the majority of people in this country, and if that's even in his mind as a federal politician, we've got some serious problems." What Rebick did was deplorable, inaccurate, and vicious. When I was asked by the press for comment, I said it was despicable to finagle somebody into a private conversation, then use it against him publicly by twisting his meaning and trying to make it appear that he had an offensive attitude towards crippled or coloured people. Of course, I took a beating in the press again.

I suppose I should have expected this kind of attack. I had no use for militant feminists and I thought NAC and their friends were uncivilized fanatics. I wouldn't raise a finger to help the feminist movement. If I was leading the government, I would cut off every cent of assistance that goes to these associations. One of the mistakes the Mulroney administration made was to financially support special interest groups who spent all their time attacking the government and its programs. That was the worst kind of foolishness.

∾

The "cripples and coloureds" was bad, but there was worse to come. In early 1993, I made a speech to the Lewisporte Chamber of Commerce in Newfoundland. The government had tabled amendments to the Unemployment Insurance legislation. At that time there was an $8.5-billion deficit in the UI fund, and the need for reforms to the UI system was obvious. The major change we were proposing was to deny UI benefits to people who voluntarily quit their job without any reasonable or just cause. Unemployment insurance is meant to be insurance against becoming unemployed for some cause beyond a person's control, such as being laid off by an employer who has no more work for him or her. However, if a person voluntarily gives up a job, then there is absolutely no reason for him or her to be paid unemployment insurance. Hundreds of millions of dollars would be saved every year by cutting off the voluntary quitters. But our amendments made it clear that an employee could be found to be a voluntary quitter only if it was clear that he or she had no reasonable or just cause for resigning. Sexual harassment constituted a reasonable or just cause for quitting.

Despite this, both the Liberals and New Democrats spent weeks arguing, falsely, that our changes would make women across the country vulnerable because thousands of them would likely quit their jobs because of sexual harassment and would lose their UI benefits.

In my speech at Lewisporte to a mixed audience of men and women, I dealt with economic issues, including the UI changes. I pointed out the fraudulent nature of the Opposition argument about sexual harassment. Then I got in trouble. "Apparently just about everybody who quits their job is being sexually harassed. We must have one hell of a lot of attractive people working," I said, and the crowd laughed. "If this is the case, I have to admit to you that I have never been sexually harassed myself. [Laughter] . . . If I were, I would certainly want to make it known [laughter] that I had been so favoured."

The CBC was present and broadcast my remarks about sexual harassment. The results were predictable – another uproar in the Commons that lasted for several days, more cries for my resignation. The NDP women's critic, Dawn Black, called me a "Crosbiesaurus." Sheila Copps condemned me. "It's just indicative of an attitude that sexual harassment is not to be taken seriously. I'm just frankly disgusted," she said. Of course, NAC's Rebick joined the throng demanding my head.

Rebick and others said my comments showed I didn't understand that sexual harassment is humiliating, not flattering. On reflection, I have to agree. This was a valid criticism of my comments, but the Opposition parties had spent weeks suggesting there was an epidemic, hundreds of thousands of cases, where women were leaving their jobs because of sexual harassment. That did more damage to the public's understanding of sexual harassment than my remarks in Lewisporte did.

The women who had attended the meeting in Lewisporte, when contacted by the press, almost invariably took the same position as grocery-store owner Jessie Green, who said that neither she nor any other woman at the meeting was offended by my comments. She said they weren't derogatory – "The joke was not meant to downgrade women. It was about the UIC." Betty Clark, the mayor of Lewisporte, told the CBC: "I wasn't offended by Mr. Crosbie's comments. I think one would have to hear his speech and the remarks leading up to it. But, you know, the remarks that were on the radio just highlighted some portion of his speech. So it was, his comments were, you know, he was making light of it and it was done in good taste in my opinion." She pointed out that I had talked quite extensively about the Women's Enterprise Bureau and had praised women for starting small businesses in Canada, often without any financial assistance from government.

I issued a statement, but no apology. I said I had made a joke about myself and the remark had been taken out of context. But the Opposition did not let up. Questioned by Sheila Copps, Mulroney came to my defence brilliantly. He agreed the issue of sexual harassment was a most serious one, and the government viewed it as such. He said no one had provided stronger leadership and greater commitment to solving the genuine problems confronting women than I had as Minister of Justice. The Prime Minister quoted two women who had heard my speech in Lewisporte. Betty Granter, a provincial government clerk, said, "It was nothing like what has been said. Mr. Crosbie was just joking, as he always does. I think anybody who was offended by it must have a problem." A Mrs. Stevenson said, "I guess it would be damaging if people thought on the whole that sexual harassment was a joke and people did not take it seriously, but that is not the way it was intended and that is not the way the people at the dinner in Newfoundland took it."

Mulroney put his case cogently:

From time to time all members of parliament, perhaps spontaneously, make a statement, a paragraph or a line or two that we would like to take back because it conveys an impression that we did not really have. But there is a sense of humour in politics that is sometimes misplaced if misconstrued. The people in the audience said that John Crosbie was not in any way trying to do anything other than treat himself in a jocular fashion, not the question of sexual harassment. That is the difference between the women in Newfoundland who heard the speech and the position of the Honourable Member who today is trying to distort it.

My office received a total of 279 letters, of which 200 supported me and 79 expressed outrage about my remarks. These numbers just about mirrored the results of a poll in the *Vancouver Province* that asked whether I should be fired. The results were 28 per cent Yes, and 72 per cent No.

Amid all of the controversy, the letters, the editorials, the debates that raged on radio and TV, I enjoyed most a letter I received from Pauline Molloy, an eighty-eight-year-old woman who lived in an old folks' home in St. John's West:

Oh dear MP John, now what have you done?
You've shocked these dear ladies with your bit of fun.
It's a pity they have not a good sense of humour.
It would help to avoid a mentality tumor.
No doubt it's an asset when in public life
To help to withstand all the stress and the strife.
So carry on John as you did in the past
May your brand of humour continue to last.
It's certainly needed in Parliament Hill
With the job you have chosen so well to fulfill.
May success be to you in matters of state
Until you reach my age which is just eighty-eight.

Besieged by reporters outside the Commons after Mulroney defended me, I complained that I was being hounded by feminists and by reporters who couldn't take a joke: "Lighten up, for God's sake. Lighten up. I joked about myself. Is that sensitive? If I wanted to go around and stay out of trouble, then I wouldn't make a joke about myself and you'd all be happy. But you've been worried now for three or four days about the shocking attack on womanhood and sexual harassment. Imagine, making light of sexual harassment! My God, what has this man done?"

No one, I noted, had complained when I gave $3.2 million to a group to fund new business ventures by Newfoundland women on the same day that I had spoken at Lewisporte. "I didn't hear the charge that I was a sexist Neanderthal. But make a speech in which you say something that can be jumped on and we'll hear from the Four Horsewomen of the Apocalypse how terrible it is, how shockingly you behave, how you should be driven out of public life, how you should be garroted, how you should be hung, how you should be decapitated."

My Four Horsewomen of the Apocalypse were Liberal MPs Copps and Mary Clancy, New Democratic MP Dawn Black, and Judy Rebick of NAC. I was not going to be deterred or frightened by this self-appointed censorship board.

As the uproar subsided, I noticed with interest a letter written to Mulroney by Glenda Simms, president of the Canadian Advisory Council on the Status of Women, which was a federal agency. Simms said her members were disturbed at my making light of a serious obstacle for women, because unwanted sexual attention in the workplace or elsewhere was unacceptable. I agreed with that completely. Simms then raised a proposal she had made before – that the government provide mandatory gender-sensitivity training for members of Parliament.

This was a serious question raised by a serious and responsible group of women. But can we take seriously the suggestion that there should be mandatory gender-sensitivity training for members of Parliament, perhaps together with anti-racism training? Are these matters on which a person can be trained? I know few, if any, members of Parliament who would need such training. Their experience of life and their experiences generally make them sensitive to issues of gender, race, and religion. They don't need grim-faced women or blacks or members of minorities lecturing them. At any rate, the subject of sensitivity training was never discussed by the Mulroney cabinet, thank heaven.

I don't want to leave the impression that my nine years in the Mulroney cabinet were dominated by confrontations with the forces of political correctness. Nor, referring again to Barbara McDougall's observation, do I want to suggest that I always said the wrong thing while doing the right thing. There were times when I did the right thing *and* said the right thing – even if the language I used might not have passed muster at the governor general's annual garden party.

It happened in the 1988 election campaign. Jim McGrath had resigned his St. John's East seat to become lieutenant-governor of Newfoundland, and we lost the ensuing by-election to the NDP. Determined to get the seat back, the Conservatives nominated my protégé Ross Reid to be our candidate in the general election. Ross had been my executive assistant when I was in Frank Moores's cabinet in Newfoundland, and he went to Ottawa with me in 1976. Ross was very personable, outgoing, and popular. In the 1984 election, he worked on Mulroney's campaign plane as ringmaster for the travelling press corps. He worked in the Prime Minister's Office, then went off travelling, returning to Canada as we started to gear up for the next election.

I was his biggest booster for the nomination, but it took a huge battle. "Jigger" Jim Morgan, the rough, tough Minister of Fisheries in Brian Peckford's provincial cabinet, wanted the nomination, too. We got four thousand Tories out for the nominating convention, the largest in Newfoundland history, and Ross won. However, someone in the Morgan camp spread the story that Ross was a homosexual. This didn't amount to much during the campaign for the nomination, but it flared up during the election campaign, and the Liberals gave it a push whenever they could. The press got interested and started asking Ross whether he was gay.

I didn't know whether Ross Reid was a homosexual. I'd never given it a thought. I knew he was unmarried and never dated women, but I didn't care whether he was homosexual, heterosexual, bisexual, or asexual. It was absolutely irrelevant. As long as people abide by the Criminal Code, they can do whatever they like, as far as I'm concerned. Ross very properly said that he wasn't going to answer questions like that, that it was no one's business whether he was a homosexual.

This alarmed many long-time Progressive Conservatives. The hard core of them in Newfoundland are Roman Catholics, and gays and lesbians are beyond their understanding. As far as they're concerned, homosexuals should be taken out and drowned like unwanted kittens. They were upset by the news that Ross might be gay, and his refusal to deny it was all the proof they needed that he was a homosexual.

My good friend and campaign manager Frank Ryan came to see me after a Tory meeting in Corner Brook to warn me that Ross's sexual orientation was becoming a big issue and that Ross had been in an unpleasant confrontation with some party members at the meeting. Conservative members of the House of Assembly from districts within the federal riding of St. John's East made it clear they weren't going to work on the Reid campaign. Frank told me the wheels were falling off and something had to be done. So I called Ross and asked him to come down to my house that evening. We talked and he told me he would not deny the rumour about his sexual orientation.

Then I called a meeting of all the Tory MHAs in the federal district of St. John's East at my offices in the Newfoundland Telephone Building. There were about six of them, plus a number of my workers. Ross Reid wasn't there. I think Frank Ryan memorized the whole discussion. I asked them what their problem was. *Well, John boy,* they said, *this is a serious problem. You see, our workers aren't prepared to campaign for Ross. This whole business of homosexuality is very disturbing, blah, blah, blah.* I just closed my eyes and listened to them all. Then I had my say. I told them Ross Reid was a fine young man who had worked with me federally and provincially. "He's a fine man," I said. "Now I don't care if Ross Reid is having sexual relations with effing cats. He's a fine man, and he's our candidate. And let me tell you something else. If there's only one worker for Ross Reid in St. John's East, it's going to be J.C. effing Crosbie. That's who the one worker is going to be – me."

Everyone just sat there. I said it again. "I'm making this absolutely clear. I'm supporting Reid 100 per cent. Now, everybody is free to do what they like, but I'm with Ross Reid." One by one, everyone jumped on board with Ross. But I wasn't taking any chances. I told Ryan that Ross was going to need a lot of help. We knew I was going to win easily in St. John's West, so I had Frank send our best workers to St. John's East, plus money, cars, and anything else Ross's campaign needed. "Do whatever has to be done," I told Frank. "Ross has got to be elected. I'm not letting him down now."

My behaviour may not have been politically correct, but it helped to produce the right result. Ross Reid won St. John's East by more than four thousand votes. He spent one term in Ottawa, helped to organize Kim Campbell's leadership campaign, and served, briefly, as Minister of Fisheries and Oceans in her doomed administration. He lost his seat in the 1993 election.

19

BATTLING THE PREMIERS

Courtesy Terry Mosher (Aislin), Montreal Gazette

ANYONE WHO SPENDS his life in politics eventually begins to wonder whether Canada is governable. The dream of the Fathers of Confederation of a harmonious federation in which a strong central government would provide national direction to subordinate provincial administrations just hasn't worked out that way. Since the Second World War, Ottawa has pushed ever deeper into jurisdictions that the provinces regard as their own. Some of them, such as the environment and offshore resources, are jurisdictions that the Fathers of Confederation never thought of when they were framing the British North America Act in the 1860s.

In the 1950s and, particularly, the 1960s, the federal government used its spending powers to create new shared-cost programs in the fields of health and social welfare, including hospital and medical-care insurance, post-secondary education, and the Canada Assistance Plan. Ottawa's objective was laudable – to establish national programs with national standards so that all

Canadians, regardless of income or region, could enjoy the same level of education and health and social services. Programs such as these were a blessing to "have not" provinces, including Newfoundland. They helped to hold the country together.

Some of the provinces, led by the more affluent ones, resented this intrusion of the federal spending power. Their resentment hardened into open hostility when Ottawa, finding it could no longer afford to pay for the schemes it had launched, started to unilaterally reduce its financial commitment to the shared-cost programs. The provinces were left holding an emptying bag. They were expected to maintain expensive national standards in health and social-welfare programs, but the federal share shrank year by year, leaving financially strapped provincial administrations to shoulder an ever-increasing portion of the burden.

The tensions between Ottawa and the provincial capitals were exacerbated by the confrontational style adopted by Pierre Trudeau's Liberal government in federal–provincial relations. This became particularly acute in Trudeau's later years as the Liberals introduced the hated (in the West) National Energy Program and set out to patriate the Constitution, unilaterally if necessary. Under Trudeau, Ottawa took the view that the provinces had nothing useful to contribute to the good governance of the nation.

The premiers, even those from smaller and weaker provinces, were not about to be pushed around. As provincial economies expanded in the 1960s and 1970s, the premiers' power increased at home, and naturally they wanted to flex their new muscles at the federal–provincial table. They seethed when they felt Trudeau was treating them like mayors of two-bit municipalities rather than as important regional statesmen, which is how the premiers saw themselves.

"The Blue-Eyed Sheik" – Peter Lougheed of Alberta – was the classic example of a premier who thought he was as important as the prime minister. Together, he and Bill Davis of Ontario whipsawed the Clark government over energy policy in 1979. The absence of a pricing agreement undermined the energy provisions of my Budget and precipitated its defeat in the Commons. The attacks of Lougheed and Davis contributed greatly to our defeat in the February 1980 election.

A province, however, didn't have to be big, rich, or powerful to produce a premier who was a royal pain to the government in Ottawa. Some of my worst moments in nine years in the Mulroney government were dealing with the provincial satraps of Atlantic Canada.

When I was a minister in Newfoundland, we had good working relationships with ministers in Ottawa. I got along well with the federal Department of Finance, and my relationship as Fisheries minister with my opposite number in Ottawa, Romeo LeBlanc, was professional and constructive. Generally speaking, good relations between St. John's and Ottawa continued as long as Frank Moores was premier. But his successor as Conservative leader and premier, Brian Peckford, was a different kettle of cod. And Liberal Clyde Wells, my old comrade-in-arms from the Smallwood wars, was the worst of the lot. His intransigence on the Meech Lake constitutional accord was a serious blow to Canada's hopes of surviving as a united country. There's no doubt in my mind: Clyde Wells put Canada and Newfoundland at peril by killing Meech Lake.

My experience with the Peckford and Wells governments was that both were totally selfish and ungrateful, no matter what Ottawa did for them. If a billion dollars in cash or benefits was delivered to them one day, they'd be howling twenty-four hours later that they hadn't received a second billion dollars. As federal politicians, we always felt at a disadvantage because provincial politicians are right there on the local scene; they can be on radio and TV and in the newspapers every minute of the day, but we were only around part of the time. It took a tremendous effort to make sure the federal government got any favourable publicity in Newfoundland. Peckford and Wells were adroit at grabbing all the credit for anything good that Ottawa did while shifting all the blame for anything that went wrong to the federal government, regardless of who was responsible.

The more we did for the province, the more they asked for, the more they attacked, the more unreasonable they were, and the more arrogant they grew.

We started having trouble with Peckford when oil was dis-covered offshore at Hibernia in 1979. It suddenly became urgent to resolve the issue of jurisdiction and control. As prime minis-ter, Clark had assured Peckford that his government would confirm Newfoundland's ownership of offshore petroleum and mineral resources by treating resources that lay under the sea in exactly the same way as resources found under land – that is, they came under provincial jurisdiction.

This seemed to satisfy the premier until the 1980 election came along. Then Peckford demanded that Clark's commitment be given in writing, which carried the implication that Joe's word was not to be trusted. During the campaign, Peckford crit-icized the Clark government on several issues, and he publicly attacked us over the northern cod, which he maintained should be fished by Newfoundlanders only. He also wanted the federal government to bar non-Newfoundlanders from operating factory freezer trawlers in Newfoundland's offshore waters. Peckford argued that, if there was to be offshore fishing for northern cod, it should be Newfoundlanders, not other Canadians or foreign-ers, who did the fishing, and that they should use wet fish trawlers only. On wet fish trawlers, the fishermen keep their catch on ice, returning to shore every week or so to unload at a processing plant. On factory freezer trawlers, the fish are processed on board, then frozen to preserve them until the vessel returns to its distant home port many weeks, or even months, later. Peckford's idea was to protect both the politically potent inshore fishery and the Newfoundland fish processors, who would lose business if factory freezer trawlers were permitted.

An election campaign was the wrong time to raise this kind of issue between two Conservative governments. When Clark's Fisheries minister, Jim McGrath, said he intended to consult with Peckford's government, the Premier snarled: "He can consult all he likes. . . . that's not good enough."

Peckford's disenchantment with the federal government continued after the Liberals returned to power in the 1980 election
and we, in Opposition, did our best to help him. Newfoundland
supported Alberta in its fight with Ottawa over the Liberals'
National Energy Program, battled the Trudeau government over
jurisdiction over resources off the east coast of Newfoundland,
and continued an ongoing scrap with Ottawa and Quebec over
the hydro development of the Upper Churchill River in Labrador
and the sale of its electricity to Hydro-Québec at a bargain-
basement price.

Peckford wanted Ottawa to make the development of the
Lower Churchill feasible by picking up the major portion of the
cost of building an electrical transmission line under the Strait
of Belle Isle from Labrador to the island of Newfoundland. He
also wanted Trudeau to use the federal constitutional power to
force Quebec to allow transmission lines to cross its territory to
carry Lower Churchill power to market in other provinces and
the United States. He got nowhere with Trudeau on either issue.
To make matters worse, the federal government intervened in
support of Quebec when Newfoundland's attempt to reopen the
Churchill Falls agreement with Quebec went to the Supreme
Court of Canada. Quebec won that appeal, and Newfoundland
is still losing hundreds of millions of dollars every year in revenue
from Churchill Falls.

By 1982, the relationship between St. John's and Ottawa was
so bad that, when the *Ocean Ranger* drilling platform collapsed
during a tremendous storm in the North Atlantic with the
loss of all on board, each government announced its own
royal commission to investigate the tragedy. Eventually, a joint
inquiry was established, headed by Newfoundland's Chief
Justice, Alex Hickman.

Relations were not that much better between Peckford and
Brian Mulroney when he became Opposition leader in Ottawa.
Initially, Mulroney played his cards close to his vest on the own-
ership of offshore resources, not endorsing Clark's policy until

the eve of the 1984 election, when he and Peckford signed the agreement that became the "Atlantic Accord."

The accord had three principles. First, the principal beneficiary of the resources should be the province of Newfoundland and Labrador. Second, the resources should contribute to energy security for all Canadians. Third, producing provinces should be treated equally in revenue-sharing, whether the resource was on land or offshore. Peckford was ecstatic. "There is no other document, including the Terms of Union, that will come as close to achieving economic and social equality for the people of Newfoundland and Labrador as this," he said. ". . . To tell you the truth I didn't think we could get everything that is in that agreement. . . . We've got a document that every single Newfoundlander who can read and write will consider the most important in the history of this rock."

The reaction in Newfoundland was so positive that Peckford called a snap election. Our federal Tory government helped handsomely. We announced a $180-million highways agreement, with $112.5 million of the total to come from Ottawa, $3 million in funding for Memorial University, and $400,000 towards construction of a new music school, among other worthy projects.

Peckford had no sooner won re-election with a comfortable majority, however, than he started biting the hand that had fed him so lavishly. When Finance minister Michael Wilson brought down the Mulroney government's first Budget, it called for the partial de-indexing of tax brackets and social-welfare payments. Peckford promptly denounced these deficit-fighting measures as unacceptable. He and his Tories voted with the Liberal Opposition in the Assembly to pass a resolution condemning the federal government and our Budget. I felt that with friends like Peckford we'd never need enemies!

The relationship with the Newfoundland government worsened when the issue of factory freezer trawlers (FFTs) flared up again. The government of Nova Scotia supported an application by National Sea Products Limited, a Nova Scotia–based company, to operate one of these controversial trawlers. National Sea felt it had to use the most modern fishing and processing techniques to stay competitive with companies in other countries. The federal government was caught in the middle between Nova Scotia and Newfoundland. After four months of study, Erik Nielsen, as acting Fisheries minister, decided to allow three FFT licences – one for National Sea, one for Newfoundland-based Fisheries Products International (if it applied for a licence), and the third for a consortium of the remaining offshore ground-fish companies.

The *St. John's Evening Telegram* excitedly reported Peckford's reaction as: "The honeymoon is over, the gloves are off and there is a strong possibility the provincial government will take Ottawa to court for allowing the use of FFTs in the east coast fisheries." Peckford accused us of ignoring Newfoundland's arguments against FFTs and of committing a serious breach of trust. Although I had opposed granting any FFT licences during the cabinet's discussion of the issue, I defended myself and the government lustily, commenting that Peckford was "conjuring up bogey men and spelling out worst-case scenarios. . . . This may happen, that may happen. Well, pigs may fly." I noted the millions of dollars we had recently poured into Newfoundland for job creation and education, and said it was now time for Ottawa to do something for Nova Scotia.

Before long, Peckford found another federal whipping boy: Petro-Canada, then still a Crown corporation, over the Come By Chance oil refinery. Some years earlier, the Newfoundland government had persuaded Petro-Canada to take over John Shaheen's bankrupt oil refinery at Come By Chance when no one else showed any interest in it. Petro-Canada mothballed the refinery while trying to find a way to reactivate it, but with no success. The company was ready to dismantle the refinery when I intervened with Bill Hopper, the chief executive, to save the facility.

An American company, Cumberland Farms Incorporated, with convenience stores and gasoline stations throughout the northeastern United States, was interested in reactivating the refinery to serve the U.S. market – but only if the price was right. Petro-Canada, which had spent $27 million maintaining the plant, agreed to turn it over to Cumberland Farms for $1. The federal government agreed to turn over the dock facilities, which it had built and owned.

Despite all these concessions, the ungrateful Peckford publicly attacked Petro-Canada for certain conditions it had attached to the gift. These conditions were eminently reasonable. Petro-Canada retained the right to take back ownership of the tank storage facilities if Cumberland was unable to restart the refinery or decided to shut it down. And Petro-Canada had the first right to market surplus product from Come By Chance in other parts of Canada if Cumberland wanted to sell product in Canada rather than in the United States, as was the plan.

Both the Premier and his Finance minister, John Collins, accused the federal government of being insensitive to regional needs and of not paying enough attention to Newfoundland. At that time, Ottawa was providing 50 per cent of the revenues of their government. I called a press conference to point out this interesting fact. "Dr. Collins is suffering from at least two human failings," I said. "One appears to be greed, the other ingratitude. He seems to specialize in biting the hand that feeds him. . . . I don't intend to criticize the premier . . . but I don't intend to keep turning my cheek every time I hear some public criticism that's unreasonable from either him or any of his ministers. I quickly run out of cheeks to turn."

The Canada–France dispute over the fishing rights of St. Pierre and Miquelon in the Gulf of St. Lawrence and the rights of France to fish in Canadian waters caused me my worst moments in the Mulroney administration. It also caused another, quite needless, confrontation with Peckford that went on for a year. Peckford and I had agreed on two points. Neither of us wanted French fishermen to have the right to catch Canadian fish in Canadian waters, but they already had that right by treaty. And we both wanted the Newfoundland government and fishing industry represented as observers at every stage of the negotiations with France.

Through no fault of my own – but through the deceit of the Prime Minister's Office and the connivance of External Affairs – Newfoundland observers were excluded from the final negotiations, and without my knowledge an agreement was signed in Paris that extended the right of the French to take unspecified quantities of fish in Canadian waters, including the endangered northern cod, while the boundary arbitration proceeded. I went to the wall in protesting this sell-out of Newfoundland's – and Canada's – interests. I came very close to resigning from the Mulroney cabinet. My protests produced an unprecedented apology to the people of Newfoundland from Deputy Prime Minister Don Mazankowski on behalf of the federal government. They also produced a public letter from the Prime Minister supporting me, in which he promised that such a thing would not be permitted to happen again. Peckford, however, was not satisfied. He persisted in portraying me as a key player in some monstrous conspiracy to sell out the birthright of our fellow Newfoundlanders.

While all this was going on, Peckford continued to attack the federal government on every other conceivable ground. He told the press Newfoundland was facing fiscal chaos and would be in a 1930s-style financial disaster within two years unless Ottawa fundamentally redefined the province's place in Confederation. He demanded a new deal in regional development, equalization payments, established program funding, and fisheries jurisdiction. In Peckford's view, "We've got, at the outside, two years and then it's 1933 all over again." Peckford said he had informed Ottawa of the perilous situation of Newfoundland in a document "that would blow your mind."

I held a press conference at St. John's a few days later, together with my caucus colleagues Morrissey Johnson and Joe

Price. I pointed out that, if the province was facing financial chaos, it was facing it despite the generous help of the government and people of Canada. I presented statistics that showed that federal funding for Newfoundland had increased to $1.164 billion a year. This would increase by $64 million in the next year. Regional development spending in Newfoundland had gone from $47.1 million in 1984–85 to $102.1 million in 1986–87. Peckford's unreasonableness was mind-boggling.

Peckford outdid himself when he appeared on national television, where he was asked whether he would campaign for the Prime Minister in Newfoundland if a federal election were called. He replied: "It would be very, very difficult and I think I would have to say 'No, I wouldn't.'"

∾

Of all the provincial premiers, the two that had the best relationships with the Mulroney federal government were Grant Devine in Saskatchewan and John Buchanan in Nova Scotia, both of whom happened to be Conservatives. Buchanan, however, was succeeded by another Conservative, Donald Cameron, and he was impossible to deal with – hard-nosed, hard-headed, confrontational, selfish, and grasping.

The four Atlantic premiers were constantly trying to get us to scupper the Atlantic Canada Opportunities Agency, which we created under Mulroney. They wanted us to turn the money that was being spent by ACOA and other federal agencies over to them to spend on whatever they wanted – mostly infrastructure, roads and things like that. The function of ACOA was to improve the economic prospects of Atlantic Canada – not just to fork over more money to improve highways in Nova Scotia or New Brunswick. The premiers just didn't want to give the federal government credit for anything ACOA did. The general public didn't realize that the regional-development programs in their provinces were 75 per cent paid for by Ottawa through ACOA. That's the way the provinces like it, of course. It's always a huge struggle to get any recognition for the role the federal government plays. I told the premiers Ottawa wasn't going to relinquish any control over the spending of its regional-development money and the premiers had no right to tell us how to spend federal money in Atlantic Canada.

∾

In January 1989, with his government reeling from a foolhardy $20-million investment in a hydroponic cucumber operation at Mount Pearl, Brian Peckford announced his intention to resign as Conservative leader and premier of Newfoundland after ten years in those posts.

A leadership convention was held at which 782 delegates chose Thomas Rideout, the Fisheries minister, by a mere twenty-six votes over his cabinet colleague Len Simms. At this time the Tories held thirty-four seats in the fifty-two-seat legislature, while the Liberals under Clyde Wells had fourteen. The closeness of the leadership race had attracted so much publicity to the party that post-convention Tory polls showed them nearly twenty points ahead of the Liberals. Rideout made the fatal mistake of following the polls instead of his head. Rather than wait until the Conservative organization was ready, he called a snap election a year earlier than he needed to. After seventeen straight years of Tory governments, the tide went out. The Liberals took thirty seats to the Conservatives' twenty-two, making Newfoundland the fifth province to elect a Liberal government since Mulroney gained power in Ottawa in 1984.

I was in Palm Beach, Florida, on vacation when Newfoundland voted. On the morning after the election, I telephoned Clyde Wells to congratulate him. It was such a discouraging conversation that I almost wished we could have Peckford back. I started by telling Clyde I was more than willing to cooperate with him to obtain assistance from Ottawa for Newfoundland. The fact that we represented different parties shouldn't prevent us from working together as Frank Moores had worked with Don

Jamieson when Jamieson, a Liberal, was the province's political minister in Ottawa, I said.

This led me to the delicate terrain of Meech Lake. In 1982, the Parti Québécois government of René Lévesque had refused to give Quebec's support to the patriation of the Canadian Constitution. In the fall of 1985, Robert Bourassa, leading the Quebec Liberals in the provincial election campaign, had set out five conditions as a basis for accepting the patriated Constitution and Charter of Rights. Bourassa's five points were: participation in naming Supreme Court judges; powers in immigration; limits on the federal spending power; recognition of Quebec as a distinct society; and a veto for Quebec on constitutional changes. The election of the Bourassa Liberals led to renewed constitutional negotiations, and on April 30, 1987, Prime Minister Mulroney and the premiers, meeting in the Gatineau Hills, reached agreement on what became known as the Meech Lake accord. The package of six constitutional amendments incorporated Bourassa's five conditions, including the recognition of Quebec as a distinct society. The accord was approved by Parliament, and the Quebec National Assembly led the way among the provincial legislatures. The rest of the provinces had until June 22, 1990, to give their legislative assent.

For all his other faults, Brian Peckford had signed the accord and he was a staunch supporter of it. The Newfoundland Liberals, before Wells became their leader, supported it in Opposition. Now, the day after Wells won the election, I tried on the phone from Florida to suggest to him, as diplomatically as possible, that it would be difficult to obtain more federal financial assistance for Newfoundland if he opposed the adoption of the accord, which was very dear to the heart of the Prime Minister and was vital to the interests of the Canadian nation. I argued that Meech Lake was of less direct interest to Newfoundland than the many practical things Ottawa could do for the province, including the development of Hibernia, which could go ahead only with massive financial support from the federal government.

I got nowhere with Clyde, absolutely nowhere. I'd known him well from the 1960s and 1970s, when we stood together against the tyranny of Joey Smallwood. As a friend, he could be a formidable ally. As a foe, he was one of the most miserable people I've ever encountered. Clyde was one of the most stubborn beings alive, and I knew that day on the phone that the Meech Lake accord was doomed.

In his most determined and certain tones, he advised me that Meech Lake was of immense importance to Newfoundland and to Canadians since it dealt with the Constitution, which would have to last for a thousand years. There was nothing more important than these constitutional issues, he said, and there was no way that he was going to be persuaded to deviate from his position on Meech Lake simply to secure federal assistance for Newfoundland. His position on the accord had no connection with any other items on the agenda between Canada and Newfoundland. Meech Lake stood on its own, he said, and surely Ottawa would not punish Newfoundland because of his principled stand on Meech Lake.

What I wanted to say to him, but couldn't, was: don't be an ass. If he opposed Meech Lake, of course Newfoundland would be punished. That's how the world works. The Meech Lake accord was vitally important to the Prime Minister and to the government and the people of Canada. We were dealing with the future of the whole country. If he sabotaged the accord, there was no way it could be business as usual between Ottawa and St. John's.

Clyde knew that, of course. But once his mind was made up, nothing would induce him to change it. Once he had taken a position or formed an opinion, that was the only right position or opinion and nothing would ever make him deviate from it. Clyde was hard-working, honest, intelligent, vigorous, intensely partisan, and articulate – but, like Britain's Margaret Thatcher, Clyde was not for turning. When Clyde declared, as he did following the election, "I will not shirk at doing whatever is necessary to protect the long-term interests of this province – including withdrawing the approval [of the Meech Lake accord] if that becomes necessary," he meant it.

People didn't understand Wells. They thought he was hostile to Quebec and Quebecers, but that wasn't it at all. He had a fanatical idea of what the Constitution should say, and how it should deal with every province. In his view, every province was absolutely equal to every other province, and should, therefore, have exactly the same powers. There was no way that Quebec, or any other province, should have any powers that Newfoundland didn't have, or P.E.I. didn't have, and so on. That's why he thought Canada should have a Triple-E Senate, in which every province would have equal representation, regardless of its population.

The Newfoundland public bought the Wells line. The reason was simple. In Newfoundland, we support the local boy when he goes to the mainland. In Wells, they saw one of their Newfoundland boys doing very well over on the mainland, standing up to the bigger players, able to articulate and to overcome the mainlanders in an argument. Looked down on in popular folklore as "white trash" and made the butt of "Newfie jokes," we Newfoundlanders delight in demonstrating to mainlanders that we have just as much on the ball as they do. The people of Newfoundland saw Wells holding up the Newfoundland side. "That's our Clyde," they said. "Boy, he's really doing it, isn't he?" They didn't understand that he was wrecking the country. They didn't realize that Newfoundland was the most vulnerable part of the country, with more to lose than any other province if the country fell apart. They didn't see it and they didn't understand it. All they could see was their champion Clyde tying old Mulroney in knots. Our party polling showed that people didn't like Wells, but they respected him. He was the sort of politician who could throw someone's mother out of a nursing home on Christmas Eve – and they'd still vote for him.

That's why Wells had so much support in Newfoundland for taking a constitutional position that was directly contradictory to the province's best interests. When it comes time to hang somebody because of how we're going to suffer as a result of Quebec's leaving Confederation, Newfoundlanders will hang the poor soul who happens to be in office when it happens. The one they should hang is Clyde Wells! He destroyed the Meech Lake accord, and Meech Lake was our best chance for constitutional unity.

The accord had already begun to unravel. The new Liberal premier of New Brunswick, Frank McKenna, as well as the new Tory premier of Manitoba, Gary Filmon, both indicated that they opposed various provisions of the accord. But what killed the accord was Wells's "principled" opposition. He had the House of Assembly rescind its approval of the accord. Then he reneged on his promise to allow the Assembly to vote anew on it. He refused to allow that vote even after Mulroney and three provincial premiers had made the trek to Newfoundland to beg the Assembly to ratify the accord.

Earlier, in the middle of November 1989, Wells joined Mulroney and the other nine premiers at a meeting in Ottawa to review the accord. At an emotional private dinner at the new National Gallery of Canada, a number of premiers berated Clyde for his unyielding opposition to the distinct-society clause. Some of their language was profane, but Wells was unbending. Under the television lights the next day, the rift burst into the open. There was an electrifying exchange in which Wells accused Mulroney of offering Quebec a "special legislative status" that would erode the foundations of Confederation. Mulroney lectured Wells about the perils of ignoring Quebec's demands to be recognized as a distinct society. It became clear to everyone at the conference that Clyde was a dangerous opponent. He appeared to know his dossier well, to be knowledgeable. He came across well on television.

His blindness to the realities of the situation were obvious, however, when he spoke a few days later to the St. John's Board of Trade. He again condemned the Meech Lake accord, stressing that his objections were based on a concern for the long-term economic security of Newfoundland and Canada's other disadvantaged provinces. He could not, or would not, see that what he was doing was putting the security of these provinces at peril. He never gave a thought to the fact that if the Meech Lake accord were not accepted and Quebec left Confederation, the remainder of Canada would have neither the means nor the will to continue to support Newfoundland and the other have-not provinces.

As the June 22, 1990, deadline for ratification by all ten provincial legislatures neared, the first ministers met again in Ottawa, spending seven gruelling days of secret negotiations in their attempt to break the Meech deadlock. Both McKenna and Filmon said they would submit the agreement to their legislatures before the deadline and that they would support its ratification. Faltering a bit in his rock-hard opposition to the accord, Wells said he would allow a free vote in the House of Assembly but would neither encourage nor oppose ratification.

I returned to Newfoundland to see what I could do to persuade members of the Assembly to vote for the accord. We commissioned a poll, which showed 42 per cent of Newfoundlanders in favour of ratification, 42 per cent opposed, and 16 per cent undecided. I sent the poll to Wells to show him that Newfoundlanders were not overwhelmingly opposed to Meech Lake, as he claimed.

It was quite a week! I met with Craig Dobbin, Miller Ayre, Richard Cashin, and other members of Newfoundlanders and Labradorians for Confederation to divide up the work of lobbying the Assembly members. We continued polling each night and, as the week went on, public support for the accord climbed until it reached forty-seven to thirty-seven for ratification. This increase was particularly evident in rural Newfoundland. We had the support of all Conservative MHAs, and it appeared that we had a reasonable chance of obtaining the votes of eight to ten Liberal members, including several from Wells's cabinet.

During the week, we had the extraordinary spectacle of the Prime Minister and three provincial premiers appearing before the Newfoundland Assembly to present their compelling arguments in support of the accord. Mulroney was magnificent! As I told our caucus in Ottawa later, no human being could have done more for Quebec or for Canada than he had. By the end of the fateful week, forty-eight of the fifty-two MHAs had spoken, with twenty indicating they would vote against the accord, eighteen in favour, and ten not declaring a position. Meanwhile, in New Brunswick the legislature unanimously approved the agreement. But in the Manitoba legislature, voting was delayed on a procedural point by Elijah Harper, a Cree and New Democratic Party MPP.

When Senator Lowell Murray, Mulroney's top strategist on Meech Lake, announced that, if Newfoundland ratified the accord, Ottawa would ask the Supreme Court of Canada to extend the deadline for Manitoba, Wells declared that Murray had put Newfoundland in an untenable position. If Manitoba could have an extension, why not Newfoundland? The Assembly, he said, was being pressured to vote against the conscience of a majority of members. At 8:30 that Friday evening, June 22, he announced there would be no Meech Lake vote in the Assembly; the Liberals used their majority to adjourn the debate. That was the end of the Meech Lake accord. Wells had reneged on his promise to allow a free vote. And what made his breach of faith more outrageous was the fact that the Prime Minister and the three premiers had come to St. John's to make their case, believing Wells would honour his commitment to allow the members of the Assembly to decide the issue. The problem in the Manitoba legislature was only an excuse. Wells wouldn't allow a vote because he feared he wouldn't win it. He knew it would reveal a deep split in his cabinet and caucus.

∾

Fifteen months later, Wells made an extraordinary comment to the St. John's *Sunday Express*, when asked whether his government was concerned about what might happen if Quebec were to separate, cutting Newfoundland off from the rest of Canada. "If Quebec were to separate," he replied, "the federal government might have more funding available for Newfoundland. Don't forget, the federal government pays more to Quebec on a per capita basis than to most other provinces."

I wrote a letter to the editor, pointing out that, in fact, Newfoundland, Prince Edward Island, Nova Scotia, New Brunswick, Manitoba, Saskatchewan, and even Ontario all received more federal expenditure per capita than Quebec, which was below the national average. Federal spending in Quebec per capita was $4,465, which was below the national average, while in Newfoundland federal spending per capita came to $6,553. For every tax dollar the federal government collected in Newfoundland, it spent $3.17 in the province; for every $1 that Ottawa raised by taxes in Quebec, it spent just $1.20 in that province.

Wells was also wrong to suggest that if Quebec were to separate, all else would remain as it was or even get better for Newfoundland. The separation of Quebec would shake Canada to its foundations. Even if Canada, without Quebec, continued as a country, I could only foresee a period of economic dislocation and hardship for the people of Newfoundland.

∾

Mulroney tried again, tabling a fifty-nine-page blueprint called *Shaping Canada's Future Together* and appointing a committee of MPs and senators to seek the views of the Canadian public. Joe Clark was in charge of this operation as chairman of a cabinet committee on national unity, of which I was a member. As our committee pulled various views together, I thought we had a package that might fly. It became known as the Charlottetown accord, accepted by the federal government, all ten provinces, both territories, and aboriginal representatives. It was to be put to the people of Canada in a national referendum in 1992.

I had strong objections to some of the main features of the Charlottetown accord, including reform of the Senate, but I felt our first priority had to be to reach a resolution to the constitutional impasse so that the danger of separation would be lessened and we could get on with other essential matters. My position on the Charlottetown accord was similar to that of historian Frank Underhill, who, when asked how he could possibly vote Liberal, replied that it was simple: He simply held his nose and marked his X. I would hold my nose and do everything I could to get the accord approved in Newfoundland.

Wells had accepted the Charlottetown accord, but back in Newfoundland he attempted to give the impression that he wasn't very keen on it. He said he would support the proposal personally and vote for it, "assuming that the legal text is written to reflect the agreement." He would ask the people of the province to authorize the Assembly to pass the necessary resolution, but he wouldn't cooperate in any high-pressure sales campaign. I tried to be diplomatic, but in a speech in Corner Brook I criticized Wells for his lack of faith in the Hibernia offshore project, his lack of economic leadership, and his nitpicking about the Charlottetown accord. I said that I was supporting the agreement and didn't need to see a legal text, adding that, if we had to wait for the lawyers, we'd all be doomed. Speaking in Fredericton, I said a No vote in the national referendum would create the costliest divorce in history for Quebec and Canada. It would mean more years of uncertainty and divided national purposes. It would mean the progressive fragmentation of Canada.

When the Newfoundland Yes committee, headed by Liberal MP (and later premier) Brian Tobin and me, kicked off our campaign, Clyde Wells, the leader who had signed the constitutional agreement, wasn't there. He told all provincial Liberals to stay away. I chided Wells – "He signed it, he negotiated it, it's his. He's the author with sixteen other people. He can't deny his own child."

Despite Wells's ambivalence and attempts to be on both sides of the issue, 63 per cent of Newfoundlanders voted in favour of the Charlottetown accord in the referendum. But not enough Canadians in other provinces followed our example. The referendum failed and the accord died.

∾

I believe in the statement of Sir John A. Macdonald about Confederation – "Whatever you do, adhere to the union. . . . We are a great country and shall become one of the greatest in the universe if we preserve it; we shall sink into insignificance and adversity if we suffer it to be broken."

Unfortunately, the loss of the 1992 national referendum and the near-victory of the separatists in the 1995 referendum in Quebec haven't awakened us. Our Canadian union is at the breaking-point today. And like other Canadians, Newfoundlanders are sleepwalking to disaster.

20

WHO HEARS THE FISHES
WHEN THEY CRY?

Courtesy Sue Dewar, Ottawa Sun

THE TOUGHEST JOB I had in my three decades in politics was my last one – Minister of Fisheries and Oceans. There were more desperate problems facing the fishery than any other sector of the Canadian economy. There wasn't much I or anyone else could do about the worst problem: the severe depletion of fish stocks on Canada's east coast, once the richest fishery in the world. And the political pressures on me, as a cabinet minister from Atlantic Canada, to do something – anything – about the fishery made the job almost unbearable.

I could have dodged the assignment. Brian Mulroney decided to make a major shuffle of his ministry in April 1991. I'd been Minister of International Trade for three years – an exciting period that covered the enactment of the Canada–U.S. Free Trade Agreement, the start of negotiations for the North American Free Trade Agreement, and international acceptance of my proposal for the creation of a World Trade Organization. Now, however, Mulroney decided to move Michael Wilson out of the Finance portfolio he'd held for seven years and make him the Minister of Industry and International Trade. The Prime Minister gave me a choice of either Employment and Immigration, which was an important and interesting portfolio, or Fisheries and Oceans.

Although Fisheries and Oceans was problem-filled and had a lower public profile than the other portfolios I'd had, it was the most important federal department for the province and people of Newfoundland, where the fishery accounted for 10 per cent of the gross provincial product and 25 per cent of the employment.

It was an unparalleled tragedy for Newfoundland when I was forced to close the Atlantic cod fishery in 1992. My action was the inevitable result of years of extreme overfishing, wildly unreliable scientific information on the size of the stocks of northern cod and their rate of reproduction, and an understandable, if misguided, tendency among politicians of all stripes to put the interests of fishermen – who were voters – ahead of the cod, who weren't.

I had another reason for accepting the post. The department was so important to Newfoundland and the problems were so grave that I didn't want to risk someone else botching the job. I'd already had a taste of that with Bernard Valcourt. Young, arrogant, and ambitious, Valcourt, from New Brunswick, was Minister of Fisheries and Oceans for fourteen months prior to the 1991 cabinet shuffle. He had an abrasive personality that was evident in his dealings with fish-plant owners, fish processors, the fishermen's union, the Newfoundland government, and other fishery interest groups. Valcourt's predecessor in Fisheries, Tom Siddon, a scientist and university professor from British Columbia, had been much easier to work with. Valcourt did not welcome my interest in Fisheries matters, was unsympathetic to the political problems that his handling of the portfolio sometimes caused, and did not feel he needed any advice or assistance from anyone.

I'd come to the conclusion that I couldn't survive politically with Valcourt in Fisheries and Oceans, and me on the outside looking in. So I suggested to Mulroney that he make me Fisheries minister and put Valcourt in Employment and Immigration. The Prime Minister agreed. He also accepted my request that I become the minister responsible for the Atlantic Canada Opportunities Agency, which gave me extra economic and patronage clout in the four Atlantic provinces. I continued to be part of the inner cabinet as a member of the Priorities and Planning Committee and of such other key cabinet bodies as the "Ops" (for "Operations") and the Expenditure Review committees.

This was the shuffle in which Joe Clark left External Affairs to become the minister responsible for constitutional affairs, Don Mazankowski became Minister of Finance, and Barbara McDougall moved to External Affairs. Kim Campbell continued as Minister of Justice, while Jean Charest rejoined the cabinet as Minister of the Environment.

A top priority at the Department of Fisheries and Oceans (DFO) was to preserve the fish stocks. This involved understanding the science of marine reproduction, improving the surveillance of fish stocks, determining the size of the catch that each species could sustain, establishing quotas in the various fishing zones, and stopping overfishing by both Canadian and foreign fishermen. As fish stocks declined and catches dwindled, we had to come up with economic assistance for fishermen and fish processors. DFO was also intimately involved in international negotiations that included such issues as the territorial waters of St. Pierre and Miquelon, the rights of foreigners to fish within Canada's 200-mile economic zone, and the limits that needed to be imposed on catches of "straddling" stocks – fish that migrated back and forth across the 200-mile line. As long as these delicate negotiations had a chance of succeeding – as they ultimately did – we couldn't risk gunboat diplomacy of the grandstanding sort that Brian Tobin resorted to in 1994 when, as the Liberals' Fisheries minister, he waged his "Turbot War" with Spain, when Canada arrested a Spanish fishing vessel at gunpoint.

Finally, DFO had to work closely with provincial governments to design and implement programs for fishermen and their industry. True cooperation between the two levels of government in Canada is as rare as snowballs in the tropics, and the federal–provincial component of DFO's mandate caused some of our worst headaches.

While Valcourt was still Fisheries minister, he and I announced a $584-million five-year adjustment program for the Atlantic fishery. A half-billion dollars was a lot of money, and it reflected a serious commitment by Ottawa to the fishery. We had previously announced $130 million in short-term aid to communities whose fish plants had closed, and $28 million to improve surveillance beyond the 200-mile zone and to police fishing on the nose and tail of the Grand Banks. The rest of the $584 million was new money – $426 million to rebuild fish stocks, to help workers to adjust to their reduced circumstances, and to help communities to diversify.

As usual, the announcement of this funding received a lukewarm response from the premiers and Fisheries ministers of Atlantic Canada. Newfoundland premier Clyde Wells found the package too little too late. This was typical. While the provincial government did nothing constructive to assist, Wells vigorously and viciously objected to, criticized, denigrated, and sneered at every attempt made by the federal government to deal with the crisis. If we'd put forward one billion, two billion, or five billion dollars, Wells and his government would have found it inadequate.

∼

Newfoundland's northern cod had been exploited by Europeans and other fishermen since 1481, eleven years before Columbus "discovered" America. Through the centuries, the northern cod was the economic foundation for the settlement and growth of communities along the east and northeast coast of Newfoundland and the coast of Labrador. Without the abundant fish stocks, there would have been no Newfoundland – as a British colony, a British dominion, or, after 1949, a province of Canada. The cod also contributed to the settlement and prosperity of a number of Nova Scotian coastal communities. In the economic life of what is today Atlantic Canada, the cod was supplemented by such other marine species as shrimp, crab, scallops, salmon, redfish, haddock, herring, pollock, flatfish, turbot, and seals. By the time I became Minister of Fisheries and Oceans, the department was administering forty species, but cod was king. Cod was the reason why Newfoundland was settled; it permitted our people to survive.

Economic diversification eventually came to Newfoundland, but the vast majority of the outports remained dependent on the seasonal feeding migration that drew the cod to the shallow coastal waters, where they were accessible to inshore fishermen. In the hundred years from 1850 to 1950, the annual catch averaged 250,000 tonnes. Occasionally, there were localized failures of the fishery, but the historical record indicated that the stocks could sustain fishing at that level without showing any obvious sign of decrease. By the middle of the twentieth century, however, new fishing technology appeared, including high-powered vessels with otter trawls that were capable of fishing in deep waters and of exploiting large concentrations of fish as they gathered to spawn along the edge of the continental shelf. At the same time, inshore fishermen began to acquire larger diesel-powered vessels, equipped with electronic navigational and fish-finding instruments, and with hydraulic net haulers that permitted the use of long "fleets" of gill nets. The inshore fishery pushed into deeper waters thirty kilometres or more from shore. The total catch soared in the late 1960s and 1970s, reaching a peak in 1968 of 800,000 tonnes, most of it taken by distant-water fishermen from the Soviet Union and Western Europe.

The stock could not sustain such intense fishing. Inshore landings fell to levels below any recorded in the previous centuries. In 1977, although the United Nations Law of the Sea Treaty had not yet been ratified, Canada declared a 200-mile management zone and adopted a management strategy known as FO.1, which would permit fishermen to take about 20 per cent of the exploitable biomass each year. For the next seven years, the annual take increased and all indications pointed to a rising stock of cod.

There were two problems with the management strategy. First, no one knew how many fish were really out there. And, second, not even the scientists had more than the most rudimentary notion of what proportion of the stock, or biomass, could be taken annually without causing the resource to go into decline.

In the prediction game, the fisheries scientists had a batting average that would embarrass a weather forecaster. Overconfident in their projections, they failed to recognize the statistical inadequacies in their bulk-biomass model. They also failed to grasp the high risk involved in taking a fish census over an enormous area. To complicate matters, they had to contend with the misreporting of catches and discard rates by commercial fishermen.[*]

At the end of 1987, the scientists advised Siddon that it would be safe to set a total allowable catch (TAC) of 295,000 tonnes for northern cod for 1988. Siddon, however, played it safe and allowed a TAC of just 266,000 tonnes.

By the late fall of 1988, it was apparent that the actual fishing mortality rate since 1977 had been at least twice the rate projected in the FO.1 strategy. Either there were only half as many fish as the scientists had estimated, or the census was accurate but the stock would sustain only half as much fishing as the scientists had thought. In 1989, the scientists changed all their calculations for the previous ten years. They said they had overestimated the spawning biomass – the cod old enough to reproduce (four years old and over) – and the total allowable catch shouldn't be more than 125,000 tonnes for northern cod. The scientists found that, over the previous ten years, the northern cod had not been reproducing nearly as rapidly as they thought. A quota designed to allow fishermen to take roughly

---

[*] The best discussion I have found of the role of science in these issues is found in Alan Christopher Finlayson's *Fish for Truth: A Sociological Analysis of Northern Cod Stock Assessments from 1977 to 1990* (St. John's: Institute of Social and Economic Research, Memorial University of Newfoundland, 1994).

20 per cent of the stock each year was actually letting them take about 35 per cent.

The scientists thought they knew a lot more than they did. They were trying to estimate fish stocks in an area of tens of thousands of square kilometres. They used statistical models and they tried to check their figures by sending vessels out to do test fishing, but there was a huge amount of room for error. The problem with the fisheries scientists was they believed in themselves too much.

A politician has to be concerned about protecting both the fish stocks and the livelihood of fishermen. We couldn't suddenly cut the TAC by more than half. If we did, for historic and political reasons, we would have had to give priority to inshore fishermen or accept the death of their outport communities. Cutting the total allowable catch to 125,000 tonnes overnight would have wiped out the offshore fishery. Two large Canadian companies were primarily involved in the offshore fishery – National Sea Products in Halifax and Fishery Products International in St. John's; both had fish-processing plants along the south and east coasts of Newfoundland. If we accepted the new TAC recommended by the scientists, both National Sea and Fishery Products International would have gone bankrupt. "We are dealing with thousands of human beings, who live and breathe and eat and need jobs – fishermen and the like, so we are not going to, because of the formula . . . immediately go to a quota of 125,000 tonnes," I told a press conference in St. John's.

Siddon, as Fisheries minister, and I, after reviewing the situation with our officials, decided to reduce the TAC for northern cod to 235,000 tonnes for 1989 only. The scientists assured us that one year's fishing at this level would not endanger the stocks.

Obviously, we needed more information. Siddon established the Northern Cod Review Panel, chaired by Leslie Harris, the former president of Memorial University, a distinguished historian with considerable experience in the problems of the fishing industry and an outport man himself.

Enjoying Question Period, February 1985.

Vote for Grand Dad, 1988.

With Prime Minister and Mila Mulroney, and Carol and Brian Peckford at Peckford's retirement dinner, March 1989.

In the office of the prime minister, 1991.

Jane with Mila Mulroney at Roy Thomson Hall in Toronto, September 1984, at a fund-raiser to help pay off my leadership-race debts.

International Trade Ministers' Meeting in British Columbia, April 1988.
Left to right: Clayton Yeutter, U.S. Trade Representative; Hajime Tamura,
Minister of International Trade, Japan; Willy De Clercq, European
Commissioner of External Relations.

The Canadian GATT negotiating team included, clockwise around the table,
from left: Charlie Mayer, me, Bill Crosbie, unidentified, Gerry Shannon,
Germain Denis, and Sylvia Ostry. December 1988.

In Washington, March 1989, with U.S. Trade Representative Carla Hills, to discuss free trade.

"Brother Serre and Sister Hills": Jaime Serre, the Mexican trade and industry minister, and U.S. Trade Representative Carla Hills, February 1991.

Jane and I meet Fidel Castro in Cuba, April 20, 1992.

Gerry Boland

At a fund-raiser in support of Jean Charest's bid for the leadership of the federal Conservative party, June 1993: Craig Dobbin, Elaine Parsons, and Jean Charest.

The family gathers for Beth's wedding in 1983. Standing left to right:
Michael and Lynn, Brian Alexander and Beth, me, Ches and Lois.
Jane is seated.

With the grandchildren
at Kaegudeck Lake,
south of Gander.

March 1997: the $5 billion
Hibernia gravity-based
structure now mated with
the topsides nears completion
at Bull Arm, Trinity Bay.
Right: The same Hibernia
structure as it was when it
was towed out from Bull Arm
to its home on the Grand
Banks in late May 1997.

At the end of 1989, we took the total allowable catch for 1990 down another notch, to 197,000 tonnes, or 38,000 tonnes fewer than in 1989. We were on the right track, but we had to move slowly for social and economic reasons.

Any reduction in the allowable catch produced an angry reaction from people whose livelihood depended on the fishery. Two hundred angry fish-plant workers booed and hissed as Siddon and I entered the hotel in St. John's where we announced the 1990 TAC of 197,000 tonnes. Within this total, the traditional allowance of 115,000 tonnes for the inshore fishery would be preserved. Although Siddon and I knew we were walking a very thin line between scientific advice and economic reality, we were trying to keep the TAC high enough to permit the continuation of part of the offshore fishery and save the jobs of people employed by at least one of the three threatened plants owned by Fishery Products International (FPI).

If we'd followed the advice of the Harris panel, the TAC for 1990 would have been 190,000 tonnes. However, I favoured a slightly higher number because I believed, if the quota was a bit larger, FPI might be able to keep its fish plant open at Trepassey in my constituency.

At the hotel, fish-plant workers, trawlermen, and union officials angrily denounced the handling of the fisheries crisis. Someone shouted out to me: "You'll be gone in the next election, buddy." To which I responded that I would not be going without a damn good fight and called the heckler a "big mouth."

The threat to Newfoundland's northern cod fishery could only be compared on a scale of disasters to what the situation in Southern Ontario would be if the entire auto-manufacturing industry was eliminated overnight. The state of the fish stocks, as the scientists were now warning us, was so perilous as to threaten the survival of the northern-cod fishery. This meant that every ground-fish plant along the province's north and northeast coast, and every coastal community thereon, was threatened with economic disaster.

At the end of 1990, Valcourt, who'd succeeded Siddon as Fisheries minister, announced the 1991 quota for northern cod would be 187,860 tonnes, down 9,140 tonnes from 1990. We projected a further reduction in 1992 to 183,000 tonnes, and in 1993 to 178,145 tonnes. Victor Young, chairman and chief executive of FPI, thought that, with these TACs, he could avoid any further offshore plant closures and that FPI could continue, with provincial financing, to operate its plants at Gaultois, Trepassey, and Grand Bank as scheduled for twenty weeks in 1991 before closing permanently.

The picture grew bleaker month by month. In October 1991, when Les Harris, the chairman of the panel, was interviewed for a CBC fisheries broadcast, he expressed grave concern about the health of the northern-cod stocks. He said he believed they had reached a dangerously low level, so low, in fact, that he worried whether the species would survive. The program then interviewed Brian Morrissey, who was then the assistant deputy minister for science of Fisheries and Oceans. Morrissey said the stocks appeared to have increased since the Harris panel did its study and, in his view, the situation was not as alarming as Harris found it. Future events showed that Harris's forecast was far more accurate than the assessment of the scientific branch of DFO.

I was still struggling to keep the fishery open. In December 1991, I announced that the total allowable catch for 1992 would be 120,000 tonnes, the lowest TAC ever. I was influenced in my decision by an estimate from the Canadian Atlantic Fisheries Scientific Advisory Committee (CAFSAC) that put the total northern-cod stock biomass at 1.1 million tonnes, of which the critical spawning biomass of six- and seven-year-old cod accounted for 270,000 tonnes. Two months later, however, CAFSAC lowered its estimate to a new biomass total of 780,000 tonnes, of which the spawning biomass was only 130,000 tonnes. In other words, the scientists were telling me that there were fewer than half as many sexually active cod as I was told there were when I set the 120,000-tonne TAC for 1992.

It was obviously impossible for the department to manage the fishery properly when the advice it received from its scientists varied so alarmingly. I started to talk about the possibility of a moratorium on fishing for northern cod.

In all of my years of political life, this was the most serious political and economic crisis I faced. The first indication of any real problem with the northern-cod stocks had been delivered to DFO by our scientists in December 1988. Only three years later, it appeared that the very survival of the species was at stake.

In addition to overfishing, there were general environmental conditions that contributed to the decline. The sea water in the area was considerably colder than usual, and the low water temperatures affected the health, condition, and size of the northern cod. A large increase in the seal population as a result of restrictions on the seal hunt caused by the unfavourable publicity generated by certain radical and irresponsible elements of the environmental movement had an effect, too. It was certain that, if the seals did not consume large quantities of the northern cod, they consumed large quantities of capelin, which was the main food source for the northern cod and for many other marine creatures.

I could not close the northern-cod fishery for the first time in five centuries without first having some kind of assistance plan in place for the twenty thousand fishermen and fish-plant workers in two hundred to three hundred communities along half of Newfoundland's 9,600-kilometre coastline. They would be left without work or income during the remainder of 1992, and for the indefinite future. My able deputy minister, Bruce Rawson, and his chief aide, Maryantonett Flumian, the assistant deputy minister for policy, went to work on an economic-assistance program. Under the program, the federal government would spend more than $500 million to compensate Newfoundlanders who lost their livelihood in the moratorium.

∾

Everybody in Newfoundland had their favourite explanation for the drastic decline in cod stocks. As many people saw it, over-fishing by foreigners was the main cause. Naturally, everybody blamed the Government of Canada, although the public never seemed to agree on just where the mismanagement took place. Some blamed the scientists, a view for which I had some sympathy. They suffered from what the Greeks called "hubris," or overweening pride, leading to nemesis.

An ocean is not a laboratory, and commercial fishermen are not research assistants. The fish are not owned by anyone, but rather are a common resource. This being so, the fishery is based on the principle that the first gets the most, and therefore everyone tries frantically to take as many fish as possible before the fish are caught by others. No one feels obliged to practise conservation. If one fisherman conserves stocks while his rivals do not, the effort is futile. The environmentally responsible fisherman suffers the consequences of the negligence of the others. In these circumstances, no one has much incentive to follow the principles of sustainable conservation. Most fishermen discard species of fish that they do not want, and those fish are lost and unreported. Many fishermen misreport what they actually catch and land at the various ports of Atlantic Canada.

No doubt the reason for the decline of the fish stocks also was connected with colder water and more ice than usual, but harvesting levels and practices played a significant role as well. We needed scientific advice more closely linked to the experience of fishermen and the fishing industry.

∾

I was constantly disappointed throughout the fisheries crises by the attitude of Premier Clyde Wells and the Liberal government of Newfoundland. Although he gave the public the impression that he was motivated by only the highest principles, he tried repeatedly to extract political advantage from the situation. He blamed Ottawa for mismanaging the fishery, although neither he nor the other three Atlantic premiers had ever urged the federal government to reduce allowable catches. To the contrary, the provinces kept pushing for higher overall quotas and a larger share of the total. They kept licensing additional fish-processing plants, even though existing plants were operating below capacity. And they approved more and more loans for fishermen to purchase fishing gear.

Wells's pet cause was "joint management" of the fishery. What he wanted was a veto over every aspect of federal fisheries management – without committing the province to invest an additional dime. Joint management would have given Newfoundland control not only over fish quotas for Newfoundland fishermen, but over some fish taken by Nova Scotia and New Brunswick fishermen as well. Joint management couldn't work unless all four Atlantic provinces, plus Quebec, agreed. That wasn't about to happen.

∾

I closed the northern-cod fishery at the beginning of July 1992. It was ironic, I suppose. Fishing is more important to Newfoundland than it is to any other province. I was only the second Newfoundlander to be the federal Minister of Fisheries (my colleague Jim McGrath being the first, in the Clark government). I was unique in having been a provincial Fisheries minister as well. And I was a Crosbie, a member of a family that had built its business empire on the fishery. Here I was, a Crosbie and a Newfoundlander, shutting down the industry that had made it possible for Newfoundland to be settled and to survive for all these centuries.

The northern cod was not my only source of trauma. In a report on Atlantic ground-fish stocks in November 1992, CAFSAC recommended severe cuts in quotas for other Atlantic species. The recommendation included a total reduction of 69,000 tonnes for three other cod stocks in the southern Gulf of St. Lawrence, off the eastern Scotian shelf, and off the south coast of Newfoundland. The scientists had found that the cod, haddock, and pollock stocks were at their lowest levels since the early 1970s.

In December, I held a press conference in Halifax to announce the management plan for the Atlantic fishery for 1993. Quotas for cod were cut by about 50 per cent, which affected fishery workers on the south coast of Newfoundland, the Gaspé region of Quebec, and the three Maritime provinces. Cape Breton was hit first, as National Sea Products announced it was closing two plants indefinitely, at Louisbourg and North Sydney.

I also closed the Newfoundland commercial fishery for Atlantic salmon, because I was sure there would be no salmon left to catch in a year or two if the fishery continued. I established a compensation plan for commercial fishermen who surrendered their licences. The recreational or sports salmon fishery stayed open, with a limit of eight fish per angler per season. Fifty years earlier, the limit had been eight fish per day! We negotiated agreements with the provinces for a comprehensive plan for stock rebuilding, and better enforcement programs were also put in place. A salmon fisherman myself, I was delighted with the encouragement I received from the public and, in particular, from fly-fishing enthusiasts.

∾

The way of life of the outports of Newfoundland has been centred on the fishery from the earliest days, but the nature of people's dependency has changed. In recent years, their economic survival has depended less on the fish they caught than on their ability to qualify for financial-support programs. Federal unemployment insurance is the lifeblood of rural Newfoundland. If a man catches fish for twelve weeks in the summer, he will accumulate enough stamps to draw UI until the following May. His wife and some of his children may work in the fish plant, processing fish in the summer, and get enough stamps to get UI, too. If a family has three or four or five people with UI coming in all winter, they'll have lots of cash. They probably live in a house on which they pay little, if any, municipal taxes, a comfortable house they may have built themselves. They can have a very good life. In the first fifteen years after the new unemployment insurance system came into force in 1972, the number of people fishing in Newfoundland doubled, while the number working in fish processing almost tripled. They weren't catching or processing any more fish. What they were doing was spreading the work around so that everyone could qualify for UI. You couldn't blame people for this. The government introduced the program, and the public took advantage of it, naturally.

Statistics told the story. By 1986, the average fishing family's income in Newfoundland was $19,850, of which 41 per cent came from unemployment insurance, 24 per cent from fishing, 30 per cent from other employment, and 5 per cent from other sources. In Nova Scotia, the average fishing family's income was $35,100 – 53 per cent from fishing, 25 per cent from other employment, 16 per cent from UI, and 6 per cent from other sources. By comparison, in Saskatchewan, the average farm family had an income of $32,000 – 34 per cent from farming, 40 per cent from other employment earnings, 26 per cent from other sources, and nothing from UI.

∾

The problems of the fishery were heart-breaking. In June 1991, about a thousand of my constituents from the Avalon Peninsula town of Trepassey brought their plight to the steps of the Confederation Building at St. John's. Fisheries Products International had announced it would permanently close its fish plant there in September, along with plants in the south-coast towns of Grand Bank and Gaultois; 1,170 plant workers and 169 trawlermen were to be laid off. As the people from Trepassey pointed out, the fishery had provided a livelihood for them and their forebears for more than four hundred years. No one, they believed, should be allowed to take the fishery from them.

These were fine, decent, hard-working people, who, through no fault of their own, were about to find themselves without jobs. I felt helpless. All I could do was to assure them that I would do everything possible to find another use for the fish plant or alternative employment opportunities. But I couldn't find anything. We had better luck in Grand Bank, where FPI closed its ground-fish plant. Clearwater Fisheries of Nova Scotia took over the plant to establish an Icelandic scallop and Arctic surf-clam processing operation, employing 220 people. The FPI plant at Gaultois was reopened by Compak Sea Foods Incorporated to process red fish, an operation that employed 250.

A special cabinet subcommittee on the Atlantic fisheries met frequently to devise a financial-support program to put in place when I had to announce the closure of the northern-cod fishery. Given the overall financial position of the government and the frightening dimensions of the deficit, I was unable to convince my colleagues that the amount of assistance they were prepared to approve was woefully inadequate from a political or human point of view. With a meagre assistance package in hand, I set off to Newfoundland for the 1992 Canada Day weekend, planning to make my announcement – and take my lumps – at a press conference in St. John's on July 2.

I'd been invited to visit the community of Bay Bulls on July 1 for a combined celebration of Canada Day and Bay Bulls Day. As part of the celebration, a Department of Fisheries and Oceans patrol vessel was dispatched to the town. Jane and I took six of our young grandchildren with us, together with several of their parents. As we drove into Bay Bulls, I noticed several CBC vehicles parked on the road leading to the wharf, and a large crowd assembled along the harbour and out on the wharf. The CBC vehicles were a sure sign that I was in for a rough time. The news media do not normally show up in Bay Bulls on Canada Day or any other day. They appear when they've been tipped off that a demonstration or similar action is planned.

It was obvious that many of those in the crowd had had a few drinks, and I was the recipient of a considerable amount of loud heckling and abuse. As an unruly crowd can be dangerous, I was worried that my grandchildren might be trampled or pushed around.

After taking a certain amount of taunting and jeering, I turned on a heckler to shout that there was no point in taking their frustration out on me because I hadn't removed the "god-damned" fish from the sea. This exchange, including my exple-tive, was broadcast across Canada that evening. We walked on down to the DFO vessel, where a member of the crew showed the youngsters around the vessel while I spoke to the crowd. Because this was in my own constituency, I knew many of the people and did not feel in any immediate danger. Nevertheless, the mood was ugly and ominous. We walked the gauntlet back to our cars to the noise of more catcalls and jeering. I couldn't blame my constituents, for they were suddenly faced with a very traumatic prospect. I was doubly determined to make sure they received all the assistance I could possibly obtain for them from the federal government.

It was clear from the scene at Bay Bulls that I could expect the worst when I made my announcement in St. John's the next day. And that's what I got. A huge crowd waited in the lobby of the Radisson Hotel, where the press conference was to be held; as on the day before, a number had been drinking. Several hundred chairs had been set up in the conference room, with closed-circuit TV to carry the proceedings to an adjoining room.

Without my knowledge, it had been decided to allow only media representatives in the room where the press conference took place. Some fishermen who tried to get in were turned away, and this angered them. As I started speaking from the head table, there was a loud knocking on the doors, which were closed and barred. Soon the crowd were trying to batter down the doors. As reporters started to slip away to cover the commotion outside, I carried on with my statement, explaining why we had decided to close the northern-cod fishery for at least the next two years.

Then I announced our pitiful compensation program. Fisher-men and fish-plant workers affected by this closure would receive

$225 a week each for ten weeks until a longer term and more comprehensive relief plan could be developed. I had warned my colleagues that $225 a week would be treated with contempt, and it was.

The security people decided to get me and my party out of the hotel before something serious happened, and we were escorted to safety.

The pandemonium in St. John's was broadcast across the country. The televised outrage of Newfoundland fishermen had a powerful effect on my colleagues in Ottawa. Within two weeks I was authorized to return to Newfoundland and announce the Northern Cod Adjustment and Recovery Program (NCARP), known to all as "The Package." Its regulations became known as "The Bible." Under this program, the compensation ranged from a minimum of $225 a week to a maximum of $406 a week. Applicants for assistance who did not wish to take any training at all received the minimum. Workers who opted for training inside or outside the fishery could receive more, up to the $406 maximum. Provision was later made for payments for the retirement of licences of fishermen who left the fishery. Within eight months, 18,000 compensation forms had been processed, with 10,768 applicants choosing training inside the fishery, 2,045 choosing training outside the fishery, and 1,600 opting for early retirement.

In my view, in the future only professional, full-time fishermen should be eligible for a licence to fish, and anyone trying to enter the industry as a fisherman should have to pass courses approved by provincial governments and the fishermen's union. We have to stop the traditional free entry into the fishery and institute severely controlled entry.

∽

While the commercial fisheries of Canada contribute only about 1 per cent of the value of all commodity-producing industries to the economy of Canada, fishing is pre-eminent in some regions. Along the Atlantic coast, about a thousand communities are mostly, if not completely, dependent upon the fisheries. Lesser numbers of such communities are found on the Pacific coast and around the lakes of the Canadian interior. The fishery of British Columbia is usually the leader in value of production, while, in the Atlantic provinces, Newfoundland leads in volume, and Nova Scotia in value, together accounting for 80 per cent of the Atlantic output.

In addition to the unprecedented problems that I encountered in the Atlantic fishery during my period as Minister of Fisheries, severe problems also developed in B.C. The most valuable fishery on the Pacific coast of Canada is the one involving the five species of Pacific salmon which have a two- to five-year cycle, from being born in rivers, migrating to the sea, and returning to the same rivers to spawn and die. As these returning salmon approach and concentrate off the river mouths, they are caught by large, modern fishing vessels. The largest catches are obtained off the mouths of the Fraser and Skeena river systems. The salmon, either frozen or canned, are a valuable export for Canada.

From an administrative perspective, the Pacific fishery differs from its Atlantic counterpart in that Ottawa has to deal with only one province, making for fewer jurisdictional issues. But the picture is greatly complicated by the need for cooperation with the United States. Huge numbers of salmon returning from the Pacific each year swim through both Canadian and American waters on their way to their home rivers. The state of Alaska is ideally located geographically to intercept these migrating salmon as they return to the rivers of British Columbia as well as to the lower forty-eight states.

The B.C. fishery also suffers from conflict between the commercial fishermen who catch the salmon for processing and the recreational or sports fishermen who are tremendously important to the B.C. tourism industry.

Further complicating the picture is the question of the fishing rights of the aboriginal peoples of British Columbia. In a landmark decision in May 1990, the Supreme Court of Canada ruled that fishing by aboriginals had priority over all other interests, except the need for conservation. Aboriginal Canadians were held by the court to have a constitutionally protected right to take fish for food, social, and ceremonial purposes. The decision had national ramifications, but its most direct effect was in British Columbia and, to a lesser extent, in New Brunswick. Unfortunately, the court did not address the issue of whether the Native people could legally operate a commercial fishery. DFO estimated that nearly one million salmon annually were caught and sold commercially by the Natives of British Columbia.

I decided to allow B.C. Natives to sell salmon legally for the first time since 1888, but only as part of an interim agreement while land-claim settlements were worked out. This was a practical as well as constitutional approach. Massive military-style patrols of the three vast river systems in British Columbia would be necessary if we were to stop the illegal sale of salmon by Natives. That was obviously neither desirable nor possible. By legalizing it, we would have some control over the management of the fishery.

After exhaustive consultations, I took a new Aboriginal Fisheries Strategy (AFS) to cabinet for approval in the late fall of 1991. AFS was a five-year, $135-million program. The thrust of the strategy was to negotiate interim agreements with each of the First Nations on fisheries management, pending final land-claims agreements. A large part of the money involved would be directed towards more federally funded habitat restoration to be carried out by Native groups along B.C.'s three main river systems. AFS would enable us to buy out commercial licences as allocations were transferred to the Native communities.

A long delay in obtaining the cabinet approval of our aboriginal strategy caused difficulties in enforcement in 1992. More than 100,000 Fraser River sockeye salmon were reported to have failed to reach the counting stations on their journey up the river system. As soon as I heard of this, I ordered an internal DFO investigation. My deputy minister, Bruce Rawson, gave me a choice. I could try to stop the loss of these salmon by increasing enforcement, or I could close the Fraser River system completely to the fishery. The next day, I ordered a complete closure of the Fraser River fishery, and I kept it closed for the rest of that fishing season, with the exception of a severely limited fishery later in the fall.

Even with this setback, 1992 was a very successful year for the B.C. salmon fishery. But all the media attention was focused on angry allegations against aboriginal fishermen and the relentless, racist bullying of the Native communities by some spokesmen for the commercial industry. Wild and irresponsible accusations flew. The truth soon became a casualty of this campaign launched by those opposed to increased Native participation in the fishery. Blockades harassed innocent third parties, nets were strung across the streets of Vancouver, and from time to time attempts were made to humiliate my officials – including the deputy minister, who was chased through the streets of Vancouver by a crowd of agitators wearing orange survival suits.

In my final few days as Minister of Fisheries in June 1993, negotiations with the United States over the Pacific salmon treaty broke down, and a west-coast salmon war seemed possible. The breakdown occurred because the various U.S. interest groups from Alaska, Washington state, and Oregon couldn't reach a consensus among themselves. Salmon was big business in both countries, with commercial salmon fishing employing about 15,000 people in B.C. and salmon exports worth $400 million a year. Recreational fishing added an estimated $1.3 billion annually to the B.C. economy.

The United States was unwilling to recognize the fact that, while Canadian salmon had flourished due to conservation measures, the number of salmon spawned in U.S. rivers had been continually dropping. Just before I left office, we agreed with the United States to set catch allocations for 1993 only. The administration of the Pacific salmon stocks by the United States and Canada still requires a proper long-term resolution.

∽

An important element of a Fisheries minister's life involves negotiating with other countries. In the case of France, it was the maritime boundary between Canada and the islands of St. Pierre and Miquelon. In the case of the United States, it was the management of the Pacific salmon fishery. But the most important, and time-consuming, part of my international effort involved negotiating, pleading, and threatening other countries, principally European, to reduce the quantity of fish they persisted in taking off Canada's East Coast. The countries of the European Community consistently abused the High Seas Fish Management system, often at Canada's expense.

In 1988, Tom Siddon, then Fisheries minister, had asked me to speak at a private reception for delegates to a North Atlantic Fishery Organization (NAFO) meeting in Ottawa. The Europeans had voted against a recommendation by NAFO scientists for sharp cuts in fish quotas for the fishing grounds outside 200 miles. Ignoring the text prepared for me by officials, I delivered a stinging attack on European fishing practices, pointing out that stocks outside Canada's 200-mile zone had been heavily overfished and that European fishermen, particularly the Spanish and Portuguese, were the main culprits. All twenty to twenty-five members of the European delegation walked out to protest my remarks.

This was the real start of my long battle against the European Community to save the "straddling" fish stocks, like the cod, that swim both within Canada's 200-mile zone and outside it, on the continental shelf of the Grand Banks of Newfoundland. At the time I spoke, the Europeans had an annual NAFO quota of 17,000 tonnes; they were taking 109,000 tonnes. My struggle with the EC nations went on for five years, ending only when the northern cod and flatfish stocks were practically wiped out in the seas off the east coast of Canada.

Later on, I went to La Toja, Spain, to appeal to thirty-five nations attending a NAFO meeting there to stop their over-fishing. Our fishermen were restricted in the amount of fish they could take within the 200-mile zone. However, they, and our fish-plant workers on shore, were being driven out of business and their coastal communities were being destroyed by distant-water fishing fleets that overfished unabatedly just outside 200 miles.

In 1991, the *St. John's Evening Telegram* published an editorial calling for "gun boat diplomacy" to stop this plunder. Somehow, I could not imagine Brian Mulroney ever agreeing to open fire on a European fishing vessel. But, as intemperate and unrealistic as the newspaper editorial was, it represented the view of a great many Atlantic Canadians. I didn't think the EC could be brought to their knees as easily as the *Evening Telegram* did.

We appointed Allan Beesley, Canada's most experienced negotiator on the Law of the Sea, to head up our negotiating effort with NAFO countries and with such non-NAFO countries as South Korea and flag-of-convenience states like Panama and Honduras. For Canada to take unilateral action outside the 200-mile economic zone would mean taking the law into our own hands, and the result would likely be armed conflict. Unilateral action would certainly not be sanctioned by the government until we had exhausted all diplomatic alternatives.

I carried our campaign to Brussels to the annual meetings at which Canada and the EC review their relationship. The EC countries agreed to the establishment of a high-level committee to resolve the overfishing dispute. Finally, they now recognized that there was a problem that needed to be resolved.

Gradually, we elevated a low-level fishing quarrel to a top-level political issue. Mulroney talked to French president François Mitterrand about it. He raised the overfishing question with the Portuguese prime minister during the NATO summit meeting in Brussels, and he and Joe Clark took it up during a meeting with the Spanish prime minister. Following the Brussels meeting, I visited Madrid and Lisbon for detailed discussions with the Spanish and Portuguese fisheries ministers. Neither Spain nor Portugal showed any inclination to settle the dispute. These countries had been sending fishermen to the northwest Atlantic waters for centuries, and it was not easy to get them to concede that a relatively new coastal nation, Canada, had any right to tell them what to do.

We initiated a major public-relations campaign in Europe to educate the public about overfishing. We stressed the concept of sustainable development originally advocated by the United Nations commission led by Norwegian prime minister Gro Harlem Brundtland. In managing renewable resources, we should use only as much as would leave sufficient resources for future generations. This was not a concept practised by the distant-water fishing nations.

In France and West Germany, I preached the need to stop overfishing outside the 200-mile economic zone. In a speech to the foreign press association in England, I explained that not only was the European Community setting excessive catch levels, but their fishermen relentlessly harvested juvenile fish. A random sample taken the previous month from a Spanish trawler contained 275 fish with a total weight of 113 pounds, or 51 kilograms. By taking immature fish, they were slaughtering a fish stock. Between 1986, when Spain and Portugal joined the EC, and 1989, European fishermen had taken 410,000 tonnes of fish – seven times the quotas allotted to the EC countries by NAFO.

I led a delegation from the Newfoundland Fishermen's Union, the fishing industry, and the Fisheries Council of Canada on a four-day visit to Portugal, where we met the Prime Minister, the Minister of Agriculture, the Minister of Fisheries and Food, and other cabinet members, as well as fishing-vessel owners. The Portuguese ship owners were completely inflexible.

We stepped up our public-relations campaign and legal initiatives by pressing for international support for conservation through the United Nations Conference on the Environment and Development, which culminated at an international Earth Summit meeting in Rio de Janeiro in June 1992. In the weeks leading up to the Rio meeting, I led a mission to London, Hong Kong, and Japan. I also addressed the Royal Institute of International Affairs in London about this overfishing dilemma. I made it clear that our patience could snap if the EC did not reduce its fishing. One possible step would be to unilaterally extend Canada's fisheries jurisdiction beyond 200 miles. "We would have to consider whatever unilateral actions a country can take that sees the livelihood of its citizens who live in the coastal areas in peril," I said. "I'm not threatening to extend jurisdiction, I'm just saying this is one possible option, all else failing."

An Opposition motion in the Commons called on the government to extend our "functional jurisdiction" to the nose and tail of the Grand Banks. We defeated the motion by a vote of ninety-one to fifty-one, but I didn't rule out unilateral action. I said the time for such drastic action had not yet arrived. We had not quite exhausted the diplomatic route.

I visited Panama to meet with the Finance minister and other senior officials to ask them to take steps to end fishing by Panamanian-flagged vessels in the northwest Atlantic. Most of these Panama-registered vessels were operated by Spanish and Portuguese owners, while some were owned by South Koreans. The Panamanians agreed to forbid vessels registered in Panama to fish in the NAFO area. From Panama, I went to Cuba, where the Fisheries minister, Fernandez Cuervo, gave us a strong commitment.

Back in Ottawa, Mulroney and I met the president of the European Community, Jacques Delors, and the Portuguese prime minister, Cavaço Silva. They were pleased that we had requested a special meeting of NAFO's scientific council to assess the state of cod stocks.

The campaign continued. In Cancun, Mexico, I attended the Conference on Responsible Fishing initiated by Mexico and attended by more than six hundred delegates from sixty-six countries. At the beginning of June, the European Community promised to suspend fishing in international waters off our east coast. It said it would stop fishing for cod on the nose and tail of the Grand Banks and that fishing for flatfish species such as American plaice and yellowtail flounder would also be suspended. I welcomed this, but suggested that European fishermen were finding insufficient cod to make it worth their while. The EC brazenly announced that it was Canadian overfishing that had been the main cause of the cod-stock decline.

The U.N. World Conference on the Environment and Development met with great fanfare in Rio de Janeiro in early June 1992. Canada sponsored a resolution, supported by 39 other nations, proposing that the United Nations convene a conference on Straddling and Highly Migratory Fish Stocks in 1993. The resolution was approved unanimously by the 188 nations in attendance. Even the European Community withdrew its opposition. And six months later, we finally reached a comprehensive fisheries agreement with the European Community, thanks to the negotiating skill of Randy Gherson, whom I chose to be our ambassador for marine conservation following Allan Beesley's retirement because of ill health. It took several years before the EC formally ratified this agreement. Ironically, Canada did not ratify it. When the Liberals came to power in 1993, they opted for the showier, more sensational route of unilateral action, as Brian Tobin, while federal Fisheries minister, launched his Turbot War with Spain. It worked for Tobin. It made him a household name in Canada and a hero in Newfoundland, and it paved the way for his election as Newfoundland Liberal leader and premier.

I chose the less dramatic diplomatic route. For several years, I had waged an intense and effective international campaign to address the problem of overfishing on the high seas. The difficulty from a politician's perspective was that diplomacy is not exciting and doesn't attract much news coverage. It's far easier to get attention by taking some sensational action, such as seizing another country's vessels on the high seas. But I was interested in having effective international rules put in place. Unless the countries of the world agreed on the need for super-vision, inspection, and enforcement, the rules would be of no use. It took years, but diplomatic solutions were more likely to be effective than extralegal measures that invited retaliation.

I was gratified to read the opinion of Toronto *Globe and Mail* columnist Jeffrey Simpson. "Mr. Crosbie has done three things manifestly right. He has closed the northern cod fishery, squeezed out of Ottawa a generous compensation plan for displaced fishermen and, now, negotiated an excellent deal with the EC." Simpson concluded: ". . . It's doubtful anyone else in politics – including his cabinet colleagues or the nitpicking premier of Newfoundland, Clyde Wells – could have displayed the courage and tenacity to achieve these objectives."

∾

The *St. John's Evening Telegram* announced I had been chosen by its readers Newfoundland newsmaker of the year for 1992, defeat-ing Premier Clyde Wells by a five-to-one margin. The paper said that I'd made some historic and unprecedented decisions:

> He shut down the 500-year-old northern cod fishery for two years in July, throwing roughly 20,000 fishermen and plant workers out of work. However, Crosbie didn't let them starve. Industry workers are receiving up to $406 a week in compensation during the moratorium. The St. John's native also banned the commercial salmon fishery on the island portion of the province for five years and his department bought out the majority of licenses. He imposed deep quota cuts on most Atlantic groundfish stocks and made headway in curbing foreign over-fishing outside Canada's 200-mile limit. But Crosbie's most unfor-gettable move was the fishery shut-down and implementa-tion of the subsequent income assistance program.

As usual, Jane put everything in perspective. She told reporters: "He might be my husband, but I also happen to believe in him. And you look – anything interesting that anybody in cabinet says usually comes from my husband."

∾

Canada maintained good relations with Cuba throughout Fidel Castro's years in power, and our relationship on fisheries questions was especially close. We have long allowed Cuban vessels to fish within our 200-mile economic zone for silver hake. This species of fish is so bony that it's extremely difficult to handle and expensive to process. Canadian processors prefer cod, haddock, and other species that have a higher value and are easier to filet and cheaper to pack. But the Cubans are hungry, they need the protein, and they don't mind taking the trouble to process bony fish. There's a lot of hake off Nova Scotia, and the Cubans, in fact, have contracted with Nova Scotia companies to process some of their catch. Over the years, a number of joint ventures have been formed between Cuba and Nova Scotia firms to utilize the silver hake.

We were in Cuba for several days. One night, the Canadian ambassador, Julie Loranger, had a dinner for us. It was very nice, but the dinner was outside in her garden and we were nearly eaten alive by mosquitoes. Our host, Fernandez Cuervo, the fisheries minister, asked if I'd like to meet Castro. On our last day in Cuba, he and his wife took us to a VIP guest house at Varadero Beach for a day of swimming and sunning ourselves. While we were there, Cuervo said Castro wanted to see us; a meeting, followed by dinner, was arranged for that evening at the government palace in Havana.

I found Castro to be tall and handsome, with an upright carriage and a keen intellect. He didn't smoke and he appeared to be in excellent health. He was interested in all the Canadians present, speaking individually to each of us and exhibiting a great deal of charm. Castro obviously had an eye for attractive women, paying particular attention to blonde-haired Ros Walsh of my staff, whom he invited to contact him if she ever returned to Cuba!

He was full of questions about all aspects of the fishery, the relationship between Canada and Cuba, and Canada in general. He was accompanied by a woman who translated his Spanish into English just as Castro spoke, so we didn't have to wait for translation. She translated my replies instantaneously into Spanish. It was my impression that Castro spoke and understood English, but wouldn't use the language because of the bitter state of relations between Cuba and the United States.

For the first hour, I explained the overfishing issue. He paid attention to every detail and called for maps so that I could show him the exact locations I was talking about. Castro was especially interested when I explained the dispute between France and Canada over the maritime boundary between St. Pierre and Miquelon and Newfoundland. He had no idea that France owned these two little pimples of islands. He ordered Cuervo to give Canada his full support on fisheries issues.

After this, Castro led us in to dinner. He served a magnificent fish that had been encased and cooked in salt. It was delicious – and it was an anomaly in that country. Many Cuban people weren't too far from starvation. Everything was rationed. If they were lucky, they had a bicycle; otherwise they had to walk. There was hardly any public transportation because there was no fuel for the buses. We were told things were so desperate that people were permitted to buy just one pair of underwear every two years.

But even if they went to bed hungry, the Cubans supported Castro and his government. They blamed their economic problems on the United States, of course, and it was easy to see that, as long as the Americans maintained their embargo against Cuba, they were going to get the blame for everything that was wrong in the country. It was clear to me that as long as the Americans persisted in their pig-headed policy of bullying Cuba, the Cubans were going to keep Castro in power.

The dinner conversation was lively. I asked Castro whether, after thirty-three years in power, he was starting to think about retirement. He was very cool to that suggestion, saying he would retire when the Cuban people thought he should. All the Cubans at the dinner quickly assured him that his retirement was the last thing they desired – "No. No," they shouted.

When I asked if they did any public-opinion polling in Cuba, Castro replied that they did, but it wasn't really necessary because he always knew what the people were thinking. He said he was considering the introduction of some kind of system of elections for positions within the party, and perhaps even general elections, although only one party would be permitted to nominate candidates. I got the sense that the Cuban leadership was open to modest reforms, but they were nervous about making many changes – such as removing censorship or freeing political prisoners – because they'd seen how regimes in Eastern Europe had collapsed when oppressive laws were lifted.

I came away from the evening with Castro convinced of two things. First, that the close relationship between Canada and Cuba should be continued and strengthened. Second, that, if the Americans would reverse their policy of organized hostility towards Cuba, drop their embargo, and open trade relations with Cuba, there would be a change of government there within months.

I concluded there might be a role for Canada to play as a bridge between Havana and Washington. When I got back to Ottawa, I wrote to Mulroney to tell him about our evening with Castro and to suggest that he meet Castro following the 1992 U.S. presidential election. Castro had indicated to me that he knew there was no point in approaching Washington in an election year because Cuba was such an inflammatory political issue to Americans. But I thought that, after the election was out of the way, Mulroney might be able to initiate a rapprochement between Castro and the White House.

I believed then, and I still believe, that with Canada's ties to Cuba and Mulroney's close relationship with U.S. leaders, he would have been a perfect catalyst to bring the two countries together. Mulroney indicated interest in my proposal, but nothing came of it before he retired the following year. I think if he'd had another year or two, he might have made the attempt to mediate between Havana and Washington. He's a superb mediator, and it would have been a great way to cap his years as prime minister.

∾

In most government departments, the minister has a chance to develop policies and implement programs to increase the prosperity of the nation and enhance the well-being of our citizens. In Fisheries, however, the challenge was to control a disaster. I wish I could say that we weren't too late in closing the fishery. I wish I could say the northern cod and other species are recovering and that the seas off Newfoundland will once again teem with fish as they did for the first five hundred years of our history. I wish I could say it, but I can't. Not yet. Probably never.

Although the fishing industry doesn't employ nearly as many people as it once did, it's still significant to Newfoundland's economy, generating about $800 million annually. The high-end species are doing well – shrimp, scallop, crab. The recovery of the salmon stocks gives us some cause for hope. When we closed the commercial salmon fishery, the situation was desperate. But now, with no nets to prevent the salmon from getting back to the rivers to spawn, the rivers of Newfoundland teem with salmon again and the sports fishery is booming.

It's likely to be the year 2000 before we'll know whether there'll be enough northern cod to support even a modest commercial fishery. If the fishery does reopen, it won't consist of thousands of fishermen going out in little boats for six or eight weeks a year. It will be fewer and larger boats – a middle-distance fleet operating within tightly controlled quotas. If Nature gives us a second chance, let's pray we don't repeat our mistakes.

21

PATRONAGE AND CONFLICT
OF INTEREST

Innis, Calgary Herald, reprinted
courtesy Glenbow Archives, Calgary, Alberta

ROSSY BARBOUR, A colourful character in Joey Smallwood's Liberal caucus in Newfoundland, had a refreshing – and realistic – way of looking at the honourable practice of political patronage. As Rossy would say in his Newfoundland accent, "To the victors belong the spiles!"

I'm with Rossy. I believe in political patronage. Leaders shouldn't be ashamed or embarrassed about looking after their supporters. Patronage is a good thing. It's essential to the democratic process. It makes the party system work. We should have more patronage, not less.

To my mind, patronage and conflict of interest are the reverse sides of the same political coin. Patronage – which simply means the support or encouragement given by a patron – is the way the spoils are delivered to worthy recipients. Conflict of interest is an abuse that needs to be controlled to prevent the spoils from falling into unworthy hands. No government does a good job of controlling conflict of interest. Mind you, most of them don't do much of a job when it comes to dispensing patronage, either.

Tens of thousands of people support political parties, year after year, election after election. Most of them don't do it because they expect great rewards, but because they believe in the cause, the philosophy, or the people who lead the party. They want to be involved and they want to help. If their party is successful and forms a government, they expect a little recognition. One form of recognition is an appointment to a position of some sort. An appointment confirms the gratitude and recognition of the recipient's party. It can be a small position that is more honorary than remunerative. Or it can be an important position that offers great prestige and good pay – anything from governor general, senator, or chairman of a Crown corporation on down. I've noticed that there's no shortage of party supporters who are willing to make themselves available for positions, large or small.

If I'd been prime minister, I wouldn't have rested until every single patronage position at my disposal was filled by a qualified Progressive Conservative. I'm not talking about appointing political supporters to the public service of Canada. The public service should be outside the patronage system, although there's no reason why governments shouldn't recruit exceptional people from the private sector, as Mulroney did, for top-level positions in the bureaucracy. I'm talking about the thousands of non–civil service positions that a government must fill. As long as the people appointed are qualified, the public has no reason to complain about their political affiliation.

Dispensing patronage is not as simple as it seems. Joe Clark, for example, offended many party loyalists by dragging his feet on patronage appointments during his brief term in office in 1979–80. Joe was always looking for Great Canadians to give jobs to; he should have settled for Good Conservatives. He filled very few patronage positions, and party supporters who had been waiting for years for some token of esteem held it against him later, when his leadership came under review.

John Turner's mishandling of patronage sealed his political fate when he followed Pierre Trudeau's parting instructions to appoint twenty-six Liberal MPs to federal sinecures on the eve of the 1984 election campaign. From ambassadorships to the bench to the Livestock Feed Board of Canada, worn-out Liberals, some utterly unqualified, were rushed by Turner to safe havens on the public payroll. It was the grossest orgy of pork-barrelling the country had ever seen. This prostitution of the system – too many appointees, too few *bona fides* – opened the way for Mulroney to demolish Turner on the patronage issue in the leaders' debate on television.

Mulroney made a mistake of his own in that debate. It wasn't what he said, but the impression he gave. He meant to leave the impression that we Tories, unlike the Liberals, would use the patronage system with restraint and would appoint only competent supporters, people of good character who had the requisite skills for the position to which they were being named. The impression he actually left, however, was quite different. It was that patronage was absolutely wrong and there would be no appointments of Conservative loyalists to federal posts, which was both absurd and impossible.

In all his nine years in office, Mulroney never learned how to manage patronage properly. He never explained to Canadians how the appointments system worked. He never made it clear that the problem with the system was not the *existence* of patronage but the *abuse* of patronage. He hurt himself by appointing some people whose only apparent credentials were the fact they were his personal friends – including his separatist friend Lucien Bouchard, whom he made Canadian ambassador to France. Mulroney was perceived to be rewarding cronies rather than recognizing hard-working Tory supporters. The government was never able to shake the perception that it was ruled by cronyism.

Mulroney didn't do himself any good when, from time to time, he named prominent Liberals or New Democrats to plum positions. The appointment of former Liberal cabinet minister

Donald S. Macdonald as high commissioner to London, former Canadian Labour Congress president Dennis McDermott as ambassador to Ireland, former Ontario NDP leader Stephen Lewis as Canadian ambassador to the United Nations, and former federal NDP leader Ed Broadbent as president of the International Centre for Human Rights and Democratic Development were seen by the public as feeble attempts to distract attention from the appointment of more Tories to other posts. The public was right. Mulroney didn't get any credit at all for being non-partisan or statesman-like when he went outside the Conservative party for talent, and we were never able to change the public's perception that we were acting in a hypocritical manner.

Although I thought those decoy appointments were foolish, I had no real objection to Macdonald's going to London; he'd done a great job as chairman of the Royal Commission on the Economic Union and Development Prospects for Canada. McDermott's appointment was a stupid waste of a perfectly good ambassadorship; organized labour wasn't going to thank us, or vote for us. But the one that really bothered me was the appointment of that puffed-up Stephen Lewis to the U.N. He was an arrogant ingrate and should never have been appointed to anything, not even janitor in the basement of the Senate.

It was another example of Mulroney's being too clever by half, of his trying to court favour with the limp left. He didn't consult the cabinet before making the appointment. Articulate and an effective speaker, Lewis had an astonishingly high opinion of himself. He wasn't shy about pushing his left-wing claptrap. On one occasion when Joe Clark was out of the country, I was acting External Affairs minister and had to respond in the Commons to public criticisms that Lewis made of Canadian defence policy. I stated that Lewis's comments were entirely out of place and did not represent government policy. If I'd been the External Affairs minister, I'd have taken his head off. It was unheard of for ambassadors or any high government officials to express in public their personal opinions if they contradicted the views of the administration.

Lewis apparently did not appreciate being told his comments had been out of place. A few days later, a gossip item appeared in the Toronto *Globe and Mail* about something Lewis said while introducing Environment minister Tom McMillan at a conference in Toronto. "You may think I spend my life introducing Conservative cabinet ministers," Lewis said. "There's some truth to that, but I am selective. You will notice that John Crosbie isn't on the platform."

This insulting and unnecessary remark was entirely inappropriate. No one in External Affairs could recall a time when public comments of a personal nature had been made by officials in Ottawa or ambassadors abroad about a member of the cabinet. However, I was told that Ambassador Lewis didn't regard himself as being "of the Department," or subject to the rules that apply to public servants. He apparently saw himself as the prime minister's personal envoy to the U.N., and External Affairs had little control over him.

I wrote to Mulroney to suggest Lewis be fired, or at least publicly reprimanded. If he hadn't been due to leave his post shortly, I would have made it my business to make sure he was removed. Mulroney didn't answer my letter, and Lewis's term was allowed to expire quietly.

On some occasions, we made the right appointment and it all went wrong anyway. I had one of my strong supporters in St. John's West appointed chairman of the Board of Referees for Appeals under the unemployment insurance system and, lo and behold, a few years later she was arrested for defrauding the UI system herself of a large amount of money. She was doing what's very common in Newfoundland. Her husband was a part-time fisherman, and she was claiming fisherman's UI on the basis that she was a fisherman, too, that she fished with him. In fact, she never fished at all; I don't think she was ever out on the water. On days when she was claiming fisherman's UI, she was presiding over appeal hearings in St. John's. They had her dead to rights.

In Newfoundland, of course, no one believes there's anything wrong with defrauding the UI. They figure the government makes the rules and, if the rules are stupid, it's the government's fault. Everyone goes after all he or she can get. Fishermen report catching fish, then, when they've got their UI stamps tucked away for the winter, they start landing fish in their wife's name. When she's stamped up enough for the winter, they start landing the fish in their son's name or their daughter's name. The whole system is ripe with deception and fraud, and the merchants and fish buyers cooperate in all of it.

∽

One of the great beneficiaries of the patronage system was Mitchell Sharp. A devout Liberal, Sharp was on the public teat for a million years. He started in the Finance department in 1942. When my father went to Ottawa to negotiate the Terms of the Union between Newfoundland and Canada in 1949, Sharp was one of the people negotiating for Canada. He was a deputy minister in the federal government in the 1950s, and a cabinet minister in the 1960s and 1970s. When we took office in 1984, we discovered that he was still there – as commissioner of something called the Northern Pipeline Agency, a body that the Liberals had set up to administer a pipeline that never got built in the Northwest Territories. We Conservatives must have been soft in the head. We allowed Sharp to carry on. His agency reported to the Minister of Transport and, when I became Transport minister in 1986, Mulroney said it was time to get rid of him. Mitchell was being paid $25,000 a year for doing nothing, part-time. We decided to terminate him.

I had to break the news to Sharp. He was seventy-five then, but he didn't take his firing lying down. He was upset. He was furious. He fought like a steer. He'd been on the government payroll for God knows how long, and he said he didn't think it was right or proper to throw him out in the cold after all he'd done, blah, blah, blah. He said it was positively indecent the way we were shafting our political opponents. I had to give him the axe; I had my instructions from the Prime Minister on that.

But I think Mitchell figured I had it in for him personally. After the Conservatives lost in 1993, Sharp came back in, this time as an adviser to Prime Minister Jean Chrétien. They said he was only being paid a dollar a year, but, even so, it's amazing that anyone could last, or would want to last, for fifty-plus years in the Government of Canada. Mitchell has survived in the patronage jungle far longer than any other known practitioner – although, in fairness, he has made some valuable contributions to the public life and policy of Canada over the decades.

∾

The first cousin of patronage is lobbying. Well-known Tories and friends of Brian Mulroney, such as Frank Moores, Harry Near, Pat MacAdam, Fred Doucet, and Jon Johnson, established firms to represent people seeking to do business with, or to obtain favourable regulatory decisions from, the government. This kind of work is legitimate. The Ottawa media, hostile to Mulroney and the Conservative party, publicized and exaggerated the importance of these Tory consultants. Although it was untrue, the perception grew that lobbyists had undue influence on government decisions.

We brought in legislation that required anyone attempting to influence the government to register as a lobbyist and to list those they acted for and in what connection. The registry was open for inspection by the public and the press. But it made no difference. The perception persisted that the government was controlled by cronies and lobbyists with tentacles reaching deep into the Prime Minister's Office and the cabinet.

I can state categorically that, in my nine years in the cabinet, I was never approached in any improper way by any lobbyist or friend or supporter of the Conservative party to take any position favouring that person's clients. The lobbying firms made sure that I or my staff was fully advised of their arguments. This was perfectly proper. No one ever suggested that I should support any particular decision because of past services to the party or myself. Frank Moores, in whose provincial cabinet I had served and who was a prominent supporter of Mulroney's, never attempted to see me or to persuade me about any business that any of his clients had with the government. Lobbyists know the real decision makers are the key bureaucrats, because 95 per cent of all government decisions are made on the advice that ministers receive from their civil servants.

On rare occasions, a decision may have such important political consequences that ministers will set aside their officials' recommendation and act on the basis of political and policy considerations rather than solely on merit. But cabinets prefer, and it's much safer, to act in accordance with the advice of bureaucrats who have examined a matter and made their recommendation.

While I was Minister of Transport, the department conducted a competition to choose a firm to develop a third terminal at Pearson International Airport in Toronto. The passenger facilities were desperately inadequate, but our government didn't have tens of millions of dollars to commit to a new terminal. We called for proposals from the private sector to design, build, and finance a terminal to supplement the existing Terminals One and Two. As this was an immensely complicated project, it involved a significant investment by any firm entering the competition. Not surprisingly, only four consortiums responded to the call.

I appointed an independent task force of officials from the Ministry of Transport to supervise, analyse, and respond to the proposals submitted; to deal with the consortiums who put in proposals; and to recommend the best proposal. At the beginning of this process, I met with representatives of the groups involved to make it very clear to them that it would be useless to try to lobby or to influence me or any of my officials. I said I would act only in accordance with the recommendations of the ministry task force. I told them merit would be the only criterion.

Each of the consortiums, of course, hired government-relations firms to lobby for them. After some months the four proposals were submitted. After analysing them, my task force reported that by far the best proposal was that of the consortium led by a Toronto firm of architects, Huang and Danczkay. Huang and Danczkay's lobbyist was Government Consultants International, of which Frank Moores was a principal. That Moores, a big backer of Mulroney's leadership aspirations, was acting for Huang and Danczkay neither helped nor harmed them. But the media seized on Moores's relationship with Mulroney to generate the myth that Moores was so influential that the government would do whatever he wanted. Yet neither Huang and Danczkay nor Moores, nor anybody else representing them, ever approached me.

My task force found Huang and Danczkay's submission best from both financial and design points of view – and that was good enough for me. Another consortium, of which Donald Matthews, another Mulroney supporter, was a member, placed second in the competition. Matthews attempted to use his contacts in the PMO to challenge the award to Huang and Danczkay, but I rebuffed all attempts by anyone from the PMO to raise the matter with me or my staff. The contract went to Huang and Danczkay, and Terminal Three has been a great success. The project didn't cost Canadian taxpayers anything.

Long after I left Transport, a similar competition was held to choose a developer for new terminals to replace Terminals One and Two at Pearson. This time Matthews, who had lost fair and square on Terminal Three, was part of the consortium that won. Unfortunately for Matthews and his associates, the contract was not signed until after Mulroney had left, and the Tory government, now led by Kim Campbell, was rushing pell-mell to annihilation in the 1993 election campaign. The new Liberal government of Jean Chrétien cancelled the contract with Matthews's group, resulting in a morass of litigation.

The legislation introduced by the Chrétien administration to restrict the Matthews consortium's claim for damages was, in my view, one of the most extreme and unjust interferences with the administration of the legal system ever seen in Canada. But the travelling public is the real victim, forced to endure airport facilities that do not live up to Pearson's status as Canada's main national and international airport.

∽

The connection between patronage and conflict of interest was brought home to me in a most distressing and personal fashion shortly after I became Minister of Justice in the Mulroney cabinet. The minister appoints hundreds of "legal agents" across the country to represent the federal government in all sorts of cases and on all sorts of files. These run the gamut from property trans-actions to the prosecution of offenders under federal drug laws, fisheries rules, telecommunications regulations, and so on. Anything that involves a federal statute usually involves a federal legal agent. This is part-time work, and legal agents are lawyers in private practice. Only people who still believe in the tooth fairy will be surprised to learn that, when the Liberals are in office, all the legal agents are Liberal lawyers. When the Conservatives come in, the Liberal lawyers are turfed out, and Tory lawyers get the business. It's petty patronage. It's the way the system works, and the legal profession knows it and understands it.

One of my first small priorities when I became Justice minis-ter was to get rid of the Liberal legal agents and replace them with fine, upstanding Tory lawyers. So, in late September 1984, about six hundred lawyers received letters signed by J.E. Hodges, senior counsel in the criminal-prosecution section, telling them to stop work on all files, except those of a pressing or urgent nature, such as bail hearings where the accused was in custody, or cases where a time limit might run out. The letter was similar to one that went out in 1980 when the Liberals returned to office after the Joe Clark interregnum.

A few months later, I was attacked by the Liberal Rat Pack in the Commons when they discovered that lawyer Peter Clark, the brother of Joe Clark, had been appointed a legal agent and lawyer for the federal government in connection with the Calgary Winter Olympics. Peter Clark was an able lawyer with a reputable law firm in Calgary, but this didn't prevent Liberal MPs Don Boudria and John Nunziata from suggesting Peter's appointment contravened our conflict-of-interest guidelines. They claimed he had been given the work because he was Joe's brother and because he was a loyal Tory supporter and fund-raiser. I thought those were valid reasons for appointing him, so long as he was competent, which he was, but the Rat Packers didn't see it that way.

The media thought they really struck pay dirt when Michael Harris, writing in the Toronto *Globe and Mail*, revealed that two of the twenty-three law firms I'd appointed as legal agents in Newfoundland and Labrador happened to employ my sons, Ches and Michael. Both were fine, upstanding young men, and extremely able lawyers, who had the good judgement to be devoted Conservatives. I was accused of having awarded "lucrative" government contracts to the firms with which my sons were associated. It was suggested this constituted a violation of our conflict-of-interest guidelines as well as an appalling example of patronage. The Commons was all atwitter when John Turner, the Opposition leader, labelled me the "Archie Bunker of Parliament – all in the family."

The Liberal Justice critic, Robert Kaplan, made a vile attack on my family, alleging that my two sons were not competent to be government legal agents, and claiming that one son had failed two years of law school. Kaplan, who had been a cabinet minister under Trudeau, behaved contemptibly. His attack was mean, vindictive, and harmful to my sons' professional careers. They were the lowest and most painful blows I suffered in politics.

The fact was that the two law firms would have been appointed legal agents even if my sons had not been associated with them. Among the twenty-three firms in the province approved to do work for the federal Department of Justice, my sons' firms were very small players. In my first six months in Justice, Michael's firm received $230 in federal business, while Ches's received $432; meanwhile, the two largest Liberal firms, which were still cleaning up old files, received $131,755 and $56,769.

The upshot of all this was that the Mulroney government, over my objections, decided to prohibit any government legal work from being given to a law firm that had a partner who was related in any way – son, daughter, cousin, aunt, uncle, father, mother – to a cabinet minister, an ordinary MP, or a senator. This prohibition discourages any law firm that wants to do business with the government from hiring anyone who has the misfortune to be related to an MP or senator.

The practical consequence of this ridiculous regulation was that we were unable to use an extremely capable law firm in Corner Brook, Newfoundland, whose senior partner, Mike Monaghan, was a great Conservative who'd run for us in the federal election of 1984 and nearly defeated Brian Tobin. But he wasn't the reason we couldn't use his firm. It was because another member of the firm, Thomas Marshall, was the son of Senator Jack Marshall. There was no earthly way the senator could have influenced anything our government did. But by virtue of employing his son, the law firm was put on the Ottawa black list until Senator Marshall reached retirement age at seventy-five. This created a positive disincentive for some people thinking of entering federal politics; they knew that, if they got elected, it could hurt the legal career of a sibling or offspring.

When the Liberals returned to power in 1993, they changed all the legal agents from one end of Canada to the other. The news media weren't interested at all. What was scandalous when Tories did it was business-as-usual when Grits did it. I thought the media would be outraged by the appointment in 1994 of Chrétien's nephew, Raymond Chrétien, as Canadian ambassador in Washington. I personally thought Raymond Chrétien was an able public servant, but I couldn't imagine the sharks in the Press Gallery letting his appointment pass without a savage attack on the Liberal administration. If Mulroney had pulled a stunt like that, we would have been excoriated from one end of Canada to the other. But, when the Liberals did it, it was hardly worthy of comment.

∾

The early years of the Mulroney administration created tremendous frustration among Conservatives over our inability to communicate our message or to set the agenda in Parliament or with the media. Despite significant legislative achievements, we received no credit from the press or public. The weakness of Commons Speaker John Bosley allowed the Liberal Rat Pack to dominate the daily Question Period. The Ottawa media had tremendous antipathy towards Mulroney and the Tories, and nothing could shake their attitude. These were years when the media were fascinated by pressure groups such as the National Action Committee on the Status of Women and others that claimed to have a large following but that, in fact, spoke for relatively small numbers of fringe fanatics. The media, driven by the same anti-Mulroney agenda, went to these groups first for comment whenever a new government policy or action was announced. These were the days when any attempt to restrain expenditures was fought tooth and nail by the Liberals and New Democrats, by the media, and by the special interest groups. Under these circumstances, our modest success in restraining public spending was a minor miracle.

The media's and the public's obsession with the so-called scandals of the first years of the Mulroney administration was reinforced by our ineptitude in handling these problems as they arose. The public perception of Mulroney and his government as being self-serving and corrupt took hold and we were never able to shake it.

Our problems began with the publication in the Toronto *Globe and Mail* of a series of stories alleging conflict of interest on the part of Sinclair Stevens, the Minister of Regional Industrial Expansion. The allegations concerned Stevens's

mixing of private business with his conduct of public business –
a situation that a judicial inquiry eventually found had, in fact,
occurred. The *Globe* stories caught us completely unaware. We
had no procedures for dealing with crises of this nature. Brian
was off travelling on official business in the Far East, leaving the
deputy prime minister, Erik Nielsen, to stonewall as the storm
mounted. It became a witch-hunt. Having used such issues ourselves to good advantage while in Opposition, it was absurd to
think we could make the allegations go away by stonewalling
them. But we did.

Sitting in Ottawa, we thought we could ride out the storm,
but I became convinced we couldn't when I went home to
Newfoundland and found everyone wanted to talk about the
Sinc stink and nothing else. Stevens finally resigned, but he hung
on at least a week longer than he should have, and this delay
further damaged the government in the eyes of the public.

I wrote to Mulroney with suggestions on dealing with conflict-
of-interest crises in the future. A fundamental problem was the
lack of time available to ministers to think or act intelligently
on issues that affect the reputation of the entire government;
our time was consumed by the Commons and by an unrelenting
succession of cabinet committee meetings. In my case, cabinet
and its committee meetings ate up twenty-five to thirty hours of
my time every week.

When the prime minister was away, as Mulroney was during
the Stevens affair, there was no effective way for a cabinet minister such as myself to intervene. There was no machinery for
involving ministerial participation in problems that were considered to come within the purview of the Prime Minister's Office.

I told Mulroney that the government's conflict-of-interest
rules were inadequate. A "blind" trust was no answer to a situation where ministers are owners or part-owners of a private
business. Even when they put their shares in a blind trust, they
still know they own the business, and so does everyone who
deals with it. A blind trust is not blind, as the Sinc Stevens
affair demonstrated.

A blind trust is suitable only for shares in public companies, bonds, or other tradable investments of such a nature that the beneficiaries no longer know whether they own the assets. Otherwise, a blind trust protects neither the minister involved nor the public interest or the political interests of the government. What's more, our conflict-of-interest rules did not deal with situations where a spouse or children might be active in a minister's private business. In my letter to Mulroney, I pointed out my own experience of having sold my interests in the Crosbie family businesses when I went into provincial politics. I noted that I'd been the author of the conflict-of-interest legislation enacted in Newfoundland by Moores's administration.

I believed then, and I believe now, that full disclosure is the best way to deal with conflict of interest. A minister should disclose publicly all his assets and liabilities when he assumes office, and he should be required to keep this information up-to-date. If it's all kept in records accessible to the public, a minister's actions can be checked against his or her holdings to confirm that nothing that is being done advances private interests. It's also essential to have an outstanding person to act as a counsellor/arbiter to whom ministers can turn for advice on how best to comply with the rules.

I'm referring to conflict-of-interest rules for cabinet ministers, and maybe senior civil servants. I don't think they need to be applied to ordinary members of Parliament. MPs don't have much chance to influence anyone or anything. Generally speaking, they're not in the game. Then there's the question of women and children. Society will have to decide whether spouses and children of ministers should be required to disclose their assets. If I was a wife, I would refuse to do it. If wives are persons in their own right, then it is an absolute insult to include them in the disclosure requirement. Forcing them to comply is based on an assumption that ministers are puppets of their spouse or that the spouse is their puppet.

The whole system is absurd because it's not really going to prevent anything. A crooked cabinet minister is not going to be stopped by a silly conflict-of-interest regulation. He'll just make his money by doing it through someone else. He won't do it through his wife. He'll use his cousin, or a non-relative.

The whole area of conflict of interest is a miasma from which politicians, once accused, cannot escape. They can't defend themselves and they can't prove they're not guilty. Nobody is safe from it. The most inconsequential things, like going on a fishing trip with someone, are said to be a conflict of interest. Even when politicians prove there was no conflict of interest, the media don't let them off the hook. Oh well, they say, there may not be an *actual* conflict, but there is an *appearance* of conflict of interest – and that's just as bad, and the politicians should therefore resign.

∾

I'd had my first sour taste of conflict-of-interest rules back in 1979, when I was Finance minister in Joe Clark's cabinet. Clark ordered all ministers, their spouses, dependants, and staff to comply with his rules and to disclose their financial affairs. The media, having an intense interest in conflict of interest as part of their constant fetish of embarrassing politicians, followed the issue closely. It was easy for me to put my investments in a blind trust because they were already being managed by a trust company and could simply be moved over. My wife, Jane, however, quite properly objected to being told what to do with her own assets when she was not in politics but merely married to a politician. My problem was I couldn't comply with the rules unless Jane agreed to abide by them, too. It didn't take the press long to discover that I was one of three ministers who hadn't complied. I was harassed by inquisitive journalists.

Jane owned $2,500 worth of common shares in a U.S. company, Allied Maintenance Corporation, whose owner we knew. "She resents being considered my chattel and being forced to place her holdings in the U.S. company in a blind trust," I told the press. A woman of strong conviction, Jane was giving no end

of grief to the people in the PMO who were charged with enforc-
ing Clark's conflict-of-interest guidelines. "I couldn't go along
with it because I am not a trained seal," Jane told the Canadian
Press. "I've lived with my husband for 27 years and I am not a yes-
woman. We battle it out. This is one that got outside [the house-
hold]." I could confirm the truth of her statements!

After a few days of media frenzy and listening to a tape of
Clark's weekly news conference at which he expressed sympathy
for the point Jane had raised, she decided to comply, because "I
think that he's such a gentleman, he's treated me so well, I just
couldn't cause him problems."

The issue was raised in the Commons at this time by Liberal MP
Jeanne Sauvé, who had been Communications minister in the
Trudeau cabinet, who was married to Maurice Sauvé, a former
Liberal minister, and who later became Speaker of the Commons
and then governor general. Jeanne Sauvé was extremely critical of
Clark's guidelines, arguing they didn't suit the times because
spouses of cabinet ministers should be free citizens and not be
"bundled up with their husbands." Sympathizing with Jane,
Sauvé told Joe he should be satisfied with oaths taken by ministers that they will not reveal cabinet confidences, and that wives
should not be required to "sacrifice their careers to the political
ambitions of their husbands." Clark agreed to review the effect of
the guidelines on spouses. In fact, Jane sold her shares of Allied
Maintenance rather than put them in a blind trust.

∿

Nine years later, Jane and I were in the news again in another
conflict-of-interest flapdoodle. By this time I was Minister of
International Trade in Mulroney's cabinet, and Jane and I were
invited to go to Thailand as the guests of Thai International
Airways on the inaugural flight of their new service between
Toronto and Bangkok. I'd been Minister of Transport when the
new air routes were negotiated and, as is customary when an
airline launches a new service, they try to grab some publicity by

inviting representatives of the federal and provincial governments, municipalities, and private-sector organizations to go
along on the first trip. I wasn't able to go, but suggested Jane go
and take our daughter, Beth.

This free trip was also accepted by Ontario Industry minister
Monte Kwinter, Toronto mayor Arthur Eggleton, later a minister in Jean Chrétien's Liberal cabinet, Metropolitan Toronto
chairman Dennis Flynn, and Quebec Tourism minister Michel
Gratton, among others. Under guidelines laid down by Mulroney,
ministers had to advise the assistant registrar general if they
received a gift exceeding two hundred dollars in value, and that
official would determine whether the gift should be made public.
If I'd gone on the trip, I would have had to report it. Because I
didn't go myself, I hadn't reported it. I was in compliance with
the existing guidelines, but the incident pointed out the need for
clearer treatment for ministers' spouses and families.

The issue of the Thai trip was raised in Parliament by Bob
Kaplan, the same vicious Liberal who had attacked the professional competence of my sons. Kaplan said he wasn't necessarily
accusing Jane and Beth of violating the cabinet's conflict-of-
interest guidelines, but he wanted to know if the government
considered such freebies to be proper. The truth of the matter
was he dragged my family into the limelight because the Liberals
were sore about the way I had manhandled their leader, John
Turner, in a debate on free trade earlier in the week.

The media, of course, were delighted with the controversy
and pleased to suggest that the trip had been most improper.
Editorial writers, it's been said, are the ones who ride down from
the hills when the battle is over to slay the wounded. That's certainly been my experience. An editorial writer in the Montreal
Gazette opined that "in allowing his wife and daughter to accept
a free trip . . . to Bangkok by Thai Airways, Trade Minister John
Crosbie stains the Mulroney government's fragile claim to new-
found morality. No political neophyte, he should know a perceived conflict of interest can be just as damaging as the real
thing – and that such an appearance plainly exists here."

It's obvious to me now, given the kind of opposition we were getting in the media and in Parliament at the time, that it was unwise for me to accept the Thai Airways invitation for myself or for my family. There's no way a politician can defend himself when the attitude is that a *perceived* conflict of interest is just as real as a *real* conflict of interest. Substance doesn't matter any more, just appearances. Anyone involved is assumed to be guilty. Politicians are not granted the presumption of innocence that is accorded without question to people in other walks of Canadian life.

22

LYNCH-MOB JUSTICE: MULRONEY AND THE AIRBUS AFFAIR

THE FOURTEEN-PAGE LETTER that was sent from the Department of Justice in Ottawa to the government of Switzerland in September 1995 was one of the most sensational documents in Canadian political or diplomatic history. Requesting assistance in certain police inquiries, the letter alleged that the former prime minister of Canada, Brian Mulroney, had been involved in a "continuing conspiracy" in the course of which he was said to have received five million dollars in bribes or kickbacks paid through a bank in Zurich. "The investigation is of special importance to the Canadian Government as it deals with criminal activities of a former prime minister," the letter said. It was signed by Kimberley Prost, a Justice department lawyer.

What was going on? I had served in Mulroney's cabinets for nine years. I knew Brian well, and I liked and trusted him. In the later years of his prime-ministry, our families became closer as he overcame his earlier suspicions of my motives, and I of his.

Courtesy Donato, Toronto Sun

421

I *couldn't* believe a word of the allegation against him. I *didn't* believe a word of it, because I knew better. The so-called scandal centred on commissions or kickbacks allegedly paid in connection with Air Canada's purchase of thirty-four A-320 medium-range jet aircraft from a European consortium, Airbus Industrie, in 1988 – at a time when I was Minister of Transport, the minister responsible for Air Canada.

There was no "Airbus Affair." There was no scandal. There was no improper lobbying. There were no kickbacks. Neither Mulroney nor anyone else in his cabinet profited in any way in the $1.8-billion deal. The competition to choose a new plane was conducted by Air Canada, with no involvement or interference from the government. The decision to buy from Airbus rather than from its American rival, Boeing, was made by the board of directors of Air Canada on the recommendation of airline officials, with no input whatsoever from me or anyone else in the government. Airbus was chosen because its aircraft was clearly superior to Boeing's for Air Canada's needs.

Not once did Mulroney speak to me about Airbus. Nor did he ever show the slightest interest in the competition. Frank Moores, who was supposed to have opened so many doors for Airbus, never approached me about the matter – and I would have refused to listen to him if he did. If Airbus Industrie paid commissions to agents on the A-320 sale to Air Canada, none of that money went to any official or minister in the government of Brian Mulroney. The "scandal" was concocted by Boeing, a sore loser, which spread baseless rumours about its rival's sales tactics. It was seized on by certain "investigative" journalists who were not prepared to let the truth interfere with their single-minded pursuit of Mulroney. They were like a Wild West lynch mob – irresponsible and out of control. The air of scandal was fertilized by the Royal Canadian Mounted Police, which conducted an incompetent and superficial investigation, feeding innuendo and unsubstantiated allegations to the Justice department; by the commissioner of the RCMP, who failed to supervise his gumshoe investigators; by the top officials in Justice, who neglected to vet the letter before it was sent to the Swiss; and by the person or persons who leaked the letter to the *Financial Post.* Above all, the "scandal" became a SCANDAL! because Justice minister Allan Rock, dreams of 24 Sussex Drive dancing in his head, became part of the lynch mob.

Distraught by this unprovoked and unfounded assault on his good name, distressed by the effect on his family, and worried about the impact on his business prospects, Mulroney sued the government and the RCMP for fifty million dollars for libel. And the government, forced to admit it had no cause to persecute the former prime minister, settled on the court-house steps, giving him the unreserved apology he sought, plus an estimated one million dollars for his legal costs. The government spent at least as much on its own legal representation; it tried to blacken the name of the man who had led Canada with distinction for nine years; and in the end it was forced to eat humble pie. Yet, incredibly, no heads rolled. RCMP Commissioner Philip Murray kept his job. So did Solicitor General Herb Gray, who was responsible for the Mounties. So did Justice minister Rock. And Prime Minister Jean Chrétien, who should have been minding the store, shrugged and carried on as though nothing untoward had occurred. The arrogance of Chrétien and Rock would have made even Joey Smallwood blush. The only casualty in this disgusting episode was the innocent victim, Brian Mulroney, who was left to repair the rents in his reputation caused by the media lynch-mobsters and by the sleazy, vindictive gang of Liberal character assassins.

∽

I was appointed Minister of Transport on June 30, 1986, moving there from Justice, and I continued in Transport until March 31, 1988, when I was made Minister for International Trade. I was in Transport throughout the period when Air Canada, then still a Crown corporation, was deciding on a new fleet of medium-range jets. The competition between Airbus and Boeing was conducted during my tenure. The decision by Air Canada's board of directors to approve the recommendation from the management of Air Canada to buy the thirty-four Airbus A-320s was made on March 30, 1988, the day before I left the Transport portfolio. The chairman and chief executive officer of Air Canada at that time was the legendary Claude Taylor, who had been running Air Canada for many years. The president and chief operating officer was Pierre Jeanniot.

When I became Minister of Transport, the decision to privatize Air Canada had already been made, with the result that the relationship between the airline and the minister was not as close as it had been. We were advised by Air Canada that it had to replace its medium-range aircraft, but we made it plain to the airline that the government was in no position to finance the acquisition of new aircraft, and that Air Canada would have to arrange its own financing.

Air Canada organized a competition among the two large American manufacturers, Boeing Aircraft Company and McDonnell Douglas Corporation, plus Airbus Industrie, the consortium made up of German, French, British, and Spanish interests. The competition lasted for two years and narrowed to a choice between Boeing and Airbus, whose rivalry was especially intense. The two companies were old enemies, and they battled each other for business and supremacy in dozens of countries around the world. Each believed its aircraft were superior, and that any decision to purchase the planes of the other company could only be the result of skulduggery. Neither believed the other could possibly win on merit. Each accused the other of being subsidized by governments, or competing unfairly in various ways. Both poured their allegations of dirty tricks into the ear of any reporter who would listen. And both hired Ottawa lobbying firms to peddle their line.

When Boeing sensed that Air Canada was leaning to Airbus, Boeing representatives went bananas. They spread rumours that Frank Moores was influencing Air Canada, of which he had previously been a director, to go with Airbus. The Ottawa Press

Gallery portrayed Moores as a fearsome figure who was so influential that he could have cabinet decisions reversed overnight to suit the clients of his firm, Government Consultants International. GCI were undoubtedly good at helping their clients in their dealings with the right people in the bureaucracy, but Moores and his associates had no special political influence, nor did they try to exert any, so far as I know.

Boeing officials constantly pressured the U.S. ambassador to Canada, Thomas Niles, complaining to him about the unfair influence that Moores supposedly enjoyed. Whenever I met Niles at social functions, he would buttonhole me to complain that Boeing was not being allowed to play on a level field with Airbus. He was a good ambassador, and he did his job, which included promoting the interests of Boeing.

In choosing the new aircraft, Air Canada had assembled three evaluation teams – one to examine bids on a financial basis, analysing cost, price guarantees, access to debt, and other financing conditions; a second to look at the technical aspects, including flying characteristics, reliability, and safety; the third to scrutinize the bids from a commercial point of view, to determine whether the chosen plane would enable Air Canada to fly new routes, how it could be configured for passengers on various routes, and so on.

I was determined that there would be no interference with Air Canada's decision making, so I asked Jeanniot to come to Ottawa to brief me. He confirmed that Air Canada was likely to purchase Airbus as a result of the recommendations of their three internal committees, all of which had unanimously recommended the Airbus A-320. He said he thought the airline's directors would accept this recommendation.

I questioned Jeanniot closely on all aspects of the competition, and he made it very clear in response to my specific inquiries that there had been no pressure from the Prime Minister, the Prime Minister's Office, or anyone else in the government to induce Air Canada to choose Airbus. He confirmed there had been no pressure, improper or otherwise, from lobbyists for either company and that the choice was a legitimate business decision made in the best interests of the airline.

At no time prior to the sending of that scurrilous letter to the Swiss in September 1995 did anyone from the RCMP bother to contact Taylor, Jeanniot, or me to inquire about our knowledge of the events surrounding the Airbus purchase. Jeanniot, who left Air Canada in 1990 and now heads the Montreal-based International Air Transport Association (IATA), is on record as saying in 1995 that there was no arm-twisting. He also said he had no contact at any time with Mulroney on this matter. As Bill James, a colourful mining executive and Air Canada director, said: "I'm sure Mulroney or somebody didn't tell Air Canada to do that, buy the Airbus and the board then did it. The board would tell them to shove it. . . . That's what you've got the g.d. board for. They're responsible for the governance of the company." In fact, the only role that the federal government played was to authorize Air Canada to make the capital expenditure once the airline had made its decision.

It's worth noting that, since 1988, Air Canada has placed two more orders with Airbus, including a $1.5-billion (U.S.) order in 1994 for six A-340s and twenty-five A-319s.

Against this factual background, it's hard to conceive how the Department of Justice came to allege in that infamous letter to the Swiss authorities that there was a "persisting plot/conspiracy by Mr. Mulroney, Mr. Moores and Mr. Schreiber [Karl-Heinz Schreiber], who defrauded the Canadian Government in the amount of millions of dollars during the time when Mr. Mulroney was in office until his resignation in June, 1993." Further, the letter claimed that there was a secret agreement among Schreiber, Moores, and Mulroney to make sure that Air Canada bought the A-320s and that Moores had opened two accounts at the Swiss Bank Corporation, one of them code-named "Devon," which was to receive money for Mulroney. It was a complete fabrication and nonsense.

In my view, the Airbus Affair, so called, was conceived because of a climate of suspicion and loathing that was created by a group of journalists who were determined to find Mulroney and his government guilty of improper behaviour. Driven by their own agenda, which was to uncover sleaze and criminality in every action of the Tory government, they convinced themselves that there had to be something fishy about the Airbus purchase. These reporters were led by Stevie Cameron, a freelance reporter and author who had already trashed Mulroney in her best-selling book *On the Take*;[*] by Trish Wood of CBC's *the fifth estate*; and by writers working for the muckraking German newsmagazine *Der Spiegel*. They ignored the truth in favour of gossip, innuendo, suspicion, wild speculation, vilification, and sinister conjecture. According to the RCMP themselves, the Mounties opened an investigation into the Airbus deal in late 1988 in response to the rumours being spread by Boeing, but they found no evidence and dropped their inquiries. They reopened the investigation later after Rock passed on to Gray rumours he had picked up from journalists.

When the RCMP went to the Department of Justice with a first draft of the infamous letter of September 29, 1995, they requested that the Swiss authorities give them access to bank accounts established by Moores and Schreiber at the Swiss Bank Corporation in Zurich. Their suspicions were wildly at odds with the facts. The fact was that Moores chose the name "Devon" because his parents had come to Canada from Devon county in England. It had nothing to with Mulroney who, as the press gleefully reported, had once lived on a street called Devon in Montreal. Moores opened the Devon account for the use of his wife, Beth, and there was never more than five hundred dollars in it.

Moores has stated that he never acted for the Airbus consortium in the sale of aircraft to Air Canada. He did work with

---

[*] *On the Take: Crime, Corruption and Greed in the Mulroney Years* (Toronto: Macfarlane Walter & Ross, 1994).

Schreiber, a German-Canadian businessman, on other transactions in Canada, including the sale of twelve helicopters by Messerschmitt Bolkow Blohm (MBB) to the Canadian Coast Guard, earning a $1.2 million commission, and on an unsuccessful attempt by another German concern, Thyssen AG, owners of Bear Head Industries Limited, to establish a plant to manufacture light armoured vehicles at Port Hawkesbury in Nova Scotia.

In the course of 1995, I was contacted on several occasions by a German reporter for *Der Spiegel* and by Trish Wood of *the fifth estate*. Each time I painstakingly reviewed what had happened while I was in Transport, assuring them there had been no improper behaviour or pressure involved in this purchase. But these maestros of innuendo masquerading as journalists were uninterested in the facts. They were determined to find some sinister and improper criminal activity involving Moores and Mulroney. Their resolve was unshaken when I suggested that Airbus had been chosen because of its quality, pointing out that Air Canada, following its privatization, had bought more Airbus aircraft, and that both Canadian Airlines and Wardair had independently purchased them, with no suggestion of any impropriety in either case.

Both *the fifth estate* and *Der Spiegel* circulated rumours that the Swiss bank accounts held monies deposited for a "prominent Canadian politician" – unnamed for reasons of libel. When Trish Wood called me in the fall of 1995, I asked her who this Canadian politician was supposed to be and she eventually suggested that it was Mulroney. I told her that this was absolute nonsense and completely untrue, but nothing I said could shake her faith in the proposition that the former prime minister was a master criminal who had lined his pockets while in office.

It is unprecedented for a prime minister or Justice minister to permit allegations of criminal conduct to be made against a former prime minister without any evidence to support such shocking suggestions. Yet either through sloth or malevolence, Rock and Chrétien permitted the letter to go to Switzerland, knowing it would be read by third parties in the Swiss government, the Swiss police, and the banks. There was no way the allegations of wrongdoing could be kept secret indefinitely. It was bound to become known in Swiss government and banking circles that Canada was making sensational allegations of criminal conduct against its former prime minister. And it was inevitable that word of the allegations would eventually leak to the press.

To obtain a search warrant in Canada, the Attorney General's department must satisfy a judge that it has reasonable grounds for suspecting that a criminal offence has occurred and that the individual in question may reasonably be thought to have been involved. But these safeguards do not exist when a search is requested in a foreign country. There is no procedure to protect a suspected person if the government decides to send a letter to a foreign government. The only protection that people like Mulroney and Moores have is the diligence, decency, and integrity of the Minister of Justice under whose name the letter is sent. Allan Rock lacked these qualities.

Neither the RCMP nor the Justice department could have obtained a search warrant in Canada because they had no reasonable evidence that a crime had occurred. Rock tried to evade responsibility by claiming he was unaware of the letter and saying that his officials didn't consult him before they authorized it, even though it accused a former prime minister of heinous crimes. In other words, Rock's defence was that his department wasn't under his control and he couldn't be held accountable for what his officials did, despite the conventions of cabinet government and ministerial responsibility.

It is exceptionally difficult to believe that Rock did not review and approve the Swiss letter before it was sent. It is even harder to believe that Prime Minister Chrétien was not informed about his government's investigation of his predecessor. But even if we give them both the benefit of the doubt and concede that they may have been uninformed, how can they explain – how can we excuse? – their behaviour after the contents of the letter were made public by the *Financial Post* in late November 1995?

As soon as the letter became public, Mulroney responded with a massive libel suit against the government and the RCMP. The Chrétien government knew then, or shortly thereafter, that Mulroney was in no way connected with Moores's bank accounts and that Mulroney, in fact, never had a Swiss bank account. But it wasn't until January 1997 that Rock and Chrétien admitted they were wrong. By then they had known for ten or twelve months that Mulroney had been falsely accused and defamed. But they kept him dangling for all of 1996. They made no move to withdraw their spurious allegations or to help him to clear his name until his libel action was at the point of going to trial. During this period, the federal government spent a fortune on legal fees and court costs for a series of technical manoeuvres – all the while knowing beyond doubt that Mulroney was innocent and Moores and Schreiber were falsely accused.

As soon as the *Financial Post* story appeared in November 1995, I contacted Mulroney to offer him my support and assistance. On January 8, 1996, the *Globe and Mail* published a letter from me in which I set out my views on the vicious character assassination perpetrated by the Chrétien government and on the reprehensible and despicable actions of Allan Rock.

Mulroney fought back brilliantly, assembling a fine legal team to assist him. But, in my phone conversations with him, I could tell that he was badly hurt and was suffering grievously from the terrible publicity's effect on his family and on those he did business with throughout the world.

One of the peculiar features of this affair, not known outside the circle of those who were friends with Mulroney or Moores, was the fact that Mulroney and Moores were no longer the close or intimate friends that they had been in the years leading up to the Conservative leadership contest of 1983 and through Mulroney's first term as prime minister. They had apparently become estranged around 1992, when Moores expressed the opinion that it was time for Mulroney to step down, to give a new leader a chance to win the next election.

Mulroney was not talking to Moores and had not talked to him or seen him for at least a year before he left office in June 1993. In the period following the *Financial Post* story, I often transmitted questions or messages from Mulroney to Moores, and vice versa. Mulroney wanted Moores to provide the authorities with full access to Moores's two bank accounts in Switzerland to show definitively that Mulroney had nothing to do with them. Moores was quick to affirm that neither bank account had any connection with Mulroney and that the allegations against him were false, but he had to be guarded in what he said publicly because he was suing *the fifth estate* for defaming him.

∾

On Sunday, January 5, 1997, I travelled from St. John's to Montreal to give evidence the next day for Mulroney at his libel trial, at which I was scheduled to be the third witness. I was staying that night with Mulroney's former chief of staff Derek Burney and his wife, Joan, in Montreal. About thirty minutes after I arrived, Jacques Jeansonne, one of Mulroney's lawyers, phoned with the news that the government had agreed to settle the case by apologizing and paying Mulroney's legal and court costs. This was a great victory for Mulroney, a settlement he could ill afford to refuse. If he'd proceeded, he would have had to meet the costs of a two- or three-month trial against an opponent who had full access to the public treasury. The settlement agreement made it clear that any conclusions of wrongdoing on Mulroney's part were unjustified, but the document was carefully drafted by the government's lawyers to protect Allan Rock and pin the blame on the RCMP.

∾

I do not suggest that the Minister of Justice or any other minister should interfere improperly in investigations involving people in public life. It would be quite wrong, for example, for a minister to suggest that the police ought not to investigate or charge some person simply because that person is a member of the minister's political party. But a minister must discharge his constitutional and political responsibilities in a proper fashion, especially where the minister has the Justice portfolio or is attorney general and is responsible for the administration of justice. In the Airbus case – a matter of great importance and sensitivity – this meant the minister should have taken pains to check and approve the actions of his officials. The letter should never have been sent to the Swiss authorities unless and until Allan Rock had signed off on it.

As a person who was involved inside the federal administration for many years, I do not believe, for one split second, that Chrétien was not informed of the serious allegations against his predecessor. The government is organized so as to ensure that the prime minister and his office are made aware of everything of any political or public importance that occurs in any department. The prime minister has an elaborate office of his own, together with the vast Privy Council Office staffed by people who are intimately familiar with every aspect of government operations and who are in daily contact with officials in every department to make sure that the centre – specifically, the prime minister – knows what is going on. There couldn't have been anything more politically sensitive, anything that would have been brought to Chrétien's attention more quickly, than the sensational charges levelled against Mulroney.

In a properly functioning parliamentary democracy, both Rock and Gray would have had to accept responsibility for the careless, damaging, wilfully and wantonly negligent actions of the RCMP and the Justice department. The ministers were accountable, and submitting their resignations was the only proper course. As leader of the Opposition, Chrétien told the Commons on June 12, 1991: "When [the Liberals] form the government, every minister in the cabinet that I will be presiding over would have to take full responsibility for what is going on in his department. If there is any bungling in the department nobody will be singled out. The minister will have to take responsibility. . . . The minute you become a cabinet minister, you take responsibility and you discharge responsibility until the end. That is the rule that should prevail. That is the one rule that can keep the confidence of the people in any individual."

Why did Chrétien, as prime minister, run away from these lofty principles? He will accept no responsibility and will take no blame. His is a vengeful, inept, and arrogant government. It is an embarrassment to our nation. It does not deserve the support or confidence of the Canadian people.

23

SAVING HIBERNIA

Macpherson, Reprinted with permission, the Toronto Star Syndicate

THROUGHOUT HISTORY, Newfoundlanders have looked to the sea for their livelihood and their future. It was fishing and fish processing, until the stocks ran out. It was shipping by sail, and later by steam, to the four corners of the globe, until supertankers and jumbo jets left our island province behind. Now it's offshore oil and gas – Hibernia, the fourth-largest oil field ever discovered in Canada; Terra Nova, southeast of Hibernia, is nearly as large; and nearby fields include Whiterose, Mara, Hebron, North Ben Nevis, and Ben Nevis. Together, they account for one-quarter of Canada's petroleum reserves.

As I write this, the great consortium led by Mobil Oil is preparing to pump the first of an estimated 650 million barrels of recoverable oil at Hibernia, about 320 kilometres southeast of St. John's, on the Grand Banks. I will feel special satisfaction when the oil begins to flow, because the development of Newfoundland's offshore resources is my proudest accomplishment

434

in twenty-seven years in federal and provincial politics. It was a long, hard battle, and there were two occasions when the Hibernia project would have died if I had not succeeded in persuading my colleagues in the Mulroney government to stay the course.

The first was in 1990, following the assassination of the Meech Lake constitutional accord by Newfoundland premier Clyde Wells. The mood of the Conservative caucus was foul, and our MPs, especially those from Quebec, would have liked nothing better than to get even with Wells and with Newfoundland. I had to persuade them to put aside their dreams of revenge and to allow legislation to provide more than three billion dollars in financing for the Hibernia consortium to proceed in Parliament. Without this package of grants, loans, and guarantees, the project would have collapsed, perhaps never to be revived.

The second occasion was in early 1993, following the decision by Gulf Canada to withdraw from the consortium. I was able to keep the project alive by talking the cabinet into doing what it had decided it would never do: to take an equity position in Hibernia by joining the consortium. It was no mean feat to persuade my reluctant cabinet colleagues to make this $290-million commitment to my province just months after it had agreed to pay hundreds of millions in compensation to Newfoundland fishermen when I closed the cod fishery.

The story of Hibernia begins in the 1960s, when Joey Smallwood was premier and I was a minister in his government. Joey, as was his wont, gave his friends John C. Doyle and John Shaheen concessions, or permits, to explore for oil and minerals on Newfoundland's continental shelf. Whether these concessions had any value or validity was a moot point because no one had yet addressed the issue of whether offshore resources belonged to the province or to the federal government. Prudent companies, however, made sure they had permits from both St. John's and Ottawa before investing in offshore exploration.

With the election of Frank Moores's Tory government in 1972, we cancelled Smallwood's concessions and set to work drawing up a proper regime of rules to govern the exploitation of the offshore. This work was begun by Leo Barry, our Mines and Energy minister, with the able assistance of Cabot Martin, a Newfoundland-born, Alberta-trained oil-patch lawyer. I took over this assignment in 1975, passing it on to Brian Peckford, later the premier, when I moved into federal politics in 1976. Although no oil or gas had been discovered to that time, we took an aggressive approach with Ottawa, insisting that, when offshore resources were found, they would be the exclusive property of Newfoundland, just as if the same resources had been found on land. We were the only province to take such a militant position. Nova Scotia trailed along in a pallid way, getting little or nothing in its offshore settlement with Ottawa. Later, Nova Scotia did secure some improved terms, thanks to the aggressive stance taken by Newfoundland.

At the time I shifted to federal politics, the Conservative caucus and party had no policy on offshore rights, and I was probably the principal person who convinced Joe Clark to endorse the provincial-rights position.

Over the years, various companies had drilled a total of fifty-nine exploratory wells in the Newfoundland and Labrador offshore before Chevron Canada Resources drilled discovery well P-15 at Hibernia in 1979, striking oil in relatively shallow, eighty-metre-deep water on the outer part of the continental shelf. This historic strike brought a sudden new urgency to the issue of ownership and jurisdiction. Under the Trudeau Liberals, the federal government claimed jurisdiction on the ground that the resources were not part of the land mass of any individual province, and hence belonged to the nation as a whole.

The discovery of oil occurred just a few months after the election of Clark's minority Tory government. We were so desperately busy – forming an administration, trying to figure out how to govern this awkward country, fighting with the Tory premiers of Alberta and Ontario over energy pricing, moving or not moving the Canadian embassy in Israel to Jerusalem, writing a Budget and watching it crash in flames in the House of

Commons – that we didn't get around to implementing our off-shore policy before we were pitched into the 1980 election.

Peckford, who had become premier in 1979 and who had won a smashing electoral victory that year – thanks, in appreciable measure, to the all-out support of the federal party – was apoplec-tic. Never an easy person to get along with, Peckford became a real menace to our re-election campaign in 1980. When Clark went to Newfoundland to campaign, Peckford insulted and humiliated him, declaring publicly that he wasn't satisfied with Clark's verbal commitment on the offshore and demanding that Clark put his pledge in writing. This to the Prime Minister of Canada, a fellow Conservative!

Having foolishly poisoned relations with Clark and the federal party, Peckford found himself totally isolated when the February 1980 election handed power back to Pierre Trudeau and the Liberals – dogmatic centralists who had no intention of yielding one inch of the offshore or one dime of resource revenue to any province.

The next four years were disastrous for federal–provincial relations, especially in the energy sector. Trudeau's National Energy Program alienated Alberta and terrified other resource provinces. While Peckford and his government slugged it out with the Liberal resource-grabbers, exploration continued at Hibernia. By 1984, eight delineation wells had found significant quantities of oil, leading the experts to estimate Hibernia's recoverable reserves at 525 million to 650 million barrels. But 1984 also brought a crushing legal blow to Newfoundland as the Supreme Court of Canada ruled that mineral and other rights on the continental shelf off Newfoundland belonged to Canada, not to the province.

(Ironically, one of the lead lawyers arguing the federal case against Newfoundland's ownership of its offshore resources was Clyde Wells. Although his federalist role was well known at the time, it did not deter Wells, when he became premier, from draping himself in the garb of a Newfoundland patriot and provincial-rights champion, thereby proving one of three things:

lawyers have no principles; politicians have no scruples; or the public has no memory. Or all three.)

In the end, it was political change, not court challenges, that saved the day for Newfoundland. In 1983, Brian Mulroney replaced Clark as Conservative leader. Mulroney had little of his predecessor's passion for provincial rights and, not long after he became leader, I arranged a meeting with Peckford. It was a disaster. Peckford was thoroughly browned off because Mulroney would not confirm that Clark's offshore policy would continue to be the Tory policy. Petulant when crossed, Peckford refused to take phone calls from Jim McGrath or me, the two Conservative MPs from Newfoundland. He behaved outrageously, denouncing the federal party and threatening to withhold his support when a federal election came along.

The situation was extremely awkward for me. Finally, I went to Mulroney and told him that my position on the offshore was clear and would not change. I was publicly committed to the provinces' having jurisdiction over and ownership of offshore minerals and petroleum, and I couldn't be a Tory candidate or support the Tory party if the policy was going to be changed. I didn't threaten. I simply told him I wouldn't be in the campaign if the issue was not resolved to my satisfaction. I couldn't campaign in Newfoundland on a different policy. Brian was a shrewd strategist. He explained he had no objection whatever to Clark's policy, but he didn't want to declare it to be his policy during the period preceding an election call for fear of handing the Liberals an issue on which to attack us in central Canada. And just before the 1984 election, Mulroney and Peckford did sign an agreement promising that a Tory administration would transfer the offshore to the coastal provinces.

But nothing was ever easy when Peckford was involved. In February 1985, with Mulroney in office, the previous year's agreement was finalized and was christened the Atlantic Accord. It established the framework for the development of oil and gas in the Newfoundland offshore and set up a Newfoundland offshore fund of $300 million – 75 per cent of it from Ottawa – to prepare Newfoundland for the development of these resources. But it then took another three years, until the summer of 1988, to translate the framework into an agreement on the principles that would permit the $8.5-billion Hibernia project to proceed. On July 18, 1988, I joined the Prime Minister, federal Energy minister Marcel Masse, Peckford, and Mobil Oil president Arnie Neilsen at an official signing ceremony at the Hotel Newfoundland in St. John's.

For once, Peckford was pleased, even ecstatic, as he declared, "I've never had a day like this before and I doubt if I'll ever have one like it again." There was cause for his ecstasy. Hibernia would be the largest capital project ever undertaken in Atlantic Canada – a world-scale mega-project made possible by $3.6 billion in federal financial support. Not only were the costs of Hibernia enormous, they were up-front. The money had to be invested long before the first barrel of oil could be pumped, and it was far more than even a consortium of big oil companies could be expected to risk without government support.

Another two years passed before all the legal documents were signed. Mobil Oil was in for a 28.125 per cent share of the ownership, Crown-owned Petro-Canada for 25 per cent, Chevron Canada for 21.875 per cent, and Gulf Canada for 25 per cent. Hibernia, however, was not yet out of the woods. The governments of Canada and Newfoundland still had to draw up legislation to guarantee the financing, and this required the approval of Parliament and the Newfoundland House of Assembly. Meanwhile, Peckford had decided to retire; a provincial election was held in 1989, in which the Conservatives were ousted by the Liberals under Wells. Clyde had always been ambivalent about Hibernia, probably because he was afraid the political credit would go to Tories rather than to him, so he denigrated the project, declaring that it amounted to no more than two fish-processing plants in terms of employment.

Having the premier belittle Hibernia made it much more difficult for us to sell it in the rest of Canada. *If Hibernia is worth only two fish plants, why is the federal government proposing to provide more than three billion dollars to make it happen?* That was a fair question, to which we had three answers. Hibernia would increase Canadian energy production and our national self-sufficiency in petroleum. Hibernia would help to overcome regional disparity in Atlantic Canada. Finally, the revenues generated by Hibernia and the spin-off commercial activity would reduce Ottawa's equalization payments by raising the tax base in the region.

When, at long last, all the legal agreements were completed, the Newfoundland Assembly passed the enabling legislation. Parliament, however, had not yet dealt with it when the Meech Lake accord blew up in 1990. Plain and simple, the accord was destroyed by Clyde Wells. The effect in Ottawa was catastrophic. Meech Lake was the constitutional centre-piece of Mulroney's policies. Next to free trade, it was the most important initiative of his years as prime minister. And it was destroyed by the premier of a province that, to Ottawa eyes, always had its hand out for more federal money. At one time Newfoundland had been viewed in Ottawa as being quaint and needy – a politically correct charity case. But now the government was caught up in the business of deficits, worrying about its financial situation, trying to cut back. It was becoming harder and harder to get any kind of assistance past the bureaucrats, and I couldn't really blame them.

Then along came Wells, contemptuously wrecking the Meech Lake agreement and, in the next breath, asking us to pass legislation to invest three billion-plus dollars in a mega-project in his province. Wells had become as dominant in his government as Joey Smallwood ever was. Clearly, it was Clyde's way or get out of the way. He thought nothing of embarrassing his own ministers as he displayed the same dictatorial habits that Smallwood had. The difference was, while it took Joey twenty years to reach a status of supreme authority, Clyde achieved it in just one year in office.

I was caught in the middle, as I so often was with Peckford and Wells. I wanted to wreak vengeance on them and their miserable governments for their appalling attitudes. But if I and my colleagues in Ottawa did that, we would simply be making the people of Newfoundland suffer for the sins of their misguided premiers. And, as an MP who needed to get re-elected in Newfoundland, I would suffer, too. I was caught in a bind. I had no choice but to forge ahead, to get the legislation through, to make sure Hibernia got its $3.6 billion.

To his great credit, Mulroney stuck with me. He could easily have said: *Well, goddammit that's it. They've just torn the guts out of my whole constitutional policy and they've put Canada in danger. Quebec may well leave. I'm damned mad and I'm not going to go along with this Hibernia nonsense any longer.* And who could have blamed him? He had only two seats in Newfoundland in 1990 and he never had more than four of the seven. It wouldn't have cost him anything politically if he'd said: *Too bad, I'm not going to do this. I'm going to show that jerk Clyde Wells how the real world works.* To give Brian his due – and me mine, because we had a pretty good relationship by this time and he listened to me – he hung in with Hibernia.

He said, "Look, yes, we're going to go ahead, but now we have a problem because the whole Quebec caucus is upset and they are all going to oppose the money for Hibernia." One week after Wells killed Meech Lake, the issue came up in caucus. I had to make a very powerful speech. I pointed out that, if we didn't pass this legislation, Wells wouldn't suffer, but everyone else in Newfoundland would. I reminded my colleagues that one-half of the population of Newfoundland had been in favour of Meech Lake – and most of them were Tory supporters. The caucus accepted my argument because, revenge aside, there was nothing to be gained by abandoning the project. However, Jake Epp, the Energy minister, and I decided not to risk putting legislation before the Commons for a few months. We wanted to let tempers cool down, so we waited until the fall. It was passed in November 1990, and the Hibernia Management and Development Company (HMDC) began operations.

After all this time, effort, and anguish, I thought Hibernia was finally off to the races. The oil companies had spent $3.8 billion on exploration and pre-development activities; they had made twenty-one significant discoveries, five in the Labrador Shelf and sixteen on the Grand Banks. But my optimism was premature. A final great crisis broke in February 1992. Gulf Canada, weakened financially by other causes, announced it was abandoning Hibernia. The contract between Gulf and its three partners committed Gulf to continue to meet its share of the investment expenses until January 20, 1993. So the remaining partners and the government had a year in which to try to find someone else to take over Gulf's 25 per cent.

The opponents of Hibernia, led by the attack-trained editorial writers of the Toronto *Globe and Mail* and by Ian Doig, a presumed oil-industry expert from Calgary, had a field day. They mounted a vitriolic campaign against Hibernia. They demanded that the federal government grasp the opportunity afforded by Gulf's cold feet to get out of the project. Mobil, Chevron, and Petro-Canada each made it clear they could not afford to pick up any of Gulf's share; in fact, Petro-Canada was openly shopping for investors to take part of its 25 per cent. Major construction work had to stop, and four hundred million dollars' worth of new contracts was put on hold. Hibernia's chances of survival were no better than fifty–fifty. For many months, another big oil company, Texaco, toyed with the possibility of joining the consortium, but, at the last possible moment, on December 15, 1992, it decided to pass. Epp immediately flew to Arkansas to meet Charles Murphy, the elderly founder of Murphy Oil, an independent that had earlier indicated some interest in acquiring a 6 to 8 per cent interest in Hibernia.

The period from December 15, 1992, to January 15, 1993, was the tensest and most exciting of my political career. Jane and I went to Florida for the first ten days of January to vacation with our St. John's friends Craig Dobbin and Elaine Parsons. We had barely settled in the sun when our holiday was interrupted by distressing news from Ottawa. There had been another cabinet shuffle and Epp was out as Energy minister, replaced by Bill McKnight, a wheat farmer from Saskatchewan. The change of ministers made it even more unlikely that Hibernia could be rescued before Gulf's obligation to support the project ended. Once that happened, the offshore development would be dead.

I immediately phoned Mulroney from Florida. He assured me he had instructed McKnight to do everything possible to rescue the project. I spent most of the rest of our vacation, day and evening, on the telephone with oil-company executives, officials of the departments of Finance and Energy, Mines and Resources, Newfoundland's Mines and Energy minister, Rex Gibbons, and my own officials in Ottawa. I also rallied Newfoundland business leaders to respond to the vicious attacks of the *Globe and Mail* and other Hibernia-haters. The *Globe*, with its influential readership in the business community, kept up its irresponsible attacks, painting Hibernia as a mere make-work project and boondoggle.

I lashed back in a letter to the editor, denouncing the newspaper's stance as arrogant, supercilious, ignorant, uncaring, callous, condescending, and insular. Although I considered my letter to be factual, subdued, and non-contentious, the *Globe* didn't want to publish it because my views didn't coincide with their own ill-informed opinions. I had to call William Thorsell, the editor-in-chief, twice before the paper finally consented to print my letter.

My efforts to defend Hibernia were complicated by a chorus of anti-Hibernia propaganda from shrill, uninformed critics within Newfoundland itself. They included the province's largest newspaper, the *St. John's Evening Telegram*, which thought it would be a good thing for the Newfoundland government to escape from "the terribly bad offshore deal known as Hibernia." While it was difficult to understand the twisted logic of the editorial, one of the main points seemed to be that, if Newfoundland received new revenue from the Hibernia project, this would be bad for the province because the equalization hand-outs it received from Ottawa might be reduced. The editorialist apparently believed it would be preferable for the province to remain forever on welfare rather than to seize an opportunity to make its own way in the world.

My role in those frantic days was later described by Cabot Martin as that of an arm-twister, an advocate in the corridors of power, and a bulldog who wouldn't let go. This was a fairly accurate description of my activities in early January 1993. But, without the strong behind-the-scenes backing of Mulroney, even the federal cabinet's support would have evaporated. To keep the project alive, the government had already offered two hundred million dollars in cash for a new partner in the project – an offer that was intended to equalize the complicated tax treatment among the consortium members. In addition, the governments of Canada and Newfoundland had agreed to back-stop some interim construction costs of the project to a limit of thirty million dollars. By the beginning of 1993, most of my cabinet colleagues were extremely nervous about investing any more public money in a high-risk scheme like drilling for oil in the iceberg-infested North Atlantic.

I knew that, if Murphy Oil took equity in the project, it would make it much easier to convince the doubting Thomases in the cabinet that, as a last resort, the government should take over the remainder of Gulf's interest.

My business allies in St. John's, led by Miller Ayre, Craig Dobbin, Cabot Martin, Chris Collingwood, and others, raised money for a large advertisement in the *Globe and Mail*, giving "the big picture – on the big project – Hibernia." As the advertisement made clear, in return for its loan guarantee, the federal government was to receive a special share of the profits of the venture over and above its normal corporate taxes and, as provincial royalties from Hibernia and surrounding fields rose, Newfoundland's equalization payments would come down. This would save the federal government approximately $1.5 billion in

1990 dollars over the life of the Hibernia field alone. The advertisement concluded that, given the size of the prize, the cost of the project to the federal treasury was a sound public investment. Then, more than thirty representatives of Newfoundland firms and associations went to Ottawa to trumpet the benefits of the offshore development. They held a press conference, which got considerable publicity, at which they stressed all the positive aspects of Hibernia.

Still in Florida, I kept in touch every day with Bill Hopper, the chairman and CEO of Petro-Canada. In times of crisis, a person quickly discovers who his friends are. Hopper proved to be a true friend. He wrote to the *Globe and Mail*, setting the newspaper straight in the most convincing terms. Hopper's intervention, along with the lobbying of my business friends from St. John's, had another effect: they helped to stiffen the spine of the nervous Nellies in the Mulroney cabinet.

I chartered a small jet to fly from Florida to Ottawa for the final scene of the drama – a meeting of the special cabinet subcommittee on energy mega-projects, chaired by Finance minister Don Mazankowski. Representatives of Chevron, Mobil Oil, and Petro-Canada were invited to attend. The outline of a deal had been reached. Murphy Oil would acquire a 6.5 per cent equity interest in Hibernia, leaving 18.5 per cent from the original share of Gulf Canada to be disposed of. After considerable persuasion, Mobil Oil and Chevron agreed to take an additional 5 per cent each, bringing Mobil's share to about 33 per cent, and that of Chevron to nearly 27 per cent.

The cabinet had to decide whether the federal government would take the remaining 8.5 per cent, at a cost of about $290 million. As we analysed the situation at our subcommittee meeting, it became apparent that, if we recommended these new arrangements, the full cabinet would concur and Hibernia would be saved. But, if we recommended against, the project would surely be doomed. The oil-company executives performed superbly. Norman McIntyre, of Petro-Canada, was most convincing as he explained the reasons for Petro-Canada's involvement in the project and the reasons why he thought the project was in the national interest. Everyone knew my views, so I had to fight to restrain myself and let the representatives of the consortium make the case that the project was indeed viable.

When the oilmen finished answering our questions, they filed from the room. Mazankowski asked whether the committee wanted to recommend that the new arrangements and obligations be accepted. To my immense relief, my colleagues all murmured assent. And Mulroney, now vacationing in Florida, approved the final package by phone. I returned briefly to Florida, then flew to St. John's to help announce the rescue of Hibernia. I told the press conference there that it was "one of the most satisfying days I have had in my political career." The night of the announcement we had a victory dinner at the Old Colony Club in St. John's, where I paid a handsome tribute to Charles Murphy. I told him that his native Arkansas was the greatest state in the union. It had eclipsed New York, California, and all the rest.

As it became clear that there was nothing else to stand between the people of Newfoundland and the development of their offshore, the compliments and congratulations rolled in. The prevalent view in Newfoundland seemed to be that I deserved more credit than anyone else for keeping Hibernia alive and for ensuring that it would proceed to the benefit of all Newfoundlanders. Elmer Harris of St. John's radio station VOCM seemed to speak for most Newfoundlanders when he commented on air:

If someone is to receive credit for going the extra mile in getting the Hibernia project up and running again, it's Newfoundland's representative in the federal cabinet, John Crosbie. John Crosbie put an extraordinary effort and determination into getting the federal money needed for the project, and without doubt, if it were not for his dedication to Newfoundland and to the Hibernia project, it would still be in limbo. The Newfoundland oil industry, which just got new life, owes its very existence to John Crosbie. On two occasions in the past twelve months John Crosbie has saved the Newfoundland economy from ruinous collapse. First it was the fisheries package and now the Hibernia development.

Daniel Yergin, the author of *The Prize*,* a brilliant book on the history of the oil industry, put the issue in perspective in an interview on CBC's *As It Happens*:

> You know, when you come down to it, the oil business is about risks, about big risks, and at the end of the day indeed the prize is out there and the prize is, among other things, large oil fields and this [Hibernia] is one of them. . . . One of the dynamic elements that also gets overlooked in the oil business, particularly from the outside, is the degree to which this is a high technology business, and certainly Hibernia is going to be an enterprise that is going to push the technological frontiers of offshore development.

The positive impact of Hibernia is already being felt. At the peak of the construction of the mammoth drilling platform at Bull Arm in 1995, the Hibernia project employed 5,384 people in Newfoundland, 137 in other provinces, and 2,312 outside Canada. The producing phase will directly employ about 800 in Newfoundland for the next twenty years and indirectly an additional 2,500 to 3,000. As the largest development project ever undertaken in Eastern Canada, with capital and operating expenditures over its lifetime expected to reach $15.1 billion, Hibernia will reduce economic disparity in the Atlantic region

---

* *The Prize: The Epic Quest for Oil, Money and Power* (New York: Simon & Schuster, 1991).

and contribute to economic growth and employment right across the country.

Newfoundlanders have learned to temper their dreams with large doses of realism. They don't expect that very many of them will get rich from Hibernia, but some people, especially those with high-technology skills, will do very well. Many of the province's middle-class entrepreneurs are already prospering. They include some of my nephews, whose businesses are profitably supplying and servicing offshore oil companies.

There is other good economic news on the horizon. Inco Limited will begin production by 2000 at the world's largest nickel deposit at Voisey's Bay in Labrador. The impact on the economy of Newfoundland will be akin to the creation of a brand-new Sudbury. The mill will be in Labrador, with the smelter and refinery located on the island of Newfoundland, at the site of the old U.S. Air Force base at Argentia, on the Avalon Peninsula. Since the closing of the base, unemployment at Argentia has been around 65 per cent, and I anticipate that the nickel-mining and -smelting operations will have a greater immediate impact on the economy of the province than Hibernia will have.

Down the road, perhaps a long way, is the development of trillions of cubic metres of natural gas that was discovered off the coast of Labrador in the late 1970s. With no economically feasible way to land the gas, the wells were capped for development in the future. The distance from market is just too great to make it practicable at this time to develop the several major finds. Ice is an even more serious problem. It's not just a question of icebergs wiping out drilling rigs; the whole area is covered by ice in the winter.

The gas is certainly there, but whether it will be developed in our lifetimes is problematic. Equally problematic at the moment are development of the hydro resources of the Lower Churchill River in Labrador and the renegotiation of the Churchill Falls agreement with Quebec to give Newfoundlanders a fair return on the electricity that is sold to Hydro-Québec.

Not all of these things will come to pass. But, if offshore oil development continues on the Grand Banks and if Voisey's Bay comes on stream on schedule – and if the cod return in numbers sufficient to reopen the fishery – all of us in Newfoundland will look forward to a future that will be brighter than our immediate past.

24

THE KIM CAMPBELL DÉBÂCLE

AS 1992 DREW to a close, it was obvious to everyone in the Progressive Conservative caucus – and to just about everyone else in Canada – that Brian Mulroney would soon have to decide whether to seek a third term or retire from public life. Mulroney had already accomplished the only two miracles I'd seen in politics. The first was to have the Meech Lake constitutional accord accepted by all ten premiers and the leaders of the territories. The second was to win agreement on the Charlottetown accord from the same group, plus the leaders of the aboriginal peoples – even though the accord was rejected in the national referendum of 1992. I thought that Mulroney might still have one miracle left in him. I thought he could lead us to re-election if he was given the proper support. And if he'd stayed, I would have stayed, too.

Following the Charlottetown referendum, there was great depression and unrest in the Tory caucus, much of it directed at the leader who had made constitutional reform his personal

Courtesy Terry Mosher (Aislin), Montreal Gazette

crusade and his party's priority. I was contacted by officials in the Prime Minister's Office who asked me to speak in support of the Prime Minister at a caucus meeting on October 29. Never being bashful about speaking strongly on subjects in which I believed, I made what others told me was a very successful speech urging the caucus members to give Mulroney their undivided support. I said that we had to let our leader lead and that he could not lead us if he was always having to look behind him to see whether he had any followers. We could win re-election if we let him do that, if we didn't niggle him to death or snipe him into senescence, or drive him to distraction or criticize him publicly, or defecate on him from great heights or quibble about his popularity, or question his credentials.

In Mulroney, we had a national leader I was proud of. He didn't follow the advice of the American politician Eugene McCarthy, who maintained that it was always dangerous for a national politician to say things that people might remember. For better or worse, people remembered what Mulroney said. We were fortunate to have, in Mulroney, the kind of leader that Walter Lippmann, the great American political writer, had in mind when he said, "The final test of a leader is that he leaves behind in other men the conviction and the will to carry on."

Although all signs pointed to defeat in the next election, I believed our record over eight years in office to be an excellent one and I thought, if anyone could carry us to a third term, it was Mulroney, with his proven toughness, leadership abilities, and political skills. There was no one else I could see in the cabinet or party – including Kim Campbell – who would have as good a chance of winning another majority.

While Brian was debating what he would do, I was busy assessing my own future. I had been in politics for twenty-seven years. Jane, who is never shy about expressing her views, was of the firm opinion that the time had come for me to retire from political life and attempt something else before I had no option other than an inactive retirement. I owed it to Jane to remove myself from the hurly-burly and the strains of politics and to live a more normal life with her and our children and grandchildren.

Between the closing of the northern-cod fishery and the struggle to save Hibernia, I had just come through a very tough year. Yet my personal popularity in Newfoundland seemed to be standing up well. *Atlantic Lifestyle Business* magazine found me to be the most influential person in Atlantic Canada in 1992. I was the only cabinet minister to be given an "A" in a Tory report card published by the *Ottawa Sun*. As 1993 began, the *St. John's Evening Telegram* announced its readers had selected me as the Newfoundland Newsmaker of the Year for 1992, outpolling Clyde Wells by five to one. In the *Humber Log* of Corner Brook, editor Fred Basha wrote, "Knowing that a John Crosbie is in Ottawa standing up for Newfoundland is indeed a precious sight, regardless of what anyone has to say. Crosbie won't be bullied, nor will he be intimidated. He is the right man at the right place in this particular time of need." And Newfoundland Television Service commentator Jim Furlong declared: "From Jack Pickersgill through to Don Jamieson and now up to the present fisheries minister, John Crosbie, the province's interests have been very well served in the corridors of power in the nation's capital. It can be effectively argued that those interests have never been better served than they are currently by John Crosbie."

Support like this made it difficult to leave and, as I assessed my future, I reached several conclusions. Under no circumstances was I interested in making a second run at the party leadership. If Mulroney stayed, I would run again. If Mulroney decided to retire, I would revisit my options. If he was succeeded by a leader in whom I had faith, who I thought could win the election, and who wanted me to stay on in some important and influential capacity, I would run again. Otherwise, I would retire.

The best published account of this period is David McLaughlin's book *Poisoned Chalice*.* As McLaughlin points out, the race to succeed Mulroney began months before he officially

---

* (Toronto: Dundurn Press, 1994).

resigned in February 1993. Chief among the candidates who were preparing to run were Kim Campbell, Jean Charest, Mike Wilson, Barbara McDougall, and Joe Clark. Prospective financial contributors were being approached, and donations solicited.

I wasn't involved in any of this. As far as I was concerned, the 1983 leadership race had clearly established that the national party believed that it was mandatory that its leader be fluent in both official languages. Obviously I was not. Having been stung once by my lack of French, I wasn't going to be stung a second time. As it turned out, of course, Kim Campbell couldn't really speak French either, but she pretended she could and the media bought it for a while.

It would take more than a new leader to overcome the public's lingering, negative perception of Mulroney and his style of politics and government. "The problem," as pollster Michael Adams put it, "is that, in the public mind, he does not have the qualities of consistency and sincerity." In the opinion of *Maclean's*, Mulroney's old-fashioned style had contributed to a sense of division in the country. While warm and sensitive in person, on television his warmth appeared effusive and his sensitivity often seemed insincere. *Maclean's* wrote: "To add to those problems the Prime Minister sometimes strayed from his own rules. He railed against patronage during the 1984 election but frequently appointed friends to government posts. He denounced pork barrel politics but constructed a prison costing more than $60 million within the boundaries of his own Quebec riding. He frequently appeared as an impediment to his own government's stated goals and therefore often failed to receive credit for the successes of his government."

Although *Maclean's* thought historians would likely view Mulroney as a transitional prime minister, I ranked him considerably higher than that. I believed he would be assessed by future historians as one of Canada's best prime ministers. And I thought that Newfoundland stood to lose a powerful ally who had done more for the province than any other Canadian politician since 1949.

Once Mulroney announced his retirement, it quickly became apparent that the front-runner was Campbell. Elected federally for the first time in 1988 from Vancouver Centre, she had made an impressive debut in the House of Commons and become a popular Minister of Justice. Every poll put her in the lead. She and her staff had been working feverishly to prepare for a leadership campaign. I was astonished to discover that Ross Reid, my colleague from Newfoundland in the adjacent riding of St. John's East, was one of her closest supporters and was going to be her campaign chairman. With my assistance, Ross had won St. John's East for the Tories in the 1988 election. The following four years were very rough ones for me, with the problems of the fishery and the offshore, and I had been disappointed that Ross had kept his distance from me. Now, he had signed on as one of the principal organizers of Campbell's campaign without breathing a word of it to me. His circumspection may have been shrewd politically, but it was certainly offensive to me personally.

I decided I couldn't support Kim because I didn't believe she had the "right stuff" for national leadership. She was a butterfly, flitting from leaf to blossom out there in British Columbia. I liked her, but, when I went to B.C., as I did frequently, I couldn't help but notice that the federal government got more criticism there than in any other province.

Although Kim was supposed to be the political minister for the province, she wasn't speaking out at all. That loud-mouthed extremist Rafe Mair, and other open-line broadcasters like him, were attacking Ottawa every day, putting out irresponsible and dangerous nonsense about Quebec and the Constitution, whining about how B.C. and the West were always discriminated against, and purveying the kind of hogwash that sells well out there. Nothing was being done to repel these attacks. I thought if Kim wasn't strong enough or committed enough to counter the abuse we were taking in her province, she wouldn't be able to counter it in the whole country.

She won the leadership because early polling put her miles ahead and because the Tories fooled themselves into thinking that by changing to a woman – and a Western woman to boot – we might be able to survive the election. I thought that other women, such as Barbara McDougall, were better suited for the job. Barbara was a much tougher woman than Kim, but she couldn't get anyone in Toronto to give her a dime for a leadership campaign. Neither could Michael Wilson. The Toronto smart-money crowd, including my old pal Bob Foster, had all jumped on the Campbell bandwagon.

Although I didn't support Kim for the leadership, I made a fatal mistake. I should have come out early with strong public support for Jean Charest. Instead, I told the Newfoundland delegation to do whatever they liked. But as such ministers as McDougall, Wilson, Perrin Beatty, Tom Hockin, and others dropped out, Reid tied up three-quarters of the Newfoundland delegation for Campbell. Convention delegates are incredibly stubborn. Once they commit themselves to someone, nothing changes their mind. By the time I came out for Charest, a couple of days before the convention, it was too late. If I'd supported him from the beginning, I think I could have gotten most of the Newfoundland delegation and some from the other Atlantic delegations. It would have been decisive. It would have been enough to stop Kim on the first ballot and elect Charest on the second.

I supported Charest because I believed he was our best chance to win the election. I found him to be competent, unflappable, and steady – qualities he has demonstrated consistently in the years since. He was an excellent communicator in both official languages, had the ability to deal with complex issues, and had dealt with a complicated agenda at the Rio summit on the environment, where he did a fantastic job for Canada.

The enormity of my mistake in delaying my support for him was evident in the results of the balloting. Campbell won on the second ballot, with 1,817 votes to 1,630 for Charest. A shift of just 94 votes would have made him leader. If I'd supported Charest from the outset and actively campaigned for him, I think I could have captured a large majority of the hundred or so Newfoundland delegates who voted for Campbell, plus others from elsewhere in Atlantic Canada.

Once Campbell became leader, I and other veterans of the Mulroney administration were effectively frozen out of the inner circle. I was prepared to do everything I could to help the party, but Kim thought Canadians wanted a real change in our politics and politicians, so she and her advisers weren't anxious to have anything to do with the senior members of the Mulroney administration.

I think I could have retained St. John's West, even in the teeth of the electoral hurricane that swept the Tories out of office and nearly out of existence. In June 1993, just a few days before the leadership convention, I arranged for John Laschinger, who was now with Goldfarb Consultants, to conduct a poll in St. John's West. Lasch found that the Liberals led in the riding with 52 per cent of the vote, to 44 per cent for the Tories and 4 per cent for the New Democrats. That was when respondents were not given candidates' names. However, when I was identified as the prospective Conservative candidate and put up against the candidates who subsequently ran for the Liberals and NDP, Tory support shot up to 63 per cent, with a two-to-one lead over the Liberal candidate. Sixty-five per cent of respondents rated my performance as being excellent or good, while 71 per cent said they wanted me to run again. The Goldfarb conclusion was that I was an extremely popular candidate who would have little difficulty being re-elected.

It was not to be. In victory, Campbell showed she lacked the sure-footedness that Mulroney had displayed when he won the leadership nine years earlier. Like other members of the Mulroney cabinet, I received a summons to meet her in the suite of offices she used during the transition. I was still ambivalent about retiring. So I determined that I would listen and consider my options carefully if Kim indicated that she was genuinely anxious to have me continue in her cabinet in an important role and if she made it clear that she valued my advice or needed me badly.

When we met, she told me she would like me to continue as Minister of Fisheries and Oceans and as minister responsible for the Atlantic Canada Opportunities Agency. But she demonstrated no warmth or real interest in my continuing in her administration. What she offered appeared to be perfunctory. I had no interest in carrying on as an appendage in the Campbell administration – or in carrying on at all unless I was enthusiastically requested to do so and assured of important tasks to undertake. I had no interest in sucking around somebody just to be in the cabinet. I was used to having some authority and power. So I declined Kim's tepid offer. I told her I would be retiring when the election was called. Campbell made no effort to dissuade me. Our meeting lasted no more than four or five minutes, and my career as a federal minister ended that week, on June 25, 1993. Campbell was, as she said, going to "do politics differently."

◠

The rest is history. At first, the new prime minister could do no wrong. When the Tories' national campaign committee met in August 1993, two months after Campbell won the leadership, they were heartened by new poll results from the party pollster, Decima Research. They showed the Conservatives leading the Liberals by six points among decided voters, 35 per cent to 29. The NDP and Reform Party each had 8 per cent, while the Bloc Québécois had 9 per cent, concentrated in Quebec. The Tories led the Liberals in Atlantic Canada by 45 to 33, while, in Quebec, we were tied with the Bloc Québécois at 33. In Ontario the Liberals still led, but by just two percentage points, 39 to 37. On the Prairies, the Tories were well in front, with 35 per cent, and in British Columbia we were neck and neck with the Liberals: 28 points for us, 29 for them.

Decima also asked respondents who they believed would make the best prime minister. Campbell led, with 46 per cent, up fourteen points since the convention. Later in August, the

Gallup poll put Campbell's popularity at 51 per cent – the highest for any national leader in twenty years.

The election campaign opened badly on September 8. Having chosen to fight the election on the issues of jobs and the deficit, Campbell was unable to present a coherent connection between the two issues. On unemployment, she gave the impression of being cold and impersonal, saying that structural unemployment was plaguing all industrialized countries, and Canadians would have to put up with a high jobless rate for two, three, or four years. While this kind of answer was accurate and honest, it was disastrous politically. So, on the very first day of the campaign, she handed the Liberals a golden opportunity and Jean Chrétien exploited it gleefully.

∾

The public doesn't understand the pressures on political leaders. They don't appreciate that a leader may have four or five emergencies while working fifteen or sixteen hours in the course of an "ordinary" day – with all the perils that this kind of high-octane existence involves. Kim didn't understand it, either. She had no sense of politics. For a national leader to complain, as she did, that her handlers weren't giving her enough time to pay her personal bills or curl her hair shows that she didn't grasp what the job required.

She had a new Russian boyfriend. One day during the campaign, an important party official needed to talk to her about fund-raising. The only place he could arrange to see her was on her campaign bus between Montreal and Ottawa. But she was in the private compartment in the back with her beau. When the official finally got to see her, her lipstick was smeared and her hair was mussed. It was obvious they'd been necking.

I have nothing at all against sex, but party leaders have no time during campaigns for courting or love-making. They have to devote every minute of the day to working on the campaign, thinking about what they're going to say at the next stop, or checking on the arrangements to make sure someone is looking after all the things that need to be done. Inattention to the essentials was typical of Campbell, and it's why 1993 was such a disastrous campaign.

It was the worst run, most dispirited, most hapless campaign I have ever been associated with. It was painfully summed up for me in a political "rally" that I attended for Conservative candidate Charlie Brett in Wesleyville, Newfoundland, on Saturday evening, October 23, two days before polling day. Charlie was a local fixture. He'd been a provincial member from 1972 to 1989, and a cabinet minister under Frank Moores and Brian Peckford, and in the short-lived administration of Tom Rideout in 1989.

Although Wesleyville, in the heart of rural Newfoundland, was renowned for its large, enthusiastic political meetings, only a dozen people turned out at the school where our meeting was held. And six of them were postal workers from another district who had been sent by their union to protest because of an ongoing dispute with Canada Post. There was no point in making speeches to twelve people, so Charlie and I sat around in a circle with them and had a chat. If this is what our new leader meant by doing politics differently, the party, I thought, would be lucky to survive.

∾

On election day, the Progressive Conservative party collected only 29 per cent of its own core vote, according to our internal polling. In other words, 71 per cent of committed Tories voted for other parties and candidates. Nationally, we got just 16 per cent of the popular vote as the once-proud party of Confederation dropped into the abyss. Kim Campbell lost her own seat, of course, and so did every Tory candidate in the land, except Jean Charest in Quebec and Elsie Wayne in New Brunswick.

The movers and shakers of the Tory party have only themselves to blame for the débâcle of 1993. Spooked by the polls, they believed that the legacy of Brian Mulroney would be an election liability, that our government's record would pave the road to defeat. So rather than defend their former leader and prime minister and proclaim his administration's accomplishments, the cowardly Conservative establishment bailed out.

They were so desperate to shed the Mulroney legacy that they didn't bother to ask whether Campbell had the experience to lead a national party, whether she was tough enough and seasoned enough to lead a cross-country campaign and to withstand the almost inhuman pressures of the campaign. In *Poisoned Chalice*, David McLaughlin quotes a former senior Conservative cabinet minister as saying, "We elected a stranger."

That's precisely what we did – and we paid a terrible price.

∾

As for me, I was not offered a patronage appointment by Campbell, nor did I want one. In the course of my career, I'd fought ten elections – one for the St. John's City Council, four provincial, and five federal. I was proud of my battle against the tyranny of Joey Smallwood. I remembered with pride the 1979 Budget I introduced as Joe Clark's Minister of Finance. If that Budget had been accepted, it would have reversed the trend to deficit financing that became so extreme with the 1980–84 Trudeau administration. For nearly nine years, I served my country, my region, and my province in the administrations of Brian Mulroney. I think the departments I ran were better when I left than when I arrived.

It was time to look for new challenges in the private sector. And it was past time to spend more time with Jane, our children, and our grandchildren. My health was not a factor, but I joked that my health would surely be in danger from Jane if I did not retire.

As Jane told an interviewer, her husband of forty years lived and breathed politics, "Every square part of him is a politician. He really had a hard time coming to terms with [retirement] . . .

and yet he knew in his own heart that he had to go." She talked about her life as a political wife who stayed by her husband's side:

> You fly in here [St. John's] and you fly out so fast. For me, it was always emptying the fridge and trying to keep the place neat so that when I came back again I'd have a clean bed. When it's only two, you can manage it and haul something out of the freezer, but that's how we lived for the past ten years. . . . I was always with him because that was the only way I suppose our marriage could survive by being with him and he was gone so much. At least I knew the pressures and things he was living under and had a feeling for it. If I wasn't with him, I mean who the hell would want to put up with that? . . . It came easy too, because I thought he was the best, and he is the premier and prime minister Canada never had, for whatever reason.

Who could have said it better than that!

25

On Reflection

Courtesy Phil Mallette, The Financial Post

WE LIVE IN desperate times. Canada came within a hair's breadth of financial, economic, and social chaos in the Quebec referendum of October 30, 1995. Just a few thousand votes stood between the people of Quebec and separation from Canada – an indecent act that the Parti Québécois government would have been only too happy to consummate. Canadians in the rest of the country seemed oblivious to the eventuality that the Yes side might win the referendum, as it so nearly did. Neither the Government of Canada nor any of the provincial governments had a contingency plan.

Too many Canadians fool themselves into believing that a majority in Quebec will never vote to separate because of the damage they will do to their own economic prospects. I believe this to be a grave delusion. It is facile to argue, as so many do, that Quebecers will always vote for what is in their self-interest, economic or other. The argument is wrong. People can easily be mistaken – or misled – about where their best interests lie. And, regardless of objective self-interest, emotion is a stronger force in determining voting decisions than reason or logic will ever be.

There's a parallel with the two referendums that were held in Newfoundland in 1948 to determine the future of what was then constitutionally an independent dominion, although executive power was vested in a commission appointed by the government of the United Kingdom. In the first Newfoundland referendum, 88.36 per cent of the eligible voters cast ballots, with 14.32 per cent supporting the status quo – continuance of the Commission of Government. Another 41.13 per cent voted for Confederation with Canada, while the largest number, 44.55 per cent, voted for the restoration of responsible government for Newfoundland – in other words, independence without the appointed commission, which had been created when Newfoundland was unable to meet its financial obligations during the Great Depression.

When none of the three options commanded a majority, a second referendum was held. The option of continuing with the Commission of Government was dropped from the ballot, leaving a choice between Confederation with Canada or a return to responsible government – which was widely understood to be the precursor to economic (and perhaps political) union with the United States. On July 22, 1948, with 84.89 per cent of the people voting, Confederation with Canada captured 52.34 per cent of the ballots, while responsible government took 47.66 per cent. The U.K. and Canadian governments accepted this narrow outcome, and previously independent Newfoundland became the tenth province of Canada in 1949.

It was obvious during the period leading up to the two referendums that the economic arguments were heavily on the side of Confederation with Canada. The Depression had been a debilitating experience for Newfoundland. For tens of thousands of our people, life seemed to hang by a thread. A vote for Confederation would be a vote for immediate improvement in their lot because they would be included in Canadian social programs, including civilian and military pensions. If voters were influenced primarily by their own economic well-being, there would have been a huge majority in favour of joining Canada. But it didn't happen. An independent Newfoundland – a much riskier economic proposition – led in the first referendum, and came close to carrying the day in the second. The people voted with their hearts, not their pocketbooks. Those who voted for a return to responsible government did so for reasons of patriotism, race, or historical experience. They had no reason to like or love Canada, because Canadians had often opposed such Newfoundland initiatives as the free-trade arrangements put in place by Newfoundland's Sir Robert Bond and U.S. Secretary of State James Blaine in 1891. Newfoundlanders came into close contact with both Canadians and Americans during the Second World War, and, by and large, we liked the Americans better. Many of us subscribed to the sentiments of an early anti-Canadian, anti-Confederation song:

> With your face turned to Britain, your back to the Gulf,
> Come near at your peril, Canadian wolf!

I believe the same forces are shaping attitudes in Quebec. Most French Quebecers will cast their ballots on the basis of emotion – as a result of their historical memories of their treatment as a minority in Canada or the appeal of being "masters in their own house." The fact that the Confederation forces nearly lost in Newfoundland in 1948 tells me that the separatist cause could well win a future referendum in Quebec.

Both Quebecers and the residents of the rest of Canada will suffer immense and immediate economic damage if Quebec decides to become a separate country. In my assessment, the greatest damage will be suffered by the residents of the four Atlantic provinces and, in particular, by the people of Newfoundland and Labrador. Since Newfoundland joined Canada in 1949, the improvement in the living conditions of Canadians and the physical world they inhabit has been astonishing, and Newfoundlanders have shared in these advances.

From the quantity and variety of food to the housing, roads, modern means of communication, schools and universities, and health and social services, the improvements have been staggering. I do not suggest that Canada has evolved into a perfect society, because it hasn't. Nor do I deny that hundreds of thousands of people still live in difficult and depressing circumstances. Overall, however, our quality of life has improved beyond our wildest dreams.

Naturally, the revolution of rising expectations has outstripped the pace of the improvements. No matter how much better life becomes, the people feel it should be even better. In recent years, there's been a tremendous increase in bitching about every aspect of life in Canada. These complaints have taken over the media completely. Anyone who listens to the radio or TV news or reads the newspapers can only be astounded at the number, variety, and volume of complaints, whines, and moans from every conceivable group. A huge proliferation of interest groups, all vocal and media-savvy, exploits the airwaves and the print media to build an audience for their complaints, real or ridiculous. No grievance is too petty or absurd to command the attention of the lords and ladies of the media. All they have to do is to stage a small demonstration, wave a few signs, and shout some slogans (the noisier and more profane the better) within view of a camera and they can count on being featured on the news that night. Reporters being too lazy to dig up real news, they welcome these pseudo protests and phony grievances. Truth, reality, balance, and common sense do not enter into the "journalistic" equation. The media and the interest groups have elevated discontent to a high place in the Canadian landscape.

∾

Separation is not an issue for Quebecers alone to decide. All Canadians have a direct and immediate interest in what happens in Quebec. We all have a right to try to influence the debate and the outcome of any further referendum. This right of intervention applies particularly to the people of Atlantic Canada, whose four provinces depend so heavily on the Government of Canada for fiscal transfers to their governments and for direct support to individuals through the Employment Insurance system, Canada Assistance Plan, Canada Pension Plan, Old Age Security, Guaranteed Income Supplement, and many other federal programs. Of the four Atlantic provinces, Newfoundland is the most dependent. In 1990, Ottawa collected $1.3 billion in federal revenue from Newfoundland and Labrador, but it spent $4.09 billion by way of transfers to the provincial government and to the people of the province. To look at it another way, the federal government raises 1 per cent of its revenue from the tenth province, yet does 3 per cent of its spending there. Every resident of Atlantic Canada has a direct, immediate, and vital interest in what happens in Quebec, because I don't believe that Canadian federalism will survive if Quebec leaves. And if federalism collapses, Atlantic Canadians will be the first victims.

In Newfoundland and, it appears, the rest of the Atlantic region, most people are living in a fool's paradise. They believe that, if Quebec leaves Confederation, nothing much will change, except that they will no longer have to bother with bilingualism or worry about the French minority in Canada. They embrace the lazy assumption that the nine remaining provinces will carry on without Quebec. They assume that all social programs, all transfer programs from the central government to the provinces such as equalization, the costs of post-secondary education, and the health system, will continue in place.

It's time for a reality check. It's time for everyone living in the Atlantic provinces to address the threat posed by the possible separation of Quebec. It's high time we Atlantic Canadians started to consider seriously the five options that face us:

- to continue as part of the present Canada;
- to become part of Canada without Quebec;

- to become part of a new Atlantic country composed of the four Atlantic provinces;
- to become independent countries again, as Newfoundland was until 1949;
- or to become states of the United States of America.

If we cannot continue as part of a united Canada, the options are cataclysmic for the ordinary person in Atlantic Canada. Despite this self-evident fact, the issue is not even discussed. Our heads are buried in the sand.

Two provinces are essential to the continuation of Canada as a nation – the two original provinces of Upper Canada and Lower Canada. If either leaves, Canada ceases to exist as a nation. It is most unlikely that Canada would survive a "successful" independence referendum in Quebec because it would not be in the financial interest of those living in Ontario, British Columbia, or Alberta to carry on as though nothing had happened. Even if we could cobble together a country out of the nine remaining units, the financial arrangements of this new federation would be completely different. The very generous transfers from the central government that provide the glue that holds Canada together would almost certainly not be replicated in a new, reduced nation.

Atlantic Canadians forget at their peril that Ontario, Alberta, and British Columbia would each be economically viable as independent countries and would each have the option of going it alone. We have no reason to expect that they would join a new federation that would continue to dispense charity to Atlantic Canada. If transfer and other support programs did continue, they would assuredly not be as generous as they are today. The best Atlantic Canada could expect would be less. The worst would be nothing at all.

It is unlikely, I believe, that the four Atlantic provinces would ever come together to form a new nation. Such a combination would not produce an economically viable entity, nor a standard of living that would be remotely comparable to what our people have today. It's also a fact that Newfoundlanders have never shown much empathy with the Maritime provinces or wanted to have much to do with them. Newfoundland and the Maritime provinces could become independent countries or the three Maritime provinces might form one nation, with Newfoundland becoming independent again. If this occurs, life will certainly be much more difficult and arduous for our citizens.

The final option would be for Atlantic Canada as a region, or the four provinces individually, to join the United States, if that country were agreeable – which is by no means a sure thing. It is not a tempting prospect for Atlantic Canadians. Individual states don't get the kind of financial assistance from their central government that the poor provinces of Canada receive. There are no huge transfer programs from Washington to the states. There is no equalization. And U.S. programs for unemployment insurance, health care, and social assistance do not approach Canadian programs in their breadth or their generosity.

Clearly the continuation of the present Canada is infinitely preferable to any of the alternatives for all the people of Atlantic Canada – *even if it means making significant constitutional concessions to Quebec to ensure that the federation survives*. This must be the guiding principle for our elected representatives in the Atlantic region. The Constitution of Canada must serve the needs of the whole country, each of its provinces and territories, and all of its citizens. The Constitution is not the servant of any politician's particular view of constitutional principle or practice. The object of the Constitution is to keep the *whole* country together and to make it possible for lawmakers to satisfy the needs of *all* our people.

The people of Canada outside Quebec have a perfect right to insist that our political leaders make several things clear to Quebecers before another referendum is held:

- There must be a clear question that is comprehensible to the ordinary voter.

- We are not going to permit repeated votes on this question over an indefinite period.
- If there is to be a referendum, the timing will be determined by all of us, not just by the government of Quebec.
- We have to agree on the percentage of the vote the Yes side must obtain for the vote to be decisive.
- Quebec cannot assume that the boundaries of an independent Quebec would be the same as they are today, because the present boundaries were substantially increased in the early 1900s.
- It must be clearly spelled out what arrangements the rest of Canada will contemplate with respect to currency, passports, and citizenship; the use of our central bank; and other such issues.
- Above all, we must disabuse everyone of the quaint notion that Quebec can leave Canada with little disruption, with Quebecers and Canadians exchanging pleasantries and treating one another in a gentlemanly and friendly manner. This will not happen. Any break-up will inevitably produce tensions, conflict, and strife – the survival of the fittest, not of the nicest. Canadians have as much at stake in Quebec's decision as Quebecers do, and we will act accordingly.

My experience in the provincial and federal spheres has convinced me that the federal system of government, where legislative jurisdiction and authority are divided between a national government and the governments and legislatures of provinces or states, is by far the best system for very large countries such as Canada, Australia, and the United States. Federalism has the beauty of flexibility. In every federal state, the pendulum of power seems to swing from the federal government to the provinces, and back again, as conditions change or as society becomes more complicated. In Canada in the 1950s and 1960s, authority seemed to swing to the federal government, while in the 1970s and 1980s the provinces acquired more power.

Apart from all other considerations, the federal system prevents absolute power from becoming concentrated in any one leader or any one group. Political leaders are inevitably affected by the exercise of power. Few want to give it up voluntarily. They become convinced that the welfare of their province or country depends on their continuing to exercise power. The apparatus of government conspires to reinforce this delusion. Our leaders surround themselves with advisers whose own influence depends upon their boss continuing to be leader, so they bend all their efforts to convincing the leader that he or she must continue in office for the good of the country. If Newfoundland had been a separate dominion with a leader like Joey Smallwood in the dominant position that he occupied for twenty years, I think it very unlikely that he could have been forced from power by normal democratic means. But in the Canadian federation, power is diffused among eleven governments and dozens of federal and provincial political parties, thereby ensuring there is never absolute uniformity of opinion and action in the country. There is always debate over the appropriate policies to follow at any given time. No one leader or party acquires enough power to become a threat to the democratic system, as happens so often in unitary states throughout the world.

∽

One of my regrets is that the Mulroney government did not abolish the Senate of Canada when it had the opportunity to do so. Never an effective body, the Senate today is a useless appendage which does more to frustrate the will of the elected Commons than to contribute to the good governance of Canada. One of its purposes is supposed to be to defend provincial and regional interests. But the provinces have never needed the Senate to protect them. They have proved to be more than capable of representing themselves in the political arena and in the courts.

The Upper House usually has a large majority of members appointed by one political party, and senators seldom vote against the wishes of those who appointed them. Due to the unhealthy dominance of the Liberal party for most of the twentieth century, this has generally meant a strong Liberal majority in the Senate. When the Conservatives were in office under Brian Mulroney, the Senate took every opportunity to harass us. It refused to pass the legislation to implement the Canada–U.S. Free Trade Agreement until we called and won a general election. It tried to block the introduction of the Goods and Services Tax, and would have succeeded in this outrageous effort if Mulroney had not exercised his constitutional prerogative to increase the size of the Senate. He appointed enough new Conservative senators to ensure the passage of the GST. After the election of Jean Chrétien's Liberal government, our short-lived Tory majority in the Upper House was able to thwart the Chrétienites on several occasions when they pulled such nefarious tricks as attempting to ram through legislation to cancel the contract for the privatization of Terminals One and Two at Pearson Airport in Toronto and to restrict the damages that the contract-holders could collect. As much as I applaud the Tory senators for standing up to the Liberal storm troopers, I cannot really defend the existence of an undemocratic second chamber. Nor can I argue that the useful work the Senate sometimes does in studying issues and improving the details of legislation is sufficiently important to justify the cost and expense of the institution.

There are those who maintain the Senate can be reformed. I disagree. I don't think it's possible for the federal government to operate properly if there is a second legislative body with senators competing with MPs to determine what government policy should be. I have always opposed the so-called Triple-E Senate, the elected, equal, and effective Senate that is favoured by the Reform Party and other faux populists. Such a Senate would be a prescription for parliamentary and governmental gridlock.

I say abolish the Senate and be rid of it. The only tears would be shed by the senators themselves as they confront the loss of their comfortable, privileged, useless existence.

∾

One of the big problems in Canada today is excessive regional-ism. Federal leaders are forever attempting to avoid decisions that can be branded in one part of the country as favouring some other part of the country. This phenomenon is peculiar to Canada. In my extensive travels in the United States, I have never heard a person in one region, say, New England, criticize any action the government in Washington might have taken to support an activity in the South or in California or in some other part of the country. Regional rivalries in the United States are muted compared with the constant shouting in Canada over Ottawa's perceived favouritism towards one region at the expense of others. This alleged discrimination becomes fodder for synthetic editorial indignation, open-line hysteria, and official outrage in the grumbling region.

For a dramatic illustration of the dangers of excessive region-alism, I look to the decision of the Mulroney cabinet to award a $1.3-billion maintenance contract for the CF-18 fighter aircraft to Montreal's Canadair, owned by Bombardier, rather than to Bristol Aerospace in Winnipeg. What particularly outraged the West was the fact that the civil servants who evaluated the bids had rated the one from Bristol Aerospace as being significantly cheaper and technically superior to Canadair's. The political cost to the federal Tories was huge as outrage over the CF-18 contract fuelled the formation of the Reform Party and con-tributed to the defection of many hitherto Conservative sup-porters in the West. It made no difference when a $200-million maintenance contract for the CF-5 fighter aircraft and a $93-million disease-control laboratory were awarded to Winnipeg. These dollops of patronage were seen as being poor compen-sation for the loss of the much larger CF-18 contract. The

Mulroney government stood indicted and convicted of favouritism to Quebec. The episode reminded me of an observation
that Samuel Johnson made about the Irish. The Irish, he said,
"are a fair people; they never speak well of one another." Or as
George Bernard Shaw said, "Put an Irishman on the spit and you
can always get another Irishman to turn him." They could have
been describing Canadians.

∾

Occasionally, I get things wrong. Because of my experiences in
Newfoundland, I thought it was impossible that there could be
any other government in Canada whose approach to economic
and industrial development was as stupid as Joey Smallwood's.
From the distance of St. John's, what I could see of the government at Ottawa led me to believe that the formulation and
administration of federal policy was far more rational and sensible than anything I had witnessed in Newfoundland. However,
my experiences in nine years in the Mulroney government
taught me how blind I'd been. The federal government was no
more intelligent or logical in its development policies than
Smallwood. The big difference was that irrational actions and
political pressures were more hidden in Ottawa than they'd been
in Newfoundland. In Ottawa, decisions about assistance for economic and industrial projects weren't made by a despot who
ignored feasibility studies; they were made in a rat's nest of
government departments, interdepartmental task forces, and
cabinet committees. When great questions of procurement or
subsidy arose in the Department of Supply and Services or
National Defence, the decision-making process became convo-
luted by the frenzied activity of lobbyists acting on behalf of
each outfit that was trying to grab a slice of the pie.

Many of the decisions made by the government or its cabinet
committees, subcommittees, commissions, or agencies were
made for reasons that were no more rational than those of the
Smallwood government. The landscape of Canada is littered

with dozens of ill-founded development projects on which hundreds of millions of dollars were expended for partisan political motives or for wrong-headed economic reasons. The heavy-water plants that were constructed in Cape Breton in the heyday of Liberal godfather Allan MacEachen are just one illustration of how money is thrown away in the name of regional economic development.

∾

It is becoming increasingly difficult to attract to the political profession men and women of ability and ideals who have an interest in public policy and public life. There are many reasons for this, one being the jaundiced view that the public takes of their political leaders, holding them to blame for all of the fiscal and other difficulties that governments face today. The practice of politics has grown more difficult and unpleasant over the last thirty years as the political system has grown more complicated and demanding, and as the media, especially television, have become more intrusive.

Anyone who seeks a seat in Parliament does so at considerable risk – the greatest being the risk of actually getting elected. Those aspiring to political life must leave their profession or business during their best and most productive years to become full-time politicians, a career that is fraught with uncertainty. They may be defeated whenever an election is called, or even be challenged for renomination within their own party.

Once elected to the Commons, fledgling politicians receive reasonable remuneration, but they soon discover that their living expenses have increased because they need to maintain residences in their riding and in Ottawa. An MP's life requires constant travel, between Ottawa and home, and to political events in other parts of the country. There will be many frustrations for him or her; much of the work in Ottawa is not meaningful, and an ordinary MP is often unable to exercise any real influence.

After six years in the Commons, MPs are eligible for a modest pension. But only if they manage to get re-elected often enough to put in sixteen or eighteen years of service can they expect a reasonable, but not extravagant, pension. By then, of course, they will have no career to return to in the outside world, having been too long away from their business or profession. They will also find that the fact they were a politician will weigh against them, because, in today's atmosphere, people are looked down upon for having been in politics. If some other political party is in power in Ottawa or in their provincial capital – especially if they are from a small, tight-knit province – their services will not be sought after, even on the shadowy fringes of politics where consultants and lobbyists operate. Brian Peckford discovered this after his retirement as premier. Unable to earn an adequate living at home, he was forced to leave Newfoundland to find employment.

Most of today's politicians could make more money, enjoy better living conditions, and have better prospects for the future if they'd never gone into public life. Anyone entering politics should either be very poor or very rich. Only people with the arse out of their pants or who are independently wealthy can sensibly risk becoming politicians. After a life in politics, I deeply regret that I cannot encourage my own children to leave their careers to take up the challenges of elected office. They would be risking their own future and the security of their spouses and children.

∞

In politics, never underestimate the importance of being number one. Towards the end of 1995, I had a chat with Brian Tobin, then Chrétien's Minister of Fisheries and Oceans, as he contemplated returning to Newfoundland to run for the Liberal leadership to succeed Clyde Wells as leader and premier. I encouraged him to do it, telling him he would be far better off, far more satisfied, and in a far better position personally if he were number one in the smaller puddle of Newfoundland than he would be even if he were number two or three in the Chrétien administration in Ottawa. It is inevitably frustrating to work as a member of a government led by someone else. No matter how much power and authority leaders delegate to you or how well they treat you, they are still number one, and, when they choose to exercise their authority, they naturally have their way. If my leader became trapped by some political circumstance and blurted out a policy pronouncement in my area of responsibility – even if he didn't know much about the subject – I had to live with it. Even if he was completely wrong, I couldn't correct what he had done. But if a person is the leader, he can make the final decision. Given a choice between being number one in Newfoundland or number two in Ottawa, all other circumstances being equal, number one in Newfoundland is the better ticket.

I had a number of opportunities to be number one in Newfoundland, but other circumstances always kept me from pursuing that option. I am satisfied that I did everything I could for my own district, for our province, and for the country, using the opportunities I had under both Joe Clark and Brian Mulroney. Who knows what the results might have been if I had pursued other options? I console myself with the thought that, even if I made bad mistakes at times, they all led to experiences that strengthened me in one way or another as a politician. Doubtless at times I was too stubborn or too opinionated or too hasty or too unheeding, but I always put everything I had into whatever I was doing and tried to serve loyally the causes I believed in. I worked seriously at the course I had chosen, with what I hope were positive results for Newfoundland and for Canada.

I am proud of Canada as a nation and of the fact that I am a Canadian. I love Canada, but Newfoundland is my homeland. I'm a Newfoundlander first, and I believe that most persons born in Newfoundland feel the same way. This may be because I was a Newfoundlander for eighteen years before I became a Canadian. It's also because of the unique history of our small island. The odds were always heavily against Newfoundland and Newfoundlanders, but Newfoundland battled on, no matter the odds. Newfoundland had to contend with the indifference of Great Britain; the bullying of friends and neighbours such as Canada, France, and the United States; and the privations that resulted from a small population scattered in 1,100 or 1,200 communities around the shores of a large island and a huge mainland area in Labrador with just the sea and the fishery to sustain us.

When others know our history and see what was accomplished by a people who had to wrestle a living from fishing and sealing, they have to admire Newfoundlanders for being a breed of tough, resilient, and enduring people. As a Newfoundlander, I always felt unique. It's still true today, in my view, that most Newfoundlanders feel themselves to be unique and, as a result, have a profound attachment to the land where they were born. Although many tens of thousands of Newfoundlanders have left to seek a better living in just about every community across Canada, as well as in the United States and in other parts of the world, they never forget Newfoundland.

Wherever I travelled throughout Canada, I met Newfoundlanders working and living in places such as Cambridge, Ontario, and Fort MacMurray, Alberta. I found Newfoundlanders in the Northwest Territories working for the Ministry of Transport or other government agencies. On a trip across Canada as Transport minister in 1987, I visited the Queen Charlotte Islands in northern British Columbia, which is the home of the Haida people. On the day of my visit, there was tremendous wind and rain throughout the Queen Charlottes, and the visibility was abysmal. Nevertheless, we were taken by helicopter to see as much as we could of the islands. In due course, we landed on a small island that we were told was inhabited only by several Haida guardians who looked after certain sacred artefacts. As our helicopter touched down in the rain storm, a young woman walked out of the woods with two children by the hand, came up to the helicopter, and looked at me and then said "How are you, Mr. Crosbie?" It turned out that she was from Carbonear, Newfoundland, though then living in Smithers, B.C., and was visiting the Queen Charlotte Islands on holiday. Even today, there is no place I can travel in Canada where I don't bump into expatriate Newfoundlanders.

I've always been proud of my Newfoundland roots and proud that my family managed to do well despite the obstacles encountered by anyone residing in pre-Confederation Newfoundland. My grandfather, father, and uncles prospered in business without apparently attracting the bitterness and dislike that is often engendered by successful entrepreneurs. They were regarded as hard-working, enterprising, fair and decent, and as approachable human beings who never put on airs.

To this day, I am ambivalent in my feelings about Joey Smallwood because I knew him to be a great Newfoundland patriot and a great lover and booster of Newfoundland. Although many of his efforts were wasteful, irrational, and corrupt, there was no doubt that he sought to develop Newfoundland and to improve opportunities for Newfoundlanders. I always recognized his positive characteristics as much as I was distressed by his defects and weaknesses. In the first volume of *The Book of Newfoundland*, published in 1937, Joey wrote: "After all the bludgeonings of Fate Newfoundland's head may be bloody but it is still unbowed. The economic blizzard has strewn the scene with considerable wreckage, but the spirit of the people is invincible." He also wrote: "Greatness Newfoundland deserves; greatness she shall have."* I had no doubt then that what he wrote was true and that he believed it. I certainly believed it – and I still do.

Someone once asked how you can tell which ones are Newfoundlanders when you visit heaven. The answer is, you can always tell the Newfoundlanders because they're the ones who want to go home.

---

* Page 3

ACKNOWLEDGEMENTS

I AM INDEBTED to the many people who not only assisted in the preparation of this book, but worked with or advised me during my twenty-eight-year career in public life. I would have very little to write about had it not been for the friendships, hard work, and support I have enjoyed from hundreds of people. I want to acknowledge some of them now, and I apologize to all whose names may not appear – not because I do not remember or appreciate their great efforts, but simply because I do not have room to include them all.

Above all, I acknowledge the love, affection, companionship, argument, and support given me by my wife, Jane. Little did she know, in the fall of 1965, when I decided to run for election to the city council of St. John's, or in 1966 when I accepted appointment to the cabinet of Joey Smallwood, what she and I would be involved in. I also wish to thank my three children, Ches, Michael, and Beth. They were in my corner throughout the twenty-eight years, supporting my ambitions, participating in campaign after campaign, and taking in their stride the abuse and notoriety that resulted when their father was covered by the news media in both flattering and unflattering ways. I am proud that they have each done well in their chosen profession as lawyers or homemakers.

In my early political days, I was lucky to have a superb personal secretary in Elizabeth Martin of St. John's. Whether in the practice of law or provincial politics, Elizabeth was an unfailing source of support and efficiency. My old law partner Fintan J. Aylward provided consistent support and encouragement, despite the effect my public activities had on our practice.

I will never forget the help and encouragement I was given by my uncles Percy and Bill Crosbie and my brother, Andrew, particularly during the years when I was at war with Smallwood. Although this situation could only harm their own business interests, they were steadfast in their belief that I had the right and duty to act as my conscience dictated.

I have always been fortunate in the number of friends and acquaintances who thought I was trying to do the right thing and believed in the same cause I did. In 1965, when I ran for St. John's city council, I had the assistance of people such as Tom and Barbara Ryan, Frank and Sonia Ryan, the late Peter Gardiner and Janet Gardiner, Morley Powell, and Rob Parker, who later was on my staff in Ottawa and was briefly an MP himself. From the beginning, I had the unwavering assistance of Reg and the late Faith Good, Joan and the late Dr. Jim Roberts, and many others. When I moved from the Liberal party to the Progressive Conservative party, I had the constant support of Maude Melendy, and, for all my political campaigns, the devotion, astounding effort, and attention to detail of supporters such as Janet Woolridge and Olive Vaters of St. John's.

When I challenged Smallwood for the leadership of the Newfoundland Liberals in 1969, I was fortunate to have the managerial skills and drive of mainlanders Jon Kieren and Boyd Simpson, and the campaign support of such Newfoundlanders as Brian Peckford (later, premier), Jim Cochrane, and Don Powell. I also had the support of three Liberal senators, Dan Lang of Toronto, Eric Cook of St. John's, and Ches Carter from

Burin–Burgeo, none of whom let his Liberal persuasions stop him from supporting our struggle to achieve a liberal and demo-cratic society in Newfoundland in the face of political tyranny.

I thank as well my colleagues in the House of Assembly from 1970 to 1972 who joined me in the Liberal Reform Group: Clyde Wells, Gerry Myrden, and the late Beaton J. Abbott. We led the way in overthrowing a corrupt, despotic, and oppressive regime. In addition, I want to thank early supporters of the PC Party of Newfoundland, including Ank Murphy, C.W. (Bill) Doody, the late W.J. Browne, and Frank Moores, for their assistance and encouragement when I made my decision to join the Tories.

Throughout my career in the government and Opposition, in Newfoundland and Ottawa, I was fortunate to meet and work with people of outstanding ability, dedication, and public-spirit-edness. Looking back, I am astounded and gratified by the charac-ter and ability of dozens of young Newfoundlanders and mainland Canadians who worked with me on my political staff. Jim Good, son of our old friends Reg and Faith Good, was a superb chief of staff for me throughout most of the years of the Mulroney admin-istration. Calm, collected, and unflappable, he was always a good source of advice with a keen sense for organization and for dealing with emergencies. Others who did outstanding work for me in Ottawa and St. John's during those years in government were Bill Crosbie, Leo Power, Bill Goulding, Cathy Beehan, Ray Andrews, Malcolm Rowe, Mac Lemessurier, Tim Powers, Fiona Innes, Elizabeth Parker, Chris Breen, Russ Corrigan, David Slade, Ros Walsh, Roy Rideout, and Janet Warren.

Ross Reid of St. John's was of great service to me when I was a minister in the Newfoundland government, Minister of Finance to Joe Clark, and in my 1983 bid for the national Conservative leadership. He became an MP himself in 1988 and was briefly a minister in the Kim Campbell government. Bill Welsh of St. John's provided tremendous assistance throughout most of my years in Parliament, looking after my St. John's West con-stituency office and attending to the many needs of the people of that wonderful district. In Ottawa, mainlanders such as Henry

Brown, Karen Mosher, Genevieve O'Sullivan, Diane Clarke, Barbara Lyon, Daniel Bernier, Colin Metcalfe, John Kane, Raylene Johnson, Guy Landry, and my wonderful secretary, Lorna Joyce, and driver, Roy Pantelone, were of superb service.

My continuing association with John Laschinger, the manager of my 1983 leadership bid, was always a rewarding and entertaining one. He is a true political soldier of fortune, dedicated to the Tory party, possessing an astute understanding of how the system works, with marvellous connections throughout the country and an engaging and sympathetic personality. I also owe a debt of gratitude to my fellow MPs Fred King, Lorne Greenaway, and the late Bob Wenman, who, with Jean Pigott and others, supported my leadership bid from the beginning and worked so hard on my behalf.

During the course of my career, I came across many able and public-spirited civil servants in the governments of Newfoundland and Canada. In Newfoundland, I remember dedicated public servants such as Dennis Groom, Dr. Stuart Peters, Cyril Abery, Dirk Peper, Gordon Slade, and Victor Young, as well as Roland Martin and the late Peter Gardiner, who came from outside to assist me when I became Minister of Finance in the first Moores administration.

At Ottawa, I was lucky to work with such splendid Canadians as Roger Tassé and Frank Iacobucci, now of the Supreme Court of Canada, in Justice; Ramsey Withers and Nick Mulder, in Transport; Gerry Shannon and Donald Campbell, in Trade; while in Fisheries and Oceans, I had the good fortune to have associated with the exceptionally talented and courageous team of Deputy Minister Bruce Rawson and Maryantonett Flumian, assistant deputy minister for policy. Little do the thousands of fishermen and fish-plant workers of Atlantic Canada who were affected by the closure of the northern-cod and other fisheries in 1992 know how much they owe to the skill and courage of public servants like Rawson and Flumian. They played a crucial role in helping me to devise and to get accepted, over great internal opposition, "The Package" that was put in place following the fisheries' closure.

I was also fortunate to have the opportunity to work with Peter Lessaux, president of the Atlantic Canada Opportunities Agency (ACOA), and Gordon Slade, vice-president of ACOA in Newfoundland, a man who accomplished much for Newfoundland in both the provincial and the federal civil services. My former cabinet colleagues Senator Lowell Murray and Don Mazankowski were towers of strength during the northern-cod crisis. Their wise counsel, keen intellect, and support were of great value both to the Mulroney administration and to me personally.

I also pay particular tribute to Joe Clark and Brian Mulroney. Anyone who knows Joe or has observed his actions, as I have since 1976, can have nothing but admiration for his steadfastness, courage, and fortitude in the face of adversity; his decent sensitivities; and his hard work. My experience with Brian Mulroney was always positive, and he exhibited great attributes of leadership during his nine years as prime minister. Brian is a warm human being, a superb political organizer and battler, and a far-seeing strategist. He came to my assistance on many occasions and, whether Newfoundlanders know or appreciate it, he is the greatest benefactor of Newfoundland since Confederation in 1949.

There are many dozens, if not hundreds, of people around St. John's West to whom I owe a great deal for their hospitality, friendship, and work on my behalf during my seventeen years as their MP. I only have space to mention Loyola Hearn, of Renews; Walter Manning and family, of St. Bride's; Bill Patterson, of Placentia; Tom Power, of Branch; Gerry Molloy, of St. Mary's; Basil Croscup, of Trepassey; and Pat Hewitt and the late John Christopher Molloy, of St. Shotts, as a few of the wonderful friends and supporters I had during those years.

With respect to this book, I want to thank Avie Bennett and Doug Gibson of McClelland & Stewart, my publishers, for their patience and support. I thank also Jonathan Webb, my editor, for his guidance and patience, and my collaborator, Geoffrey Stevens, the political journalist and managing editor of *Maclean's*. It was decided that my manuscript needed to be sent to a literary "fat farm" to be reduced in bulk, and Geoff has accomplished this slimming task and rewritten my original manuscript with great skill. Since there are many issues on which his limp liberalism does not coincide with my enlightened conservatism, our collaboration produced many lively exchanges. I thank Ruth Hiscock, my Tolt Road neighbour, for her great work in typing the manuscript and for her always positive and upbeat attitude.

Finally, I hope the reader enjoyed my story and found this book of interest, just as I found my career in politics to be full of interest and fulfilment.

Hogan's Pond, Newfoundland
May 1997

INDEX